MAINE COAST

By Bill Caldwell

Gannett Books

Guy Gannett Publishing Co.
Portland/Maine

Dedication

For all those good companions and shipmates who have hauled the anchor, scrubbed the decks, shared the joys and chores of cruising with me
in Steer Clear—especially Barbara, Stan, Bearson and Jean, Gayle and
Joe, Karen, Tom, Mike, and Kevin. Welcome aboard, always!

First edition 1988. Printed in the United States of America. Published by Guy Gannett Publishing Co. Portland, Maine 04101, August 1988
ISBN #0-930096-98-3

CONTENTS

I
ALONG THE COAST

It's not often a man can write with impunity about his mistress. But a boat can't talk back.

This is a love story about some of the most tender —and some of the most scary—moments in a man's life.

The setting is a small boat, cruising and gunkholing along the coast of Maine for 20 summers.

I hope it is as much fun to read as it has been to write.

But—fair warning. This is not a "Where-to-cruise-and how-to-do-it" book about maintaining boats, approaching harbors, plotting courses and picking marinas. This is a "how-to-enjoy-it" book about the Maine coast.

In a way, it is a book of love letters, an album of snapshots and memories, about a man and a boat enjoying the sea.

These are love letters of a different kind; about coves, islands, seabirds, whales, people, seals, storms, sunsets, moonlight, dawns, close shaves, a sampling of the joys and perils my boat, "Steer Clear", and I have shared together.

We make an odd couple. But after poking into so many coves together for so many years, we've grown indispensable to each other. I'll never want to own another boat. And I doubt that "Steer Clear," at her age, is looking for another owner.

I first met my boat on a September day in 1968. But it was no thunderclap of love at first sight. She lay isolated in her cradle in a far corner of a boatyard on the grassy slopes of the Cousins River, outside Yarmouth, and she was not a pretty sight. She had been on the bank, untended and unloved for two years. Tarpaulins, cracked and wrinkled as the hide of an elephant, covered her. My friend and boat-advisor, Charles Bradley, helped untie the knots and throw back the tarp, so we could take a look at her naked.

I think my heart bounced at the sight, but I took care to hide such feelings. Charlie was all business. He took out his knife and an ice pick, and went to work, probing the wood everywhere for dry rot. He grunted, found a little and finally pronounced her to be in "pretty fair shape." To me, she looked big, beautiful and a bit too much for a novice to handle.

That was the beginning of a love affair which has endured 20 years and still goes on.

The boat and I were an odd pair to wind up together for so long. She was used, third hand, when I became her fourth owner.

I was a 47 year-old newspaperman, who'd only recently moved to Maine. I knew little about boats and the Maine coast, having lived and worked only in big cities in the U.S. and overseas. But slowly, there came a bonding between us.

Within two years, the love affair became a triangle between man and boat and the Maine coast. Perhaps these snapshots of this triangular love affair will entice other men and women to enjoy, explore, lie on anchor and be happy on their boats in their coves. If so, Steer Clear and I will die happy, and watch you fondly from afar.

Race to Monhegan—Yearly race of about 100 yachts from Portland to Monhegan Island and back is a major event for sailors. This air shot by Don Johnson, once a regular on Steer Clear, includes the spectator fleet.

I

MEET THE BOAT

"Steer Clear" is the right boat for a man with shallow pockets, who likes to get out among the islands, gunkhole up rivers, live aboard, and be safe.

That's a big order, but she fills it. However, Steer Clear is no yacht. She's a poor man's boat. She is small but gallant; old but comely; comfortable but Spartan. Above all, she's safe and she's simple and she's got two reliable Palmer engines, sound insurance for a very amateur mechanic.

When I bought her, she looked intimidatingly big to me. When I paint her by myself, she grows bigger every hour. When the job is finally done, I'd swear she was 80 feet long. In fact, she's 30 feet long—plus three more for the pulpit off the bow. She's a Bristol boat, made from four pieces of strong marine plywood; one piece for each side, one for the bottom and the fourth for the stern.

At first, I didn't like those words "marine plywood", because they had a flimsy sound for a seagoing boat. But Langdon Quimby, the father of Bristol boats in Rhode Island, built her for himself in 1953. And he knows the secret. "Lang Quimby probably knows more about all phases of plywood manufacture than any other man in the country; and is much sought after by the Orientals and the Canadians, who make the most of the hardwood plywood," wrote Robert W. Winchell, an expert on these boats. For good measure, Winchell said that Quimby, aged 68 at the time, and his wife on her 65th birthday, dove 65 feet in scuba gear.

Bristol also built 70-foot air-sea rescue boats for the Air Force and Navy from the same kind of marine plywood, as well as many 40- and 50- foot sportfisherman, still in use by Nick Lopez in Florida. Lopez calls Bristols, "the best sea boats made."

Steer Clear at 35 years sits bobbing on her summer mooring outside my home in Buttermilk Cove, ready to take me cruising. "I reckon she has 10 more good years to go," said a marine surveyor recently after he had checked her over before launching time.

Equally reassuring, especially to this all-thumbs mechanic, is the fact that she has twin engines, two 135 h.p. Palmers. If one acts up, I can shut it down and keep going on the other, since a single 135 h.p. engine is ample power for a 30-foot boat.

Forward is the main sleeping cabin, with twin bunks larger than on many far bigger boats. Midships on one side is the galley and on the other side is the "head" (toilet).

The twin engines are boxed in, sound-proofed and further quieted by large foam rubber cushions covered in deep blue vinyl. These make warm day beds, because of the heat from the engines. They are as sensuously pleasing as heating pads when, after a day's cruising, we put the anchor down and stretch out. These convert into beds of 6 feet, 3 inches for overnight guests.

For greater creature comfort on extended cruises, I had the midships enclosed by roof and glass, and then had white canvas and plexiglass drop curtains made to enclose the stern deck. Now in the evening, we drop the curtains and stay warm and dry. This gives a salon or living room area from helm to transom about 15 feet long. I've also installed cabin heaters for cool nights on fall cruises. There are reading lamps in six places and a good stereo system for music. We have, of course, a radio telephone and two standby radio receivers and transmitters, plus depth finders. There is no Loran or radar. If we get caught in fog, I use dead reckoning, to run from buoy to buoy on plotted courses, regulated engine speed and a kitchen timer. If fog shuts down while I'm on anchor, I stay put until it lifts—a safe, easy, pleasant solution. It took years for me to discover it.

The best innovation on Steer Clear is our "poor man's flying bridge". This needs an explanation, plus some imagination, to picture it. We cut hatches into the cabin roof above the helmsman's position and the navigator's seat amidships. These hatches easily swing up and open. On sunny days two people can sit up there in the fresh air and sun, and run the boat. We sit on heavy canvas slings, which act like gimballed seats. I steer the helm with my feet and sea-educated toes. For extra comfort in winds, I installed forward and side windscreens of heavy plexiglass, which are a boon on long passages.

There are a few handsome touches aboard. All bookshelves, drawers, and closet doors were made by a craftsman-joiner out of fine mahogany and are kept brightly varnished. There is plenty of storage for clothes, dry foods, lines, bumpers, a fair-sized ice box, stainless steel tanks for

Steer Clear in her home waters, Buttermilk Cove, at the head of Harp-swell Sound. Author is in "poor man's flying bridge," steering the helm with his feet. Note low registration number on bow — ME 48B. Bristol, twin engine, marine plywood, built 1953.

100 gallons of gas and 30 gallons of drinking water. There's a good ship's library of charts, books and music. And a handsome rowing skiff astern.

And that's the boat Steer Clear, Bristol-blue hull, white topsides and dolled up to style with a gold bootstrap two inches wide at the waterline, with hand-carved blue and gold nameboards on the stern and midships.

Admittedly, I invest plenty of time and money in keeping her safe and pretty as I can. And she repays it all in the peace and joy, the beauty and sometimes downright nasty worry which she gives me, year after year.

Now, let the cruise begin with 14 pieces about the Maine coast in general. Then we'll meander downeast, region by region.

THE MAINE COAST: FOR THE BIRDS

I'm home from the boatyard and my big nose is twitching with those wondrous smells of varnish, caulking and paint, turpentine and fresh engine oil. It is almost launching time again. All along the Maine coast, canvas is coming off, hulls are being scraped, bottoms are being painted. These are the magic days of anticipation. Launch Day is just around the bend.

The anticipation of pleasure soon-to-come may be the most delectable of all human emotions. Right now, I'm brimming over with happy anticipation; but my body cannot express happiness as well as my dog's can. Nothing can express joyous anticipation the way a dog does. Two minutes before feeding time, my dog is in ecstasy, shaking nose to tail, vibrating, undulating, bouncing and prancing—and all for a can of the same dull dog food she has been getting every day, year after year.

I wish I could show my feelings with that kind of body language at least once a year, on Steer Clear's launch day. But ahead of launch day, my heart is out among the islands, anticipating our return to snug coves and remote beaches.

Migrating sea birds are already back on their favorite islands. They have flown millions of miles between them, through storms and headwinds, over oceans, to get back to Maine islands to feed, to mate, to build nests and raise their young. It would be nice to be doing the same.

Thanks to the efforts of many concerned people, there are more nesting birds on the Maine islands now than at any time in the last 180 years. The islands of Maine teem with birds aloft, on the water, under the water, in trees, in burrows and nesting on tiny, dangerous ledges. To enjoy the islands fully, you need to watch and enjoy the birds.

A good guide and companion to help you enjoy the birds and the wildlife, the fish and the rocks of these islands is Philip W. Conkling of the Island Institute. He has been on 450 of them and he tells about their ecological systems in his book "Islands in Time."

Will warblers by the thousands come swooping in when Steer Clear gets back to her favorite islands? One day in early May, the island spruce forests are silent. On the next day, there is a wind and weather shift, and suddenly wave after wave of songbirds arrive and fill the silent woods with joyous warblings.

Gulls in the wake of a fishing boat at Monhegan.

The cormorants are back already, hungry and tired after their long flight north. God played a mean trick on these unloved, ungainly birds, which in Maine we call by less fancy names—shags or worse. Shags spend much of their life underwater, yet God chose not to put the water-shedding oil in their wings which He gave to other sea birds. So shags must sit atop buoys,ledges and pilings looking ridiculous, while they hang their wings out to dry, like so much laundry.

For years, fishermen and wardens waged war on fish-eating cormorants. They killed so many that cormorants were virtually extinct on the Maine coast for 45 years, from 1880 until 1925. In the last 63 years, those remaining few have multiplied and remultiplied by tens of thousands, feeding mostly on trash fish, making dive-bomber dives as deep as 30 feet under water to nab them.

The cormorant is a dirty bird if ever there was one; their filthy nests exude excrement which kills trees. When hundreds nest on a single island, they'll eventually kill every tree on it. When baby cormorants are hatched, they come into the world without feathers, ugly, scaly beasts which look more like lizards than birds.

Herons by the hundreds will be back again to nest and breed on Wreck Island in Muscongus Bay. I love to see them stand on one leg, erect and motionless, watching for fish and then suddenly strike out their long necks like lightning to catch their meal.

These huge birds are awesome and noisy in their ponderous flight. But to see one land in tree branches is a hilarious, hair-raising sight. The long, spindly legs tremble and clutch on branches quivering under their weight; and then the huge bird tries to climb into a twig nest that is always far too small.

Eider ducks are already here in droves, mating on the islands now. The bright-plumed males, having performed their biological function, will soon fly off in bachelor groups for a carefree summer at sea, leaving 25,000 dull-colored females to hatch 150,000 eggs.

When the chicks hatch in early June, there will be an ungodly massacre on the islands. The baby chicks break out of their shells at almost the same time and then race toward the sea for safety. But gulls will devour 50,000 before the tiny chicks reach the waterline. Once in the water, the young eiders raft together for safety, and mother hens swim guard around the flock. Even then, submerged loons will often snatch and swallow a chick whole, striking from below like a bandit in ambush.

The ospreys arrived back in Maine in early April. They had a long flight from their winter havens in South and Central America. The older birds come back year after year to the same nests. If winter storms have damaged last year's nest, they'll rebuild in the same spot, just adding more and more big twigs to their straggling homes.

We have been watching ospreys come to the same nests for 20 years. They are big and handsome hawks to see; but they sound ridiculous. Their weak, miserable, high-pitched cry sounds as though it should come from something smaller than a sparrow. By August the young ospreys are so big they dangle over the sides of their nests; but they still sit there, crying to their parents to bring food and fill their wide-gaping, importunate mouths.

Finally, the parents have to boot the loutish children out of the nest and give them flying lessons. The young look too big to be such cowards, but they tremble on the end of tree limbs, scared to move, imploring mother to come to their rescue.

It is hard to believe now, but gulls were once close to extinction along the Maine coast. Food stores in the cities bought thousands of dozens of gulls eggs. A few days before an island was to "be egged," men would row ashore and walk the island and smash every egg. When they returned a few days later to collect the eggs for sale, they knew all eggs were freshly laid.

Ladies demanded bird plumes for their hats and by 1896, breast and wing feathers from gulls were fetching $12 a dozen. The slaughter of gulls and terns was so intense that in 1902 the Maine legislature passed a law making it a crime to sell or ship bird feathers. Today there are so many gulls in Maine and so few town dumps to feed them, that our gulls are heading out for the bigger and better dumps of New York and New Jersey.

Out among the blessed islands now there are puffins and petrels, egrets and eagles, terns and guillemots, auks and gannets, sandpipers and yellowlegs. Birds no bigger than my fist have crossed oceans to get here. When we humans cross the same oceans, we need jumbo jets with a maze of navigation instruments to find our way. We need flight attendants to bring us food and drink. But these simple birds do it all, alone. Today they are here by tens of thousands to enjoy summer in Maine waters.

And I can't wait to join them.

Fish cleaning, gull feeding time, Casco Bay.

LAUNCH DAY BRINGS WAVES OF PLEASURE

Steer Clear is overboard!

My boat has been launched again, and my world has a new glow.

It's hard to explain how much "Launch Day" means to infatuated boat owners. Launch Day has the joy of a wedding; the thrill of a reunion with an old flame; the anticipation of leaving on a journey; the sense of liberation and new life-to-come which a prisoner feels when he walks out the prison gate.

It means more than birthdays, Mother's Day, Father's Day and the Fourth of July. So be kind to boat owners in the spring, for their metabolism goes haywire as they come under the spell of Launch Day.

There are more than 115,000 boat owners in Maine who register with the state Bureau of Watercraft. But mighty few of them match the boat owners pictured on the covers of glossy boating magazines.

Those covers are apt to show a Mr. Money Bags sipping gin and tonic on an expensive yacht, surrounded by bosomy beauties in bikinis. Maybe that happens in the marinas of Miami or on the azure waters of an exotic anchorage in the Bahamas. But not in Maine. About 75,000 of the 115,000 registered boats in Maine are little fellows, 16 feet or under; about 35,000 are 17 to 25 feet long; only 4,000 are 26 to 40 feet; and a mere 248 are between 41 and 65 feet long. When you get up into the luxury size, over 65 feet, only 31 are registered in Maine. Almost 7,000 Maine registered boats are commercial workboats. Thin pickings for the gin-and-tonic, bosomy-bikini crowd.

Look in any boatyard, or in many back yards, in May and you'll see the typical Maine boat owner. He (and she) is smeared with paint, spotted with caulking compound, speckled with varnish. Or they are mucked up with oil and grease as they rejuvenate an engine suffering the arthritis of winter. But in their laughing eyes, you'll see that fanatical gleam which marks a boat owner ready to go overboard.

I found out strange things about the taste buds of mice, as I got ready to go overboard.

This winter the mice had a field day in my boat box filled with odds and ends from the galley. A sophisticated breed of Maine mice they turned out to be! Their favorite food was a concoction called Vodka Italiano. I had never tried the stuff, don't even remember how it got aboard. But the mice adored it.

The rascals ate their way through the outer packaging, then shredded 20 little silver foil packages inside which each contained a drink-size package of this Vodka Italiano. Some mice with less sophisticated taste buds wintered well on 24 packages of Sweet and Low.

One of the most horrifying revelations that comes to light when I'm getting our boat ready for cruising is the amount of "stuff" we carry. Eight life vests; four sets of foul weather gear; six outsize boat cushions; four mattresses and eight pillows; enough plates, cups, glasses and tablewear to equip a small restaurant, plus an incredible number of pots, pans, coffee-makers and kitchen utensils.

Once a station wagon load of this kind of stuff is stowed aboard, I fill the wagon all over again with a half-dozen docking lines, spare anchor and anchor chains, a supply of engine and transmission oil, 12-volt light bulbs, tapes for the tape deck, books for the foggy days, typewriter and copy paper, even a computer for writing and sending columns to the Press

Herald, wet suit, snorkel and goggles, two tool boxes, spare oarlocks for the dinghy, two pairs of binoculars, 40 charts for navigation, flares for emergencies, first aid kits, navigating instruments, fuel for auxiliary heaters, a back-breaking load of canned foods and folding chairs for the after-deck.

My pristine, newly painted boat, embellished this year with expensive improvements, looks a mess.

"Do I really need all this junk aboard?" I ask every year.

THE GULF OF MAINE: HUGE AND DENSE WITH INVISIBLE LIFE

You can't see 20 feet beyond your nose. Visibility is worse than in dense fog. But what blocks your vision is not fog. It is plankton, multitudes of millions of tiny living creatures so dense you can't see as far as a person can jump.

You are underwater in the frigid Gulf of Maine. The opaqueness, the murkiness is not a sign of pollution; it's a sign of fecundity. By contrast, the clarity of the Caribbean is not a sign of purity; it is a sign of barrenness.

This Gulf of Maine is one of the five richest, most fertile bodies of saltwater in the world, so dense with living creatures that they "muddy" the waters. Though they are too tiny to see, billions of plankton together make a mass so thick that you cannot see through them. These are the vital, basic parts of the food chain which keep our human race alive. Yet even marine scientists know very little about them.

However, new information is continually being gathered by the Department of Marine Resources, the Bigelow Laboratory at Boothbay Harbor, the University of Maine, the Maine Maritime Academy at Castine, the Maine Geological Survey in Augusta and a recent consortium of all five, called ARGOM—Association for Research on the Gulf of Maine.

Although Maine scientists are finding out more each year about myriad aspects of marine life, they don't yet understand its whys and wherefores. Nor does anyone, anywhere in the world. Mankind is becoming expert about outer space, which we began investigating only a few years ago, yet is still rather ignorant about the sea, which we've "known" for thousands of years and which comprises 75 percent of our world.

For 500 years, the Gulf of Maine has been feeding the world with fish, shrimp, clams and lobsters. By the 1600s, more than 300 foreign fishing boats were here, harvesting Maine fish to feed Spain, Italy, France, England, Portugal.

After World War II, when Europe and the Soviet bloc were in desperate need for food, the Gulf of Maine became a bigger food supplier than ever before, the hunting ground of fishing fleets from across the world. In July 1975, the Coast Guard reported 334 foreign vessels fishing in the Gulf of Maine. The Soviets alone had 204 vessels, of which 156 were large factory ships.

These foreign fleets so decimated fish stocks that the United States passed a law in 1976 extending the U.S. ocean boundary to 200 miles, just beyond the outer edge of Georges Bank in the Gulf of Maine. However, the World Court has since awarded to Canada half of Georges Bank, the richest fishing ground in the Gulf.

Nevertheless, Maine fishermen have been earning more than $100 million a year from their catches in the Gulf. Other fishermen from Canada and Massachusetts, earned an additional $200 million. The total economic impact of Gulf of Maine fisheries (in boats, fuel, food, gear, ice, shore crews and so forth) is an estimated $1 billion a year.

But without multitudes of invisible plankton, there would be no multimillion fish catch in the Gulf of Maine. That's why researchers are working to find out more about the whys and wherefores of the plankton, the water currents, the temperatures, salinity and living habits of the 38 types of commercial fish which flourish in the Gulf.

The Gulf of Maine is huge, more than 35,000 square miles, equivalent in size to the combined land areas of Connecticut, Massachusetts, Delaware, Rhode Island and New Jersey. It stretches from Cape Ann in Massachusetts to the Bay of Fundy in Canada and almost 200 miles out to sea, beyond the outer edge of Georges Bank. Yet the World Almanac fails to mention the Gulf of Maine.

The Gulf is almost separated from the Atlantic by the encircling arms of Cape Cod and Nova Scotia. In between are many great fishing grounds, such as the Grand Bank, Browns Bank, Jeffreys Bank and the greatest fishing ground of all, Georges Bank. There the continental shelf rises, the saltwater shallows and consequently these Banks get greater life-producing force from sunlight—photosynthesis.

Deepest parts of the Gulf are in Jordans Basin, off Mount Desert, and Wilkinson Basin, in the western part of the Gulf, where water is over 500 feet deep. Shallowest water is on Georges Bank, where the depth in places it is only 40 feet. Beyond Georges, the Gulf of Maine meets the Atlantic Ocean, where depths plunge to an average of 12,000 feet.

But it is more than photosynthesis from the sun which makes the shallow Gulf of Maine so rich and fertile. David Townsend, one of the 20 "principal investigators" (marine scientists with Ph.Ds and years of on-site research) at Bigelow Lab in Boothbay Harbor, explains how the Gulf benefits from vertical and horizontal mixing.

Vertical mixing is from bottom to top. "In winter, the water temperature at the surface is about 42 degrees," Townsend says. "But down at the bottom, it is warmer, up to 48 degrees. That warmer, saltier water flows into the Gulf of Maine deep down, from the Gulf Stream. When it rises to the surface in spring, the warmer water brings up enormous quantities of nutrients and nitrogen." In the surface waters, up to 50 feet down, the rays of the sun can reach these nutrients, and that results in photosynthesis. This photosynthesis causes an explosion of growth called plankton. This plankton makes splendid food for slightly bigger though still very tiny animals called zooplankton. Zooplankton are a favorite food of carnivore fish, such as pogies and herring, which feed close to the surface. As billions of food particles drift downward, bottom-feeding fish such as cod and haddock eat well. So they too, swarm to feed in the Gulf of Maine.

Horizontal mixing is caused by the fresh water "spring runoff" from the big Maine rivers which flow into the Gulf. The enormous runoff amounts to 250 billion gallons of water a year, most of it from snow melt. "The fresh water run-off is enough to raise the level of the entire Gulf of Maine by 1½ feet," says Townsend. The snow melt far inland brings with it a rich mixture of land nutrients and minerals which add to the richness of the Gulf of Maine.

Due to the earth's eastward rotation, the rich fresh water circulates counterclockwise. But at the deep Northeast Channel, dense ocean water pours in and increases the speed of the counterclockwise flow. Thus, the mass of different nutrients from deep ocean and shallow rivers mix and mingle and circle round and round the Gulf, while the photosynthesis from the sun performs its magic of growth and transformation. As a result, water in the Gulf of Maine is so dense with life that visibility is cut to 20 feet.

Emperors of the Sea: The Great Sperm Whales

ABOARD STEER CLEAR — At night aboard this little boat anchored in an island cove far out to sea, it can be deliciously terrifying to read about whales so big they could flail us to splinters with a mere smack of their massive flukes.

Last night in my bunk, with the ocean lapping a few inches from my ear, I relished reading about sperm whales in Hank Searls' book, "Soundings". As I read, I knew there were sperm whales not far from me in the Atlantic, calling to each other with voices I could not hear.

Somewhere out there tonight a massive bull is "blanging" to his herd with a sound so loud it would break the eardrums and deafen a man in the water. Other whales may be hearing it hundreds of miles away, understanding the code of the herdmaster's "blangs".

A great bull sperm whale plowing through the ocean may be 65 years old, weigh 70 tons, measure 65 feet long. His massive head measures 20 feet wide. Inside it is the largest brain known on this planet.

Biologically a sperm whale's brain is identical to man's brain. But it is seven times the weight and volume of man's brain. Its thinking cortex has five times the convolutions and 10 times the nerve cells of a human brain.

Sperm whales possessed this enormous brain 30 million years before mankind's ancestors came down from the trees.

So, imprinted on that massive brain of each sperm whale sharing the ocean with my tiny boat are inherited memories of 30 million years of ancestors, plus the whale's own years of experience cruising oceans depths almost unknown to mankind.

A bull in his prime can plunge from the ocean surface as deep as 7,000 feet, into the black abyss of the Atlantic, where the pressure is one and a half tons on every square inch of his vast body. Down at those depths, each cubic foot of air he sucked into his massive lungs on the surface is compressed to a bubble two inches in diameter. His lungs, which measure 7 feet long on the surface, are compressed to the size of a cod fish.

A steel-ribbed nuclear submarine would collapse at a depth of 6,000 feet; but a sperm whale's 16-foot-long ribs of bone barely begin to bend.

With the miraculous sonar and computer inside the whale's gigantic brain, he can read the topography of the caverns and mountains on the ocean bottom, can decipher the temperature and salinity of water miles distant. His sonar will discover and report the size of a giant squid thousands of feet below. Giant squid are his favorite food. He will compute whether the squid will yield enough protein to be worth the energy he would have to expend to reach it and fight it. His sophisticated detective apparatus can even penetrate throught the hide of a female whale and judge the size, well-being and sex of his calf which she is carrying inside her, reports Hank Searls.

The gestation period from conception to birth of a sperm whale calf lasts 16 months. At two months, the fetus is only 3 inches long. By the fifth month, it has grown to 200 pounds. At birth in the 16th month, a baby bull calf weighs two tons and is 12 feet long. On the first day of life, he must learn to swim at two miles an hour, plunge to 100 feet and stay under water for 15 minutes.

For the first two years, the baby will nurse on its mother's milk, probably the richest food on this planet. It will suckle every half hour, drinking 50 gallons of whale milk in a day, and gain 100 pounds of weight every day for a year.

To provide so much nourishment, the mother must hunt and eat voraciously. To make her life more arduous, the mother must virtually tug her 10-ton baby beside her through the ocean for a year.

The young bull has a long, frustrating development to full maturity. At the age of eight years he may weigh 40 tons, as much as his mother, and measures 40 feet long. His maleness urges him toward sexual activity (his testicles weigh 5 pounds each). But he has no teeth. His 8-inch-long curved teeth do not penetrate through his gums until he is almost 25 years old. Not until then will he be able to do battle with the adult bull harem-master for possession of any females. So during this long boyhood, the young bull must remain on the outskirts of the harem, doing sentry duty and helping to hunt giant squid.

Giant squid, usually living more than 2,000 feet deep in the ocean, are murderous carnivores. They can weigh 1,000 pounds. Their 10 arms have sawtoothed edges which rip through tough whale blubber like a flenser's knife. Sperm whales detect the giant squid through their sonar; the whale's weapon is sound.

First, the sperm whale makes a stealthy approach to within less than 1,000 feet. Then at short range, the whale lets go with an enormous blast of sound, a short-range "blang" that will stun the giant squid into a moment of immobility. At this moment, the whale must get its 15-foot jaws latched onto a vulnerable part of the squid. The squid, using its longest 12-foot tentacle will try to clamp shut the whale's blow hole.

The fight is on. The giant squid tries to wrap its longest tentacle over the whale's blow hole, using its other nine arms to slice the blubber. The suffocating whale is fighting to drag the 1,000-pound squid to the surface 2,000 feet above, so he can get air; and the squid is releasing black ink to disorient the whale.

Dragged to the surface from its habitual depths, the change in pressure weakens and explodes the squid. The whale tears off the tentacle suffocating its blow hole, gets the needed air, and then shreds the squid to ribbons with its eight-inch teeth. Soon the whale has gobbled down almost 1,000 pounds of vital protein.

That protein is needed for long journeys through parts of the ocean where feeding grounds are scarce. A bull whale may eat enough to add 1,000 pounds of blubber in seven days, before setting off to a distant destination with his herd. On long journeys, pods of whales interchange information. By their blanging sounds, pods of whales contact each other over hundreds of miles.

Their ancient language is delivered in standard information patterns. Hank Searls reports that after the whales make contact, the first batch of information transmitted concerns precise location, a description of the ocean bottom or seamount where each is, pinpointed precisely with detail on the water salinity and temperature. The next batch of information exchanged concerns feeding grounds along the route they have followed. Only after these information exchanges are completed does their transmission become more personal and intimate. Then pods may swap news and gossip about births and deaths and about shipping encountered—freighters and submarines or whaling vessels.

In my bunk, I feel awed by the realization that even as Steer Clear bobs at anchor, the ocean beyond me may be filled with such transmissions and such voyages.

These herds of giant sperm whales transverse the oceans endlessly, cruising at about four knots, though a bull in battle can briefly reach a speed of 20 knots. These giants normally swim below the surface for 50 minutes out of each hour, then surface for 10 minutes. I have on rare, lucky occasions heard the weird exhaling of a whale, blowing out as it surfaces. Then for the next ten minutes on the surface, a sperm whale will inhale hugely, once a minute, replenishing the oxygen in its bloodstream; and then submerge for another 50 minutes.

At times a sperm whale pod may meet and mingle briefly with its small cousins, the 20-foot-long pilot whales or black fish. Mankind has captured and trained some of these and reportedly used them for espionage under water. There is a report, unconfirmed by the Defense Department, that cameras were mounted on trained pilot whales and that for a year they were stationed off Elsinore, photographing every Soviet submarine which left the Baltic.

Mankind has worked hard to teach pilot whales, dolphins and porpoises some of our tricks. But what a new world of undreamed knowledge mankind could uncover if our minute brain learned how to tap into the enormous brains and 30 million years of experience which lie within a sperm whales's head.

Maine had a brief fling at whaling, when the money went out of fishing, at the end of Mr. Madison's war. Under the Treaty of 1818, Maine fishing boats lost the right to fish within three miles of British dominions. Our boats couldn't put into Nova Scotia to buy bait, seek shelter, take on water and food or make repairs. After Maine's fishing fleet dropped from 10,000 tons to a mere 760 tons, a scared Congress gave out subsidies to Mainers to build new boats, and the tonnage jumped back to 11,000 tons by 1820.

To make quick money out of these subsidies, a group of Mainers started the Wiscasset Whale Fishing Co. They bought a hull being built on the Hitchcock ways in Damariscotta, fitted it out as a whaler, christened it Wiscasset and sent it out to hunt whales under the command of Capt. Richard Macy.

Three-and-a-half years later, the Wiscasset came back with 2,800 barrels of sperm oil. Out it went again, but this voyage was a flop. The Wiscasset returned with a mere 900 barrels of whale oil. Discouraged, the whaling company sold the vessel. And that was about the sum total of Maine whaling.

But in New Bedford, Mass., 329 whaling ships were making rich men out of their owners, who used the windfall money to build the most extravagant ship captains' homes in New England. Harpooning a big whale in those days was as good (for the owner) as bringing in a "gusher" oil well is today. One 50-foot whale might yield 8,000 gallons of whale oil. Whale oil in 1850 was worth a dollar a gallon; it lit the lamps of the world until the discovery of petroleum in 1859.

Crews on whaling ships got the blunt end of the stick, while owners got rich. Their pay after a four-year voyage might be $200. And living and dying in the fo'c's'le was awful.

Whaling killed seamen, and Arctic ice killed their ships. In one year, 1865, the confederate raider Shenandoah burned 25 whale ships caught in Arctic ice. In 1871, 33 more whaling ships were trapped and crushed by ice. More than 1,200 crewmen escaped, helped by Eskimos. But more died.

One magnificent book put whaling into America's conscience - Moby Dick by Herman Melville. In 1841, Melville, then a 22-year-old who was out of work, went to sea from New Bedford aboard the whaling ship Acushnet, bound for Cape Horn and the south Pacific. Melville couldn't stick out the hard, dangerous, cold, wet, smelly life. He jumped ship in mid-voyage, after 18 months. In 1851 he published Moby Dick, telling the first-hand story of whaling and thereby created one of the greatest of all American novels.

In those days, U.S. whaling ships alone were killing 10,000 whales a year. By the 1980s, more than 30,000 whales were being killed a year, mostly by Japan and the Soviet Union. In April 1985, President Reagan pressured the Soviet to reduce whaling. He cut in half the amount of fish the Russians could take from U.S. waters and hinted that he might prohibit the import of all Soviet fish products, a trade worth $17 million. That hurt Russia. So the Soviets promised to stop all whaling in the Antarctic after 1987. Japan also was pressured by Reagan to quit its $50 million-a-year whaling business or risk losing its $500 million-a-year fishing harvest from U.S. waters.

Bowheads, humpbacks, right and blue whales are close to extinction in some areas already. This economic squeeze on whale slaughter by Soviet and Japanese commercial whaling may ward off the extinction of some of the largest animals ever to have lived on Earth.

SURVIVAL: HOW TO STAY ALIVE IN ICY MAINE WATERS

How long can you survive in Maine waters?

Robert S. Pratt, the University of Maine Sea Grant Program's expert on cold water survival, was talking to a room packed with Maine fishermen and their wives. They hung on every word, as if their lives depended on it.

But not only fishermen risk drowning. Maine people and visitors go onto and into the water on Maine's 2,500 ponds and lakes, 5,000 rivers and streams, and along almost 3,000 miles of coast. The inland water area of Maine amounts to almost 2,300 square miles. People drown in fresh water as easily as in salt water.

Pratt himself came too close to drowning in his own back yard. "We skate on a frozen pond back of our house. My kids and I had been skating together all afternoon," Pratt said. "After dark, I went back to skate alone under the stars, so I'd sleep well. The ice broke and suddenly I was in icy water, out of sight and hearing from the house. My first thought was "Darn! I've ruined our ice." Then I tried pulling myself out. I couldn't, because the ice kept breaking away in my hand. My next thought was, "I can't drown out here, alone in the night. I teach survival." Eventually, he got his fingers into a crack and slid up onto the thicker ice. He made it back to his house.

He was lucky. Hypothermia comes very fast in icy water, and its first effect is to make your hands and feet almost useless. Without strength in your hands, you can't pull yourself up onto ice, or even grab hold of a ladder to get back on a boat.

How long can you survive in Maine's cold waters, even in summer? Pratt says the first 60 seconds spell life or death. That is when people decide whether to give up. "On one well-known Maine island," says Pratt, "some fishermen carry 'prayer stones' aboard. When a fisherman who can't swim has to leave a sinking boat, he drops his prayer stones inside his boots, to sink him fast. That man has decided early that he will drown."

So the first step to survival, says Pratt, is to change your attitude from dying to living. Next is to learn basic ways of how to survive. Third step is to own and use the equipment required to help you survive.

Pratt's first lesson in how to survive came as a surprise.

"Don't swim. Don't tread water. Don't try the drown-proofing technique," warns Pratt. "All three will make you lose precious body heat and hasten hypothermia, which is your first enemy."

Hypothermia means loss of heat in the vital organs. The marvelous instincts of the body fight hypothermia automatically. Soon after anyone is thrown into cold water, the brain orders the blood supply to stop flowing to the arms and legs, extremities not vital to life, and uses the heart's energy to pump blood only to where it is vital for maintenance of life—the brain, the lungs, the trunk of the body.

"So don't move your arms and legs, which will force blood there. Stay still. Protect heat loss from the core of your body by folding your arms across your chest, by bringing your knees up to your stomach. Get into the womb or fetal position, the way you do when you climb into a cold bed with cold sheets on a winter night. If several of you are in danger, get together in a tight circle, wrap yourselves around each other for warmth as well as flotation," advises Pratt.

Hypothermia develops even in water of 50 degrees and higher, not only in icy water. Normal body temperature is 98.6 degrees Fahrenheit. If water chills the blood to 97 degrees, uncontrollable shivering starts. Between 96 and 94 degrees, the heartbeat drops to very slow; less blood circulates; the victim becomes glassy eyed, acts as if drunk; the blood-starved brain slows down on sending commands. As body temperature drops the heart slows until it comes to a standstill.

"Keeping warm, preventing the loss of body heat in critical areas, is the key to survival. This is where equipment comes in to help you," says Pratt. The purpose of all survival equipment is to keep you afloat and keep you warm. "The warmer it keeps you, the longer you will live. For example, the ordinary lifejacket approved by the Coast Guard might keep you afloat and warm enough so you'd last an hour or two on a summer day. But a float-coat with neoprene insulation and a hood will increase your survival time to about eight hours. And if you are wearing a full survival suit which keeps your head, chest, legs and arms warm and dry, you could survive 24 hours," says Pratt.

In the last few years, there has been a surge of interest and action by fishermen in survival techniques and gear. Pratt estimates that today 50 percent of Maine's commercial fishing boats over 30 feet carry survival suits for everyone aboard. Big offshore vessels also carry expensive liferafts. Extensive publicity about survivals, rescues and drownings have made most fishermen acutely aware of the need for such gear, according to Pratt, who has delivered 150 lectures on how to survive in Maine's icy waters.

"The biggest job is to get people to practice using the gear they have bought, and to wear it when near the water," he says. "We are fighting the John Wayne syndrome. Few fishermen dare to be seen at the dock wearing vests or float coats. They like to seem so tough that if their boat sinks, they'll walk home."

To make vests and float coats less conspicuous, manufacturers are making them to look like regular jackets and light enough to be worn when working on deck. "When you buy one, pick a bright color—orange, brilliant red or yellow. Don't choose blue, because on a blue ocean against a blue sky, you won't be easily seen," says Pratt. He tells fishing boat captains that the best skippers make their crews practice getting into their clumsy survival suits in the dark, on a rolling sea, until they can all do it in a minute.

Pratt is on the faculty of the Sea Grant Program at the University of Maine. He is a professional marine biologist, but has been assigned to instruct fishermen and pleasure-boating groups in survival.

Pratt is going beyond survival in his talks with fishermen. He is urging local groups to drill in search techniques. "Every fisherman along the Maine coast will willingly go out searching for a missing boat. But chances of finding that missing boat or the men floating in survival suits are hugely increased if groups of local fishermen train themselves in organized search procedures.

"The East Casco Bay fishermen have organized and trained themselves into a fine search operation. They are ready to train other groups. And so is the Sea Grant Program."

A tragedy spurred the East Casco Bay fishermen to organize themselves into a skilled search group. The tragedy was the loss of the men aboard the boat, Spring Tide. The crew went overboard when their boat caught fire within sight of shore. They had survival suits aboard, and they wore them when they abandoned their burning boat. So they were surely alive in the water when other local boats came searching for them. But good as each boat was, the fishermen were not trained as a group to work together in an organized search pattern. Time ran out. When the men were finally found, they were dead. Out of that experience emerged the expert search group among the fishermen of East Casco Bay. This group now helps other groups organize themselves into trained search squadrons. But few have yet done this. Nor have Maine's yacht clubs, according to Pratt." If any group wants assistance, we will provide it free. Call the University of Maine Sea Grant Program, either at Walpole or at Orono," says Pratt.

LEARN THE LOBSTER LINGO

"In the summer of 1952 my brother Paul hauled a trap in the cove at Metinic which had 82 lobsters in it, 14 of them counters."

This is one of the first sentences by Kendall Merriam in his book, "The Illustrated Dictionary of Lobstering." It is a sentence to stop anyone in his tracks. Lobsters are scarce today. The idea of 82 lobsters in one trap, even if only 14 are big enough to keep, is an impossible dream today.

Merriam's little book is a dictionary of a few hundred words and terms heard in most Maine harbors and lobster pounds.

Here is a sampling, which could be a handy reference when you are eating lobster on an outside deck, watching the fishing boats.

Anchor rode: A piece of line used for anchoring.

Bait bag: A small, knit, mesh bag filled with bait, placed on the bait string of the trap by means of the bait iron.

Berried lobster: A female lobster with eggs on her tail. Egg-bearing females must be thrown back in Maine.

Blue lobster: A rarity of the sea, some say one-in-a-million. Lobsters occasionally have yellow, green, red or white shells. Lobsters having two colors, split down the middle lengthwise, have been seen.

Brim: Lobster bait. The head, backbone and tail of redfish, from which the fillets have been taken.

Cage: Framework of bronze rods surrounding a lobster boat's propeller to prevent the propeller cutting off or fouling on pot warp (see pot warp).

Car: A wooden, slatted box, usually 10 feet by 15 feet by 3 feet, kept in the water to store lobsters in until they are sold. A small car holds 1,500 to 2,000 pounds of lobster.

Door: The top part of a lobster trap, which is on hinges. Opened to take out lobsters and put in bait. Hinged on straps of leather or rubber.

Highliner: Lobsterman who consistently has highest catches in his area.

Kitchen: first chamber in a lobster trap. Followed by the parlor. Lobsters get to the parlor by going through the kitchen (where the bait is). Parlor is also called the bedroom.

Pot: Another name for trap. Years ago, traps were pot-shaped.

Pot warp: A twisted, three-strand rope attached from the trap on the ocean bottom to the marker buoy on the surface. Used to haul the trap up to the boat.

Pound: Storage area for holding lobsters keeping them alive. Substantial risk of loss due to disease or cannibalism.

Shedders: Lobster during moulting stage. The lobster sheds its whole shell in order to grow. Occurs late summer and early fall. Shedders or soft shells bring a lower price.

Short: A lobster under legal size.

String: A particular line of traps, usually of the same warp length. Also all of the traps one lobsterman fishes, as "He has a string of 550 traps."

Sternman: The man who empties the traps, rebaits them, puts them overboard. He is usually paid in shares, profits of the catch.

Tomalley: The liver of the lobster. Essential to lobster stew.

Toggle: Toggles once were empty liquor bottles, but today are doughnut-shaped pieces of Styrofoam; used as a flotation device tied part way down the pot warp to keep it off the bottom. Toggles ride on the surface, 10 feet or so from the lobster buoy.

Twine: Thin cord used in knitting bait bags.

Wet smack: Small boat once used for carrying lobsters to market long distance. Wet smacks had compartments with holes to the outside, so the seawater could flow through the hull and keep lobsters alive.

Now, you know the language, here are a few facts about the sex life of lobsters.

The average lobster caught in Maine weighs about 1 1/4 pounds, is about five years old and may already have shed 20 times. Each new shell is large enough to allow the lobster inside it to grow about 15 percent before the shell gets too small. Then the lobster again sheds the tight shell, and grows a new shell, a few sizes larger.

The meat in shedders is sweeter, some lobster lovers say. No doubt a shedder is much easier to eat because the new shell is soft. You can easily break the claws and tail with your fingers. The disadvantage is that there is also more water in a "softshell" or shedder than in a hard shell. This is one reason shedders are bargain priced; another is that shedders don't stand up to shipping, and so must usually be sold locally.

A lobster's sex life is tied into shedding, too. This is the time when females are impregnated. Just after females shed their hard shells and are exposed and vulnerable, the male lobsters impregnate them.

But there is a quirk to the biology of a female lobster. Although impregnated, her eggs are not fertilized for another year. The impregnated

50 years ago, when lobsters were big and lobstermen wore felt hats.

female lobster has within her a compartment, called a semen receptacle, in which she carries the male sperm.

In a separate compartment she carries her eggs. A year after being impregnated, she will extrude those eggs from the inside of her body to the outside of her shell and in the process will pass them over the semen receptacle for fertilization.

A female of legal minimum size and five years old carries 9,000 eggs on her swimmerettes—tiny claws. Only about nine baby lobsters will survive after hatching, and many of these will die in the early stages of life. A more mature female may carry up to 40,000 eggs, of which fewer than one in a thousand will survive the initial stages of life.

KEEPING LOBSTERS IS LIKE PLAYING THE STOCK MARKET

Keeping lobsters is a tricky business, about as risky as playing the stock market. And you keep lobsters for the same reason you play the market—to make money. To win, you buy low, sell high. Maine has the capacity to store six million pounds of lobster in "pounds".

Essentially, a lobster pound is a live stockpile of lobster kept in a contained area and sometimes given controlled feedings. In this way, a pound for lobsters is like the fattening-up, grain-feeding yard for beef cattle. The idea is to fatten up the lobster too, and thus get far more money for a fat lobster than you paid for a thin lobster.

But if you can make a pile, you can also lose your shirt running a lobster pound.

For example, lobsters can and do escape in large numbers. Overnight, you can get a mass escape of $20,000 to $50,000 worth through an undiscovered break in the "wall," far below the water line, so it is invisible.

Lobsters are cannibals. The strong eat the weak.

Lobsters get sick. Disease can spread like wildfire among them, and can kill off all the profits.

A disease called redtail is the dread killer. Some pound owners have lost more than half their stock in a season from redtail. That means losing half their money.

Pollution can kill lobsters. A bit of oil on their gills can spell sudden death.

If the incoming tide fails to mix new oxygen with the old water deep down at the bottom of the pound, the lobsters lying on the bottom may die, asphyxiated from lack of fresh oxygen.

But of course there is the good side, the money-making side to keeping a lobster pound. If all goes well, you may buy at $1.90 cents a pound and sell at $3.90 or more. If you do this with 100,000 pounds, you have made $200,000.

On Southport Island, near Boothbay Harbor, there are two lobster pounds, one with a capacity for 150,000 pounds, the other for 100,000 pounds.

At Friendship, there is a six-acre pound that can hold more than a quarter million pounds of lobster. (This pound got hit catastrophically in November 1963 by an oil spill).

Some of the other big pounds are at Milbridge, Hancock, Hewlett Island, Boothbay, Deer Isle, Vinalhaven and Small Point.

There are two dozen or more pounds in Maine with capacities from 50,000 up to 450,000 pounds. The biggest, at Hancock, has a capacity of almost half a million pounds. Together these lobster pounds have a capacity of 4.3 million pounds of lobster.

In addition, another million pounds can be held in big "cars," which are huge crates floating in harbors. They hold about 1,000 pounds each.

Lobstermen themselves often hold back their daily catch till the price goes up. They use crates, most holding 80 pounds, which they tie onto their moorings. Sometimes this works well, and they can hold to sell on a rising market. Other times, they wish they'd sold earlier at any price.

For example, Fred Boynton of New Harbor recalls the day a friend came along wanting 35 pounds of lobster for his little girl's birthday party.

"I went down and hauled a crate of my lobsters. Found a few dead ones. So I hauled my other crates. Found 200 dead in five crates. Well, it had been awful calm down there with no wind or circulation, and there was a lot of seaweed caught around the float and I think they smothered for lack of oxygen.

"The only other thing I can figure out is that one of those draggers came in yesterday for water, and the water for cooling his engine was discharging overboard right near my crates. That water is very hot and it's possible it heated the water up enough to kill my lobsters."

Finally, there is the human predator. Some scoundrels in outboards come into a strange harbor in the nighttime. They cut loose a few crates, tow them to a cove nearby, empty them and steal another man's livelihood. Along the Maine coast, that is a dangerous game. And not many fools risk trying it.

Lobster pound downeast at Sorrento. Note the wooden retaining "fence". Up to $100,000 worth of lobsters are kept in big pounds, waiting for the right price to sell.

"Keeping lobsters," hoping the increase in price will more than offset losses in the pound, is the Maine coast version of playing the stock market.

SEABIRDS ON MAINE ISLANDS

Alan E. Hutchinson is the seabird expert at Maine's Department of Inland Fisheries and Wildlife, which manages the wildlife on 275 islands and ledges along the length of the Maine coast.

Hutchinson says Maine has 12 species of seabirds, including three in the Alcid family; the puffin, the guillemot and the razorbill auk. Maine islands are the southern limit of the breeding range of all three. Maine therefore is the only part of the United States where these three birds nest.

We nearly lost these wonderful birds at the turn of the century because their feathers were sold at good prices to New York milliners who stuck them by tens of thousands into ladies' hats. Then ladies' fashions changed, protective laws and regulations were passed, and the Alcids came back to nest again on Maine islands, but only in a minor way even now.

Puffins are still extremely scarce. About 125 pairs nest on the cliffs of Matinicus Rock, some 24 miles to sea from Rockland. A few have been brought back artificially to Eastern Egg Rock in Muscongus Bay, not far from Monhegan Island. But there are only two nesting sites of the razor-bill auk and together they number only 25 pairs.

The gay, bobbing, little guillemots have made a splendid comeback. About 3,000 breeding pairs are making nests on 115 islands.

Gulls of three kinds—the herring gull, the great black-backed gull and the laughing gull, with its strange cry and smart skullcap have come back in tremendous numbers.

Herring gulls are everywhere. More than 25,000 pairs breed on Maine islands.

The great black-backed gulls are relative newcomers, who arrived in Maine in the 1920s. Now over 200 islands support about 10,000 nesting pairs of black gulls. They've become predators, but their lives are still protected by federal law.

Laughing gulls are fairly scarce. But their numbers have been on the increase, now amounting to 230 pairs on six islands.

Unhappily, the terns, my favorite seabirds, have been having a bad time from the black-backed gulls. Their numbers have been on the decline since 1940, when the gull population began exploding. The common terns nest on 24 islands. But they numbered only about 2,000 pairs in 1986. Even fewer in numbers are the Arctic terns; and still scarcer are the Roseate terns (about 80 pairs) and the least tern (only 21 pairs on two islands).

Eider ducks have made a tremendous comeback after being hunted almost to extinction. Today some 25,000 pairs are nesting on about 250 islands. Cormorants are everywhere too, with more than 16,000 pairs nesting on well over 100 islands. Herons, which were almost extinct in 1930, are back today, with 1,000 pairs building their huge twig nests on about 18 islands.

Yet, out of Maine's almost 3,000 islands and ledges, only about 350 of them have nesting sites for seabirds, according to a 1986 survey by state biologists.

MAINE COLONISTS BEAT PILGRIMS HERE

The Pilgrim Fathers are touted as the founders of our country. But that's a bit of Massachusetts promotion. The nation began on the coast of Maine, long before a Pilgrim set foot on Plymouth Rock.

The truth is that Maine was settled so far ahead of Massachusetts that farms on Maine islands and the Maine coast fed those so-called "first settlers" from the Mayflower, when they were starving in the winter of 1621.

First to voyage to Maine were the explorers, treasure seekers, and navigators, men such as Giovanni Caboto, who charted Maine waters in 1497. Giovanni da Verrazano was sailing here in 1524; Esteban Gomez named Casco Bay and Campobello in 1526. These men were looking for gold, silver and a passage to the Pacific and China and India—all in vain.

Then came the English. John Walker planted the English flag at Camden in 1580; Martin Pring and Edmund Jones sailed "Speedwell" and "Discoverer" to Monhegan, North Haven and Vinalhaven in 1603; John Smith sent home shiploads of Maine fish from Monhegan in 1614; Richard Vines was flourishing at Biddeford Pool in 1616, and 120 men at Popham established a colony there in 1607—14 years before the Pilgrims arrived at Plymouth.

They chose a bad spot. Popham was exposed to the worst of the weather in that dreadful winter of 1607. Half the 120 settlers died and the rest were evacuated home to England within two years.

However those unsuccessful colonists at Popham were the first Europeans to build a boat in the New World, and a mighty good boat it was. Their 30-ton pinnace, "Virginia," named for the reputedly virgin Queen Elizabeth of England, sailed between England and the New World for 20 years before she was wrecked in a storm off Ireland.

Long before the Pilgrims landed at Plymouth, Maine had settlements at the Isles of Shoals, Kittery, York, Saco, Parker's Head, Damariscove Island, Pemaquid, and Monhegan Island.

Early settlers on the Maine coast were so relatively established by the time the Pilgrims arrived that they filled a ship with stored food they had grown and shipped it to Plymouth to save the Mayflower people from starvation in the winter of 1621.

Fish and the Catholic Church were the odd couple responsible for Maine becoming the real birthplace of our nation.

In the early 16th century, all of Europe and most of England were Catholic. And half the days on the Catholic church calendar were decreed meatless days. That meant fish on the table. European waters could not provide all the fish needed. The early explorers, who came to Maine seeking gold and silver and the route to China found none of these; but they found fish, fish in vast quantities never seen in European waters. Fish became the silver mines of Maine.

What attracted fish by the billions to these waters 400 years ago? The same natural phenomena which still make the Grand Banks and Georges Bank, two of the best fishing grounds in the world today.

Water over these banks is shallow, less than 200 feet, compared to 2,000 feet in the ocean just off the banks. This means sunlight can reach to nourish plant growth on the ocean floor. That plant life is the Maine attraction to enormous schools of cod and haddock and other fish.

Two major currents, one cold, one warmer, meet over the Grand Banks and Georges Bank. The cold current, flowing from Labrador, is enormously rich in plankton, those microscopic bits of salt-water life which are a delicious food to fish. The warmer current from the south brings algae, favorite food of mackerel and herring.

This is why 400 years ago foreign fishing fleets were in Maine waters, reaping the fish harvest.

Those early fish boats averaged 200 tons and carried 50 men in dark, dank quarters. The reason such small boats carried so many men was that half of them worked on shore, drying, salting, corning the fish, while a second crew manned the boats to catch more fish. Soon some shore gangs decided they'd rather sleep on the Maine islands than go back aboard those smelly, wet, dark, and overcrowded boats at night. So they built shelters to sleep in.

During the day, while the vessel was off fishing, the shore crew would take breaks from drying fish to walk the islands, to snare rabbits, catch birds, kill a deer. Before long these farm boys from the west country of England took to planting a few crops.

Some asked to be left behind on these Maine islands when their boat sailed home to England with 400,000 pounds of dried fish smelling in the hold. They were given basic provisions and hunting guns with the understanding they would have the fishing station ready next spring. These first settlers began a profitable winter trade in furs with the Indians. Each year, more men chose to stay on the islands or along the coast of Maine rather than endure the rough and smelly voyage back across the Atlantic, and then face a nagging wife, or the sheriff back in England.

Years before the "Mayflower" sailed into Plymouth, 300 or more foreign fishing boats were working in Maine waters every summer. Old log books and ship records indicate that as many as 30 boats would seek shelter on a stormy night at Damariscove Island, near Boothbay Harbor.

In Maine at Thanksgiving, we can do better than sentimentalize those late-coming Pilgrim Fathers. Better we drink a toast to Sir Ferdinando Gorges, the father of Maine.

Sir Ferdinando, despite his Spanish-sounding name, was born in Somerset, England about 1573. He fought so well for Queen Elizabeth against the Spaniards at the time of the Armada, he was knighted for bravery and rewarded by being named Governor of Plymouth at age 30.

In 1604 he clapped eyes on an Indian birch bark canoe, the first ever seen in England. Martin Pring had carried it back as a souvenir from Maine, after his voyage here in 1603. The Indian canoe proved to be a tremendous piece of travel promotion. The sight of it hooked Sir Ferdinando Gorges to a lifetime addiction to colonize the New World, particularly Maine.

For the next 40 years, Sir Ferdinando sunk every penny he had, every ounce of his wheeler-dealer energy, into promoting and financing expeditions to the Maine coast.

Gorges was the man behind the Weymouth expedition in 1607; behind the ill-fated Popham colony later that year; behind three voyages by Capt. John Smith; behind the fiasco of Henry Challons, who got so far off course that he was captured by Spaniards in Puerto Rico. Calamity after calamity struck down the dreams and hopes of Sir Ferdinando. But he would never quit.

Finally, King James I named Sir Ferdinando, now into his sixties, to be Governor General of all New England, giving him king-like powers. He got ready to arrive in great style. A new man o' war was built for him. But it turned over at its launching and never sailed. Nor did Sir Ferdinando. He stayed too loyal for too long to the Crown.

After Charles I was deposed and decapitated, by Oliver Cromwell, the Roundheads threw Sir Ferdinando into jail, as a royalist. He died in prison, at 74, broken and broke. He never set foot in Maine, which he had done more to establish than any man. Today in Maine, his monument is the drab, abandoned Fort Gorges in Portland Harbor.

BUOYS: 1,200 SENTINELS ALONG THE COAST

A red nun bobs and sways outside my porthole.

Sailors coming into harbor always pass a red nun on their right. Sailors going out to sea always leave a red nun on their port or left side. Red Right Returning—that's the slogan.

Red nuns, black or green cans, flashers, doleful bells, cacophonous gongs, spindles, reflectors—they all speak a language to boatmen more detailed and informative than land people might guess.

Buoys speak a language which a foreign ship with no knowledge of the local tongue can understand; and thereby be guided safely into a harbor never seen before.

Yet, the language of the buoys can also deceive. When it does, the result can spell disaster—as Portland Harbor knows.

Changed positions of buoys helped cause two disastrous oil spills in Portland Harbor.

In 1972, the 810-foot oil tanker Tamano, coming into Portland, hit Soldier's Ledge. The shipowners contested that buoy was off station by 215 feet, after the Coast Guard had serviced the buoy two days before the Tamano hit Soldiers Ledge and ripped a gaping hole in the ship's hull and spilled 100,000 gallons of Bunker C oil into Hussey Sound. It cost $4 million to clean up the mess.

Nine years earlier, in 1963, the tanker Northern Gulf hit Western Cod Ledge, ruptured its hull and spilled vast quantities of oil. Subsequent investigation showed that buoy was off station by 400 yards, and had been so for nearly eight months.

Lawyers defending the Coast Guard against shipowners in court suits, argued that a ship should be navigated by bearings on fixed objects on shore or by soundings, and should not rely on buoys which are only floating aids to navigation, subject to being moved by wave or wind action.

Buoys—even though waves and winds do move them—are much bigger and heavier than they look, since only a small part of them shows above water. The biggest sea buoys are 60 feet long, with most of the length under water; they weigh as much as 17 tons.

Outside of Portland Harbor, the sea buoy at Jeffreys Ledge weighs 12 tons. Sea buoys are anchored by "deadmen", huge blocks of concrete, which weigh between 2 and 8 tons each. The enormous anchor chains which run between buoy and anchor weigh a ton a "shot." (A "shot" is 15 fathoms or 90 feet.) If a buoy is moored in 100 feet of water, the anchor chain should be 500 feet long, five times the depth of the water. The chain alone would weigh more than 5 tons.

The United States has 10,000 buoys, far more than any other nation. The Coast Guard is responsible for the maintenance, repair, painting and positioning of all 10,000.

In the first Coast Guard District alone, which runs from Montauk Point, Long Island, N.Y., to West Quoddy Head on the Maine-Canada border, there are 2,766 buoys. About 1,275 of them are in Maine waters in 1988.

Buoys began when our nation began. President George Washington approved $264 to build a buoy for Delaware Harbor. An Act of Congress in 1797 provided for 16 buoys for Boston Harbor. In 1843, all buoys on the Maine and Massachusetts coast were wooden spar buoys, painted black, white and red, but without any numbering system. They spoke no language.

Then in 1850 Congress passed a law requiring that buoys be colored and numbered, and the buoy language began.

Since then any vessel invariably steers its course into a U.S. harbor leaving red buoys with even numbers on its right, or starboard side, and black buoys with odd numbers on the port or left side. The safe channel is in between them, leaving red to right and black to left, coming into harbor and the opposite leaving harbor.

But there are buoys without numbers. What do they mean?

Buoys without numbers but with horizontal stripes indicate rocks below; they may be passed on either left or right. Numberless buoys with stripes are mid-channel markers and may be safely passed close-to on either side. Still other numberless buoys are fitted with perches, cages, even signposts; these mark abrupt turns in the channel or obstructions ahead.

Buoys have different shapes. The red nuns are conical or pointed, and the black or green cans are flat-topped. This difference in shapes is for identification when numbers or colors cannot be read. (Many black cans are now painted green for improved visibility.)

What does a sailor do in fog or night, when these buoys cannot be seen? Well, many buoys are fitted with bells or lights or whistles.

Bell buoys started about 1855; whistling buoys were invented in 1876 by J.M. Courtenay. Gas-lighted buoys first came to New York Bay in 1882. By 1910 compressed acetylene gas was used to light buoys. Now most are

The author relaxing aboard Steer Clear, safe in a snug harbor.

powered by special-type batteries, triggered off and on by the rising and setting of the sun. There are 450 of these large lighted buoys along the Maine coast.

In fog or storm, in dead of night or early dawn, there is no more valued friend to a boatman than a buoy. If the light goes out on one, or the bell is silenced, the Coast Guard hurries to replace or repair it.

But gales and storms have swept away even 17-ton buoys, with all their tons of chains and anchors. A loose buoy in the ocean can be as dangerous as a loose cannon careening around the deck of an old time frigate. Some buoys which broke loose along the New England coast have been found weeks later, washed up on the shores of Ireland.

I look out my porthole at sunup to make sure my red nun is still there, bobbing and swaying, and has not been swept off to Ireland. And in my mind's eye, beyond that nun, I envision 1,275 buoys along the Maine coast, incessantly on lonely duty in every weather, guiding sailors to safety.

I'm grateful. But if there is reincarnation, I pray to heaven I never come back as a buoy.

Our First Chartmaker: Mathew Fontaine Maury

ABOARD STEER CLEAR — We have been gunkholing and poking into coves we never knew along rivers we seldom travel. They've become our refuge in time of trouble at sea.

This morning the marine weather reports have been issuing hurricane warnings. We heard reports of thick fog, 45-mph winds, swells 25 feet high on Georges Bank. So we headed up the rivers, and gunkholed, enjoying calm waters, warm sun and discovering new hideaways.

Gunkholing means that we poke our way at the slowest speed possible, in part to relish the beauty, in part to keep an ever-cautious eye on the charts. While one of us aboard spots seals and herons, terns, kingfishers, killdeer and new houses—the helmsman keeps track of precisely where we are on the chart. Parts of some Maine rivers are tempting traps for the unwary.

The rocks, the shoals, the long-fingered mussel beds and the depth of water are all marked on the charts, every one of them. But charts usually cover a lot of water; the details are marked small. Among a myriad of similar inlets and coves on the rivers, it is easy to mistake one for another. You pay with grievous consequences if your attention to each inch of the chart gets sidetracked by seals or the flights of startled ducks.

But the amazement is how much accurate detail is contained on every navigation chart. Put all the charts together and every bit of the entire U.S. coastline, every twist and turn of every navigable river in the United States, has been charted with painstaking accuracy.

The depth of water, which can vary dramatically in a very short distance, and the characteristic of the bottom—muddy, sandy, rocky—is plotted. To assemble and plot all these details on just one chart covering only a tiny fraction of the total coastline must take many man-years of precise work. And we have two dozen charts aboard this small boat just for Maine.

The man who began this system of navigation charts in the U.S. was Mathew Fontaine Maury. Most of us who use these charts have never heard of him.

Mathew Fontaine Maury was an obscure young midshipman in the U.S. Navy in 1825, when he circumnavigated the globe on a four-year voyage aboard Vincennes. In 1839, a stagecoach accident lamed him for life. He was appointed to shore duty, as superintendent of the depot of Charts and Instruments.

There he wrote a book called the Physical Geography of the Sea. That book soon made Maury's influence felt on navigation all over the world. His book is indeed the very foundation of the science of oceanography.

Before long, Maury had organized a worldwide network through which ships of all nations filed copies of the logs of all their voyages, together with their observations on winds and tides and currents. With painstaking brilliance, Maury assembled and organized this mass of information into navigational charts; and the mariners cooperating with him received copies of those charts.

Soon Maury's charts, and his records of winds and currents, shortened the passage of American East Coast vessels to Rio de Janeiro by 10 days, to Australia by 20 days and around the Horn to California by 30 days. When the Civil War broke out, Maury resigned his post to join the Confederate forces, became the agent of the Confederacy in Britain, and did not return to the U.S. until 1868, when he became a professor at the Virginia Military Institute.

The only consistent mention of his name today is a line at the bottom of pilot charts which still carry the inscription "Founded on the research of Mathew Fontaine Maury while serving as a Lieutenant in the United States Navy."

Maps and charts were once treasured secrets. Sea charts were the key to an empire and the way to wealth. As such, they were hidden documents. Lloyd Brown in his book Story of Maps says no true mariners' chart existed during the first 1,000 years after Christ.

The first book of charts—The Mariner's Mirror—was compiled by a Dutchman, Lucas Waghenaer. It was published in 1584 and covered western Europe from the Zuyder Zee to Cadiz.

The East India Company, that great mercantile corporation based in England, employed their own chartmakers, who prepared secret atlases of sailing directions to the wealth of the Indies. Their top map maker, Alexander Dalrymple, left to become official hydrographer to the Admiralty, which began its survey of the coasts of the world in 1795.

Hard on his heels came our Lieutenant Mathew Fontaine Maury. From these two men have stemmed the vast world network of navigation charts.

Today we buy these gold mines of information for a few dollars at almost every port. Without them, every voyage would be a high risk danger.

They are crammed now with scientific information, gathered by advanced scientific instruments. But even the ultra-modern United States Pilot, which contains computer directions for loran, still draws on the lore of the ancient sailors.

"Navigators," it says "should observe the bird life . . . Shags are a sure sign of the close proximity of land . . . the snow petrel is invariably associated with ice . . . Blowing whales usually travel in the direction of open water."

Today, every time I use our charts, I give a smile of thanks to that almost forgotten young lieutenant with an unforgettable name—Mathew Fontaine Maury.

LOONS AND SANDPIPERS

ABOARD STEER CLEAR — Seven loons are laughing, diving and fishing, within 100 feet of where we are anchored. Never before have we seen so many loons at once, so close.

The loons came early this morning, at first light. And first light today was thin, watery, ghostly, a mere glimmer of sun vainly trying to fight its way through the white cocoon of fog that swathed the world.

A westerly wind blew and moved wraiths of fog mysteriously across the flat, steely-gray surface of the sea. Out of this eerie white vapor came the wild cry of loons laughing. For a moment, it sounded like the cry of the world at birth.

That was when seven loons drifted into sight on the current. One by one, they emerged into sight until all seven were in a tight circle. As they fished, they dived under the water. Sometimes only one or two would be on the surface. Then five. Then none. Then seven. Then three.

The young loons seemed a soft, pearly gray. The adults were black-necked, with black backs flecked with a checkerboard of white.

Whenever I aimed my camera, five of them would duck. When I lowered the camera, all seven would surface, glance my way, then duck again as I tried for a picture.

These loons are out here on salt water for a summer holiday. They do not nest here, because receding tides can leave 100 feet of dangerous ground between nest and water, where they would be an easy prey for predators.

Loons cannot walk on or fly from dry land. So they build their nests at the edge of fresh water lakes. When danger threatens there, they can usually just slide out of the nest into the lake.

Once on water, loons are fast-swimming experts who can dive to safety, hide far below the surface for a long time, swim out of sight, then resurface far from the spot where they were. But, happily for boatmen, many loons like to summer out by the islands.

But my favorites are the tiny sea birds. I love to see them scamper on spindly legs for food on the flats at low tide. They are the sandpipers and the phalaropes. There are 30 kinds of sandpipers in North America. As a rank amateur in bird watching, I know only a few. The spotted sandpiper, with thrush-like spots, is teetering around everywhere, bold as brass. The cunning sanderling plays tag with the waves, racing out on tiny legs as each wave recedes, grabbing some invisible speck of seafood on its trailing edge; then as the next wave comes in, the sanderling wheels and races up the beach, just ahead of it. There is something funny about this tiny seabird running so fast to keep its feet dry, their neat little stems of legs flashing yellow in panic retreat.

But the little seabird I love best has the least lovely name. It is called the semipalmated sandpiper and has dark legs that flick along at such speed they seem to be a gray blur. They are no bigger than a sparrow— except for those long spindly legs. They have a kissing cousin called by the delightful name of the least sandpiper. There is no prettier sight on a beach at low tide than the sight of these lively, lovely, delicate, seabirds racing on matchstick legs across wet, food-filled sands.

MAINE WORMS EXPLODE ON FOURTH OF JULY

Maine marine worms trigger faraway happiness over the Fourth of July weekend. More Maine marine worms are bought by distant fishermen over the Fourth than at any other time of the year. Few of God's creatures is happier than the fisherman in New Jersey who hooks his fish with a Maine worm on Independence Day.

Picture tens of thousands of city families who flee their asphalt jungles for happy respite on the ocean shores over the Fourth.

At dawn they leave, loaded into family cars, special buses and excursion trains, heading for the beaches of the Atlantic and Pacific oceans. Some pile picnics, sodas and beer into rowboats and outboards. Some simply shed their city shoes and socks, roll up their trousers and wiggle

48

white toes in the sand. Braver city fishermen stride into the ocean and, saying a prayer, cast their lines into the sea.

They are celebrating Independence Day with the oldest endeavor known to man; going to the water to catch fish for supper. The essential link between them and their fish is a Maine marine worm.

Every Fourth of July is peak season in the number of Maine blood and sandworms shipped to America's eager fishermen.

Where do the Maine worms go? Here are some destinations to which the Maine Bait Co. of Newcastle shipped worms for a recent Fourth of July. Fishermen in Rye, N.Y., bought about 187,000 sand worms from the Maine Bait Co. But Wantagh, N.Y. topped them with orders for 252,375. Greenport, on Long Island, went higher, buying some 330,000 worms. At Atlantic Highlands, N.J., fishermen bought more than half a million. Down at Annapolis, home of the U.S. Naval Academy, the preference turns from sandworms to bloodworms. These Maryland fishermen bought 338,250 Maine bloodworms to celebrate the Fourth with fireworks and fish.

The champion of bloodworm buyers is Myrtle Beach, S.C., which took well over a million. In Texas, they were pikers, with Corpus Christi and Galveston buying only about 180,000 between them. But the fishermen of San Rafael, Calif., swear by Maine worms, and bought 790,000 of them. Far in the Pacific, where you might not think fish fancy the flavor of Maine worms, fishermen at Waimanalo, Hawaii, bought 18,000.

Down in the Virgin Islands at St. Croix, 10,000 hooks were baited with Maine worms. And in Marseilles, France,—hold your breath—they bought more than a million bloodworms from the Maine Bait Co. in Newcastle.

Ivan Flye, who started the Maine Bait Co., is a small-boned, rather delicate, bespectacled man who began as a wormdigger in 1938. By 1983, Flye was selling five million worms a year to customers around the world, and his sales were still going up. Along the Maine Coast, worm dealers are shipping out a million worms a week.

Where do the worms come from? Out of the mudflats at low tide. About 1,200 licensed Maine wormdiggers, using short-handled hoes with 8-inch tines, dig for them in the way you dig for clams.

In the good times, a wormdigger gets about one goodsized sandworm for each turn of the hoe. Bloodworms come harder, usually one for each four turns. A good wormflat yields a harvest worth at least $4,000 an acre per year. A successful digger, working all low tides, may make $20,000 a year.

Never look down your nose at the lowly worms. "The bloodworm is undoubtedly the most valuable catch, per unit of weight, of any regularly harvested marine animal in the world. The sandworm is the second most valuable marine species per pound in Maine." So states the Atlantic States Marine Fisheries Commission.

Maine produces about 90 percent of all the sandworms and bloodworms sold to saltwater sportfishermen in the United States, shipping more than 50 million a year. There's no sign that nature's supply of them is diminishing.

ISLAND LIFE: FOR FEWER PEOPLE WITH MORE MONEY?

Nearly half of all Maine islands—about 1,300—are uninhabitable ledges, averaging in size a half-acre of almost barren rock. These are mostly owned by the state. Their combined size amounts to only 600 acres.

The other 1,700 islands are privately owned. Their combined size amounts to 250,000 acres. They average five acres each; most have trees, grasses, bushes and a landing place for a boat. Together, these privately owned islands amount to 95 percent of the land area of all Maine islands. Only 5 percent of Maine island territory is in the public domain, belonging to state, town or federal governments, as of 1988.

The Maine islands are where modern America began. The first white settlers from Europe and England landed, lived and fished from these Maine islands long before they started to settle on the North American mainland. These islands were the centers of population and trade in the early days of the white men in Maine.

Today only 1 percent of Maine's islands support year-round communities; fewer than 20 percent of our islands have summer houses on them—so far.

But all of Maine's islands are within a day's driving time of half the population of the United States. Some of the biggest islands outside of Casco Bay—North Haven, Vinalhaven, Islesboro, Swan's Island, Matinicus—are linked to the mainland by passenger and car ferries; excursion boats run several times a day in summer to Monhegan and Isle Au Haut.

Traffic on the ferries has been steadily increasing. New ferries are bigger and carry more cars. A dozen islands have air strips. A few have heliopads. Outboards can reach many islands in fair weather, and 30-foot inboards with radar can reach almost every island, fair weather or foul. Getting to and from most Maine islands is becoming a little easier and quicker every year.

Most Maine islands are today very underpopulated by man or beast. A hundred years ago, these same islands supported more families, more farms, more sheep and cows by far than they do now.

Islands, including the biggest near Portland, Rockland and Camden, have fewer than 10,000 year-round islanders living on them. Not many people for 1,700 habitable islands. Every year-round island community, reports the Island Institute, would today welcome more year-round residents, especially young families who fit in to the island way of life.

Some year-round island communities complain of the summer invasion, especially by day visitors. Isle Au Haut, a superbly beautiful, mountainous and wooded historic island off Stonington, has fewer than 70 year-round residents, and 10 of these go ashore in January and February. (A hundred years ago, there were 275 year-round residents, a number which dwindled to 25 one winter in the 1960s.) Come summer, over 300 summer residents swell the resident population of Isle au Haut to more than four times the size.

But the trouble spot here is the one-day excursionist. More than 3,700 one-day tourists and campers poured in one recent summer day to visit Isle Au Haut, partly because half the island is now part of Acadia National Park. In addition, 1,500 visiting yachts dropped anchor in island harbors along the Maine coast.

Year-round island families on Isle au Haut have been overwhelmed and at times angered by the invading "hordes" who overran their only road, played havoc with their small trails and gawked at the "natives," those strange folk who left ignition keys in their cars, left cash on the island's gas pump for the fuel they took, left homes unlocked.

The open hostility between islanders and park authorities has eased. Park authorities agreed to cut the day-visitor traffic in half, by limiting space on boats from Stonington. The islanders passed zoning ordinances prohibiting the building of any hotel, restaurant, camping grounds or other such development. Yet Isle Au Haut, like dozens of beautiful Maine islands, would welcome a few young working families who'd become year-rounders.

Frenchboro, sometimes called Long Island Plantation, six miles to sea from Mount Desert Island, is today balanced on the brink of survival. Down to fewer than 50 year-rounders, with 17 more coming out to summer homes, the islanders want more year-rounders, especially young couples, "breeders," as they are sometimes called by islanders.

When the one-room, one-teacher school is closed, Frenchboro may join the ranks of Criehaven, Hurricane and other Maine islands which once supported flourishing year-round communities but where now only summer camps and cottages and a few fishing families remain.

Isle Au Haut and North Haven scorned state or federal aid, fearing there would be too many strings. So they formed their own development corporations with local money. Isle Au Haut built a new fish weir. It paid for itself in one year. North Haven has a number of projects being hatched. In 1988, Monhegan Island defeated a proposal in the state legislature to limit the number of day visitors. "We'll handle our problem our way" said the islanders to the Legislature.

If organized change on the islands by islanders themselves does not occur, the future is bleak. But there is an island solution on the horizon which is welcomed by islanders who are willing to organize and work to make it happen. The Island Institute, is trying to make it happen, in different ways, on different islands.

IT'S A FRAGILE PLANET

I'm often embarrassed by the overflowing armload of books I carry off from the public library to the boat. I wish I could be like the person ahead of me, who checks out just one book and goes off happy.

People who spot my armload of books think I'm boning up for a major project. Nothing so virtuous. The armload is a sign of insecurity. I worry that if I take only two books, I won't like either. So I take out four. If I'm going off on my boat, I take eight, in case I get caught in fog or heavy rain. A purgatory-at-sea for this graphomaniac is to be weather-locked in a remote cove with nothing good to read on board.

Last weekend, I discovered a new perspective on the familiar Atlantic Ocean, thanks to one of the books I grabbed before heading out on Steer Clear. The book is "The Atlantic: A History of an Ocean" by Leonard Outhwaite, published by Coward-McCann.

Maine enjoys the longest coastline on the Atlantic Ocean of any state.

This ocean affects our lives and livelihoods, our climate, our food, our industry, our transportation; yet the ocean is a topic too seldom touched upon in most Maine schools.

I've been hooked on the mysteries and magnitudes of the deep canyons and high mountain peaks hidden below the Atlantic. Oceanographers enthrall me with dramatic place names such as "the Deep," "the Abyss," "the Trench." Now my newfound teacher Outhwaite has given me a new perspective. The Atlantic, he contends, is really shallow when compared to the area it covers. Outhwaite brings our enormous Earth and all its vast oceans and continents down to a scale humans can comprehend—a steel sphere 5 feet in diameter. The result is full of surprises.

For example, how deep a gouge should we make in the 5-foot metal sphere to represent the deepest of all Atlantic canyons, the 28,000-foot-deep Cayman Trench, just north of Puerto Rico?

The answer is a scratch, 1/25th of an inch deep.

From where we humans sit, we think of mountains as towering and oceans as deep. We think of clouds in the sky and the rarefied atmosphere where spaceships fly, as being very high. But a mere 60 miles up—the distance from Portland to Camden—Earth's atmosphere becomes a vacuum. All the useful air which man can breathe, where winds can blow, where lightning can flash and thunder roll, where rain and snow can fall down on our Earth - all this would take place in a thin film far less than 1 inch high on the 5-foot steel sphere, representing Earth. This is the eggshell arena in which we act out our human drama.

The Atlantic and the Earth's other oceans, provide the moisture and the temperature needed by mankind, animals and plants to live. Without our oceans, Earth would be as arid, as icy cold and as fiercely hot as our barren satellite, the moon. On the moon, without moisture and without temperature control from oceans, heat reaches 200 degrees when the sun is shining and drops to 200 degrees below zero when the sun sinks.

As I read his book lying in a bunk of Steer Clear, Outhwaite explained in language I could understand, that the thermal capacity of air to that of water is in the ratio of 1 to 3,000. It takes 3,000 times as much energy to warm one cubic foot of the Atlantic as to warm one cubic foot of Maine air one degree. It works the same in reverse, which is why the Gulf Stream keeps us warm. One cubic foot of Gulf Stream water cooling one degree will raise by one degree 3,000 cubic feet of air.

The vast Atlantic is not just a huge pool of saltwater filling up troughs gouged eons ago out of the Earth's surface. It is a thin sheet of life-creating water curving around the world, touching five continents. We speak in awe of the "ocean deep" but, in comparison to its extent, the depth of the Atlantic is barely thicker than the paper this is printed on.

"It is in this filmy scum of rock and sea and air, wrapped thinly around the core of our world," writes Outhwaite, "that we live out our destiny in privation or richness, in war or peace. This is our ultimate base and we must preserve it as well as master it. The knowledge that we stand so insecurely upon so thin a paring of the world's space does not destroy the human responsibility.

"Man need not be too humble because, as far as he can know, he is the only actor on the stage . . . He has discovered and so, in a way, helped to create the universe."

I put down the book and went out on deck into the rain and east wind, to check Steer Clear's anchor line. From the bow, I looked out at the world and the Atlantic. They seemed not only awesome but also fragile.

Maine clam diggers in 1947.

II
KITTERY
TO PORTLAND

KITTERY BUILDS SUBMARINES

FRISBEES: OLDEST FAMILY GROCERY IN THE U.S.

GOURMET PASTRY AT STRAWBERY BANK

TUNA HUNTER AT OGUNQUIT

WINSLOW HOMER: THE GREAT PAINTER AT PROUTS NECK

HANDSOME CHURCH AND OLD TIME FIRE FIGHTING

THE CAPT. LORD MANSION AT KENNEBUNKPORT

OIL BARGE ALONG THE MAINE COAST

Portsmouth-Kittery Naval Shipyard, home to submarines. Old naval prison is far right.

II

*Maine begins and New Hampshire ends in Gosport Harbor amid
the nine islands with the magical name—Isles of Shoals. The spoils
are almost evenly divided. Maine has the five northern islands, Apple-
dore, Duck, Cedar, Malaga and Smuttynose; the four southern islands
belong to New Hampshire—Star, Lunging, Seavey's and White.*

*The Isles of Shoals were settled before the Mayflower reached
Plymouth. They rise with startling whiteness out of the ocean, nine
miles to sea from Kittery. They were so beautiful that Captain John
Smith, the lover of Pocahantas, the explorer who at age 26 helped settle Jamestown in 1607, named these little islands after himself—
Smith's Islands. Never before or after, did Smith name any other island or harbor after himself, despite all the lovely places he first charted and named. But the name of Smith's Island did not last. Early
fishermen, those practical seamen, changed the name to Isles of
Shoales, because this is where the ocean shoaled or shallowed.*

*Steer Clear too seldom heads west of Casco Bay, which is our loss.
For the coast from Kittery to Cape Elizabeth is a fascinating and
handsome fountainhead of early colonial history, and the taproot of
the first great monied families of Maine. And so a few stories to entice you with the flavor of the fabled York County coast.*

KITTERY BUILDS SUBMARINES

KITTERY — It pains me to write Portsmouth—and not
Kittery—Naval Shipyard. Given half a chance, I always call it the Kittery
Yard. The shipyard *is* in Maine, not New Hampshire; it *is* in Kittery, not
Portsmouth. Portsmouth is its mailing address, left over from 186 years
ago.

When the Yard was begun in Kittery as an official U.S. Navy shipyard in 1800, Kittery had no postal service, and Maine was a district of Massachusetts. So the Navy sent its official mail to the nearest post office, which was across the river in Portsmouth, New Hampshire. The Navy addressed the mail to the Portsmouth Naval shipyard. The wrong name and wrong address have stuck. And that is why the Kittery yard in Maine is still called the Portsmouth Naval Shipyard in New Hampshire.

No naval shipyard in the U.S. can rival Kittery in long history. Nor can any equal its experience with submarines. Kittery was the first naval shipyard to build a submarine—in World War I, in 1917. Kittery then built seven more World War I submarines.

In World War II Kittery built half the entire U.S. submarine fleet. On a single day in 1944, Kittery launched four new submarines. Kittery had a work force of 20,000 then (compared to 7,600 now). They built 75 submarines during that war.

Since World War II, Kittery designed and launched the first nuclear submarine in any naval shipyard (Swordfish—1958); designed and built the fastest submarine of its time (Albacore—1953); designed and built the world's deepest diving submarine of its time (Dolphin—1968); built the first nuclear submarine to dive under the icebergs and the first to travel submerged through the Northwest Passage to the North Pole (Seadragon—1958). Seadragon's maiden voyage was a long, hard one; 11,231 miles from Kittery to Hawaii. And this Kittery sub traveled 10,415 miles of her maiden voyage underwater or under ice.

Tragedy struck another Kittery-built submarine, the Thresher, on April 10, 1963. While on trials, she failed to surface from a dive 220 miles east of Cape Cod. She sank in 8,400 feet of water taking her 129 men to their deaths.

But the roots of Kittery go far back. Walk 200 yards from the submarines and you are in Quarters A, the handsome, huge white house where the yard commander lives. This home was built in 1724, 50 years before George Washington defeated Lord Cornwallis. The first admiral of the U.S. Navy, David Glasgow Farragut, died in this house in 1870, when Ulysses Grant was president.

But for Kittery, Farragut's death is only yesterday. Men were building ships here in 1690, when this land was called Puddington's Island after John Puddington who dried fish on its banks. Kittery built the first three naval ships built in America for the English navy—the 50-gun Falkland in 1690, the 32-gun Bedford in 1696 and the 60-gun American in 1749.

The first American ship was built here, the Raleigh, a 32-gun frigate. They built her in 60 days and launched her six weeks before the Declaration of Independence. The second ship of the Continental Navy was built on the same blocks, and went to sea as Ranger, under the command of John Paul Jones, the father of the U.S. Navy. This Kittery ship was the first vessel to sail to Europe flying the 13 stars and stripes of our new nation's flag.

The canny Jacob Sheafe, who ran a tavern near the shipyard and kept his ears pricked for moneymaking gossip, heard the new government might buy Fernald Island for its own shipyard. So in 1794, Sheafe bought the island for $650 from John Fernald Jr. Three months later he sold it for $2,500 to William Dennett, who in turn sold it for $5,500 to the government. In 1800 this became a navy shipyard, and has been so for 188 years so far.

This yard on a summer afternoon is a mountain of memories . . . The Marine Barracks high on the hill is a reminder that in July 1776 George Osborne of Kittery was commissioned as the first Marine captain aboard the first American warship, the Raleigh . . . that Marines from Kittery brought back and guarded in the prison here some 1600 Spanish officers and men captured at the battle of Santiago in 1898. The prison here held close to 3,000 captured Axis soldiers and sailors in World War II. This prison began as a cage 12 feet square built in 1662 to punish settlers who smoked on the Lord's Day.

I am awed by the billion dollars worth of nuclear submarines here today. Yet 200 years from now, will we remember them and their commanders as we remember John Paul Jones and the Ranger? Are these scientific monsters, with their 2,000-mile missiles, short-lived and ephemeral? Are they only expensive but not valuable?

FRISBEE'S: OLDEST FAMILY GROCERY IN THE U.S.

KITTERY — The oldest family grocery store in the United States is Frisbee's on Kittery Point, the southernmost tip of the State of Maine.

Frisbee's was first opened by Daniel Frisbee in 1828, when John Quincy Adams was president and Maine was just eight years old as a state. The family store is now run by the fourth and fifth successive generation, Frank and David Frisbee and their children, more than 160 years later.

"The fifth generation is already working in Frisbee's store," says Frank. "My younger brother David has his daughters Paula and Sheri working here. My son Frank C. Frisbee III, is working here. And so is my wife Evelyn—she runs our Captain Simeon's Restaurant where the original store stood, on the wharf behind the present store."

Frank and David, the owners and operators of Frisbee's, were born over the store.

In 1828, when Daniel Frisbee opened the store, he bought the land from the Cotts family. They had acquired ownership from the Commonwealth of Massachusetts. Massachusetts had confiscated the valuable waterfront land from Sir William Pepperell, the first millionaire in these parts. Pepperell had sided with the English King at the time of the American Revolution, and his land and properties were confiscated because of his loyalty to the crown.

Frank Frisbee, the boss of today's store, keeps a small library of Frisbee memorabilia.

"The stock in trade of the store in 1828 included skunk oil, gunpowder, flints, ox yokes, bear grease and lots of rum. Great schooners, home from voyages across the world, unloaded their cargoes at Frisbee's wharf. Frisbee's sold barrels of molasses, rum, spices, drygoods and dress materials, straight from the ships.

"Frisbee's was a ship chandlery as well as a grocery and drygoods store. Our great-grandfather did a handsome business in stocking out-going vessels with everything they required."

Today a corner of the grocery is filled still with ship supplies—marine paints, caulking compound, nails and rope. Frisbee's still has one foot in the sea, supplying food, drygoods, wine, beer and fuel to ships which come into their float.

The backdoor of Frisbee's has always been the famed Kittery-Portsmouth harbor, where ships have been docking for 400 years. Frisbee kids have grown up with one foot in the store and the other in salt water.

"For 24 years, David and I ran a waterski school from our wharf out back. We taught 800 kids how to enjoy water skiing before we got too old and too busy. Now we have the Pepperell Cove Yacht Club out back. When we were putting in its foundations in 1954, on the site of the very

*David and Frank Frisbee, owners of Frisbee's store, oldest family-owned
grocery in the U.S., at Kittery Point.*

first Frisbee store, we found six bottles of rum. Rum was a great business then. These bottles had been carefully and safely hidden. We sniffed
the rich old rum. But didn't have the courage to drink it.''

Today you can drive the winding road out to Kittery Point, watch the
sea and smell the lilacs in profuse bloom. At Frisbee's you can walk
through the old store, see the old floor still left in a few places, see parts
of the old ceiling—and chat with the fifth generation of Frisbees. Nearby is the Frisbee School, named for their great grandfather Frank Frisbee.

On the wharf in back of Frisbee's, you can look out to Whaleboat Light
and on to the Isles of Shoals. Stand quietly and in your mind's eye you
may see the harbor filled with old sailing vessels of the first settlers. This
is where some of the first settlements in Maine were built in the early
1600's.

"Now we have moorings out here for over 211 boats—sailing craft,
pleasure cruisers and lobster boats. We still do a lot of lobster trade over
the wharf,'' says Frank Frisbee.

When Frank came back from the navy in 1951, he made Frisbee's into a self-service store. Until then a Frisbee waited on you, cut your meat, ground your coffee, and fetched whatever items were on your shopping list.

"Each morning until World War II, the store sent a man with a horse and wagon to knock at customer's doors. He'd take down their orders and deliver the goods later in the day," says Frank. "I helped make the deliveries when I was a boy."

The old ways are, of course, changing. But Frisbee's still has the very special atmosphere that rightfully clings to the oldest family grocery store in the United States. Frank and David wear neat short sleeved shirts and always wear ties. They wear the long white aprons that once were the hallmark of good grocery stores.

"We still make the Frisbee corned beef for which customers drive hundreds of miles," says David. He explains how Frisbee's has been doing it for one and a half centuries.

"We start with cold fresh clear water. Add salt and keep adding until it is salty enough to float a potato. Sometimes we use an egg instead of a potato. Then we put in top quality beef, about four pieces weighing 10 pounds each. We put the beef into the brine on Monday and by Thursday it is ready—Frisbee's famous corned beef."

The great and the wealthy who used to summer here on huge estates and in vast rambling cottages were customers at Frisbee's. Old account books tell the story of enormous orders from the estates of John M. Howells, designer of New York skyscrapers and son of William Dean Howells, the 19th century writer; and from the homes of Mrs. Decatur Wright, Mrs. Anna Payson, Ambassador Edmund Crocker and dozens more. Theodore Roosevelt, Margaret Truman, Mark Twain and the great eagle carver James Bellamy have all been customers of Frisbee's.

Frisbee's moves with the times. Frank Frisbee, for example, has been president of the Maine Grocer's Association; now behind the old desk in America's oldest family grocery is a computer and a red phone marked "Hot Line": plus a picture of Frank with Miss America.

Walk slowly through the old store and you'll see visions of cracker barrels, barrels of molasses and salt and flour; of an iron potbellied stove and stories being told by the men around it—men who include father, grandfather and great grandfather of the Frisbees running the store now. The history of Maine and the United States is written here.

Look across the road as you leave the store and you'll see a single head-stone. It is in memory of Sir William Pepperell, 1696-1759. Pepperell was the leading figure in the colonial days of Kittery Point. His birthplace, the mansion he built, and his tomb all are close to Frisbee's store—built on land confiscated from him.

"We take care of Sir William's marker and his tombstone now," says Frank Frisbee. "It's come full cycle."

Here on the southernmost tip of Maine, on a summer day, you see the sparkle of the harbor, you see out to Isles of Shoals and Smuttynose; and at your back is the fifth generation of Frisbees minding the oldest family store in the United States. In a fast changing world, it is a comforting moment of continuity.

GOURMET PASTRY AT STRAWBERY BANK

PORTSMOUTH — A reward due all cruising crews is a fine dinner ashore now and then, at a table set with crystal, fine china, and heavy silver, with a French chef to prepare dinner and attentive waitresses to serve it.

So we docked Steer Clear at Portsmouth's town dock and walked across the waterfront park to 20 Atkinson Street in the Strawbery Bank district of Portsmouth and feasted. There Fritz Albicker in the Strawbery Court restaurant was making sinfully delicious pastries, tortes, meringues, crois-sants, cakes, and gugelhopfs. Yes, the restaurant is in New Hampshire. But Fritz keeps his classic cruising boat, a 32 foot Huckins built in 1929, at Eliot, Maine, and that's qualification for including his fabulous pas-tries in a book on cruising the Maine coast.

The tiny historic house at 20 Atkinson Street is a gem, beautifully re-stored to its authentic Federal colonial charm by Burton Trafton Jr., who sold it for $80,000 in 1974 to Fritz Albicker and his friend Les Taylor. As soon as I tasted the pastry I asked to meet the genius who made it; and that is when Fritz Albicker told me his story.

"In Basle, Switzerland, my father, and his father before him, were the leading bakers in the city. When I was 17 my father apprenticed me to the leading patissier in all Europe—Anton Bachmann. I worked under him 12 hours a day, six days a week for four years until I was 21. I didn't get paid a penny. Instead, my father paid Backmann $1,000 to let me work as his apprentice. In 1943 that was a lot of money. But Bachmann was the grand master. And I still have my handwritten book of recipes learned from him.''

But after years as a chef, Fritz Albicker chose to ''work the front of the house'' in the great international hotels of Europe during the 1950s. Then he came to America. ''From 1964 until 1973 I was second in command of the Ritz Carlton in Boston, and before that I had been in charge of all foreign dignitaries who stayed at the Plaza in New York, in the days when the Plaza was the Plaza.''

Cruises to Maine from Boston, aboard his classic 1929 Huckins, taught Fritz to love Portsmouth-Kittery harbor so much that in 1974 he bought Strawbery Court and began making pastries again. He gave me this recipe.

''For my classic French puff pastry I mix three kinds of flour. Your American flour by itself is too vigorous. The glutin in it is too active. And I use only unsalted butter. Eggs must be less than one day old. I make my dough early in the morning or late at night. The time of day matters. I fold my dough in one thousand times. Between each 12 minute ''tour'' I let it relax for three hours. Then another ''tour,'' folding and stretching. Six tours in all. Plus six hours of rest for the dough before it is ready. I make enough dough for 64 croissants and three dozen petits parmers. That is the polite word for pig's ears.''

This classic French puff dough keeps well in the freezer. ''When my pastries and cakes are done they improve by maturing three days in the refrigerator at 50 degrees. This permits a better fusion between meringue and butter cream. They keep in a home refrigerator for a week. But give them 30 minutes to breathe at room temperature before you serve.''

Fritz says that customers come to feast on his pastry and cakes since he serves ''tea'' from 2 p.m. till 4 p.m. He sells the special cakes at the special prices they merit.

''The Rum Meringue Torte you are eating'' he said ''consists of 10 separate layers. I use hazelnuts finely ground and made into a special meringue. My French biscuit is drenched in rum syrup and mocha butter cream.''

A classic 1929 Huckins cruising boat, a classic Mercedes parked outside a classic 1815 Federal gem of a house—and inside those cakes. Dressing up, going ashore and deserting Steer Clear for this dinner across the border into New Hampshire is worth it.

Lady Pepperrell House, Kittery.

TUNA HUNTER AT OGUNQUIT

OGUNQUIT — Carl O. "Sonny" McIntire hunts and harpoons tuna fish. He makes his living—a good one—from ironing tuna weighing from 200 to 600 pounds each.

Leaning out over the ocean at the tip of the 16-foot pulpit, his throwing arm high in the air, Sonny hurls his harpoon at the head of the massive fish swimming below the surface. If Sonny throws exactly right at the precise second, his barbed iron dart will strike behind the eyes and hold.

If Sonny misses, his 12-foot pole and harpoon float miserably in the water and the giant fish is long gone. There is dejection-after-anticipation among the crew aboard. But if Sonny hits—which is often, because he is a top tuna hunter—the giant tuna plunges steeply, racing downward to throw out the barb and regain freedom in the ocean depths.

As the massive fish plunges, hundreds of feet of heavy line go streaming out after it until the flag and a wooden pole or barrel flies off the deck into the water. This is the marker. Wherever the fish swims, it will tow the flag marker. Fish and flag may go racing off, hell bent for freedom, burning up miles of ocean. Or the fish may sound, plunging to the depths, taking the pole and flag with it. Or the fish may have been hit a mortal blow and die immediately, close by the boat. Sometimes a harpooned tuna, hundreds of feet of line, flag and pole all disappear, never to be seen again.

Most often Sonny and his boat and crew follow the flag, circling, waiting, watching until the wounded fish tires itself out and stops. Then the flag and pole stand upright, motionless in the ocean. The boat comes alongside. The crew recovers the flag and begins the hard job of carefully, slowly hauling in 300 or more feet of line, with perhaps 500 or more pounds of tuna at the end of it, held by a barb weighing about three pounds.

The job of hauling in the tuna requires more than muscle. It requires skill and a delicate touch. The dart can pull out easily if you pull in one direction when, deep in the ocean, the fish decides to angle away on a different course. If that happens, the fish, perhaps worth $4,000, is lost. The dart which holds the tuna is only about three inches across and six inches long, shaped like an arrow head.

Sonny McIntire, one of the leading tuna hunters working out of Perkins Cove, Ogunquit, is a tall, black-haired man of 48. His boat—named Ave Maria by his wife—is 32 feet long, plus the 16-foot pulpit off the bow. It has a 20-foot mast with a crow's nest and steering position at the top, for spotting the telltale ripple of a swimming tuna or the backfin breaking water, or, more rarely, spotting a school of tuna leaping through the air and splashing back into the sea.

When the tuna are spotted, the man in the tower carefully steers toward the target fish, creeping in on the prey until he has the boat within hurling range of Sonny's harpoon—normally less than 20 feet.

Ave Maria is a fiberglass boat, built by Holland in Belfast in 1982. Sonny and Richard Damaren installed the power plant, a 240-horsepower Iveco diesel, and rigged the boat for tuna fishing.

On the day Sonny talks about hunting tuna, he is tied to the wharf in Perkins Cove. He has been installing and lining up a new drive shaft, and the deck floor is open and covered with tools.

Bringing a tuna alongside. The fish was "ironed" by a harpoon thrown from the pulpit off the bow.

"The big fish haven't gotten here yet. They'll be up here before mid-July, we hope." Half a dozen other fishermen from Perkins Cove are sitting on the gunwales of Ave Maria, downing a few beers and taking tuna.

"The price is low early in the season when the oil content of the tuna is apt to be low. We may get as little as $2 a pound then. When the oil content is high, the price may go up to $12 a pound," Sonny says.

Last year was a bad year for the Ave Maria. Sonny harpooned only 15 fish.

"Our best year recently was 1984, when my father and I got 80 fish."
One unforgettable day in 1984, Sonny said, they landed nine big tuna,
averaging 400 pound each, dressed.

Japanese buyers come up from Newburyport to buy the dressed fish,
ice them and air-express them to the Tokyo market. A "dressed" tuna
weighs about 21 percent less than when it is harpooned and hauled in.

"I cut off their heads with a chain saw. Monstrous big heads weighs
as much as 150 pounds," says Sonny.

Sonny remembers a string of good days in 1984 when his boat brought
in five tuna. A boat which brings in 50 fish averaging 400 pounds dressed
might earn as much as $200,000 between June and October.

That sounds like a lot, but expenses run high. Sonny and his 26-year-
old son, Billy, and his other son, Shane, run as far south as Block Island
and as far east as Mount Desert, chasing tuna. He fears costs may soon
go higher still. "I worry about how much longer before we have to hire
a plane and pilot to spot tuna for us, instead of having a lookout man
atop our 20-foot mast. Spotting from planes is the way to go. But the cost
skyrockets."

Tourists by the tens of thousands are flocking to Perkins Cove. An endless stream of slow-moving cars creeps along the single road, searching
vainly for a place to park. Onetime lobster shacks and fish houses have
been remodelled into boutiques and restaurants. A memorable thrill for
tourists is to push the button which raises the wooden drawbridge under
which fishing boats and tour boats pass all day long, going and returning to moorings in Perkins Cove.

Nevertheless, Perkins Cove is still emphatically a fishing harbor. One
proof is that the prime parking spots beside the wharfs are marked with
large signs which state "Reserved for Fishermen."

WINSLOW HOMER: THE GREAT PAINTER AT PROUTS NECK

PROUTS NECK — If you end up adulated in art muse-
ums and your work fetches millions of dollars, you become a "revered
master." The world seldom remembers Winslow Homer of Prouts Neck
as a workaday human being—a quirky fellow who bought 144 pairs of
socks at a time; a live-alone bachelor on the Maine coast, who cooked
for himself, ate well and drank joyously; a chap who was a good friend

of the local stationmaster, the mailman and a reprobate town drunk; but who slammed the front door on pompous visitors from Boston and New York.

Maine's Winslow Homer, born Feb. 24, 1836, is so high on a pedestal that we forget the man behind the painter at Prouts Neck, overlooking Saco Bay. Yet it is his foibles which warm a "revered master" into a loved human being.

Today, let's celebrate Winslow Homer with a few stories about the human side of one of America's great painters.

Long before he was a "revered master," Homer was a hustler, knocking out a torrent of illustrations and meeting deadlines for the news magazines of his time.

Homer was a 19-year-old artist-journalist, chasing stories as a war correspondent or drawing sexy covers for sheet music songs (equivalent of today's covers for hit tapes or records), songs with names such as "Katy Darling" and "Wheelbarrow Polka."

Homer turned out at least 220 engravings for 11 different magazines between 1857 and 1875. He did 127 illustrations for Harper's Weekly alone, and covered the Civil War for that magazine, drawing the grunts more often than the generals, doing for Civil War soldiers what Bill Mauldin did for the GIs in World War II.

Homer began at the bottom, grinding out calendar and sobsister illustrations for the Boston printer H.J. Bufford, who paid Homer $5 a week for his art.

Like many journalists, Homer rocketed to popularity while covering sports. He did a two-page spread of a football game at Harvard which became his smash-hit. Action pictures of the game bounced Homer into the front rank at Harper's Magazine.

On the family side, Homer could not stand his father; he drew cruel cartoons of him. One cartoon mocks his father's refusal to take a bath; another shows him as a circus freak. When Homer thought his father might come calling at his studio, he locked the door and hung a sign on it: "Coal Bin."

But Homer was close to his mother, a gifted painter herself. She was a Maine girl, Maria Benson from Bucksport. In the 1870s, about the time Homer was famous and 40, she and her son had a joint exhibition of their work at a New York gallery.

Homer never married, though he lived to 74. Some think he had an unforgettable mid-life love affair with a redhead, who showed up often in his paintings of stylish ladies during the 1870s. One small oil painting of the redhead—titled "Shall I Tell You Your Fortune?"—stayed in Homer's studio all his life. But suddenly in 1879 the redhead disappeared forever from his work.

The next year, at the vulnerable age of 44, Homer said goodbye to New York and Boston—and perhaps the redhead—and went to live alone in a fishing village on England's North Sea coast.

Here, something or someone seemed to change Homer the man, his outlook on life and his painting style. He stopped painting pretty ladies with parasols and turned to robust fishwives. He painted wet, rough wool and oilskins instead of chiffon dresses; storms instead of sunny days at the beach; working men and women on the brink of disaster at sea instead of elegant ladies and children picking berries on a summer day.

In 1882, Homer came home and moved to Prouts Neck, Maine, where his brother had built a house, and there he lived and painted for 27 years, until his death in 1910.

Homer wintered in the summer cottage at Prouts Neck 100 years ago, and bone-chilling it must have been in those Februarys. "I made a mistake in not getting a bigger stove," he wrote to his brother. "I wear rubber boots and two sets of drawers."

To avoid shivering because of his too-small wood stove, Homer began buying six kerosene stoves at a time, so he'd always have extra heaters handy. Remember, he was also the middle-aged bachelor who used to buy 144 pairs of socks at a time, since he cared neither to darn nor wash them.

But Homer was not a helpless bachelor around his house. He had a housekeeper named Mrs. Hamilton. She was not total joy to him. "Mrs. Hamilton is leaving Thursday, which adds to the beauty of the situation," he wrote to a friend.

Homer liked to cook, eat and drink. His letters show it. Witness this letter to his brother Charles: "I brought down (from Boston) a leg of Canada Mutton, two spring chickens, Bermuda onions, six bottles of old rum, an Edam cheese, six bottles of rare old vatted whiskey."

On another occasion, Homer wrote to Charles: "After a visit to father in Boston, I got home to Prouts Neck about one o'clock. I opened my fish and cooked two shad roes and cut up a cucumber in cold water. Then with a quart of South Side Scarboro cider on the side, I knew I was again in my own house."

Charlie and Winslow were close friends as well as brothers. They went fishing together for salmon at a remote camp 100 miles north of Quebec. Homer went to this fishing camp 21 times. The only way to get there was by canoe, a hard trip Homer relished and frequently painted.

As they were breaking camp after one successful trip, Homer and his brother gave each of their four guides a bottle of whiskey. Those backwoods Frenchmen were too canny to risk breaking the bottles as they were shooting the rapids. So they drank the four bottles on the spot. Homer talked for years afterward about his ride down the rapids with four drunken guides.

Homer was a gardener during his 27 bachelor years at Prouts Neck, growing his own vegetables and flowers. Homer used to pick flowers to take as gifts when he went visiting.

"When he came calling," wrote a neighbor, "he'd always dress up in a high collar, a derby hat, and put a flower in his buttonhole. He'd walk along the cliffs carrying a bouquet of flowers in one hand and a glass of imported sherry wine in the other."

Was he a recluse? That's been written. Certainly, he chased away city visitors whom he did not want dropping in on him at Prouts Neck. But he often invited the stationmaster, Elbridge Oliver, or Harris Seavey, the mail carrier, or Alvin Brown, who owned the fish house down the beach, or Henry Lee, his handyman, to come in for a smoke, a drink and a visit.

Sometimes these local friends would tear apart Homer's newest painting. The stationmaster looked at Homer's now famous painting of The Fox Hunt and said "Hell! Win,—them ain't crows!" So Homer walked down to the railroad station. There he and the stationmaster spent three days feeding corn to crows while Homer drew sketch after sketch of the crows. He then went back to the studio and repainted the crows in The Fox Hunt—a painting worth close to a million dollars today.

HANDSOME CHURCH AND OLD TIME FIRE FIGHTING

KENNEBUNK — Outdoors, the rains came down in torrents, drenching 130 arriving guests. But indoors, the evening was full of warm Maine surprises in the First Parish Unitarian Church of Kennebunk. Steer Clear lay, buttoned up tightly, at the dock in Kennebunkport.

One shoreside surprise was the Fire Society of Kennebunk. In 1988, it is celebrating its 175th consecutive annual meeting. Firefighting buffs began meeting in Kennebunk in 1812—before Maine became a state in 1820—and they are still meeting to talk fires and eat turkey served by the Evening Alliance.

Another surprise was a shock. I was told that, as the after-dinner speaker, I would speak from the pulpit in the church upstairs.

What a pulpit!

The huge mahogany pulpit had a strange beginning. Legend is that 100 years ago a lookout aboard a Kennebunk schooner in the Caribbean saw a huge Honduras mahogany log floating in the ocean. The skipper coveted its size. But there was no winch to hoist it on deck. So he looped a line around the massive mahogany log and towed it all the way home to Kennebunkport. Here a ship's carpenter fashioned it into this pulpit.

I think about the heaving and hauling, the swearing and yelling, the blessing and cursing laid on that mahogany log as it was towed home from the Caribbean; and the pulpit seems less awesome.

The ceiling of the First Parish Church is a special Maine surprise, too. Here are 6,000 square feet of extraordinarily fine trompe l'oeil painting. This "trick the eye" painting makes it seem that the ceiling and walls are carved with handsome designs in wood and plaster.

"I sat for two years in the congregation, wondering why they never put flowers in those beautiful niches beside the altar. Then one day I walked up close to them and discovered they were not niches. They were trompe l'oeil painting. And for 104 Sundays they had foxed me!" says Betty Joyce of the Evening Alliance.

Nobody knows who did these "trick-the-eye" paintings. The church has detailed records of almost every aspect of its long history from 1743; and its expenditures are detailed to the last penny except for the glaring omission of an entry about payment for these amazing paintings.

Who did these paintings? That's the mystery.

Kennebunk was part of Wells, and Wells was part of Massachusetts, when 32 families invited Daniel Little, schoolteacher, to be the first full-time minister of the church in 1751.

This church began because 241 years ago it was a long ride by horseback to the nearest church seven miles away in Wells. Babies, because of the high rate of infant deaths at that time, were baptized on the day they were born, if possible. So new mothers with new babies had to ride seven miles strapped behind their husbands on horseback, to get the infants baptized.

The handsome steeple is designed after the style of Sir Christopher Wren, designer of St. Pauls in London. The bell in the belfry was made by Paul Revere in 1803. Before Maine became a state, it rang out every weekday at seven o'clock in the morning, noon, and nine o'clock at night; and the strokes of the hammer rang out the day of the month. When this Revere bell sounded the fire alarm, it was heard 12 miles away.

The long pews with hinged doors were sold "best seats to highest giver." On cold winter Sundays women brought live coals in hand-stoves and foot-stoves. Men brought heat in liquid form, to warm them from the inside out during the sermon.

This was a big-hearted church from the start. In 1760 it sent funds to Boston, burned out by fire. When 170 sailors from Marblehead were lost in violent storms in 1770, this Kennebunk church sent money to the widows and children. It proved a warm, dry haven for the drenched skipper of Steer Clear on a stormy night.

THE CAPT. LORD MANSION AT KENNEBUNKPORT

KENNEBUNKPORT — This is a hard town to dominate. On every serene, tree-lined street there are pristine gems of Americana, homes beautifully built 200 years ago and meticulously maintained today.

Out by the ocean are the enormous Victorian summer cottages and Vice President George Bush's large family compound on Walker Point. So the competition is fierce.

But dominating all else in grandeur, size and location is the Captain Lord Mansion.

First built in 1812 by a local ship owner, it is now one of the most fabulous bed and breakfast inns in the country. I stayed there for two nights this week in opulent 19th century comfort in a room named the Bark Hesper, one of the 16 guest rooms named after the sailing ships built by Capt. Nathaniel Lord.

Bev Davis and Rick Litchfield are the owners and innkeepers. Sitting under a pair of huge chestnut trees on the spacious lawns, Litchfield told me the story of the mansion, and how he and his wife bought the 24-room house 10 years ago.

"Today, June 15, is the 10th anniversary of the day we took ownership, and quaked in our shoes at the enormity of what we had done. I was 33 years old then and my wife Bev was 30. By the time we signed the papers, we'd sunk every cent we had into the new venture. We knew nothing about running an inn. Our bank account was drained down to $15. Thank heavens, Bev had $285 in cash left from the yard sale when we sold our house in Schenectady, N.Y. That bought us groceries for our first weeks in Maine."

Litchfield and Davis met each other in Albany, N.Y., in 1976, just two years before they bought the mansion. Rick was the account supervisor in an advertising agency that handled the advertising for McDonald's. Davis was the regional advertising manager for McDonald's.

They fell in love, working together on ad campaigns, and planned to marry. But McDonald's was moving Davis to new assignments around the U.S. every 18 months. So they both decided to quit their jobs and buy an upscale restaurant on Cape Cod or the Portsmouth-Kittery area, or possibly the Lion and the Unicorn on Route 1 in Kennebunkport. And then get married.

"We looked in vain for a year. Then a realtor called to say he had that morning received a flier in the mail about the Capt. Lord Mansion. It was St. Patrick's Day, 1978, so we drove over to look, thinking it was a restaurant, serving three meals a day. When we got here, we found it was a boarding house for seven elderly ladies.

"We loved it, were bowled over by the price, and were told we had 90 days to get the financing if we wanted to buy."

The price was $425,000—a lot of money now, but 10 years ago it was a great deal more.

"No other house in Kennebunkport had commanded such a high price, not even the biggest and best oceanfront estates," said Davis. But the couple managed to get $70,000 together between them as a down payment. The bank allowed them to assume the first mortgage and the owners agreed to take a second mortgage for the balance.

Rent from five elderly lady boarders, all over 80, who stayed on in the new Capt. Lord Mansion, covered the first mortgage payments. But not the fuel bill. The uninsulated huge house needed 8,000 gallons of heating oil that first winter.

The new owners scraped, sanded and papered most of the 24 rooms. Litchfield put on a new roof, got help to put in new hot water heaters

Captain Lord Mansion, Kennebunkport
The town, a mecca for summer visitors, still keeps the splendor and the charm of old ship captains' and ship owners' homes.

and added 12 new bathrooms to the existing five. They added insulation and cut the fuel bill from 8,000 to 3,000 gallons of oil a year.

The couple celebrated their first year as innkeepers by getting married. And, after all the work, they looked forward to being innkeepers to crowds of summer guests. But the summer of 1979 brought the second gasoline crisis. Only three rooms were booked for the big July 4 weekend that year.

Then in 1981 Kennebunkport began to boom. The inn, fully restored, improved and furnished with antiques, rated "four diamonds" by travel authorities, was widely praised in magazines and newspapers. Business rose to near capacity. Then, within 14 months, two children were born, and the family moved into private quarters close by and hired a staff which now numbers 14.

Room rates in summer are $90 to $155 a night. Occupancy rates near the 100 percent mark in summer, and drop to an average of 70 percent in winter, when the 11 guest rooms with fireplaces burn 30 cords of firewood.

Classic Kennebunkport doorway.

Kennebunkport is, forgive the pun, a hotbed of B&Bs. Today there are 40, compared to six when Rick and Bev started their B&B in the Lord mansion. According to Litchfield, Kennebunkport has at least six B&Bs equal or superior to the best anywhere in America.

The Lord mansion, built by Nathaniel Lord in 1812 so he could keep his boatbuilders busy when the war with England closed most shipping, was built to be the finest house in Arundel—as Kennebunkport was then called. The house remained in the Lord family until 1972.

"We are only the second owners outside the Lord family," says Litchfield.

The huge yellow house still dominates the center of Kennebunkport today, as it did 176 years ago. One big difference is that in 1812 it cost about $5,000 to build.

"Now it might bring $3 million or $4 million if it were for sale. But it isn't," says Davis, who gave up her job at McDonald's, drained the joint bank account—and married the innkeeper.

OIL BARGE ALONG THE MAINE COAST

I went along for the ride—what a ride! Aboard the tug "Intrepid," pulling and pushing 10 million gallons of gasoline from Boston to Portland.

We joined the gas-delivery-voyage at night in a grubby, down-at-heel section of Boston, which looked more like a movie-set for a scruffy dope-drop than a multi-million dollar oil terminal.

The 10 year old, 135 foot tug would cost over $5 million to replace today. The huge, ugly hulk of the 535 foot barge we'd push and pull has a price tag of $13 million, empty. Its cargo of 10 million gallons of gasoline is worth another $10 million, retail. "You're stepping aboard a $28 million package", said Ralph Hooper, part owner of Interstate and Ocean Transport, the Philadelphia firm which owned and operated 36 tugs and 53 barges. The Hooper shipping business began with Maine built schooners working out of Thomaston more than 100 years ago.

But sea surge and swells which would never have stopped those Thomaston schooners delayed our ocean-going tug, despite the fact its twin diesels can generate 5,700 horsepower. Intrepid was 48 hours late arriving in Boston from Philadelphia. The captain had to drop anchor for 24 hours in Buzzards Bay, waiting for northeast winds of 35 mph to moderate and for a high tide to help the heavily loaded barge, with its 31,000 tons of oil, pass safely through the Cape Cod canal. Once through the canal, they'd had to slow engines back to four knots because of eight to 15 foot seas. Again at 9 p.m. Friday night off the sea buoy at Boston Harbor, the seas were running too heavily to risk towing 10 million gallons of highly inflammable gasoline up the north channel. So from midnight Friday until dawn Saturday, the mammoth tug and barge circled around the sea buoy. By ten o'clock Saturday morning, skipper Macon Squires of South Portland headed his 31,000 ton baby slowly up Boston's north channel. About noon he had two tugs alongside, and at 12:55 p.m. the barge Ocean 250 was alongside the Mobil dock in East Boston.

First delivery. For six hours, Ocean 250 pumped gas at the rate of 420,000 gallons an hour into the thirsty tanks of East Boston. After she'd delivered two and a half million gallons, Ocean 250 was closed down, secured, made ready for the next delivery to Portland.

It was night time when, with signal whistles blowing their warning, Intrepid and Ocean 250 eased away from the gas dock to midstream in the Chelsea river. Two tugs—the Daley and Walton—came alongside to help us. Then, an hour before midnight, began some of the hairiest, tightest, most skillful pushing-and-pulling, and twisting-and-turning I ever hope to witness from any ship's bridge.

The task was to turn around. To turn around 635 feet of tug-and-barge, laden with eight million gallons of gasoline, in a river only 800 feet wide, and do the maneuver at low tide, at night.

First obstacle was a drawbridge dead ahead. Bad enough by itself, since our barge is 85 feet wide and the bridge span is 100 feet wide. But the added complication that night was that a motorist had abandoned his car on the bridge, right where the span is supposed to lift. We wait while the car is towed away. We suck in our gut and squeeze through. And let out a sigh of relief as we clear without the slightest bump.

Now skipper Squires from South Portland squeezes me into a so-called elevator. It is an open-wire, semi-enclosed cage which can lift one man in comfort and two in intimacy to the high bridge, 70 feet above the keel. From this tower, the skipper gets a bird's eye view, seeing over and beyond the bow of the barge 600 feet ahead.

He slows engines to a crawl. In soft-voiced sentences of few words, he orders his tugs: "Daley, give me a push . . . Walden, ease off." His accompanying tugs acknowledge each command with a whistle blast, but no voice response. These are tense, taut moments. Searchlights focus their brilliance on rocks and mud on shore, perilously close as Squires backs and fills, turning this 635 foot long combination of tug and barge in a dark river 800 feet wide. Finally his infinitely slow, painstakingly patient seamanship results in a 180 degree turn. We move, a behemoth on the night river, and squeeze under two more narrow span bridges. By 1:10 a.m., we release Daley, our last tug.

A new maneuver begins. Outside Boston Harbor, the surge is too strong and the sea too choppy for our ocean tug Intrepid to push the barge, Ocean 250, to Portland. Despite Intrepid's 5,700 horsepower, we must tow the barge. So now we come to dead slow, let the huge barge lose her momentum. Then we reverse out from the V cut in the stern of Ocean 250, where Intrepid does her pushing. Once clear, the 5,700 horses in her two diesels are shoved to full ahead and we turn and race ahead of the bow of barge Ocean 250. Three tankermen on the barge now lasso the mighty hawser and bridle we have thrown to them. The three crewmen, work under lights, handling winches, lifting shackles of gargantuan size. Finally the tow line is secured. Now we move ahead, straining to move the dead weight of the 31,000 tons of barge and fuel behind us. Slowly—slow is the key word in this work—we are both underway. By 3:15 a.m. we clear the Boston sea buoy and head down east to Maine. At 5:30, Tony Ruello, the Sicily-born cook, is serving us breakfast of Philadelphia scrapple and fried eggs. The new day at sea dawns sparkling bright, as we come abeam of Cape Ann at 6:15.

As we run by the Isles of Shoals, the sea surge is breaking in big clouds of white spray over the ledges and over the bow of Ocean 250, riding 1700 feet astern of Intrepid.

We stand out in the February sun, on deck, cruising at 7 knots, and talk about the hawser that links Ocean 250 to us. "All steel, two and a half inches thick" says Hooper. "Costly stuff. Price is $27,000 for 1800 feet, the length of the tow line." Every 15 months it is replaced.

Three years ago, the hawser cable broke outside Boston Harbor in surging seas. It was too rough for Intrepid to pick up the emergency cable that always dangles over the decks of Ocean 250. So for three days and rough nights, Intrepid circled her drifting barge, protecting against her drifting into dangerous waters. Finally the seas quieted and Intrepid recovered the emergency line, rigged up a new hawser and headed into port.

Loren Percival, 52, from Delaware is chief engineer. For 21 years he worked the giant diesels on the menhaden fishing boats, then 15 years ago he came to the big tugs. "My twin diesels—5,700 horsepower between them—burn 5,000 gallons a day—we use up 28,000 gallons on the round trip from Philadelphia to Portland." Two assistant engineers on Intrepid are graduates of Maine Maritime Academy, Dan Williams of Greenville Junction and Wayne Soucy of South Berwick. Pete Bryant of Portland is an Able Seaman aboard.

For lunch Tony Ruello serves large veal steaks, the richest of Italian spaghetti, Greek salad and multiflavored ice cream. We talk of working life on tugs. Pay is good, averaging $30,000 a year for the crew. They work two weeks, get two weeks off, and can take a month's holiday too. Often they choose to work instead, raking in extra pay. But sea duty is around the clock, with 84 hour work weeks. The skipper of course makes a good deal more money; and has the luxury of a very large panelled private stateroom and bath. His room has built-in TV and radio, desk, sofa. Skipper Squires, originally from North Carolina, recently transplanted to South Portland, has 10 men in his crew, including three tankermen who work Ocean 250.

The cost of delivering gas to Portland via Ocean 250 is just over one cent a gallon. The cost of running the Intrepid-Ocean 250 combination is about $12,000 a day. "All told," says Hooper, "our outfit Interstate and Ocean Transport delivers about 250 million barrels, about 11 billion gallons, a year to U.S. ports. That is enough to keep America running for 14 days."

At 2:40 p.m. Sunday afternoon in choppy seas, surging swell, and bright fair weather, we are off Cape Elizabeth. We cut speed from seven to four knots, and slowly, slowly, begin to take in some of the 1700 feet of hawser cable. Heading up the channel into Portland Harbor, the hills, spires and skyline of the city are beautiful. All the crew on the bridge agrees this is the most handsome harbor in the east.

Over the radio, we learn another barge is unloading at our dock, and we will be delayed two hours.

The hawser is almost up. Fresh water hoses wash off the salt, to inhibit rust. Now at dead slow we on Intrepid break our link to Ocean 250. The barge drifts momentarily, while we race to separate, turn and run aft. In perfect, but very slow and gentle seamanship, Squires nudges Intrepid into her V-notch astern Ocean 250. The three tankermen again scramble onto the barge's afterdecks, and in long-practiced teamwork they start her hydraulic power and get ready to drop her two bow anchors. Splash go the enormous 5,000 pound anchors. Up goes the black balloon, signifying to all ships that Ocean 250, laden with gasoline, is at anchor.

By 7:30 p.m., she is alongside the unloading dock helped by Portland tugs to her berth. The gas delivery starts. Portland wants 65,000 barrels, 2,730,000 gallons of gasoline, for the cars and trucks of Maine.

By 3 a.m. Monday Intrepid and Ocean 250 are on their way out to sea again. They'll be back, on average, three times a month, delivering gas to Maine.

III
CASCO BAY

Portland pilot boats, old and new, come past Portland Head Light into Portland Harbor.

Old timer at the slip in Kennebunkport.

III

Casco Bay is the first splendid jewel in Maine's wondrous necklace of island-dotted bays which grace the coast all the way to Canada.

But I didn't realize what a jewel until Elmore Wallace first cruised Steer Clear throughout his beloved Casco Bay, island by island. Elmore is gone now, but the story about him is right where it belongs— first in this section on Casco Bay.

The bay is huge; 18 miles wide at the entrance, 200 square miles in total. A boast is there are 365 islands in Casco Bay. Untrue! That tall tale was first told in 1700 by a Maine native, talking with a straight face to Colonel W. Romer, His Majesty's chief Engineer for the Colonies, who had been sent to Casco Bay on a surveying inspection. The colonel chose to believe the number of 365 islands, in preference to going out and counting them. So Col. Romer reported to London that "Said Casco Bay has a multitude of islands, these being reported as many islands as there are days in the year." Thus, the islands of Casco Bay became known as "the calendar islands." Truth is there are 136 islands, including ledges.

Indians and white men loved them and fought over them so often in the 1670s that James Andrew built a small fort on what is now called Cushing Island. More than 800 soldiers were stationed on Cushing as Indian fighters, according to the records of 1754. Much later the U.S. Government poured millions of dollars into building forts on major islands, beginning at the time of the Civil War and continuing until World War II. You'll find a story about these forts in the pages just ahead.

So huge is the bay, and so deep are its shipping channels, that in one anchorage alone in World War II, the U.S. Navy anchored up to 60 ships at a time. They assembled here to depart in convoys across the North Atlantic in the 1940s.

Portland, as the name implies, was a major gateway for enormous amounts of cargo and passenger traffic by sea and rail. This story too is told on the following pages.

Casco Bay was first charted by a white man in 1524 by the Italian explorer Verrazano. The Bay was christened a year later by the Spanish explorer Estafan Gomez. He named it Bahia de Casco, because it was shaped like a helmet, called casco in Spanish. A young Englishman, 27-year old Christopher Leavitt became the first white settler in Casco Bay. In 1723 Leavitt and 10 men from his crew built a stone house on the island still called House Island.

Casco Bay is packed with history, islands, swimming coves and beauty. A special advantage is that many of these islands can be easily visited by ferry or tour boats running out from Portland.

Steer Clear has a fair acquaintance with many of them, thanks to Elmore Wallace. Later on, I kept Steer Clear in Harraseeket Harbor, South Freeport, and spent several summers among these lovely islands. Here follow a baker's dozen of stories on Casco Bay.

ELMORE WALLACE: A SPECIAL KIND OF MAN

CASCO BAY — An invisible shipmate sails on Steer Clear with me as I cruise slowly among the islands of Casco Bay during the halcyon days of summer. I am happy, feeling his unseen presence toward sundown as I pick passage into an isolated cove and set anchor for the night.

He had shown me the way, years ago. He had been there, too, on the fishing tides, wishing me fisherman's luck as I trolled for bluefish. At anchor in an island cove, after dark, salt-caked and sun-baked after a wonderful day, he'd sit with me in the stern, watching the rising moon throw a swath of silver across the silent ocean. And he'd tell stories of Casco Bay.

The name of my invisible shipmate? Elmore Wallace. He died in August, 1985 at 75; and these islands of Casco Bay will seldom see his like again.

Elmore loved these islands in a special way. He knew every one of them as intimately as he knew the back of his big, capable hands. These islands were in his blood as a boy, in his blood as a man, in his blood even until he died. Part of his heart will forever be out here, among his islands.

Elmore first showed me these islands many years ago; Elmore first guided Steer Clear into the snug coves of Casco Bay islands to which Steer Clear keeps returning. Small wonder I feel his presence aboard.

Elmore, on that long-ago first cruise among these islands, was the "boat handler"—his kindly name for being my mentor and guide when photographer Don Johnson and I were on assignment to produce feature articles for the Maine Sunday Telegram on the islands of Casco Bay. We got Elmore, who was then working in the building maintenance department of the Portland newspapers, to come along as "boat handler."

There will never be another "boat handler" to come close to Elmore. He didn't only handle the boat expertly, he mothered it. He refused every chance to go ashore with us on the islands. He gave the same answer two dozen times: "I'll stay with the boat."

I can see him vividly even now; a tall, strong, lean man, wearing his standard lumberjack shirt, his heavy, dark green wool trousers, held up by both a belt and suspenders. And his fisherman's cap, with its salt-stained khaki cloth, a fixture on his head. His hair was gray; his face was weather-tanned and the skin was creased from his constant gentle smile. His eyes were as blue as his sky and his ocean. His voice was always soft, yet deep and gravelly. His hands and forearms were enormous. They made the helm of Steer Clear look like a toy as he handled it and worked the throttles and gears.

I don't remember Elmore ever glancing at the charts which I spread so carefully on the helmsman's table. He knew every rock, every ledge, every cove, every beach, every marsh, every wildflower on every shore, every sea bird, every seal, every porpoise, almost every mackerel, bluefish and giant tuna. He knew every island, every house, every shanty and he knew most of the old-time fishermen and their boats on Casco Bay.

Why not? His father, Joseph B. Wallace, had spent his life on Casco Bay, working as a marine warden for 25 years and going out among these islands for his fun, too. He took his young son Elmore fishing out here to catch lively tinker mackerel and later to chase the big tuna. His father lived, and finally died, aboard a boat on Casco Bay. Then Elmore followed his father's course.

In 1938, a decade out of Portland High School, Elmore too, joined Sea & Shore Fisheries as a warden on the bay. Years later, Guy Gannett, who owned the Portland newspapers, looked for the best man possible to run his boats and to run his hunting and fishing camps in the north woods. And he found Elmore Wallace. For Elmore knew the lakes and the woods, the inland birds and fish and wild animals as well as he knew everything that moved in or near the ocean.

The imprint and legacy of Elmore will always be part of Steer Clear. He was among the best tuna fishermen on the Maine coast, landing more than his share of 600- and 700-pound tuna on rod and reel; and few men could match him throwing a harpoon.

Elmore tried to make a tuna fisherman out of me; but he did not have much success. He installed stainless steel holders for tuna rods into the catwalks of Steer Clear; and they are still there. He rigged the big plate in the aft cockpit to secure the fighting chair against the weight of a 700-pounder fighting on the other end of the line. He equipped Steer Clear with harpoons and barbs and tuna buoys and huge old washtubs full of line, coiled carefully to run out fast and smooth when a big fish was "ironed." I see him now, poised out on the pulpit, tense, his harpoon at the ready—and then springing into action, throwing the dart with uncanny accuracy and strength, through the water into the vulnerable spot on a swimming giant tuna.

I see another side of Elmore; his enormous hands working with curved needle and waxed thread, rejoining the slit belly of a fresh caught mackerel with all the delicate touch and phenomenal speed of a surgeon. Elmore could sew a big tuna hook inside a mackerel so that neither you nor a tuna would ever know it was there. When Elmore had finished his surgery, those dead mackerel bait would swim on the line off the stern of the boat, looking exactly as though they were alive.

From Two Lights to the old Portland Lightship, to Halfway Rock, to Seguin, past Boothbay, past Pemaquid Light and east to Monhegan Island, Elmore and I chased the big tuna. He loved the sea, the weather, foggy, foul or sunny, the seals, the sea birds, the stars and almost all mankind. Only Maine can breed a man like Elmore Wallace. Only a man like Elmore can love and relish Maine to the hilt.

I feel blessed to have known him and to feel his presence still as a shipmate on Steer Clear.

PORTLAND HARBOR: A GOLDEN PAST—AND A GOLDEN FUTURE?

Take Casco Bay and the current hot proposals for the future of Portland Harbor and the Portland waterfront. Some of them may seem far-fetched visions, laced with strong doses of optimism. But to see the future more clearly, look at the past more deeply.

In 1872, 65 trains a day were arriving and departing from the Portland waterfront. Twice a week, luxury steamers left for New York and far more often for Boston. In 1874, six million feet of lumber left Portland docks for the West Indies alone; and on their return trips those ships brought sugar and molasses for Portland's huge rum distilleries. Along one street alone, 30 commercial lumber companies flourished.

The great grain elevator which used to dominate the Portland waterfront had a capacity of 200,000 bushels, and adjacent warehouses could store over 450,000 bushels of wheat. In 1899, 22 million bushels of wheat from the Midwest and Canada poured into Portland. Freight trains a mile long hauled wheat from the prairies to Portland's waterfront. And a stream of cargo ships swallowed over 13 million tons of wheat a year into their holds at Portland docks and hauled that golden grain to Europe. Alas, no more.

A hundred years ago, Portland Harbor was not only a huge cargo port, but a busy passenger port too. In 1891, seven shipping lines were carrying more than half a million passengers every year past Spring Point Ledge. Alas, no more.

Most of those passengers were headed to and from New York and Boston, preferring the overnight boat to the train. Now we have neither passenger boat or train. Other passengers streamed into Portland from Europe. Indeed, Portland was a human gateway to North America. In 1913 over 26,400 aliens came through immigration on the Portland waterfront.

While all this profitable water commerce was going on among civilians, the military was becoming a huge presence and big spender in Casco Bay. Portland Harbor became the third most heavily fortified harbor in the United States, dotted with island forts and thousands of troops travelling regularly between the islands and the Portland waterfront.

The waterfront was the boom center and business hub of the city. Besides the passenger lines, the fleets of cargo ships and the extensive military construction on the islands, the waterfront was humming with fishing and lobstering boats and canning plants. By the 1850s, when cod were the leading fish on the market, Maine was the leading cod fishing state, employing 1,300 vessels and 9,000 men on the cod side of the fishing industry.

In 1880, Maine's lobster catch topped 14 million pounds (it is about 19 million pounds in 1988). A hundred years ago, about two-thirds of the lobster catch went to the canneries. In the 1880s, Casco Bay lobstermen usually fished between 40 and 60 traps (compared to 500 to 1,500 today), and they averaged about five lobsters per trap, more than double the catch per trap today.

But even so, the lobstermen complained the catch was down from the 1850s, when the average catch per trap had been seven lobsters, each weighing about five pounds. In those days they got only about a dime a lobster no matter its size. Today a lobsterman may get only one "keeping" lobster, weighing about one pound and a quarter per trap, but the price is about 100 times higher than in the 1880s.

Combine the fishermen, the ocean-going crews, the arriving and departing passengers, the stevedores, the military, the shipping agents and chandlers, the repair shops and boatbuilders, add the trainmen from 65 trains daily, and it is not hard to see why the Portland waterfront was the commercial life-blood not only of Portland but of southern Maine. These thousands of men spent heavily, as most waterfront men have always done, in the taverns, hotels, rooming houses and dance halls.

Is all this waterfront boom only a memory of a bygone age? Or is this past a prologue to the future?

This past can be prologue to a resurgence of Portland's waterfront, updated to the 21st century. For the essential endowments are here still, with even greater economic potential.

For example, Casco Bay is almost 300 miles closer to European ports than any other major port in the U.S. With today's fuel prices, a saving of 600 miles, round trip, is a saving not only of fuel but of two days at sea. In dollars that can mean $30,000 per ship per round trip.

Portland Harbor stevedores, once new cargo piers and equipment are installed, will load and unload faster, with less pilfering, less delay and lower overhead than workers in any major U.S. port on the East Coast.

The Portland shipping channel is deeper than the shipping channels in Boston, New York, Philadelphia and Baltimore. The harbor is unobstructed by bridges. Anchorages are spacious enough to hold more than

Portland's waterfront with Back Cove in the distance, and Franklin Arterial linking the Harbor and the cove. This picture was taken in March 1986, and the development of the waterfront and the BIW dry dock (foreground) continues.

half a hundred ocean-going vessels. When the navy operated a refueling depot in World War II on Long Island in Casco Bay, as many as 60 warships waited with room to spare to take on bunker oil. As recently as the 1970s, 438 big tankers from the Persian Gulf and Venezuela unloaded six billion gallons of crude oil a year at Portland, making this one of the biggest oil ports in the East.

Over 100,000 people now live close to Casco Bay, but perhaps fewer than 10 percent have been out into the islands on their doorstep. Casco Bay is huge, more than 200 square miles. The entrance is 18 miles wide and the average width is 12 miles. The United States Coastal Pilot, a staid and reliable book, states there are 136 islands and ledges in Casco Bay.

The Indians who loved and used these Casco Bay islands christened this glorious bay "Ancocisco," which means the place of herons. White men, unable to twist their tongues around that word, shortened it to Casco. Perhaps. Another story is that the Spanish explorer Estaban Gomez (Stephen Smith) named it "Bahia de Casco" when he sailed in here in 1525, because its shape resembled a helmet.

Christopher Levett, at age 27, was the first permanent white settler. He built his stone house on a Casco Bay island in 1623, after searching the coast from Isles of Shoals to Cape Small for the perfect spot.

For 23 years I've been looking at Casco Bay from the windows of my office at the Portland Press Herald. I've looked up from my typewriter with joy at sunsets, storms, fog, sea smoke; seen the passage of ships winter and summer, spring and fall, night and day. I've sailed in the bay in small boats, and seen the islands from the bridge of a supertanker. These islands are so filled with history, romance, adventure, terror, hardship, scullduggery and kindliness that no man in a lifetime could know more than half there is to know about them.

What has happened is only half the story. Most of the story—and perhaps the best—may lie ahead. But the first few centuries since white settlers came to Casco Bay have been a glorious prologue.

CASCO BAY ISLANDS: MECCA FOR TOURISTS, PLAYGROUND FOR LOCALS

Have you ever set foot on an island in Casco Bay?

The islands are the Cinderellas, the poor sisters, of modern Greater Portland. Yet they are where our roots began, where the first settlers built

Elmore Wallace and author in Casco Bay on Steer Clear.

the first homes, began the first farms, raised the first families in this part of Maine more than 350 years ago.

More than that, the islands were once the jewels in Portland's crown. Less than 100 years ago, the nearby islands of Casco Bay were the greatest tourist mecca of Maine. These islands were the playground, the theater district, the hotel center. They were, in short, the Old Port, the Civic Center, the Old Orchard Beach, the Kennebunks, the Boothbays and the Camdens of Maine—all rolled into one.

There was more traffic between the Portland waterfront and the nearby islands of Casco Bay 100 years ago than there is today at the Portland Jetport. More people went to see the productions at the Gem Theater and the open air vaudeville shows on Peaks Island than crowd into the Civic Center today to see the Maine Mariners play ice hockey or hear a pop music concert.

Big ferries of the old Casco Bay Steamboat Company shuttled hundreds of thousands of passengers. One timetable from 100 years ago lists island hotels and boarding houses. It shows the Ottawa House on Cushing, run by Charles E. Davidson, had accommodation for 250 guests with rates from $3 to $4 a day.

On Peaks Island, there were 21 hotels and boarding houses. Biggest were the Peaks Island House and Coranado-Union House, operated by R. E. Rowe, which had rooms for 600 guests. Traffic to Peaks was so heavy that Peaks had three steamboat landings—the Forest City Landing, Trefethen's Landing and Evergreen Landing.

The same timetable lists three major hotels on Long Island, the Granite Spring Hotel, with rooms for 150, Dirigo House with rooms for 100 and the Casco Bay House, with accommodation for 60. Prices started at $1 a day.

Peaks Island was then the busiest spot in Casco Bay, a combination of Atlantic City and Coney Island—part resort, past amusement park. Among the attractions were the Forest City Skating Rink, and the outdoor vaudeville acts at Greenwood Amusement Park. A famed balloonist named Prince Leo was a top drawing card. The Prince would climb into his balloon, ascend hundreds of feet into the air, then parachute down. A Professor Oldwie advertised that he walked on water. He did. He wore two outsize floats as shoes, and plowed across the water like a cross-country skier over snow.

A fleet of steamers traveled in the summer between Portland and Peaks Island. A day's outing cost 25 cents, which included the boat ride, plus a chance to see the open air vaudeville acts. Records show that the little steamer Cadet—one of the smallest in the fleet—carried 64,681 passengers in the summer of 1890. This boat alone averaged 5,398 passengers a week.

Peaks Island claims to have been the first summer resort in the nation to boast a real summer theater, located first at the old opera house in Greenwood park, then at the Pavilion, finally at the Gem Theater. By 1895, showman Bartley McCullum was bringing top stars from New York and San Francisco to head the bill at Peaks Island. Broadway's fabled George M. Cohan produced some of his early hits at the Gem Theater. John Ford, the Portland boy who became one of America's greatest movie directors, started his movie career by working as an usher at the Gem Theater on Peaks Island.

Speaking of Broadway stars and Casco Bay Islands, famed song writer Cole Porter was a camper on Bustins Island. He treasured a photo of him made in 1905 holding two big fish he had caught. The boys' camp Cole Porter attended was run by Donald MacMillan who later became Admiral and led explorations to the Arctic in the schooner Bowdoin.

Yacht Basin at South Portland, looking at Portland skyline.

Exclusive, expensive summer colonies developed during the 1880s on other Casco Bay Islands. Great Hog Island, which earned its original name because it was a 250-acre pig pen, changed its name to Great Diamond Island, because summer residents wanted a more mellifluous address.

By the 1880s Great Diamond Island Association was the hub of Portland's wealthy. Members built large summer cottages, operated their own golf course and tennis courts, even ran their own steamboat, Isis, to carry them back and forth to their offices in Portland.

With the threat of World War I, the federal government turned many of the Casco island resorts into fortresses. Guns, troops, equipment and barracks poured in and the tourists and the summer colonies pulled out.

The decline of the islands as resorts and playgrounds began with World War I, and World War II again increased the military dominance. Millions of dollars were spent making Casco Bay one of the best fortified harbors on the Atlantic Coast, but no shot was ever fired in anger by the U.S. military.

After the military finally pulled out in the 1950's, the islands were offered as gifts to the state of Maine and the city of Portland. Neither the state nor the city would accept them. Many of the islands went onto the auction block and were sold dirt cheap, mostly to out-of-staters, for a few thousand dollars during the 1960s.

Today, 365 years after Christopher Levett built the first house here, the Casco Bay islands, where it all began, may be in their ascendancy once again.

JEWELL: BEAUTIFUL, AND RAVAGED

JEWELL ISLAND — If God is in His Heaven, then He is missing something by not being on Casco Bay. Never was sea and shore, coast, cliff and spruce more sparkling bright and beautiful on this perfect summer day. "Steer Clear" is heading seaward between Peaks and Long Islands, with Hope Island and Cliff Islands coming up to port. Our destination is Jewell Island, outermost of the western islands in Casco Bay, lying halfway between Cape Elizabeth and Harpswell Neck. The legendary treasure of Captain Kidd is supposed to be buried at Jewell. The facts are that Captain Kidd never came near the Maine coast, and that Captain Kidd never had much treasure anyway. Nevertheless, treasure seekers have turned over tons of earth and sand at Jewell Island searching for Kidd's buried treasure.

We pass Overset Island. Its 8 1/5 acres were bought from the U.S. Government in 1967 by William and Rosemarie Harrington of Manomet, Massachusetts. They reportedly paid about $400 for each island acre. One more island Maine sold for a song only 21 years ago.

Now we cruise by Vaill Island, still another Casco island bought by people from away. Vaill, just off the southeastern tip of Long Island, was bought in 1963 by Carl Hess of East Berlin, Connecticut. Mr. Hess paid $19.80 a year in taxes to the City of Portland for his island acreage.

Off to port now are the lovely, hidden sand beaches along the seaward side of Long Island. Long Island is where King Resources hoped to moor supertankers, 1,200 feet long, each mammoth vessel unloading about 21 million barrels of oil, to be piped ashore to new storage areas King Resources planned to build on Long Island. King Resources went broke before their oil terminal was built. In 1988, this part of Long Island was sold for only $800,000. The asking price was low because the huge fuel tanks buried underground by the U.S. Navy are a future liability.

Philadelphia wealth looms next to port. Down Luckse Sound, atop Hope Island, stands a huge lodge. A group of Philadelphia friends, with an eye for beauty at a bargain, bought Hope Island for themselves. They keep it as a private club of their own, complete with their own power plant, own water supply and own boat service. In 1987, Bette Davis starred in the film "Whales of August," made on this island.

Now—Jewell. And what a jewel of Casco Bay this uninhabited 221 acre island is! Originally, George Jewell, of Saco, Maine, bought the island from the Indians in 1637 for the proverbial horn of powder and bottle of rum. But guess who bought Jewell Island in 1950?

John B. Absmeier of New York City. He picked up most of Jewell cheap, as surplus government property. Absmeier also bought the priceless Little Chebeague Island, again as a surplus bargain from the government. The purchase price for Little Chebeague was reportedly about $13,500, payable over 25 years. For 143 acres on Jewell including wharf, water towers, gun emplacements and barracks, the reported price paid by Absmeier was $33,000.

The City of Portland might have bought most of Jewell for a mere $4,000 down; and might have bought its half of Little Chebeague for about $800 down! The State of Maine's Park Commission made no effort at all to keep these precious islands.

If Maine had earmarked them as "historic sites," then the federal government would have handed these and other Casco islands to the state as a gift. Maine didn't. Neither the state nor Portland wanted them, even as a gift, in 1950.

We cruise slowly up Jewell's shore, admiring the long, sheltered harbor, the rugged cliffs, the high wooded bluffs. We skirt shoals and ledges, and round the tip by Inner Green. Towering and stark are two concrete military look-outs, 70 feet high.

Jewell has come full cycle. Some 265 years before the U.S. Government of World War II built mammoth gun installations and watch towers on Jewell in 1941, settlers from Harpswell had built their own watch towers on Jewell in 1676, to keep watch against their enemies, the Indians. The blood of Indians and settlers are intermingled in the soil on Jewell.

Ashore, this gorgeous island is fragrant with sweet smells of wild flowers, wild roses, wild peas, honeysuckle vines, daisies. We climb to the remnants of the old McKeen cottage; long since horribly vandalized. The McKeen family, direct descendants of the first president of Bowdoin College, became owners of Jewell in 1894.

In the hot midday sun, we walk for another thirty minutes to reach the ocean tip of Jewell and stand atop Knife-Edge Rock, and look down into the cove where Captain Kidd's treasure has been vainly sought.

A narrow path is all that is left of the broad roadway once laid down by the military, now totally surrendered to lush and lovely vegetation.

But staunch and solid, stand the 70-foot high concrete watch towers. We climbed one tower, floor by floor. And found the passage of almost

50 years since G.I.s had manned them has barely made a dent in their solidity.

Time, however, dates those scribbles which visitors seem driven to write upon walls. A whimsical graffiti on the fourth floor of this watch tower tickled the fancy of this reporter, who had been in London at the time the scandal in question broke; "Dr. Stephen Ward Loves Mandy Rice-Davies"—P.S. "So does John Profumo."

We come panting to the top floor, push open the heavy door-in-the-floor, and see all Casco Bay spread below. This panorama of Maine's coast is breathtaking. The view alone is more than worth the trip out and the climb up. "This, I think, should belong to the people of Maine!" Today it does. The state finally bought it—for $200,000.

The history of Jewell Island crowds in. The story goes that in 1676 Richard and Margaret Potts, with their children, came to Jewell from Harpswell Neck for refuge from attack by Indians. Soon after, on the second day of September, 1676, fine weather blessed Jewell. Consequently, Richard Potts and the other men from Harpswell who were seeking safety for their families on this outer island, sailed over to cut corn on nearby Green Island, where corn grew rich, thanks to perpetual fertilization by gulls. The women, taking advantage of the fine day, carried their washing down to the brook.

Alone on lookout in the camp was nine year-old Thomas Potts, who had just been taught how to load and fire his father's musket. Suddenly young Thomas Potts spied eight sea canoes less than a mile away, each carrying four Indians, paddling from Cliff to Jewell. The boy fired his warning shot. Hearing the alarm, the men on Green and the women at the stream rushed back. By the time the Indian canoes reached the rugged shore, the settlers were ready for them, and drove them off.

Down from the watch towers, we walk the narrow trail which leads to the massive concrete bunkers where our World War II Army installed eight-inch guns. The bunkers are underground. We pace the sweating, dark concrete tunnels; 100 winding yards long, eight feet wide, ten feet high, the tunnels lead to ammunition storage vaults. Massive iron doors hang from huge hinges at either end. Millions of dollars, millions of yards of concrete were poured in wartime into this now peaceful island. The brutally great gun bunkers are overgrown today with sweet smelling wildflowers. Wild roses climb upon the empty ammunition depots.

The open ground nearby, which the military cleared, is a huge over-

grown meadow now, and songbirds flutter out from nests in the collaps-
ing barracks. Below, foaming surf beats and retreats from the Knife Edge
rock, where a sentinel gull stands watch.

Amid this beauty and this remoteness and this history of Jewell, a man
feels happy; and alone, and separated from today's world. But, he somehow feels linked closer to the world of the Potts family of 1676 than to
the soldiers of 1943 who manned these shores, or the oil tanker coasting
by Halfway Rock in 1988.

Enriched with a kind of benediction from a morning amidst wild beauty and enduring land, everlasting rock and everchanging waves, we go
back to "Steer Clear" to open a cold drink and boil up a pot of lobsters.

TWO ISLANDS TO LIVE AND DIE FOR: STAVE AND LITTLE CHEBEAGUE

STAVE ISLAND — "Young seals" murmured pilot El-
more Wallace quietly, while he edged "Steer Clear" between hidden
ledges and into the cove at Stave Island.

At first, we mistook the baby seals for a silvered and knotted log of
driftwood floating in the blue water. But as we come closer, we see a dozen
baby seals—whitish in their young fur—are huddled together, close and
silent, basking in the sun on a ledge barely above water.

Photographer Don Johnson sneaks forward to the tuna pulpit to make
pictures of them. SPLASH!

Everything that had looked like a silver bump on a driftwood log now
slides into the water and disappears. The seals are gone. The little ledge
which supported them is revealed.

"We'll tie to this mooring" decides Elmore. He knows each gully hole
and hidden rock after sailing in these waters for 50 years, 14 of them as
a Sea and Shore warden. "I'll stay with the boat. You and Don go ashore."

Stave is as pretty and unspoiled as any island in Casco Bay. Not as large
nor as magnificent as Jewell; not as close to civilization as Chebeague;
not as wild as Whaleboat, nor as flat as Bangs or Stockman or Ministerial
Islands. But Stave has the finest kind of many beauties, mingled in perfect yet careless balance.

A sheltered cove, with black rocks for surf to beat and foam upon; a
small blanket of white beach, for a man to stretch out and sleep upon

in the sun; steep cliffs to climb, then breathless at the top, to look out to sea from; lush ferns, sweet smelling wild flowers and ripening bushes of berries to be tempted by; and green-blue pines, evergreens and underbrush for the wind to whistle through, and for birds to rest in, and under which a hot man can find shade, quench his thirst, and be grateful to be out on Stave.

Abner Harris, founder of the Harris Company, ship chandlers, used to own Stave. The weir and lobster pound he built there still stand, tumbled about a bit by more than 50 years of waves and storms. But they bespeak still all the work which men put into building them. They bring memories of the thousand upon thousands of lobsters caught by scores of fishermen who once sold to Abner Harris, lobster dealer.

The water in the old lobster pound is warmed well—fairly well—thanks to the restraint of the weir, and to the heat from the stones. It's a grand place to skinny-dip far out at sea.

Abner's old fish house still stands near his old lobster pound, facing the cove where Steer Clear bobs at the mooring. The home he built up on the hill is there still too, with a path cut through the lush fern leading up to it.

Austin Harris, Abner's grandson, tells us that Abner sold the island in the mid-1940s to Charles Olsen, a Cape Elizabeth fisherman.

To relish a spell of utter loveliness, of total peace from people, to hear sea birds call, drop your anchor off Stave. If you need excitement, then watch the tide rise and fall. That will give you 12 hours of excitement. If you need brain work, stay the night out on Stave Island and count the stars overhead. If you get hungry, catch a mackerel, dig clams, maybe mussels, and then top them off with fistfuls of island berries, an elixir of sunshine and salt water spray.

Then if you like to rub salt into your envy, go back to the mainland and look up the tax records in Cumberland for Stave Island.

All the heaven that is called Stave was on the books at a total taxable value of $10,000 in 1970.

LITTLE CHEBEAGUE—Late in the afternoon of the unforgettable, unforgotten day spent on Stave, we dropped anchor for the night off the beach of Little Chebeague and rowed ashore in the dinghy for a look around before cooking supper.

Little Chebeague beach is about half a mile long, shaped like a shallow crescent. As the tide ebbs, the beach widens until it becomes a clean stretch 200 feet wide from dunes to water's edge. This is one of the finest beaches in Casco Bay, and the anchorage is close in and holds well.

The delightful little island is only two throws of a stone to 'civilization' and all the amenities. Long Island is just across the channel; and a sandbar, which can be walked across at low tide, joins Little Chebeague (about 200 acres) to Great Chebeague (about 2800 acres). Great Chebeague has telephones, paved roads, electric power, a hotel and golf course, ferry service and about 400 year round inhabitants, rocketing to 2000 in summer. But no one lives on Little Chebeague today.

During World War II, the navy set up a fire-fighting school here. The only remnant of it is a steel hulk on the beach where the navy set fires, and navymen learned to put them out, as training to become firefighters on aircraft carriers.

Before World War II, before the navy requisitioned Little Chebeague, over a dozen summer homes had been joyously used on the island for two generations and more. Today those homes arc tumble-down ruins. But, surrounding their foundations even today are remnants of once lovely gardens of roses and lilies.

"When I was a boy, 50 years ago, I used to row over from Long Island" said Elmore Wallace "and get milk from the cows the farmer kept in these meadows."

The grass in those meadows is shoulder high now. Small mice scuttle in it. Young birds who can't yet fly seek shelter in it, after crashing in attempted takeoffs. And the lovely, warm smell of hot summer lies fragrant on the meadow.

Ancient shutters creak on broken hinges in a vandalized house, as the breeze from the sea stirs up a moaning through gaping walls.

But it is not ghostly in these abandoned meadows and there is no meanness in the tumbled down porches. Only an air of sorrow, tinged with all the joy and happiness young people once had here.

The sun is setting fast. Back on the beach, the tide is out.

Two children who have laughed and played for an hour on this beach are now fetched by their father in a skiff from his sailboat. They up anchor and depart.

Little Chebeague is ours. We see the sun sink; then the moon rise; and feel the air cool, hear the bell buoys clang. The stars come out. The night here is still, so still that the voices of youngsters calling goodnights to each other on Long Island, across the water, sound close.

The tide is coming now. We go to the dinghy, row out to Steer Clear.

I put off going to bed, loathe to lose consciousness.

The night is still and beautifully soft. But the day! What thanks can ever be enough for a summer day spent on Stave, a summer night spent at anchor off Little Chebeague?

WHAT LIES AHEAD FOR THE GLORIES OF GREAT CHEBEAGUE?

GREAT CHEBEAGUE — The American Indian can be a very smart man indeed, especially when it comes to real estate. As proof, take the fact he sold Manhattan Island cheap; but fought like the devil to hang onto Great Chebeague in Casco Bay.

Indian Chief Madockowando was top man on Chebeague when the first white settlers came. Each June, in those days, Madockowando would lead his people from the inland forests. In a long parade of birch bark canoes they'd cross the water to spend the summer on Chebeague. They caught fish in tremendous quantities, salting much away for the hard inland winters; they killed porpoises, and used the hides to make snowshoes; they captured whales and seals, extracting the oil. And they, like Chebeaguers today, lay in the sun and swam from the beaches. And they loved summers on Chebeague, 400 years ago and more.

The Indians sold Manhattan, but not Chebeague. Up until as late as 1870 a small group of the Penobscot tribe still summered regularly on Chebeague.

A fine way to enjoy an hour on Chebeague is to go down to the wharf, and swap talk and visit and gossip. The pretext is that you are waiting for the ferry to bring its load of supplies and passengers from the mainland.

The Doughtys are there on the wharf. Doughtys are in every part of Casco Bay. They've been on Casco Bay for 200 years. The name Doughty is synonymous with good fishermen.

And probably there'll be Rosses and Seaburys, Rickers and Bennetts, Webbers and Johnsons on the wharf too—and others whose roots go deep into Chebeague's past. That is a long way back.

For the recorded past of Chebeague dates back to 1620. Then Chebeague was listed as a 'colony of the Royal Crown of England.' Sir Fer-

Great Chebeague Island looking toward Yarmouth.

nando Gorges was the island's first white proprietor, an absentee owner who lived and died in England. But in 1650 Sir Fernando sold the island to a Boston merchant named Merry. Merry never came to the island either, but he boosted his ego by changing its name to Merry Island. However money spoke louder than vanity to Merry and he sold Chebeague to John King for $500.

Later a Walter Gendall of Yarmouth owned it and held it despite the fact he was charged with treason by a Massachusetts court, and had to buy a pardon for twenty pounds. But the Indians killed Gendall. And soon Chebeague underwent a change in name and in purpose. Chebeague was given to two deacons of the First Church of Boston as recompense for their "goodly deeds." And Chebeague was renamed "Recompense Island."

But only briefly. In 1743 Colonel Thomas Westbrook bought it. Westbrook was a moneymaker, with his eye on the big white pine. For Col. Westbrook was the agent in Maine for the English navy; and the 120-foot tall pines he sold at Stroudwater for $500 each made fine masts for the English navy, and a fine profit for Col. Westbrook.

But except for the wise Indians, none of these early owners of Chebeague had the good sense to set down roots and live on lovely Chebeague. That plain piece of commonsense had to wait until Scotsman Ambrose Hamilton came to the island, built a log house on the north end, and fathered 12 children and presided over 71 grandchildren here.

This manly effort by Ambrose gave the Hamiltons a head start to becoming the leading family of Chebeague. By the 1850s the Hamilton "stone fleet" of thirty sloops was hauling Maine granite to build the Washington Monument, the Naval Academy at Annapolis, the Board of Trade in Chicago.

Today some 2000 people summer on Chebeague. Only about 300 or so live on the island year round.

That is a small number considering that Chebeague is almost five miles long, a mile wide, and has paved roads, a school, library, power, telephone and electric service.

A year-round population of 300 or so is small, especially considering the lovely beaches, the tree thick hills, the ideal boating, the views—and the fact that Chebeague is only 10 miles from Portland. But the distance is by water.

In 1950 a small group began to petition the state legislature for a bridge and a park on nearby Little Chebeague, joined by a sandbar at low water. They argued that with only an increase in the height of this natural causeway, both islands could be linked for car traffic, and the beauty of both could be preserved, buttressed by a flourishing economy.

A legislative committee reporting to the 103rd Legislature, urged the building of the Chebeague bridge. Says their report: "Chebeague Island is made up of some of the finest residential land in the country. It has miles of sandy beaches and shore front, numerous coves that delight boating and picnicking enthusiasts . . . But because of inadequate transportation, inadequate educational facilities and inadequate job opportunities the young people are leaving the islands . . . Today people will not live, shop or play in areas not accessible by car."

This Legislative committee urged that a bridge be built from Littlejohn to Chebeague, and predicted that accessible island-living on Chebeague would attract 5000 year-round residents. This, they said, would help to boom all of Greater Portland and Southern Maine. Their recommendation was soundly rejected in a state-wide referendum, thank Heaven.

Chebeague is lovely as it is today. Welcoming the ferry, swapping the news on the wharf, will always beat counting the cars crossing a bridge.

The Indians knew a good thing when they had it. They had Chebeague. And for hundreds of years, they flocked here.

FORE STREET: THE FILLED-IN HARBOR

PORTLAND — The young waiter in Portland's Old Port Tavern served us steak teriyaki and spiced it with the remark "Ships tied up where you are sitting. This whole dining room was ocean. That stone wall of this dining room was a seawall. Portland harbor used to run right up to Fore Street."

Across the street from the Old Port Tavern is an old brick building which is now stores. It was built as a house.

One night 141 years ago a widow sleeping in this house got a terrible scare. A visiting skipper in Portland had tied his coastal schooner just outside her house. The great tides of Portland harbor ran out while the skipper and his crew were ashore; his ship's level dropped with the tide; and the bowsprit and figurehead of his vessel punched clean through the window. The figurehead of an old pirate nudged the widow in her back as she lay sleeping that night of 1851. She woke screaming, they say, in delight; delight soured to disappointment, the story goes, when she found her night visitor was only a wooden pirate.

For a hundred years schooners tied up at Fore street. Today asphalt instead of ocean is there. All the land on seaward side of Fore street is man-made. Commercial Street is built on fill. A mile of fill, hundreds of feet wide, drove back the ocean; all done at a cost of $80,000 back in 1853.

A Bangor lawyer was the driving force for pushing Portland further out to sea. His inappropriate name was John A. Poor—odd name for the most enterprising railroad pioneer of his time.

Poor's dream was to make Portland the booming winter port for Canadian wheat when the St. Lawrence river froze over. To promote his dream of a Canada-Portland rail link, lawyer Poor, with his partner William Pitt Preble drove a sleigh through dead of winter all the way to Montreal— and mapped a railroad line. When the rail line was mostly built, Poor sweet-talked the City of Portland into $2 million of bonds—a huge sum in the 1850's—to build a spur to the Atlantic and St. Lawrence Railroad. On the heels of that, came Poor's persuasion of the city council to fill the harbor, build Commercial street and thereby link the Portland, Saco and Portsmouth terminal at High Street with the Atlantic and St. Lawrence Terminal at India Street. Soon the Grand Trunk took over; the Maine Central added unification to scattered lines; Portland became the great railroad as well as shipping center of the region. Up went the 200,000 bushel grain storage silos; the huge railway station; up went the most handsome Customs House in the northeast. After its completion in 1871 that Customs House began collecting duties of close to a million dollars a year from the booming port of Portland. Much of the boom was due to Mr. Poor of Bangor.

As a result of the fill, Fore Street was left high and dry, with no ships and no sailors and no waterfront. Gone were its grogshops and gaudy bawdy houses, gone were the free-spending sailors.

Gone today are most of our old landmarks here. Who walking these streets today knows that Richard Tucker and George Cleeves built the very first home in the region at the spot where Fore and Hancock intersect? They built that house in 1632. Longfellow was born near that spot in 1807 and the sea ran up to his front door. Later the family moved to Congress Street, into the Longfellow-Wadsworth house, now a museum.

It is fun to stand where Fore and Exchange streets meet and think about the widow with the bowsprit in her backside; and dream of schooners tied the length of Fore Street. In those days Exchange Street was called Fish Street for obvious reasons. Enterprising storekeepers have done a lot to restore the old buildings and make Exchange Street lively and prosperous today. Maybe they will erect a sign to the first of their kind. Nathaniel Deering was the first bold man to open a shop on Exchange Street, more than 200 years ago, right after the English Capt. Henry Mowatt bombarded and shelled to rubble 414 out of the 500 buildings in Portland (then called Falmouth). Thus Portland in 1775, then Falmouth, became one of the first casualties of the American Revolution.

A WATERFRONT KID MAKES GOOD

PORTLAND — The tough little Italian kid who flunked out of Portland High and enlisted in the Army and was on his way to Korea by the time he was 17, has done for the Portland waterfront what the Portland Establishment didn't have the guts to do. He's put his own cash on the line to revitalize his part of it, without tapping the public till. "I gambled all I had on my dream boat there on Long Wharf," says Tony DiMillo, with a gambler's gleam shining in his hard brown eyes.

DiMillo's dream was the gigantic DiMillo's floating restaurant that wines and dines 1,100 people in luxury and gives a stranger a spectacular view of Portland Harbor and the islands of Casco Bay.

DiMillo's dream boat is big; four steel decks, 216 feet long and 65 feet wide. She is floating by Long Wharf, off Commercial Street, secured against storms by eight mammoth dolphins, each with 14 pilings. Her 200 big windows give every guest a water view.

"I've spent $400,000 on her so far and I need another $800,000 fast to get her open for business," DiMillo told me in February, 1982. "But once I open, customers will be spending $4 million a year eating and drinking aboard her." Indeed they did. But Tony DiMillo's dream sounded a bit crazy then, when the Portland waterfront was largely decrepit and down-at-heel.

DiMillo was 48 then, the father of nine children, and a controversial buccaneer, to say the least, on the Portland waterfront and especially in the banking community. Finesse and finance never have been his strong points. DiMillo often looks and talks like a tough, streetwise operator who has clawed his way up the money ladder the hard, rough way. Why not? That's his record, and he wears it like a proud badge.

"I don't know a damn thing about fancy finance, write-offs and tax shelters. I was taught to make a dollar, save some, plough it back and make another. But I guess that's dumb today. Accountants talk to me about how smart it is to lose money these days to get a write-off. Then on income tax day that loss somehow turns into a gain. But I gag on that kind of arithmetic."

DiMillo now owns a large slice of the prime central waterfront in Portland. He owns six Commercial Street buildings and a huge parking lot going down to the water. He built and owns DiMillo's Marina and Long Wharf where his floating restaurant is now.

"Bankers told me I was nuts when I asked to borrow money to put in the marina. They said no one would ever keep their boat in downtown

Tony DiMillo, the street kid from Munjoy Hill, who is a big owner of Portland waterfront, including DiMillo's floating restaurant.

Portland. Now look at it—filled with millions of dollars worth of yachts. When I asked for financing for my floating restaurant, the bankers still said I was nuts. And they offered no money for DiMillo and his dream boat.''

DiMillo's floating restaurant was built as a car ferry in 1949, when heavy steel was plentiful and cheap. In her early years she ran out of Norfolk, Va., and later out of Newport, R.I. When she was 20 years old, she was transformed into apartments, then made over again to house a yacht club on Long Island Sound. There, DiMillo saw her and bought her.

DiMillo paid about $65,000. He had the ferry towed to Portland in May, 1981 to undergo eight months of costly tearing out and rebuilding.

"We tore out the kitchens, freezers, bathrooms, dining room, dance floor, and bandstand that were put in when she was a yacht club," DiMillo said. "We gutted her, reinforced and strengthened her. We enclosed her bow and stern, and then put in 200 large thermopane windows to provide perfect views. We covered her steel decks with concrete to make them level and smooth for carpets and dance floors. We poured concrete three inches thick amidships and six inches thick at the sides. You can figure what that cost me, when the main deck alone is over 14,000 square feet."

DiMillo's dream came true. It is now a floating restaurant with tables for 250 people, a cocktail lounge for 150, plus an enclosed upper deck with three function rooms that accommodate another 400, with an open deck astern where, on summer days, another 200 can drink or dine as they watch the harbor scene.

But this dream boat is more than an exciting enterprise. It is also a revealing story about the resurgence of Portland and a wiry, black-haired waterfront kid whose roots are here.

Tony DiMillo grew up a few blocks away, one of six kids in a poor family. "We lived behind the Portland Co., on the wrong side of the tracks. This waterfront was our backyard. We went clamming here. Somedays we'd 'borrow' a rowboat and explore the wharves. I never dreamed I'd own a big chunk of this waterfront myself and have a floating restaurant and a marina here."

When DiMillo came home from the Army in Korea, he began with a tiny quick-food spot called Tony's, at the foot of Munjoy Hill, in 1958. Then, briefly, he ran The Steak House at Congress and Forest before taking a stab at the big time with Anthony's, off Monument Square, which he sold to John Martin. It was for years "The Art Gallery" restaurant.

Following a short misadventure into a supermarket in South Portland, he opened DiMillo's Lobster House on Commercial Street in 1966. ''We began with tables for 55 customers. Expanded until we had room for 175 and did $1.5 million of business a year.''

This kid who flunked out of Portland High and grew up tough and streetwise here on the waterfront is now the owner of a big chunk of it.

Down the street is the Bath Iron Works' great drydock. Up the street is the International Ferry Terminal. Between is the new multimillion-dollar fish pier and new ferry terminal. All are great improvements, on a bigger scale than DiMillo's. But each one of them is backed by bond issues, city and state and federal money.

But here, one Portland kid put everything he owned or could borrow on the line. You can't help but admire this waterfront kid who made good in his own back yard.

FORTS: THE SENTINELS OF CASCO BAY

President Reagan had his vision, nicknamed Star Wars, for defending the United States against possible attack by the Soviet Union with nuclear missiles, and the cost is—pardon the pun—astronomical. But on Portland's doorstep, many millions of dollars had been spent by earlier presidents to defend the United States against possible attack by darn near every Western nation—The French, the English, the Spanish, the Germans—and even attack by fellow Americans from the South during the Civil War.

Between 1775 and 1945, throughout the first 170 years of our nation, the federal government kept spending vast amounts of money and manpower to build forts and guns, watchtowers and ammunition cellars, mines, searchlights and submarine nets to keep possible enemies out of Casco Bay.

Casco Bay bristled with enormous guns, enormous forts, enormous underground tunnels and thousands of very bored soldiers and sailors. The cost of it all is mind-boggling. And the very best thing about it is that in all those 170 costly years not a single shot was fired in anger against an enemy.

Except for one night of beet-red embarrassment during the Civil War. The forts of Casco Bay were already massive and many. And on this night of shame, these forts distinguished themselves by failing to spot, let alone stop, a single confederate raider boat, Tacony, from sailing unchallenged into Portland Harbor, cutting the anchor lines of the government revenue cutter Caleb Cushing, boarding it and putting the captain and crew in chains.

The Confederates towed their prize out to sea. The forts of Casco Bay stood uselessly by. But some fiery lads ashore commandeered a pleasure boat, the sidewheeler Forest City, threw a few firearms and militiamen aboard and raced out to rescue and recapture the government cutter.

But if they were undistinguished in war, these old forts on Casco Bay are engineering marvels, even now.

I spent awestruck hours in the great gun bays and underground tunnels of Fort Scammel on House Island. We had a hard time tying Steer Clear to an old stone pier, and an arduous scramble to get up to the fort. But 125 years ago, 30-year-old Brig. Gen. Lincoln Casey, master builder, landed millions of bricks and thousands of huge granite slabs onto this rough island shore and bossed hundreds of laborers into constructing an engineering marvel in shape, size and endurance, which would be impossible to duplicate today. And he did it with a mere $60,000 appropriated by Congress in 1862 to protect Portland Harbor against Confederate raiders.

This same 30 year-old wonder boy built Fort Gorges and Fort Preble in Casco Bay, Fort Knox on the narrows of the Penobscot River opposite Bucksport and Fort Popham at the mouth of the Kennebec. Later, Casey built the Library of Congress and completed the stalled work on the towering Washington Monument.

Fort Scammel, named for a Revolutionary war hero, has more to delight the eye than massive engineering. There is architectural beauty of form here, too, far below ground. The huge main hall and the munitions magazines, buried deep, are of wondrous and elegant proportions. Three staircases of granite spiral gracefully upward from the drinking water supply and the dungeons at the bottom of the fort.

Sunlight and eerie moonlight pour through gun holes in the granite walls to create weird and haunting patterns in the caverns with arched ceilings where enormous guns once commanded the shipping channels of Casco Bay.

The whole fort is roofed with solid earth, many feet thick, where sea grasses and wildflowers now grow in wild profusion. The earth roof was a military shield, to safeguard the fort from shells fired by the newly invented rifled gun barrels aboard ships.

Forts built before the Civil War were usually built at water level, so that cannonballs fired from muzzle-loading cannons could be ricocheted across the top of the water to hit enemy ships. Fort Preble, where Southern Maine Vocational Technical Institute now stands in South Portland, was built at water level.

House Island, where Fort Scammel stands, is the island where 27-year-old Christopher Levett, first white settler in Casco Bay, is believed to have built a stone house in 1623 for himself and the 10 men who sailed with him. Wildly enthused about the islands and the mainland he saw from Casco Bay, Levett left his 10 men and sailed back to England to recruit more settlers. He never returned. He was drowned at sea. His men left House Island.

More than 150 years later, in 1794, the new Congress of the United States authorized $76,000 for the construction of harbor forts and $96,000 to fortify them. Four years later, prodded by an insistent George Washington, Congress appropriated $400,000—a huge sum then—for more defenses for U.S. harbors. As tension mounted with England, Congress in 1808 authorized $1 million more for harbor defense.

And that was the year the federal government bought 12 acres on House Island for $1,200 on which to build a fort. It also bought five acres in South Portland to build Fort Preble, directly across Casco Bay from Fort Scammel. Work started immediately. Portland's newspaper, the Eastern Argus, carried an advertisement on May 26, 1808, for materials wanted: 200,000 best hard-burned bricks, 70 tons of square-hewed pine, 12 inches square of 32, 24, and 16 foot lengths, 15 pieces forty feet in length, and 3,000 two-inch pine planks for roofing.

This first Fort Scammel was only an eight-sided wooden blockhouse, with a porthole and gun on each side of the upper floor.

The Civil War triggered a boom in forts on Casco Bay. Fort Scammel and Fort Preble were rebuilt and hugely enlarged. The wooden blockhouse on House Island was replaced with two vast granite redoubts and 71 great guns, one 15-inch cannon, 38 ten-pounders, 18 thirty-two pounders and more were mounted at stupendous cost. Across the water at Fort Preble, 72 great guns were installed on the enlarged fort. Deeper into Portland Harbor, the federal government started building Fort Gorges in 1858, finished it in 1864, and armed it with 194 short-range guns to guard against an enemy raider getting to the wharves of Portland.

Fort Gorges in Portland Harbor is the engineering marvel that was never gunned, never manned, never saw a shot fired in anger. Built 1858—by Gen. Thomas Casey, builder of the Washington Monument, it is named for Sir Ferdinando Gorges who at the time of Queen Elizabeth I of England was the first "Proprietor of Ye Province of Mayne."

The fort boom went on. Between 1873 and 1975, the federal government bought land for more forts at Cape Elizabeth (Fort Williams) at Crow Island (Fort Lyon) and at Great Diamond Island (Fort McKinley).

A stubborn Maine man, Francis Cushing, went to court three times to stop the feds from taking 125 acres of his Cushing Island to build yet another fort. But the feds got it and built Fort Levett there. After another court fight in 1904, Jeremiah M. Johnson lost nine acres on Long Island for more fortifications. In 1906 the feds took 19 acres on Peaks to build more forts and in 1913 a fort was even built on little Crow Island, across from Fort McKinley on Great Diamond.

Fortification fever heated up again with World War II. To protect the massive fleets and convoys anchored in Portland Harbor, island forts were modernized; guns with tremendous ranges were installed. One monster gun was installed on Peaks Island at a reputed cost of $1 million.

But no shot was ever fired in anger from any fort in Casco Bay. After World War II, forts and island property owned by the federal government were offered virtually free to Portland and to Maine. After the city and state refused to take them, they went on the auction block.

Fort Scammel sold for $1,200 in 1951, the same price the feds paid for 12 acres of it in 1807. Fort Gorges was given to the city of Portland, which has done nothing with it. Fort Preble became SMVTI, the Southern Maine Vocational Technical Institute. Fort Levett on Cushing Island was sold in 1956 to a New Jersey man, who paid $33,750 for 125 acres, dozens of buildings, roads, docks and 15 fine brick residences. Fort McKinley on Great Diamond, on which millions had been spent, was sold to the same New Jersey buyer for $42,350. For that price, he got 200 acres, scores of buildings and houses, a hospital, a theater, miles of tarred roads, sewage and water systems—all in good order. Fort Williams, which did not close until 1962, is now owned by the town of Cape Elizabeth.

Today those prices paid for islands and multimillion-dollar forts on Casco Bay would hardly buy one room in one condo on one island.

ADMIRAL PEARY'S ISLAND IS NOW A STATE PARK

EAGLE ISLAND — This beautiful 17-acre island on the outermost fringe of Casco Bay is a place where big dreams have come true. Little dreams too, for the 5,000 visitors who come ashore these summers. Most come by private boats but a cruise boat, Kristy K, leaving from DiMillo's marina in Portland, has been bringing out 25 percent (or about 1,000) of the visitors, according to the Maine Bureau of Parks and Recreation which manages the state-owned island.

Vivid proof of how dreams came true here is easily seen by anyone who goes ashore to the big house during the summer, when Eagle Island, now a state park, is open to the public.

Eagle Island was the dream home of famed Admiral Robert E. Peary, the first man to reach the North Pole. Peary planned his final successful drive to the North Pole on April 6, 1909 in his Eagle Island home. Twice before, Peary had tried and twice failed to reach the Pole.

Peary's dreams of a home on Eagle Island however began long before his dreams of reaching the North Pole.

Peary's widowed mother brought him to South Portland when he was 3 years old. While he was a student at Portland High, young Peary went out to Haskell's Island, looked across the water to Eagle Island and dreamed a young boy's dream: Someday, somehow, he would own that island and live on it.

The dream lived on inside his head while Peary went to Bowdoin College (class of 1877), but at age 21 Peary had no money to buy an island in Casco Bay, cheap as they were then. During the next several years, while he served in Nicaragua with the Navy, Peary saved his pay with one goal in mind—to buy his dream island.

By the time he was 26 years old, in 1881, Peary had money enough just to buy the land of Eagle Island. But the only house he could afford was a tent, pitched 100 feet above the sea. It took Peary 20 more years to save money enough to build his house on the island. Then from his home in Washington, D.C., Peary signed a tough contract with a local builder to build him a very small house at a very low price.

By 1904, five years before Peary discovered the North Pole, his first house was ready. It was later moved, renamed "The Igloo," and used as a guest house. Not until 1912 was Peary able to start building the splendid large house which still dominates Eagle Island, and in which Peary, his wife and children lived each summer.

In 1967 Peary's daughter, Mrs. William W. Kuhne, gave Eagle Island to Maine. She was the famed "snow baby," born in the Arctic aboard Peary's Maine-built ship, the Roosevelt. In 1970, the island was opened to the public as a state park. Since then, tens of thousands of people from across the United States have made pilgrimages to this spectacular and special island.

In the house, they can still see letters, diaries and notes made by Peary, still see his worn admiral's topcoat with its gold braid long tarnished, still see wild birds which ornithologist Peary shot and stuffed, still see pictures he took of the frozen North. Standing on the terrace, visitors can still see the lights of the six lighthouses which Peary watched at night.

Gone now are the great heads of polar bear, musk-ox and walrus which Peary brought home from the arctic. Gone is the rocking chair he once used as a cradle for the "snow baby" in her first year of life off the Greenland coast. But still intact and curious is the unique three-faced fireplace, with its triangular chimney, which Peary designed. And indelible on the minds of all who have stood on Eagle Island, and imperishable long as Eagle Island stands, are the wild and glorious views in every direction.

The season is over by October. The moorings are empty. Eagle Island is battening down for another winter. But this island of special dreams will be alive and glowing in the memories of every one who has visited here, seen its beauty and felt the awesome spirit of the first man to reach the North Pole.

ROYAL RIVER—ROYAL PASSAGE THROUGH HISTORY

ROYAL RIVER — This was the day to take Steer Clear out of Casco Bay up the Royal River to Yarmouth for winter storage. This time there would be no postponement.

Balmy days of sunshine and blue skies in early November were such a delightful tease that we had stretched the boating season to the limit. Several times we had gone to the boat and off-loaded a carful of the stuff one accumulates through the summer. We had intentions of hauling out each time. Each time the good weather teased us out to the islands for one more final cruise.

But by the end of the first week of November, I was playing with dice loaded against me. A bad blow might burst on Maine any day with hurricane fury.

The last trip of the year is, to me, a ceremony I like friends to share. Perhaps it would be closer to the truth to admit it is too sad a trip to make alone. So six of us met at the slip in Harraseeket Harbor, South Freeport, where Steer Clear was docked. We met at 1:30 p.m., just as the rising tide was starting to come. I wanted to be going upriver on an incoming tide.

The finality of the last trip of the year began even before we left our slip. This time, instead of simply casting off the docking lines, we had to untie them from the cleats on the slip and take them aboard with us.

Steer Clear would not be coming back.

Running out past Pound o' Tea, the tiny island at the Harraseeket Harbor entrance, we had the entire Casco Bay almost to ourselves. Hundreds of times this summer, I had threaded Steer Clear through the lobster pot buoys set close to Pound o' Tea in such a routine way that I barely noticed their colors. On this last trip I did, saying a silent goodbye to each. I said the same kind of silent farewell to each can and nun which mark the channels between the islands. As we ran slowly down between Moshier Island and the tip of Great Chebeague, I eyed coves where we had dropped anchor and places where we had swum or fished. In my mind's eye, I played back the film of the days of summer on Casco Bay.

"Throttle way down, Bill, we are coming up on the buoys at the mouth of the river," warned navigator Jim Saunders. "We'll be making sharp turns by mudbanks, and the tide is still only minutes past dead low."

Saunders loves his boyhood river. He knows the long history of the Royal River well. Each turn, every landmark on the banks holds memories, some of which he shares.

"My father used to like running upriver at night. He ran without lights. He said there is more light than you'd ever guess at night—provided you have no lights on your boat. He made it without a hitch almost all the time, but once in a while we did spend long hours struck on a mudbank, waiting for the rising tide."

Somewhere in history, the Royall River lost its last "l."

The first permanent settler here was William Royall, who arrived at North Yarmouth about 1635. In 1673, well advanced in age, he deeded his land and buildings to his two sons, William and John, in consideration of their perpetual support of himself and his wife, Phoebe. His four grandsons were born here by the Royall River. One grandson, Isaac, made his fortune in Antigua; and his famous son, Col. Isaac Royall, built the lordly mansion in Medford, Mass., which is still preserved as a museum. A Loyalist to England, Isaac Royall fled to Nova Scotia at the start of the Revolutionary War and never returned to Massachusetts after his rich estates were confiscated. But he endowed one of the most famed chairs at Harvard, the Royall Professorship of Law.

Second only to William Royall as a Yarmouth pioneer was John Cousins, born in England in 1596, who bought two beautiful islands at the mouth of Royall's River, one of which still bears his last name—Cousins Island—and the other bears his nickname—Littlejohns.

We were taking Steer Clear up to the Yarmouth Boatyard for the winter. John MacDonald, then the owner of the boatyard, had comforted me before my first trip up the Royal River by saying it was "well buoyed all the way. In addition to Coast Guard buoys, you'll see plenty of stakes with red and green flags painted at the top of them. They will guide you fine."

Well, I found all the stakes. They were aboard the lobster boat Molly O, which had pulled them for winter on the previous day. But navigator Saunders did us better than the stakes would have.

Mudflats, marsh grasses and lots of ducks, ospreys and patient herons give a special beauty to the Royal River when the tide is low. But the amazement is that so many huge ships were built and launched on this mud-flatted river more than 100 years ago.

There have been shipyards here since 1740. By 1865, Yarmouth men were building ships so fast that the brig Emma was constructed in 90 days. The owner even signed a contract in January for Emma to carry a cargo to Cuba in April; and in January his men were still out in the winter woods, cutting timber for the frames that would go into Emma. But on April 3, Emma sailed out for Cuba.

The Admiral was the largest ship ever launched in Yarmouth. It left in 1875, 260 feet overall, 2,209 tons, with iron masts and spars and wire rigging. It carried a crew of 27 and cost $150,000, including the Brussels carpets in the main cabin. I'd like to have seen a 260 foot ship coming down this narrow channel between mudflats.

On July 4, 1848, the new Montreal-to-Portland railroad made its first stop at North Yarmouth. During its first month of operation, 6,357 passengers got on or off at Yarmouth Junction. Today no passenger trains serve Yarmouth—or any town in Maine. An even stranger transportation fact is this: In 1916, the large farm between the Old Grand Trunk and Maine Central railroads at Yarmouth Junction was one of the largest shipping stations in the world for horses and mules. During World War I, more than 76,300 horses and mules were kept, fed and then shipped from Yarmouth to the battlefields of Europe.

Steer Clear's run from South Freeport and up the Royal River to Yarmouth took less than two hours of an idyllic November afternoon. But, thanks in part to Saunders' local knowledge, we traveled hundreds of years, from the first settler, William Royall, who landed here more than 300 years ago, to a senior at Yarmouth High School who was docking a $20,000 speedboat next to Steer Clear.

EXPLORING A LANDMARK: CASCO CASTLE AT SOUTH FREEPORT

SOUTH FREEPORT — When I lived in New York, I got so used to the Statue of Liberty that I never went to visit that spectacular landmark. The year Steer Clear was berthed in South Freeport, I had a minor version of the Statue of Liberty to beckon me back to Harraseeket Harbor. The chart for Casco Bay marks it simply as 'tower'. Before this landmark too became just a familiar mark on a familiar shoreline, I decided to see it up close and find what it is and how it got there.

The strange stone tower, which from the sea looks like the battlements of a medieval English fortress, is not easy to reach by land. When I got close, I was warned to keep out by No Trespassing signs. I inquired at the houses nearby, and met a bevy of Plummers, good people who have lived close to the strange tower since it was built.

There is nothing medieval about it. It was built in 1903. One fine Plummer man told me, ''I was a baby lying in my crib, when outside my window, masons were building that tower. The first word I learned to say was 'hod-a-muck.' ''

I thought ''hod-a-muck'' was better than ''goo-goo'' as a baby's first word, but asked how a baby picked up language like that.

''That's the cry masons high on the tower shouted down to workers below. When the masons were ready to lay more stone, they cried 'hod-a-muck!', meaning 'Send up a bunch of mortar!' ''

The strange tower at South Freeport is all that is left of Casco Castle, once a spectacular, luxury hotel with 100 rooms overlooking Casco Bay.

The Plummers showed me old pictures of the great wooden hotel, with banners flying from atop three turrets, complete with apertures from which medieval archers might have fired arrows at the armies of an upstart warlord.

The medieval fairy tale castle even had a moat which guests crossed on a wobbly 300-foot-long drawbridge. The drawbridge was, in fact, an old suspension bridge which had been a footbridge in Lewiston-Auburn and was brought down here, piece by piece, and reassembled.

Guests in the old Casco Castle Hotel reached the adjacent 100-foot tower by another smaller suspension bridge, high in the air. They then climbed a wooden circular staircase to the top of the tower, and from there enjoyed spectacular views across the islands of Casco Bay in one direction and to the White Mountains in the other.

Those steep, winding steps to the top must have been a challenging climb for turn-of-the-century ladies in long skirts and tight corsets and their men with high celluloid collars, handlebar mustaches, derby hats and stove-pipe trousers—especially after a sumptuous dinner in the hotel's formal dining room.

But the prices for those dinner in 1903 seem bargains. The engraved menus of that era offered a Casco Castle Shore Dinner for 50 cents. It consisted of lobster stew, steamed clams with drawn butter, boiled lobster, fried clams, doughnuts, spring chicken, coffee and fresh fruit.

The price for a room with a view was $12 a week, and every room had its own fireplace. An orchestra played for dancing in the ballroom nightly; there were baseball games each weekend on the hotel's own ballfield; and a saltwater swimming pool and a sand beach for those brave enough to try the ocean.

The hotel grounds, with elaborate flower gardens and a zoo featuring monkeys, peacocks, buffalo and moose, covered 60 acres. The total cost for building all this was $25,000.

Amos Gerald of Fairfield was the owner. He'd made a fortune building and promoting 12 electric railroads in Maine. And his Portland and Brunswick Street Railroad ran frequent excursion trips to his Casco Castle Hotel.

But fire gutted the hotel in 1913, ten years after it had opened, and shortly after an unprofitable summer. Only the stone tower escaped destruction, though the stairs inside were burned.

Tattered streamers of old flags whipped in the breeze atop the 100-foot tower on the day the Plummers told me of their memories of the once great hotel which commanded Casco Bay over 80 years ago. I asked how the banners got up there, since no stairs are left to reach the top. The Plummers told me that a young neighbor, who had been an instructor in rock-face climbing at the Outward Bound School on Hurricane Island, rappelled up the face of the tower and planted big, beautiful flags 100 feet up there. Since then, winds and storms have shredded them. But there is no one here now who is willing to rappel sheer stone face of the old tower to get them down.

I missed my visit to the Statue of Liberty because I let that landmark become old-hat to me. But now when I come into South Freeport Harbor, steering by the old medieval tower, I feel a tiny surge of virtue at having tracked down this landmark before it became just another part of the Casco Bay landscape.

INDISPENSABLE MAN: ARCHIE ROSS OF BUSTINS ISLAND

CASCO BAY — Archie Ross, barefoot, bearded, small, lively and forever laughing, seems the best-known man on the South Freeport waterfront.

Ross looks like a leprechaun, escaped from County Tipperary to holiday on the coast of Maine. But in fact, he was born in 1920 on Great Chebeague Island, biggest of the 180 islands in Casco Bay.

Ross runs the boat which links South Freeport to Bustins Island, three miles away. He is the indispensable man to the 350 people who summer on Bustins Island. In his 36-foot boat, Ross ferries them back and forth, making more than 25 round trips weekly.

"My boat and I do the equivalent of a quarter way around the world every summer. Every four years, we make the equivalent of a circumnavigation of the globe, over 25,000 miles, just going back and forth to Bustins Island from May to October" says Ross.

Ross's boat has served him long and well. He has put his fifth new engine into it, since it was built at Handy Boat in Falmouth by Harold Sawyer in 1950. "Back then, my trademark expression was 'Judas Priest', and when they launched the boat, they hung a name sign on her—Judas Priest. But some religious families whom I ferried back and forth to Bustin didn't much like that. So I changed her name to the Marie L, after my mother Marie L. Ross," he says.

After a Chebeague Island boyhood on lobster boats, Archie Ross worked for Walter Swett, running the old Nellie G, which had been converted from steam to gasoline, carrying passengers from Falmouth Foreside to Cousins Island, Littlejohn Island and Chebeague Island. "Later, I ran Nellie G III, which is still running out of Portland."

Ross began the Bustins Island run from South Freeport in 1946. He remembers carrying Admiral Harold MacMillan out to Bustins in earlier years, when the Arctic explorer ran a boys' camp there. Ross's original boat on this run, the Victory, was lost when he attempted to rescue a schooner during a hurricane. That is when the people on Bustins Is-

Archie Ross, the happy pixie of Harraseeket Harbor, runs the essential ferry to Bustins Island.

land raised money through suppers, raffles and poker games to help Ross buy the Marie L as their new ferry. They still subscribe $5,500 a year to keep Ross on the summer run plus a fee per trip per passenger. But the money is not enough to keep Ross through the winter. So from October to May, he and his partner Caroll Lowell build lobster boats at their Even Keel boatyard on the Cousins River.

Between trips on the Marie L., Ross talked about the tremendous changes he has seen in Harraseeket Harbor at South Freeport. "There was just a dirt wharf, six feet narrower than today, when I began working here. No marinas. No boatyards. No Harraseeket Lobster and Lunch restaurant. Only one small brick building on the wharf. All the buildings you see today are mostly on filled land, built up behind bulkheads."

He looks out to the 500 moorings for pleasure boats at the slips at Ring's marina and South Freeport Marine and at the Harraseeket Yacht Club. "I remember when there were only three pleasure boats here. A black schooner called Wild Goose, owned by Dr. Rodgers; a little green sailboat and a 24-foot cabin cruiser. And there were just eight local fishermen with their lobster boats moored here."

Passengers for Bustins Island begin drifting down to the wharf for the next run. Many of their cars have out-of-state licence plates. They arrive with loads of summer gear, from guitars to garden plants, from clothes to kitchen utensils. And every one of them greets Ross with a hug or a handshake, as though he were a member of their family whom they had not seen since last summer. Ross beams, grabs their load of luggage and hustles in his bare feet to stow it aboard the Marie L. He is so much a part of the Bustins Island community that when he married in 1953, the wedding was held at Bustins Island Community Hall and 500 guests, including almost every person on the island, came to the candlelight ceremony.

If and when Archie Ross gives up the run which links Bustins Island to the mainland, no one knows what will happen. "There will never be another Archie Ross," says one Bustins Islander. "So we'll have to pray for a good substitute, because without Archie around, Bustins Island may float out to sea, lost to Maine forever."

A HALF-CENTURY OF SAILING THE MAINE COAST

UPPER GOOSE ISLAND — The Emma lay in the cove, and the Bennetts waved from the open deck, and my day was made happy. Every June for 60 years, two of the most delightful people in Maine set off in one of Maine's most unusual boats on perhaps the most enjoyable cruise anyone in Maine will have.

Their idea of heaven-on-the-salt-water may not be yours and is not mine. We are probably too old and too soft to endure the hardships which Paul and Emma Bennett of South Freeport call pleasures.

The Bennetts have both turned 80 years. He is lean, tall, curly-headed with a wiry beard, grizzled-gray. She is white-haired, blue-eyed, pretty and forever laughing.

Their boat is a classic, too. It is a 27-foot double-ender, a St. Pierre dory, built for the Bennetts in 1967 by that master craftsman of small wooden boats, William Shew of South Bristol. It is built of solid white pine on white oak, lapstrake fashion, with decks of teak. So the boat is as tough and seaworthy as the dories used by the St. Pierre fishermen from the Maritime Provinces in the hard weather of the Grand Banks. The 22 horsepower Palmer engine has logged 2,000 hours.

The Bennetts go to sea in Emma for two months every summer. They go east as far as Cutler and Lubec, gunkholing among their favorite island coves all the way, moving along at a gentle five knots.

Every August 1, they celebrate their wedding anniversary at sea together. That is the way it's been for more than half a century.

"We spent our wedding night together aboard the Boston-to-Bangor boat, on Aug. 1, 1931," says Bennett. "And that first night together, we made a promise we'd spend every wedding anniversary in a boat at sea along the coast of Maine. And we've done it."

Mrs. Bennett grew up in Dixfield, while Paul Bennett lived on the family farm in nearby West Auburn. "My father worked in the woods, making $15 a month as a teamster, driving his white horses on a tote team. He got $3 a month more for shooting deer to feed the lumberjacks in camp. Here is a picture of him and his team, made in 1905," says Bennett. It is a dog-eared photo of a life long gone from America. I wonder what teamster Bennett would think of his photo being looked at more than 80 years later, on the deck of a cruising boat.

Young Paul Bennett dreamed of becoming a forester and was accepted at the School of Forestry at the University of Maine in 1927. "I sent in $7 deposit as key money for a room in Oak Hall and $25 deposit on tuition, and went off to college in Orono."

He graduated in 1931, slap at the bottom of the Depression. But he was lucky enough to land a job with Great Northern Paper Co., cruising for timber around Mount Katahdin. A year later the Depression hit even the Maine woods; Great Northern didn't cut a stick that year and Paul was laid off in 1932.

"By then, I was married to Emma. Her brother had sat next to me in high school. In my world then, he held the keys to heaven, because he owned a motorbike. I went home with him to tinker with it and fell in love with his sister almost as much as with the motorbike. When I landed the job with Great Northern, I ran all the way to a telephone at Clayton Lake and called Emma and told her I'd be right down to marry her. I didn't fancy a long cold winter sleeping alone in the north woods."

Emma went to Town Hall, got a marriage license and bought winter underwear. Then she married Paul and caught the night boat to Bangor with her new husband.

Bennett found a new job with the Koppers Co., selling tar and asphalt to towns throughout Maine and the Maritimes. His wife traveled with him for most of 30 years, getting to know the town selectmen and highway bosses.

But in the summer of 1972 when they were cruising aboard Emma, Bennett put into Matinicus Island to visit his great friends Cheney Ripley and Ken Ames. "Ripley is a rare man," says Bennett. "He makes dulcimers, writes poetry, plays the saw and the piano and writes beautiful calligraphy. I used his phone to call the Koppers office in Portland and they told me I was laid off. Because of the cut-off of Arab oil imports, there wouldn't be enough tar and asphalt for me to sell. I was so mad at having to let down 62 customers across Maine that I quit and took early retirement."

The blessing of that early retirement at age 66 was that it allowed the Bennetts to enlarge a two-week holiday cruise into a full two-month cruise Down East. So every June since 1972 they head off to visit their furthest Down East friend, lobsterman Simeon Dobbins of Cross Island, near Cutler.

The Bennetts bought their white clapboard farmhouse in South Freeport with 3.5 acres running down to the water where their boat is moored, 55 years ago. "We paid $1,500 for it then. We borrowed the money from my folks," says Mrs. Bennett, "and paid it back with interest." Emma and Paul have raised four children in their comfortable house, which was built more than 175 years ago.

Though well into their eighties, this couple have more fun living together aboard their small boat than most people do on a luxury yacht. They seem perfectly matched to each other and to their St. Pierre dory. I can see them now, celebrating their 57th wedding anniversary; Emma cooking a special supper over an alcohol stove on an open deck, Paul with his longbilled fisherman's hat crooked on his bushy head of hair, regaling his bride and anyone within hearing distance with wonderfully told seafaring stories. Then they will break out a special noggin, drink their toast of love and laughter together, and throw the glasses into the sea.

GOOD MORNING! WAKING UP AT WHALEBOAT ISLAND

LITTLE WHALEBOAT ISLAND — I woke at dawn, unzipped my sleeping bag and took three steps from the sleeping cabin of Steer Clear to the helmsman's wheel and looked out to sea.

Fog. White, milky fog. But not everywhere. The shoreline of Little Whaleboat, an uninhabited Casco Bay island, 100 feet from where we are anchored, is clear. Wet, yellow-green seaweed drapes granite ledges; birch trees glisten silver-white; and raucous fish crows caw, shattering the silence of dawn.

The sea is a mirror-flat surface of pearly gray, a welcome change from last night when a 25 mph wind from the southwest kicked up turbulent whitecaps and rolled the boat. My loyal, lonely seagull is back in his position, 20 feet astern, where he patiently rode the waves all day yesterday, hoping for food. Off the bow, I have another constant companion, a seal who pops up his head every few minutes for an inquiring look, twitches his whiskers and vanishes. But he allows me time enough to focus the binoculars on his face—kindly bulbous eyes and a head as big as a mastiff's.

A great blue heron stands motionless at the head of the cove, fishing. Long neck, spindly legs, he is a gaunt, elongated, unlikely bird, and looks like an El Greco painting. He can't find a fish for breakfast here. Slowly, he lifts one spindly leg and its great webbed foot, then the other, and pads away stealthily to try his luck in another fishing pool.

The sun, a deep orange ball misted by white fog, is above the island tree line now, and splashes a narrow path of pale gold on the leaden sea. The sun's warmth wakens sleeping gulls, who protest with a cacophony of early day screeching.

Now a swivel-necked cormorant swims alongside Steer Clear and fixes me with his cold, red eye. "Harmless," he seems to think, and dives for breakfast. Long neck down, body below the surface, he leaves only a swirl on the water where he was.

Then, 30 feet away, he surfaces, a slithering fish thrashing in his beak, trying to escape death. Up goes the cormorant's head, his curved neck stretches out straight, and down the long throat the fish slides to dark death.

Now, an hour after dawn, the climbing sun turns the fog into glaring white vapor, too dense for eyes to penetrate. Islands further down the bay vanish in the glaring whiteness which totally obscures most land and sea. Yet the tallest treetops on the highest islands are weirdly visible, hanging in space, unconnected to the world below.

The breeze picks up, stirred to life by the rising sun. It plays tricks with the white vapor, blowing it aside to unveil an island shore here and an island cove there, until the islands of Casco Bay look like ethereal paintings from a children's book of Camelot, imaginary islands of chivalry and Guenivere, Excalibur and Sir Lancelot.

Perspectives are strange. Lobster buoys loom huge, three times their actual size. Sound plays strange tricks too. I hear the engines of invisible lobster boats, noise travelling far ahead of sight.

Finally, I see the first early morning boats, rounding a distant island. Their white hulls emerge from the milky mist and suddenly gleam brightly, starkly luminescent when rays of the rising sun strike them. They stop to haul traps. Sound dies as engines are throttled back and gears are shoved to neutral. Then the engines roar again, and the boats race on to haul another set of traps.

The misty world around me is coming full awake. Five ospreys circle overhead, emitting their high-pitched, squeaky cry, so incongruous out of majestic hawks. I spot their sprawling nests atop dead trees.

A pair of ducks fly by very low, wings barely clearing the surface of the ocean, necks outstretched, noiseless except for the whispering murmur of their beating wings.

A platoon of eider ducks paddles out from the rocky shore. The motherly hens are taking ten baby balls of fluff out for a morning lesson in how to forage for breakfast.

Suddenly, a prize sight; a handsome pair of loons, one glossy black, the other beautifully speckled in black-and-white, come gliding close to Steer Clear.

There is a burst of excitement. The female snags a dead fish floating under the surface. But it is too tough, too large for her to swallow. She pecks at it hard and angrily, then dunks it time and again deep in the water, to soften it, and pecks again, furious because it is still unswallowable. A dozen times she does this, getting angrier each time. In disgust and disappointment she finally tosses it away, and swims off with her mate to find a more manageable meal.

The bay is busy now with workboats sprinting between lobster traps and young boys in outboard skiffs nosing into shallow coves to haul. I hope there will be lobster money in their jeans for a date tonight.

By my watch, it is not yet seven o'clock. But this sea and island world is already peopled by working men. Boat engines roar. Boat radios blare and hard rock music—the sound to haul by—shatters the quiet.

Time for me to get Steer Clear underway. I turn on the blowers to clear out any gas fumes that may have accumulated overnight under the engine hatches. I turn on the depth finder to check on the water under the hull. Turn on the radio for the weather report from Eastport to the Merrimac River. Start the engines. Go forward to the bow to haul in the anchor, buried deep in sticky mud which comes up smelling of the centuries. The fog is lifting and a good day lies ahead.

The magic of day's dawning, the special loneliness of the misty world when no man was stirring near this island cove and all was primeval mystery, is gone. Yet there lingers in my mind an oasis of serenity.

If the root of human distress is a sense of alienation from the natural order of the universe, then a fountainhead of human happiness is this hour alone in a small boat at dawn, when the islands and the sea are soft and calm, empty of the present but brimming with the ancient past, exuding the peace that comes from having endured through centuries of storms and change in man and nature.

BATTENING DOWN FOR A HURRICANE

CASCO BAY — By 2:30 Friday afternoon, boatyards along the Maine coast are like churches. Seldom has heaven heard so much praying from wet and weary men in yellow slickers. A hurricane is on the way.

In the dockmaster's shed at the harbor where Steer Clear is in a slip, the owner and his wife huddle with exhausted yard crews. "Now we are only waiting for it to happen. Praying, waiting. Everything that can be done to secure the boats has been done. It's too late to do anything more," she sighs. It had been a long, hard Thursday and Thursday night for the

Aftermath of a hurricane.

yard crews, and an even harder Friday since sun-up. A hurricane is rampaging along the East coast, closing in on Maine.

"Forty yachts pulled. Double anchor lines rigged on 20 more out on moorings. Walkways and finger slips secured with hawsers," says boat-handler Peter Tucker.

Pulling a yacht is harder than it sounds. First, two boat-handlers must get out to the yacht in an outboard, come alongside in a stiff wind and heavy chop, pre-hurricane weather, and clamber aboard. Off come the sails, bagged on the boom, plus everything loose on deck. Then comes the job of towing the yacht from its mooring to the marina and then the big job of de-masting. Then, with the wind and rain, begin tricky maneuvers to get an $95,000 yacht safely embraced by the massive slings of a travel lift. Then come the heart-stopping minutes of tension as the costly yacht is lifted bodily out of the water, high into the air, dangling, swaying, helpless, awkward. Finally the slow haul through the wild air to the cradle on land.

The job can take two men three or four hours. Forty yachts have been hauled at this one yard in the past 24 hours, since the hurricane began her dervish dance along the Northeast Atlantic coast.

Some 350 moorings in sheltered Harraseeket Harbor have boats bouncing on them. Hurricane winds can break mooring lines, and a multi-ton yacht, broken loose, can smash wildly into other boats as the gale blows it across a crowded harbor, wreaking more havoc than any bull in any china shop. This is why owners and yard workers have been out in the driving rain and wind, working on every moored boat, adding anti-chafing gear, adding double pennants for double security, an extra link of strong rope to marry the boat to the anchor chain and thence to the 1,000 pound block of granite on the bottom.

Steer Clear is going to ride out the hurricane at her finger slip. She has sea room, for the boat next to her has gone. Eric Horn, who works in the marina, comes down to help me rig more lines. Three lines to port, three to starboard and two off the bow. Now Steer Clear should stay tethered tight as a wild pony in a stall. Might buck and kick, but she won't get away—I hope and pray.

Five sea miles to the west, in Falmouth Foreside, at Handy Boat, the crews have been working past midnight the last two nights, preparing for the hurricane to hit. Here three travel-lifts are at work. Yards, parking lots, every foot of open space, has a stormed-scared yacht sheltering on it. Even so, another 300 yachts are out in the open sea, bucking the storm from their moorings. They are bucking hard and angrily already, by 4 p.m. Friday. The waves and the wind are far worse here than in Harraseeket Harbor, for here the winds from the southwest have a clear stretch of eight miles of open water across Casco Bay to build up power and clobber these much-loved, much-pampered yachts. The beauties may be in for the roughest night of their lives tonight.

Walter Cronkite and his CBS shipmate Andy Rooney phoned from Christmas Cove to ask if Handy's could haul out their 42-foot boat to safety during the storm. "Wish we could help," they were told. "But there are 100 boats ahead of you, waiting to be hauled." But Cronkite's handsome boat finds safety closer to Christmas Cove. Goudy and Stevens Yard in East Boothbay, just across the Damariscotta River, hauled Cronkite's boat to safety on dry land.

The sky is lowry, the rain pelts and the wind gusts and rises. The air is heavy and strange. Something bad feels about to happen. The radio says the hurricane is passing Bridgeport, Connecticut, with 100 mph blows. She may hit Casco Bay and all these beautiful boats with 75 mph punches in a couple of hours. By now there is not a darn thing more a boatman can do. Except stop fearing the worst and start praying hard for the hurricane to spare his boat.

Ducks along the Maine coast at sunrise.

IV
CASCO BAY
TO BOOTHBAY

GUNKHOLING RUN: FROM YARMOUTH TO GURNET

STEER CLEAR SALUTES A POET FROM RAGGED ISLAND

THE CRIB BRIDGE AT BAILEY ISLAND

THE BIRDMAN OF BAILEY ISLAND

MOON OVER BUTTERMILK COVE

ROUGH SEAS AT SEGUIN, PEACE AT HARPSWELL

NO FISH STORY: FISH CATCHES MAN

COLD FEAR STALKS STEER CLEAR

PARTY TONIGHT WITH THE SEALS AT OVEN'S MOUTH

FILBERT IS CRABBIEST DOG AROUND

In the winter Steer Clear goes south, all the way to Yarmouth, which is 15 miles by car from my home on Buttermilk Cove, outside of Brunswick. But from May till November, Steer Clear comes north, to a mooring within 80 yards of where I live. When I'm in an upbeat mood, I'm apt to boast "My boat is moored right outside my house." Not quite the case. The boat is close but I cannot quite see Steer Clear, hidden behind a jut of rocky land on which high pines grow. And I cannot row out to her directly from my house, because the water in front drains out to mudflats at low tide.

In fact, its a job getting out to Steer Clear with gear, guests, and food for a weekend on the water. But that's a handicap I suffer gladly, most of the time, but especially when I'm taking out "yacht club" types from the suburbs, people who are accustomed to stepping from clubhouse to afterdeck.

To get from house to Steer Clear, you must first drive down a rutted dirt road cut through a forest. You park in an opening cut out between pines. Then you walk steeply downhill, lugging your stuff until you come to the fish house and dock, owned by a friend. The friend is a very busy lobsterman, and on some days his bait is very ripe.

The skiff is tied at his dock, and often must be bailed after summer rain. Then it's loading time for guests and grub, which is not a simple maneuver for city folk without experience of getting into a tippy skiff from a dock bobbing on the tide and slippery with bait grease. Then we row 80 yards to Steer Clear and clamber aboard. This is a high-stepping maneuver, involving lots of leg display for ladies who wear skirts.

Thank heaven, there is idyllic Maine coast scenery of a workaday kind to enthrall them.

Now they have to wait through my caution-and-check routine. First, I turn on the blowers for five minutes to rid the boat of any possible gasoline fumes lurking in the bilges. Next, I take a yardstick to measure the amount of fuel in the tanks by hand and eye, being a true disbeliever in deceiving gauges. Next I open both engine hatches, not so guests can be reassured by the sight of 270 horses in their combined power, but so I can manually check the vital signs, the levels of oil and cooling water for the engines, and visually check all hose connections. Next I lift a hatch cover in the deck to open three sets of petcocks, two of which open to permit sea water to flow into the external cooling systems around the outside of the engine blocks, and one of which opens the gas line which feeds fuel to the engines. (All petcocks get firmly closed whenever I leave the boat untended.) Finally I check the radios, and depth finder to be certain all are receiving and transmitting. Only then do I shut off the blowers and start engines. I let both engines idle for two minutes, while I watch the temperature and oil pressure gauges respond. Then, very briefly, I check the transmission by putting the hydraulic gear into forward, and then into reverse and finally back to neutral. Over-cautious? Well, my worst accidents so far have been bad scares, two of which are recounted in this section.

Now I get a guest to go forward to the bow and cast off the mooring (when solo, I do this little chore.) It's a shock to a novice to find that by throwing off one loop they have set loose the boat. That is when the fun begins. Whichever course I choose to head toward the ocean, it piques the interest (to put it modestly) of first-time-outers. The choice is either to poke down the winding, stake-marked, shallow channel through Long Reach (described in the following pages); or to run the tide race under the Gurnet Bridge.

Tides often make the choice for me. I still won't risk the Long Reach back channel, the staked, winding run, within one and half hours of low tide, because it shallows out too much for this chicken sailor. And I won't risk going under the Gurnet Bridge within 90 minutes either side of high water, because there's not enough clearance. Clearance is 10 feet at high water, and the span is 25 feet.

Under the Gurnet bridge, the tide race can sometimes be scary. Going against it, as the New Meadows river pours into Buttermilk Cove, means I must throw formidable power (between 2,500 and 3,000 r.p.m.) onto both engines to overcome the push of the rushing water. Even so, the tide race is so strong that Steer Clear makes only three knots of forward speed, compared to 14 knots at the same r.p.m. in open water. What's more, the tide rip, compressed by the narrow span of the bridge, creates whirlpools which could slam a less powerful boat against the bridge. To avoid this requires a strong correcting pair of hands on the helm. It can be a white-knuckle job for a few minutes until we are in the calm and lovely water of the New Meadows River.

Clearance under the old Gurnet bridge used to be lower than the 10 feet it is today. Roland Coffin, the lobsterman who lives beside the *bridge and runs "Ben's Lobster," had a unique way, I'm told, of negotiating his lobster boat under the bridge at close to high water. "He'd come at the bridge stern first. Then, if he saw he couldn't clear, he'd throw the power to her hard and shoot back into open water and wait for the tide to drop a mite," says a long-time neighbor of his.*

That's a trick which Steer Clear will never try. This sailor has no thirst for danger, no hunger for risk taking. I had enough of both. But when danger comes, as it inevitably does, I get my kicks after the danger is over. While it's going on, I hate it and simply swear I will never get into the same fix again. So if the tide is running too hard against me, I wait happily and comfortably, because I know that in a little while that tide is going to change.

GUNKHOLING RUN: FROM YARMOUTH TO GURNET

YARMOUTH — Did the minister do it? Maybe. Because ten minutes after we took a minister on board, the fog lifted, the rain stopped and Steer Clear happily cast off her dock lines and left the Yarmouth Boat Yard on her first trip of summer.

The fog-lifter is Christopher Sims, from St. Mary's Church, Falmouth Foreside. He had turned 60 when he was ordained. Sims had had a long wait for his collar. He had started at the seminary soon after he turned 20, but got side-tracked into becoming a successful businessman. In his mid-60s now, Sims makes a jovial priest, with the expansive girth, twinkling eyes and laughter-rich voice of a year-round Santa Claus.

We had other fog-lifters aboard, helping the one with heavenly contacts.

One with political influence was Helen Schlaack. She'd been mayor of Brunswick for six years. Another, with scientific clout, was Joe Sukaskis. He'd studied at the Julliard School of Music, then trained in nuclear science, switched to broadcasting, now is working at the Maine Public Utilities Regulation Commission. The third fog-lifter was his wife Gayle Sukaskis, who spent part of her young life flying through fog and rain with Pan-Am.

At 10 a.m. we five were still standing on the dock, huddled in foul-weather gear, gloomily watching fog roll up the Royal River. Marine Weather Radio was still forecasting rain, fog and 8-foot seas, no weather for Steer Clear's first trip of the year with guests aboard.

Suddenly the fog lifted, the rain stopped and the vote to head out was unanimous. By the time we reached our destination at Buttermilk Cove, near the Gurnet Bridge, four hours later, we were to enjoy gunkholing of the finest kind.

Gunkholing is a sport which should be played in very slow motion. The penalty for playing too fast is going aground and getting stuck on a mud-flat, where you can spend hours slapping mosquitoes while you wait for the tide to come in and lift your boat off.

Gunkholing is boatmen's talk. Sensible people seldom hear the word, but it has won its way into Webster's dictionary. However, Webster's definitions are gruesome.

"Gunk," says Webster, is "sticky or greasy matter, usually objectionably messy or smelly." Webster defines "gunkhole" as a "shallow cove or channel nearly unnavigable because of mud, rocks or vegetation."

The Royal River at Yarmouth is a gunkhole at low tide. Even at high tide, people who make a bad turn around one of the hairpin bends end up gunkholing in the worst way: They run aground at the rate of three or four boats most summer weekends, according to Merrill (Mike) Kimball, a lobster and mussel fisherman on the Royal River.

The Coast Guard knows the Royal is a tricky river to navigate. So in one mile of river, there are 15 Coast Guard buoys to mark the channel. "But there's a trick to them," says Kimball. "The numbers run from 1 to 18; yet there are only 15 buoys. They took a couple out, but didn't change the numbers yet."

Steer Clear had been up and down the Royal River only three times before, each time with expert help from Jim Saunders, a Maine newspaperman, who cut his boating teeth on the Royal River as a boy. This time I had to go without Saunders, but I had Kimball's stakes to guide me.

Under a contract with the town of Yarmouth, Kimball sets out 35 stakes to augment the 15 Coast Guard buoys in marking the winding channel. Kimball, with a helper, sets most stakes into the soft, ancient mud using only his body strength. But a few stakes must be set in hard sand, using a post-digger. Its a strange sight to see Kimball anchor his boat, climb out hefting a postdigger, and start digging a hole in the river bed.

Our run down the Royal River was made two hours before high tide. The new depth finder just installed on Steer Clear showed ample water under the hull all the way—nevertheless, we crept along slowly. I wondered how the Admiral, largest ship ever launched in Yarmouth, sailed down the Royal River without going aground. The Admiral, launched in 1875, was 260 feet long, carried a crew of 27 men and its captain's cabin was so luxurious it had Brussels carpets on the deck.

We crossed Casco Bay, leaving Moshier Island to port and passing south of French Island and then turned seaward between Whaleboat Island and the South Harpswell shore. The fog had totally cleared. The rains had stopped. But the wind was so chilly and damp that we dropped the cabin curtains to increase warmth inside Steer Clear. We steered the long, safe course, going out to the bell buoy beyond Little Birch Island, then making our turn to Potts Harbor, coming outside Horse Island and easing our way into the gas dock at Dolphin Marina. There, we topped Steer Clear's fuel tanks with an extra 40 gallons and took aboard Chuck Booth, our pilot for the gunkholing which lay ahead. This is Steer Clear's first trip up Long Reach to a new mooring at my new home on Buttermilk Cove.

By 1:30 p.m. we cleared Potts Harbor, a tight obstacle course of buoys, and cruised toward Harpswell Sound, getting a fine water-level look at the cribwork stone bridge which links Orrs Island to Bailey Island. It is clear sailing up Ewin Narrows, under the new high bridge there, until the real gunkholing starts as we make a sharp turn right at Doughty's Island into Long Reach.

One look at the chart is enough to scare most boatmen away from here. The passage is narrow, winding and the water is shallow. There are no buoys. These waters absolutely require local knowledge, which is one reason we have Chuck Booth aboard as pilot. He knows the way. So with Chuck Booth, a Brunswick realtor, plus my depth finder working overtime, we gunkhole, very slowly against a strong outgoing tide.

Low tide will be at 5:45; it is close to 3 p.m. as we start the last, scary leg. This passage is beautiful, remote, extremely quiet. We share the water and the shores only with bulbous-eyed seals, ospreys, egrets and great blue herons.

The depthfinder, taking electronic soundings from under the hull, leaps erratically. One moment the alarms shriek, warning the water is down below 8 feet, then shriek louder signaling it is down to 4 feet. I go almost dead in the water, stock still, engines in neutral. The alarm stops. The depth finder jumps to show 8 feet. We edge forward. Shortly the alarm shrieks again. And again. But Chuck Booth says we are o.k. I push Steer Clear very slowly on.

Now we have stakes to guide us. I bless the man who set them out. These stakes are set by the good will of one local lobsterman, Roland Coffin. To me, they are godsends.

Finally, Steer Clear makes the last turn out of Long Reach into Gurnet Strait and Buttermilk Cove. Booth says "Split it down the middle and head to your mooring." This mooring for Steer Clear is provided by a kind neighbor, Jimmy Coffin, who has his lobster boat and wharf across Buttermilk Cove from me. We are now close to waters which drain out completely. Only 20 yards from the mooring in one direction is nothing but mud. Yet, only a few dozen feet in the other direction, the depth plunges to a 90-foot hole. Divers know that exact depth. Some 20 years ago, they dove on the spot for a car which had careened off the old Gurnet Bridge. A bigger, new Gurnet Bridge has replaced it. Steer Clear is moored halfway between that bridge and our house on Buttermilk Cove.

Roland Coffin set out those stakes we steered by, so at sundown I go to Ben's Lobster by the Gurnet Bridge and there I find Coffin in his workshop, bending wire for his traps.

"I've come to thank you, Roland," I say. "What for?" he growls. "For setting out those stakes I steered by," I answer. He puts down his tools and looks at me amazed. "Why, I've been setting out those stakes for 50 years, since I was 15, and you're the first person to ever thank me."

STEER CLEAR SALUTES A POET FROM RAGGED ISLAND

RAGGED ISLAND — Steer Clear is caked with salt on her decks again; and salt is caked on my flesh again—and the world seems a far, far better place.

Salt starvation is an invisible soul sickness; you don't know what's been ailing you until you're cured, suddenly in one day. A day in early May, gray and glowery though it was, dished up the cure. Eight hours out on the water, the first in six long months, worked miracles on a man who has been landlocked since November, when the boat was hauled out for winter.

There's something special about the moment you cast off docking lines for the first trip of the season. True, there's something special about "firsts" of every revolving season—the first fiddleheads, the first lobsterbake, the first crocus, the first peas, the first snowfall, the first rose of summer. But the first day you cast off docking lines has a special bite to its sweetness—it's spiced with a tiny pinch of anxiety that something may go wrong.

Little worries on a powerboat are that a spark plug won't spark, that a fuel line will be clogged by a speck of winter dirt, that the seams will leak; or, on a sailboat, that a halyard will stick or a batten break. And too, there is an awkwardness to reusing boat skills and habits that have been rusting all winter. Routines such as bringing in all bumpers, letting out the dinghy or checking oil pressure, tachometers, depth finders, compass headings, temperature gauges—none are routine on the first time out in a new season. You've got to drill yourself again—like getting back on skis for the first run of winter. Within a few hours, thank heaven, this first-time-out tenseness eases. And the plain joy of being on a boat again brings the old happy zest to your heart.

With three good friends aboard, we cast off the dock lines for the first time this year. There is a tenseness to this first 20-minute slow run to the sea.

Eyes and concentration tense up a notch, a bit like the tenseness a Maine driver feels when he hits Boston's Expressway at rush hour. Then, as you pass the buoy which marks the division between river and ocean, an invisible load drops off your shoulders. Here is open sea, islands and lots of water under the keel. The season's first sight of the myriad islands of Casco Bay brings a rush, a high in spirit, a surge of gratitude to be running a boat in Maine waters, loveliest in the world.

I turn the helm over to my trusted boat handler, Joe. But, I'm always a persnickety worrier at sea. I spread ocean charts on the navigation table and get out all my toys, the course-plotting instruments. The charts already have my courses well plotted. Yet there is comfort in rechecking and coming up again with exactly the same courses.

With that chore done, I indulge for sybaritic moments in the most romantic reading in the world—a nautical chart. The unique feel of the huge, heavy paper, so long, so wide, is a happy change from memos, newspapers and books. The sea secrets a chart reveals are forever fascinating. Shadings of light and darker blues reveal hills, valleys, even mountains under the ocean; marks and hieroglyphics indicate the unseeable—from sunken wrecks to eel grass to unexploded bombs; special kinds of hen tracks tell me whether six fathoms down under me the bottom is mud, sandy or rocky, information my anchor needs to know too.

Most romantic of all, the chart is filled with imagination-firing names which have clung to ledges and islands for hundreds of years, seamarks for tens of thousands of boats; Pound o'Tea, Whaleboat, Eagle, Turnip Ledge, Charity Ledge, Bold Dick, White Bull, Carrying Place Head, Bombazine, the Gurnets and three score more rich names in only a few miles of Maine's fabulous coastline.

Sand pipers in flight along the coast.

Heading east, before we turn north by the big gong off White Bull and head toward Cundys Harbor, I keep eyeing every detail of Ragged Island. Ragged is the right word for this forbidding and relentless island where Maine's most bewitching, romantic and talented poet, Edna St. Vincent Millay, chose to live her last summers.

Born in Rockland, Millay lived and wrote in Union, Camden, Ragged Island, Greenwich Village and Spain. She won the Pulitzer Prize for poetry before she was 30 and set her world afire with the erotic intensity of her poems, the red haired sexuality of her beauty and the virulence of her political poems— "Conversation at Midnight" in 1937, dealing with the events leading to World War II, and "The Murder of Lidice" in 1942, her account of the rape of a Czech town by German soldiers.

Millay sowed plenty of her poetic and her personal wild oats in Greenwich Village in the Flaming Twenties. By the time she reached 32, after a whirlwind courtship, she married a Dutch importer, Eugen Jan Boissevain, and in 1939 they bought Ragged Island for $900. On this Maine island Millay summered alone and wrote her lyric poems for 10 years. Then in 1950, at age 58, she had a heart attack, fell down a flight of stairs at her farm near Austerlitz, N.Y., and lay dead, alone for eight hours until discovered. Edna St. Vincent Millay (named St. Vincent in honor of St. Vincent's Hospital, which saved her brother's life) was rooted deep in Maine; her ancestor, Anthony Emery, settled in Maine in 1648. She, her work and her Ragged Island are jewel in Maine's crown.

We blow a long wail on the foghorn, sea praise to her poems, as Steer Clear cruises by Ragged Island on the first salty day of summer.

THE CRIB BRIDGE AT BAILEY ISLAND

BAILEY ISLAND — The crib bridge between Orrs and Bailey Islands looks lovely in daylight but can put knots in your gut in the dark of night if you are trying to decide whether or not to run under it for the first time in a 32-foot boat. Ledges surround the approaches like snarling dogs guarding the entrance to a jealously protected place. I came face-to-face with those ledges one night.

I peered through the dark, over swirling currents, and eyed those close-by ledges, camouflaged by slithery seaweed which clung to the granite against the force of the tide. I looked and didn't like what I saw in the night, so stood off while I focused my big high-intensity spotlight.

The Crib Bridge, with small channel for boats, between Orrs and Bailey Island.

The Crib Bridge, joining Bailey and Orrs Island, is an unique engineering feat.

The beam ripped through the black of night, vividly revealing the ugly mass of ledges. The sight tied a tight cold knot in my gut, which signalled a short, clear order to my head—"Don't!"

I threw the engines of Steer Clear into reverse until we had backed well away from the approach to the cribstone bridge and out of the worst of the fast current. I decided to anchor for the night in the dubious spot where we were.

But how to get the anchor down? I didn't want to risk leaving the helm and engine controls unmanned and then skidaddle forward along the catwalk to the bow, unfasten, drop and set the anchor, a job which would take three minutes. My mate, Dr. Stanley Evans, was off in the skiff doing another job. His wife Jean had undressed for bed, and was in her bunk.

Then I heard her call out, "Want me to drop anchor?" I did, I most certainly did. Promptly this able woman with Maine Indian blood in her veins hitched up her nightdress and edged herself along the catwalk to the bow.

The latches on the chain and anchor lines were unfamiliar to her, so it took Jean a little while to discover their tricks. Finally I heard the anchor splash, the chain run out and then I called forward to Jean, "Keep it short. Only 20 feet!"

The depth-finder showed only eight feet under us. Astern, to starboard and to port, were jagged ledges. I was scared we might fetch up on them if we had too much scope out—but scared too that we might drag if we had too little out.

Her shout, "Anchor down and holding!" came out of the night—the sweetest words my ears could hear.

But Jean, mother of a 3-month-old daughter (my godchild) and a 2-year-old son, is a loving and a worried wife. No sooner was she back inside the boat, nightdress sea-salted, hands anchor-scuffed, than she commanded me, "Now get Stan back on board!"

Stan was out there in the blackness in Steer Clear's dinghy. Thereby hangs this story, with this moral to it: Never ask a stranger if there's enough water for you to stay at the dock. If they tell you, never believe them.

After two lazy and happy days and nights of cruising, Stan, Jean and I decided to go ashore and enjoy dinner at Rock Oven, a good waterfront restaurant next to the crib bridge. We ran west from Small Point to the eastward side of Bailey Island, with Stan on lookout with binoculars as my buoy-spotter and doing a fine job.

We had a hard time spotting from a distance the buoys which mark the safe approach to the crib bridge. They are not Coast Guard buoys, but privately-maintained, slender poles extremely useful but not easily spotted by a lookout in strange waters.

Passing between the markers, we saw the dock at Rock Oven. Tied to it was a sport-fishing boat named Hey Jude, rigged with tuna tower and harpoon-throwing pulpit.

It was bigger than Steer Clear, so we pulled in behind it, tied up to the big, secure dock and went ashore for dinner at 6:30 p.m., with my depth-finder showing 8.5 feet under us. Low tide was due at 8:40 p.m., and I doubted we'd lose over four feet of water in the time we'd be at dinner.

However, I asked two young men on the dock if there'd be enough water in the last two hours of the falling tide. They said we'd have plenty of water because a bigger boat was permanently docked just ahead. In the restaurant, a gracious hostess said our boat would be fine.

But it wasn't. When we got back, we could see bottom less than two feet below the propellers and the tide would be falling for another 45 minutes.

That's when I decided to move out, even in darkness, into narrow, unknown water rather than risk grounding out, and perhaps damaging my propellers and drive shafts.

But how to move? If I started the engines, the propellers would dig into mud. The only chance was to tow Steer Clear out into deeper water, without power. The one way to do this was to put Stan Evans into the skiff, tie a line from Steer Clear to the skiff and have him row like blazes, towing Steer Clear into water deep enough for me to start engines safely.

He did it wonderfully well, but very slowly. As soon as Steer Clear had more water under her, I fired up engines and cast Evans and his skiff loose while his wife and I motored out to deeper water. Once there, we'd pick up Stan and be on our way, going under the crib bridge and into Harpswell Sound. That's when I sized up those ledges in the night and chickened out of running the crib bridge. That's when Jean in her nightgown dropped anchor and we brought Stan back aboard.

"Lord, I thought I heard you hit ledge," he said gravely. "Then I realized that scary scraping noise I heard was the anchor chain going out, not you hitting rocks."

Bailey Island—During the tuna fishing tournament at Mackerel Cove.

Jean and Stan went exhausted to beds in the main sleeping cabin. I stayed topside, watching the water drop on my depth-finder and seeing the ledges which hemmed us in come closer with every inch of water we lost, until finally low tide was over. We would have been in trouble had we stayed at the dock.

The numbers on the depth-finder began to climb at last, as the tide changed from outgoing to incoming. Every 40 minutes through the night, I went forward and let out more anchor line to give us better holding power against the incoming tide. As the tide came toward full (about 2:30 a.m.) the ledges which had looked so threatening at low water looked kindly now. I slept for two hours. The boat held fine and steady. At daybreak, we ran under crib bridge. It was a piece of cake. Relieved, we set anchor in Harpswell Sound and ate breakfast.

The cribwork bridge is one-of-a-kind in the world, an embodiment of Maine canniness. In June 1926, the first load of 14,000 tons of granite arrived, and work began. After two years of work, the 1,200 feet of ocean water between Orrs and Bailey Islands was spanned—and it cost $120,000.

Bailey Island—A newer view, with a Casco Bay ferry coming to the dock.

Since that day when the bridge was first used 62 years ago, more than 90,000 tides have flowed and ebbed through its cribwork and not budged a single granite block out of the crib. Recently the unique bridge was awarded high honors of a kind—it was named a National Historic Civil Engineering Landmark.

But the idea of a bridge linking the two islands had led to bad blood and bitter fights between the voters of Orrs Island and Bailey Island. The fight began at Town Meetings in 1872 and went on until the bridge opened in 1928. One town meeting would approve the bridge and the next would veto it, in a see-saw battle. The case went to the Maine Supreme Court— and even the War Department. Finally the State Legislature approved funds to build it in 1926.

Until the crib bridge was built, a boatman in his dory linked the two islands. He waited on the Bailey Island side with his eye peeled for a white flag on Orrs Island. Anyone who wanted to get across hoisted that white flag and paid 15 cents to get rowed over. It cost 25 cents to get rowed back.

THE BIRDMAN OF BAILEY ISLAND

BAILEY ISLAND — Pete Rogers is one of of the biggest, brawniest lobstermen on the coast of Maine—close to 6 feet 6 inches, 260 pounds, broad in the shoulders, black-bearded, blue eyed and a Bailey Island fisherman for 34 of his 44 years. But Rogers' heart is part tender mush and part black murder when he talks about the seabirds he loves and those he hates.

He loves the rafts of baby eider ducks, guarded by mother hens fore and aft, port and starboard. The sight of them turn this giant's heart to tender mush. He hates the black-backed gulls which circle above these rafts of babies, then swoop, kill and devour newborn ducklings by the thousands. This sight inflames his heart to black murder.

"I boil over when I see those black-backed predators gobble down a raft of 24 eider ducklings," he says. "Those gulls are unholy terrors, with a 7-foot wing span. The baby eiders are maybe 4 inches long, enough for just one gulp for a black-backed gull." Rogers says a single black-backed gull can eat five baby eiders in a morning, probably more than a dozen a day. With thousands of black-backs in Maine and their numbers constantly increasing, Rogers says they devour many thousands of baby eiders, songbirds and terns each May and June.

Rogers used to carry a gun aboard his boat. To even the odds a bit in the uneven battle between baby eider and giant gull, Rogers would shoot at the black-backs the moment they started to swoop down for the kill. Two years ago, he shot 130 of them, knowing he risked a steep fine, because it is against federal law to shoot a black-backed gull.

Rogers grew up on Mackerel Cove at Bailey Island, where he and his brother and his brother's four boys all live and fish. Rogers men have been fishing out of Bailey Island for generations. Seabirds are their daily companions when they are out hauling traps.

"When I was in high school, 2,000 pairs of least terns—beautiful seabirds—nested on Monument and Turnip Islands," Rogers recalls. "Now there are none. Those black-backs ate 'em right out." Scores of fishermen have carried guns, as Rogers did, to help the helpless rafts of baby eiders survive attacks from their murderous predators.

Few sights are more touching, more intimate, more peaceful pictures of happy family life than a raft of baby eiders and mothers paddling in fluffy convoys in an island cove or in the sheltered waters of a granite

Pete Rogers, the birdman, lobsterman of Bailey Island. To protect baby eider ducks from being eaten by black wing gulls, Rogers has shot these predators which now are protected by law.

ledge. These lovely, lively rafts of 20 to 30 tiny ducklings, escorted by several guardian mothers "baby-sitting" the broods of others as well as their own offspring.

The babies in the rafts are a week or two weeks old in the early days of summer. They hatch out from mid-May until mid-June or so, and soon are learning to swim, dive, find food, quack and wag their tails. Only the escorting mothers realize the dangers of imminent death which these babies seldom survive. Murder is around the bend at sea here as much as on a city street.

Death comes from above, from the black-back gulls, and from underneath the water too. The laughing loon has a gangster side to his character. He swims near the raft of babies, then dives down and attacks silently from below, like a submarine. From underwater, he lunges up, snapping to grab and devour a baby duck.

The escort mothers see the attack coming only at the last second, and are helpless to fend it off. The babies don't seem to know what has happened to the missing chick. They simply close the gap and keep on in joyous play.

In the next moment, one of the black-backed marauders starts his downward dive. Mother ducks spot this one sooner. They stand up on the water, yelling warnings to the babies, beating their wings, creating little waves with their wing tips and three webbed toes. If luck is with them, the black-back is warned off. The babies are scared, and instinctively climb up onto the mother's back for safety.

But most often, if Rogers or other fishermen return to the same spot next day, the raft of babies left alive may have dwindled down to five or six.

Today there are 25,000 eider ducks in Maine waters with babies in tow. Each colony of baby ducks brings you to laughter, to tears, to applause, to scolding and to praying for their safety as you watch them play, and know that most of them will die as infants.

But the laws of the land are against Rogers and other protectors of the babies and in favor of the black-backed killers. Under the Migratory Bird treaty between the United States, Canada and Mexico, it is a serious offense to shoot, poison or harm gulls, no matter how many thousands of baby eiders, least terns or songbirds the black-backs kill.

There was once good reason for protecting gulls. They were almost extinct, hunted to the vanishing point along the Maine coast.

Two of man's activities almost killed off the gull population. One was "egging." The eggers would row or sail out (no outboards then) to islands where nests held thousands of gull eggs. They'd collect all the fresh eggs and sell them at market by the barrel load.

The other activity was "gunning." In the years when ladies wanted feathers in their hats, New York milliners paid gunners in Maine 40 cents apiece for white gulls and 20 cents for immature brown gulls. That was big money at the turn of the century. In 1899 one New York hat maker even furnished guns and ammunition to Maine's Passamaquoddy Indians to kill gulls.

The slaughter stimulated formation of the first Audubon Society, which launched a crusade to stop the killing of gulls, eiders, terns and other seabirds. State and federal laws were eventually enacted to protect the gulls. Today there are more than 10,000 nesting pairs of the black-backs in Maine. These bullies are now driving out terns, eiders, songbirds and even other gulls.

We amateurs talk about "seagulls." But experts say gulls are mostly land birds, scavengers which prefer the easy pickings of a garbage dump or the gurry and waste thrown overboard from fishing boats.

Watch a fishboat coming home, cleaning fish on the way, and a hundred herring gulls seem to surround it, screaming out and diving for scraps. Eat dinner on the deck of a harborside restaurant and beggar-gulls strut brazenly close to the people and the food, picking up a free meal from Maine visitors, who think gulls are cute.

Experts insist there are over 40 different kinds of gulls, but along the Maine coast we mostly see three types—the herring gulls, the bigger black-backs and the laughing gulls. The herring gull (we have about 30,000 nesting pairs in Maine) is the one you see most often, sitting on pilings, messing up boat decks and scavenging garbage. Laughing gulls are smaller and have black heads, so they seem to be wearing a small sailor's black watch cap. Herring gulls live longest. One wild bird is known to have lived 31 years and a captive bird 49 years. They mature slowly. They are brown, not white, for the first years of their life.

But the black-backs are by far the worst predators. Maine's fish and wildlife experts recognized this when they poisoned the gull population of Petit Manan to bring back the terns and other birds driven off by gulls. Other programs to control the overpopulation of gulls by poisoning them or smashing eggs before they hatch have been considered for Matinicus Rock, West Goose Rock, Egg Rock, Turnip Island and the Cuckolds. But the biologists hesitate because of certain criticism that they'd be "playing God."

Yet, man is playing God every time he throws out garbage or feeds a crust to a gull. Rogers played God when he shot 130 black-backs two years ago. The baby ducklings which survived because of Rogers are glad he did; but the law enforcers and the black-backs were not.

MOON OVER BUTTERMILK COVE

BUTTERMILK COVE — The cove outside our house near Great Island will feel the pull of the full moon tonight. High tide will be higher, the cove will be jammed with more water. Hospital emergency rooms will be jammed too. Moonbeams from a full moon exert their mystic pull on the bodies and brains of men and women as much as they do on tides. All creatures will be stirring wildly in the light of the full moon tonight. Ambulance sirens and blue lights of police cars will be piercing the night. When the moon is full, ambulance drivers, police on patrol and hospital emergency rooms feel the tide of business rise higher.

The coming and going of the tides, their height and their drop, radically affect life on Buttermilk Cove. So we pay heed to the phases of the moon, because the moon's phases govern the force of the tides on Buttermilk Cove, and everywhere else on the saltwater seas of the world.

Tides rise and fall twice in the time between two rising moons, about 24 hours and 50 minutes. The range of the tide outside my window varies from total drain-out to brimful, according to the position of the sun and the moon. When the moon and sun are pulling along the same line, as they do at full moon and new moon, the tide rises higher than normal and is called a spring tide. When the sun and the moon pull at right angles to each other, as they do when the moon is in its first and third quarters, the tide rises less high than usual, and this is called a neap tide.

Men have known for thousands of years that the moon pulls the tides. The Roman naturalist Pliny wrote about this force before 100 A.D. But the physical laws governing the height and time of tides were not worked out until English scientist Sir Isaac Newton, thanks to the fall of an apple, discovered the law of gravity in the 1600s. Now little give-away tide tables give us advance notice of the precise time and exact height of the tide at every major harbor in Maine for the entire year ahead. It is comforting to find one thing in this world upon which a citizen can rely with total confidence.

Yet as I watch the tides rise and fall, I wonder why the moon gets most of the credit. What about the sun? The sun, after all, has 27 million times more mass than the moon, so why doesn't it exert 27 million times more pull on the waters on Buttermilk Cove? Part of the answer is that the sun is 390 times further from Buttermilk Cove than the moon. Therefore, scientists say, the tide-producing force of the sun is only 46 percent as great as the force of the moon. Yes, say these learned men, the sun does affect the tides, but not as much as the moon. Tides caused by the sun are less than half as high or low as tides caused by the pull of the moon.

I don't understand how the moon does it, but the moon's gravity pulls the water nearest to it away from the solid parts of Earth. At the same time, the wondrous moon manages to pull the solid Earth slightly away from the water on the opposite side of the world, the part of Earth which is farthest away from the moon at the time. Thus, the moon's gravity produces two bulges on the oceans of the world. One tidal bulge always stays right under the moon. The other tidal bulge always stays on the opposite side of the Earth.

Buttermilk Cove in winter seems, at a surface glance, to be empty and deserted. The boats of summer are long since gone. Gone from sight too are most of their moorings; some hauled ashore, others bent down on their mooring lines so they spend the winter submerged a few feet below the water, thereby avoiding being cut loose by the cutting edge of ice on the surface. Lobster traps have been hauled for the winter. They sit, coated with snow, along the banks, in neatly stacked rows, where they will freeze till spring. The few lobster boats still working the waters nearby have mostly switched to fishing gear. They are rigged in winter for scalloping or shrimping.

Gone too are the diggers who, in warmer weather, come when the tide is out to dig in Buttermilk Cove for bloodworms. Yet below the mud where, in warmer weather, their high rubber boots and the long tines on their short-handled digging forks left moonscape patterns in the prehistoric slime, millions of life forms still live—enduring the bitter cold in hibernation.

Gone are many birds of summer. But not the gulls, the everlasting, ever - hungry gulls still swoop and scavenge. Impervious to winter cold, they sit haughtily on chunks of ice and float and cry their grievous cacophony to the icy air. When the cold fist of winter night seems to freeze all life on the cove, the tide still runs in and out, under the ice. And from the trunks of the enduring, patient trees come the eerie groans and cries and grunts of these stalwart pines, protesting the relentless grip of the cold night penetrating their core.

ROUGH SEAS AT SEGUIN, PEACE IN HARPSWELL

ABOARD STEER CLEAR — We got half drowned off Seguin. We shipped seas over the bow every few seconds, all the way from the Cuckolds outside Boothbay Harbor, to Mark Island Monument outside Bailey Island.

That leg of a rough trip took us 90 minutes. We shipped sea over the

Fish House on Bailey Island. Photo was taken in 1938 by George French.

bows 300 times. And the seas were "confused," as mariners say. They came at our boat every which way: one moment head-on, the next off the starboard midships and seconds later a big one would roll us from the port quarter.

In these conditions there is no way of easing the banging and the drenching. You endure in the knowledge that once you are out of this mess, life is going to seem lovely.

Indeed it did. We turned at Bailey Island and ran up Merriconeag Sound to tie up to a friend's dock in South Harpswell, collapsed in two chairs on deck and silently enjoyed just being still, being motionless, being on an even keel, being without waves slamming at us. We sat in the sun smiling that silly kind of smile you wear when you've come through a bit of nastiness nicely.

The day was filled with wonderful contrasts. That tough passage was followed by peace at the dock of the graceful white farmhouse with meadows running down to the sea. An hour later we were driven by car to the Elijah Kellogg church, built in 1844 and one of the loveliest in Maine, to join in the celebration of Harpswell Days.

Seguin. There's no sailor on the coast who isn't moved to hate or gratitude, or both, at the very mention of Seguin. And that's been true since President George Washington commissioned the building of Seguin Lighthouse. Today it is on the National Register of Historic Places. Seguin Light is a midpoint mark, 20 miles from Monhegan Island and 20 miles from Cape Elizabeth, a lonely sentinel high atop an island.

Seguin Light first flashed its signal to sailors on the night of March 29, 1796. The man who lit the lamp that night was Johann Ladislas, Count Polersky, a soldier of fortune who had left his home town of Rosheim, in Alsatia, to fight in the American Revolutionary War.

Later, Emperor Napoleon offered Ladislas an opportunity to return to the French Empire and inherit his title and lands; but the keeper elected to stay on lonely wild Seguin in preference to going back to Europe and his wife, the countess. He is buried in Dresden Mills.

Seguin was a devilish spot even to early Indians. One story about how Seguin got its name is that an Indian, pressed into service as a local pilot by white explorers, came to the rough water at the mouth of the Kennebec and said, "Sea go in." Another story is that Seguin is the Indian word for "place where the sea vomits."

Not only can the water between the mouth of the Kennebec and Seguin be rough, confused and miserable, but there is a rare magnetic disturbance here which turns reliable compasses into liars. North is no longer north for about half a mile east and west of this distortion area.

Past Seguin, past Small Point, past Bailey Island, coming west, lies Harpswell Sound. Here we dock Steer Clear, change clothes and go to church. I'm to speak from Elijah Kellogg's pulpit in the afternoon celebration of Harpswell Day.

Elijah Kellogg was a sailor-priest at Harpswell who preached for 60 years here, between calls to more pretentious pulpits. He wrote the Whispering Pine series of boy's books and also built and manned his own small boats.

At the Apprentice Shop in Bath they've built a replica of an Elijah Kellogg boat. The Harpswell church named for him, the church where he held his first ministry, is handsomely and lovingly kept in fine repair.

Harpswell's original church across the street was built about 1727 and maintained by town funds until Elijah Kellogg demanded and got a church separated from local politics. The old church is now the Town House, with the town clerk's office in the balcony, over the box pews of the old town fathers.

Harpswell Sound—South Harpswell is still a fishing village, though very near to the city of Portland and to Brunswick. Coming out of Casco Bay, Steer Clear turns here to make for her mooring in Buttermilk Cove.

No FISH STORY: FISH CATCHES MAN

FIVE ISLANDS — This is the story of how a local Maine fisherman single-handedly pulled a 500-pound tuna and a 170-pound man, both hooked together, up out of the sea and onto the deck of his boat.

Kenneth Pinkham, from Five Islands, is the skipper who hauled a fighting fish and drowning man out of the ocean. Brad Moore, in his twenties and a cousin of Pinkham's, is the man who was saved from a strange death from drowning after being hooked by a fish.

I first heard the story from Susan Morrison as she related it in Commercial Fisheries News. She got it from Robert Gowell of the National

Fisheries Service in Portland. But Pinkham, the hero of the affair, shrugged it off saying, "Don't see how a newspaper can make a story out of it."

Pinkham and his crew aboard the Dorothy E., a 34-foot Maine-built boat named after Pinkham's wife, were hunting big tuna 15 miles at sea. It was the day before the end of the tuna season, and they were eager to hook into big, high-priced fish and come home with a great wad of money in their pockets. The weather was clear and the seas were smooth that September day, but the big tuna were scarce.

Then, over his radio, Pinkham heard his friend Gene Atwood, aboard his big dragger, calling Pinkham, suggesting that Pinkham bring his boat closer to the big dragger and try for tuna there. The dragger, said Atwood, had been throwing overboard lots of fish scraps and junk fish, which might be enticing bait to tuna.

Atwood was right. Five minutes after Pinkham had brought the Dorothy E. close to the big dragger, and strung out his lines and hooks, a big tuna struck one of his six lines. The crew hauled in hard, and the big fish came in fast. When it was close alongside, the crew got a harpoon into it.

Before they had a chance to haul up the other lines and hooks streaming out behind the Dorothy E., a second big tuna hit hard into one of the other hooks. Thrashing wildly in the water, the second tuna got itself wound up in the other lines, and quickly there was an unholy mess. Finally it broke free. The crew quickly hauled up the tangle of lines and hooks on deck to straighten out the mess. But as they were doing this, the first tuna they had caught was still very much alive, thrashing alongside and too ferocious to bring on deck, despite the harpoon in it.

The crew gave the tuna more rope so the fighting fish could run out or sound and tire itself before they brought it on board. As they paid out more rope, the rope snagged into the lines of hooks they were untangling. One of those hooks caught in Pinkham's shirt. The other men managed to hold the rope from running out for a moment, while Pinkham got the hook out of his shirt.

As soon as Pinkham was clear, they yelled "OK. Let'er go!" and the rope spun on out. The harpooned tuna took off, taking the tangle of lines and hooks along with the rope. As they zoomed overboard, one of those sharp hooks sliced deep into crewman Brad Moore's hand, snagging him hard as it flashed by.

And it took Moore with it. The sounding tuna pulled Moore and all the lines and hooks with it. In a split second, Moore was in the air, flying off the boat and down into the ocean.

Pinkham saw the freak accident happening in front of his eyes. In a split-second reaction, the burly Pinkham grabbed the disappearing harpoon rope in his hands, dug in his heels and hauled back hard with all his strength.

He had close to 700 pounds of fish and man at the end of that rope. But, with adrenalin pouring emergency strength into his body, Pinkham held on and hauled back, fighting the 500-pound fish which was pulling Moore deep into the ocean.

Somehow Pinkham gained, pulling in the rope and fish and man together until, inside a minute, he had fish and man both on deck. With one arm he held the huge fish; with the other he propped up the half drowned 170 pound, bleeding Moore.

"Don't get out of the boat again!" Pinkham shouted at Moore whose hand was still impaled on the hook and who was still attached to the fish. Someone tossed Pinkham a pair of wire cutters and he cut the line and hook which attached Moore to the fish.

A motorboat rushed Moore to shore where a car rushed him to the hospital where his torn hand was sewn so well that it is now almost normal. Moore says he has no memory of his moments under water, being pulled to near-death by the huge tuna to which he was attached.

Pinkham says the 500 pound tuna dressed out at 350 pounds. But he paid little heed to the dollars that earned him. With his young cousin as his catch "I felt like the richest man in the world," he says.

COLD FEAR STALKS STEER CLEAR

ROBINHOOD — Rain, merciless, mean and angry, attacks out of the black night, beating on the boat deck, drumming so fiercely on the wooden cabin roof that rain noise drowns out the screams of the near-gale. That wind is blowing forty and gusting to fifty miles an hour, barreling right out of the Atlantic. It wallops this section of the Maine coast, gets compressed by hills and woods, and comes rampaging up the narrow gut to where we are anchored, and punches and pummels Steer Clear hour after endless hour through those black and fearful hours of 1 a.m., 2 a.m., 3 a.m., 4 a.m., until, at long last, first light comes creeping into the world—comforting, reassuring as a nurse's hand stroking your forehead when you come sweating out of a scary nightmare in a strange hospital bed.

All through the stormy night, Steer Clear had been bucking and pulling against the anchor line. Awake in my bunk, I'd listen to the creak and groan of that anchor rope, straining to hold fast to the bollard while the wind and sea tried to break its grip. An old saying kept jangling through my head, fraught with a meaning I didn't want to understand: "Hanging on by a thread."

The thread was the anchor line. At the end of the anchor line, buried in mud somewhere below and in front, was the anchor—merely a few pounds of high-tensile steel to hold tons of boat and the three souls in it.

Two friends, Gayle and Joe Sukaskas, were aboard with me for a summer weekend cruise, and this was their first night.

I peeked into the cabin to see how they were taking the wild storm. They looked as though they were sleeping through it and I was mighty grateful, because near-hysteria aboard was unneeded. But it was brave pretense on their part, I found out later. They told me in the morning that they had been laying awake, rigid, silently praying.

Ears and head are in torment through the wild night, bombarded with noises of the gale and rain, torrents beating against the boat, and the boat bouncing and dancing in circles like a wild pony on the end of a rope. "Hanging by a thread."

Suddenly the storm dies. At 7 a.m., the wind starts dropping fast. The water around the boat, which has been pounding the hull furiously in the black night, gentles and smoothes. By 7:30 a.m., the mean, miserable, sullen sky begins to smile. First a patch of blue, then a Dutchman's breeches, soon a whole sky of summer blue, with sun shining onto our sodden and battered boat and crew.

We tidy the cabins. Roll up and stow sleeping bags; dress in shorts. Gayle rolls up the stern canvas to let in the summer sun and balmy breeze. We set up a table in the stern cockpit and eat hungrily—muffins, eggs, sausages, fruit and hot coffee. We laugh about the lonely fear which had gripped and chilled each of us through the night. It all seems so far away, almost unreal, now that the sun is out and the sea is calm.

How quickly most of us can forget the trauma, erase the memory of fear. That's a gift we are born with—and too seldom grateful for. Would we get into a car, a plane, a boat, climb on a horse, a surfboard, skis, unless we forgot past moments of terror and fear? Too real, too vivid a memory would immobilize us, glue us to home, bed, easy chair.

How many scares in 20 years of boating in Steer Clear? More than I can remember now. But surely there must have been at least two nights every year like the one just described. Anxiety is, thank heaven, usually the worst part—worrying if the anchor will hold; not daring to sleep for fear that if you do, the anchor will drag and the boat could be swept away and dashed against a ledge.

The best insurance against dragging is scope, always much more scope than seems necessary. So I do lengthen the scope in stages. When we first get the anchor down, we wait for it to settle, then reverse engines hard, in short bursts, until the person on the bow working the anchor line is almost pulled overboard by the hard pull of the hard-set anchor, and yells and waves furiously to stop engines.

About 20 minutes later, I amble forward and quietly let out 30 feet more of scope. After dinner dishes are washed, especially if there's a chance the wind will pick up in the night, I amble out on deck again, saying I'm taking a look at the stars. But I let out still more scope, until the anchor line seems to be running out forever, at a shallow angle.

In rain, it's hard to climb into slicker and slosh forward to do this chore. But that's better than having to do it hours later, at midnight, better than pulling oilskins over pajamas and stumbling over wet, dark decks to let out more scope. That is the pits, and I've been there.

It is scope, scope and more scope which keeps a boat secure in a storm. Yet I still lie awake on stormy nights. Even with lots of scope I never can put enough faith in my long anchor line to sleep easy.

Daylight chases away fear. A convenient, selective memory soon forgets nighttime gales and the lonely fear that feeds on listening to the groans and strains of the anchor line. And that's the blessing that leaves cruising men and women eager to go out again.

PARTY! SEALS DANCE IN OVEN'S MOUTH

OVEN'S MOUTH — The seals had a ball last night. In the Oven's Mouth, they came out to dance by the light of the moon. The noise of their funmaking was infectious. Aboard Steer Clear, we listened, enchanted. Then as the seals splashed and crashed around the water, as they snorted and blew through their snouts, as they opened their mouths wide and shouted out strange groans and sneezes, we began to clap and laugh and join in the fun with the celebrating seals.

It was an eerie night. The Oven's Mouth can be the quietest salt water sanctuary in Maine waters. The approach to it is through a narrow passage which at low tide seems like a miniature Norwegian fjord, with miniature cliffs bordering the throat of water which leads into the Mouth. When the tide flows fast, in or out, strong eddies that verge on whirlpools can spin a punt.

Once inside the Oven's Mouth, a boat can be lucky enough to have this great silent body of strange water entirely to itself—except for the seals and the herons.

When the tide is low, great blue herons fly in, their vast wings spread 70 inches from tip to tip, beating the air in slow motion. Each takes up position on a separate fishing territory. They stand like gaunt sentinels, motionless on long spindly legs, with long necks elongated to full stretch, long sharp beaks at the ready to stab and swallow every unwary fish.

The herons fly in at late afternoon. Three of us climb off Steer Clear, secure on anchor, and get into the skiff. This skiff was built for me in Bucks Harbor, off the Eggemoggin Reach, half a dozen years ago, on lines as graceful as a Whitchall. But this one is made of fiberglass, so it is lighter and easier to haul above the tidemark when exploring island coves. Because it is so long and light, the skiff floats like a leaf on the still waters of the Oven's Mouth. I need to pull on the long oars only once in a while, for between strokes the skiff keeps dancing along silently. This stealth helps when coming close to herons and seals.

Each pair of herons lays a clutch of four pale green eggs. But the mortality rate is high. The ground below heron nests is often spattered with broken eggs and small broken bodies of baby herons. Those nests of twigs are huge, yet so poorly built that many a baby falls out.

In a perverse trick of nature, herons kill the island where they nest. The guano or excretions from colonies of herons is so strong that it kills vegetation and trees. After a score of years it kills all growth on the nesting places and the heron colony must move to start another island colony, leaving death and devastation behind them, gruesome hallmarks of their homes.

Back aboard Steer Clear, our three-man crew (Joe and Gayle Sukaskis) cooks and eats a sailor's dinner. Before we have finished our coffee, mosquitoes attack, seeking their bloody supper. They attack in mass. Swiftly we drop all the aft cabin curtains of vinyl and plexiglass in a vain attempt to minimize their access to our flesh. But we are too late. Hordes of mosquitoes are already aboard.

Then we humans put on a show for the animal life of the Oven's Mouth. Three of us on Steer Clear perform the Mosquito-Catchers Jive and Jig. Each armed with a swatter, we whirl and twist in hot pursuit of our foe. The person who has the most mosquito scalps at the end of the half-hour battle wins the last slice of pie.

Victorious over the winged invasion, we sit down to count the scalps. And that is the moment we hear the seals going wild.

At first we could not figure who or what was making the weird sounds. So, with mosquitoes repelled for the night, we roll the side curtains back up again to see better and get the cool, soft night air.

From astern come frantic sounds of dire distress. From the awful snorts and coughs and from the huge shadowy shapes on the ledge, we identify a big male seal in an awful fix. The 400-pound goliath had caught a fish too big or too bony to swallow. It is, we guess, stuck in his throat, perhaps alive and flapping still, and stuck halfway up and halfway down.

The great seal is throwing a fit. The night is loud with his coughs and hiccoughs, snorting and blowing, and every kind of noise a panicked seal makes when trying to free a fish stuck in his throat. It is an agonizing sound. We wish we could get close to the sufferer and help by clapping him hard on the back to dislodge that fish in his windpipe. The dire commotion goes on for thirty minutes. Finally the stuck fish goes either up and out, or down, the gullet.

Peace and stillness return, except for the deep breathing of the worn-out old seal, who lies motionless and panting, trying to recover.

That's when the young seals came out for their night on the town. They came as noisy and brash as teen-agers burning rubber, driving fast in tight turns, on the town parking lot at home.

The sounds are so strange to our ears we could not recognize it as the noise of seals cutting up. Eight of them come whirling and dancing around Steer Clear. One after the other they leap out of the water and come crashing, thumping down, belly-first, thwacking the water, creating a weird explosion of sound to rip the serene night air. Round and round they cavort, chasing, leaping, diving, thwacking in the greatest good spirits. They yell for the pure fun of it. They blow, they snort, they bellow, they bark in celebration of Young Seals Night Out.

The carefree fun is infectious. There is something so lovable, so fool-

Oh! Those bulbous eyes. Maine is the breeding place for harbor seals of the entire East Coast. We have 10,000 or so harbor seals in Maine. Females come upriver to give birth. The Oven's Mouth, off the Sheepscot and Cross Rivers is a playpen and dancing spot for seals.

ish and innocent about the glassy snout, the bulbous eyes and the comic-book whiskers of a seal that humans watching them suddenly feel fine and light-hearted. Within moments, all of us aboard Steer Clear are laughing and clapping with shared happiness as we watch the seals cavort and play and shout.

The seal game lasted close to an hour. Then those earless seals may have heard some siren song from far away, for they all dove and never came back to play again that night.

Harbor seals are so widespread in Maine waters that more than 40 harbors, ledges and coves are named "Seal." We have seals by the thousands. A big seal can eat 50 pounds of fish in a day and will tear through and ruin fish nets in hot pursuit of a meal.

Under pressure from fishermen who were losing too much of their livelihood to seals, the Legislature passed a bounty law in 1900, authoriz-

162

ing town clerks to pay one dollar for each seal nose brought in as evidence of destruction. But the connivers outsmarted the law and punched out dozens of "noses" from a single seal skin. After paying $25,000 in bounties, the state rescinded the law. Now seals are protected by a federal law and anyone touching, let alone shooting, a seal is liable to a fine of $10,000.

Seals are the friendliest faces in the sea. Yet they are wonderfully complicated physically. For instance, when a seal dives, its heart rate drops from 80 to 10 beats a minute, enabling it to stay underwater chasing fish for as long as 15 minutes. As soon as the seal comes up for air, heartbeat and circulation return to normal.

Sea creature or land creature? A seal is both. It can waddle but not walk on land. It sunbathes in the air on ledges above the water, then goes swimming for a day. A seal is born on land. Pregnant mothers come ashore to give birth. Yet, a seal pup can swim as soon as it is born.

Young seals know no fathers. And the mothers know not which of the dozens of seals who mate her every season is the father. But mother and pup are extremely close. Seal mothers suckle their young for two weeks and thereafter the pup (only one pup at a birth) must catch its own fish. However, mother and pup enjoy so close a bond that on a ledge with a hundred other seals, they instantly recognize each other by smell and voice. Male seals are completely liberated from all responsibilities of parenthood.

About 25 percent of those cute, white-furred seal pups die before they are a year old. If they survive, they are likely to live 20 or 30 years.

Solemn as seals look, they certainly love a good time. I doubt any playboy or playgirl ever had more fun on a night on the town than those seals cavorting around Steer Clear that amazing night in the Oven's Mouth.

FILBERT IS CRABBIEST DOG AROUND

CROSS RIVER — Filbert is the name of a nutty dog with two passions. One is crabbing from a skiff, the other is sleeping in parked cars. I went crabbing with Filbert. It was an experience I shall remember forever.

Let me introduce Filbert. He is a mutt, an off-duty police dog in mufti, who claims to be 40 percent Alsatian. He is eight years old, but has not grown up much physically, and barely at all mentally, since he was a pup.

He belongs to my friend Charlie McMichaels, a brawny man with a brassy voice and a golden heart, who was known as "Pappy" when he was construction boss of oil pipelines being laid across the deserts and swamps of Texas, California and Louisiana.

Charlie got the dog from his stepson, a sophisticated computer expert who lives in a sophisticated city condominium where no nutty dogs like Filbert are allowed. So Filbert joined Charlie on Cross River, near Boothbay, where both have retired to spend their days crabbing, lobstering and building docks and porches on Charlie's house.

All three of us went out to haul crab traps, and Filbert had the best time of all, killed the most crabs and made the most noise.

The moment the dog saw Charlie pulling on his high hip boots, Filbert began jabbering and prancing. As we walked to the dock and untied the spring lines which hold Charlie's work boat, Filbert started giving tongue like a hound dog on a hot scent. He yelped in excited, frantic cries, leaped into the boat and made a doggy stab at casting off the lines with his teeth.

Once we were underway, Filbert sat on his seat amidship, looking calm and almost dignified.

But as soon as we slowed and circled to pick up the first trap, Filbert lived up to his name and went nuts. When Charlie began handhauling the first trap, Filbert jumped on the seat beside Charlie and went into his act. Filbert's job is to bite off the kelp and seaweed which clings to the line as it comes over the side of the skiff.

"This nutty dog watched me yanking off the kelp on our first few trips together," said Charlie. "One day Filbert decided he could do a better job than I could. Now, pulling off kelp is his great passion in life, even ahead of sleeping in parked cars."

Sure enough, as a yard of slimy brown kelp began coming out of the water, Filbert bared his teeth and nipped and tugged at it until he had torn it free of the line.

By now his black snout was far over the side of the skiff and his eyes were glued to the water. He yelped with excitement as the toggle came up, took a quick nip and let it pass. For the really big moment was coming—his first sight of the wooden slats of the trap breaking surface.

The traps throw Filbert into spasms of delirium. His steady yap goes up the scale until it is a shrill continuous cry. The dog's voice and body are all aquiver with expectation of the catch inside.

Charlie wrestles the heavy trap onto the platform at the stern, flicks open the leather catch, flings back the trap door and reaches in to grab the crabs. The sight of those crabs crawling is too much for Filbert. His cries turn hysterical.

Charlie's gloved hand grabs the crabs which are too small to keep and pick, and he throws them back to grow bigger. You can see Filbert's heart break each time a crab is tossed back. If Charlie drops one into the boat, Filbert makes a frenzied leap at it, bites it, kills it, but refuses to eat it.

Charlie tosses the big crabs, the keepers, into a large rectangular tub of red plastic. Filbert makes no attempt to get near these crabs. I asked Charlie how he trained this nutty dog to stay away from the container filled with lively, scratching crabs, each waving pincer claws in the air.

"The crabs taught him, not me," says Charlie. "They bit him hard on his black nose and held on. He yelled bloody murder. After three times, he had learned his lesson. Now he never goes close to the crabs in the container."

Filbert and Charlie go crabbing or lobstering every day in season. They've been doing it together for years. By now, any sensible dog would have become bored. But not the nutty Filbert. He hits peak excitement when the thousandth trap breaks surface, just as he did when he saw the first trap coming up out of the ocean.

He still savages each piece of kelp and seaweed as though it were a cornered rat. I don't know how his heart stands the fever pitch excitement day after day.

Seals however do not excite Filbert a bit. We come by ledges on which a dozen or more seals are sunbathing, and the dog won't even raise his head. Even when a swimming seal bobs its whiskered face up out of the water alongside the skiff, Filbert ignores it.

Crabs are a different matter. This Filbert, who is so city-bred that he still has to be walked on a leash before bedtime, is the crabbiest dog in Maine. His only other passion in life is to scramble through the half-closed window of a car, anybody's parked car, curl up in the back seat, go to sleep and dream about catching crabs.

V
BOOTHBAY AREA

Windjammer Schooner "Roseway" in outer harbor at Boothbay.

V

Boothbay Harbor is a magnet still to me, and for the past three summers Steer Clear has almost cut her own track in the waves from her mooring by Gurnet Bridge, down the New Meadows River past Seguin, past the Cuckolds, to a Down East Yacht Club mooring off the town landing in Boothbay Harbor.

Steer Clear lies so often on that mooring that I want to pay a little tribute to it and the unique D.E.Y.C. which maintains four moorings in the inner harbor for its members. This yacht club is unique in ways which so appeal to me that I've been a member for years and years. First, it's cheap. Dues in 1988 went up from $30 to $50 a year. Second, it has no yacht club, no dining room, no bar, no dances. It has, however, these four fine moorings just off downtown Boothbay Harbor, and a slip where you can tie up a dinghy. It stages a summer cruise down east (which I've never been on) and a few island picnics. But most of all, for me, the drawing card is that mooring.

This mooring is the finest gawking spot in town. Its the Boothbay Harbor version of a seat at a sidewalk cafe in Paris, when it comes to watching the world go by. But here your passing parade is afloat and ashore, the hulls of yachts; and the jaunty jibs, or sometimes billowing spinakers, of ladies shopping on shore.

I can sit, reading or writing, in the stern of Steer Clear and look up to watch sight-seeing boats and million-dollar yachts, young kids in dinghies, elderly couples coming by launch into town from Squirrel Island to buy groceries, and, across on the working harbor, the lobster and fishing boats. At night, there are few finer sights than the illuminated spire of Our Lady of Peace church, with the sound of its carillons chiming across the water.

In summer, this is a gaudy, frantic, fascinating hub of busy tourism, a spectacle best enjoyed from a distance from a boat out on a moor-

ing. Coming to this mooring in Boothbay after a stint alone out in the islands, is a bit like a cowboy from Montana hitting Times Square. I love it, for one or two days and nights. And I then bolt for the peace of a lonely cove.

Almost everyone from almost everywhere has special memories of Boothbay Harbor from sometime in their life. I have met matrons of 50 and 60 who remember fondly their first job as a summer waitress here when they were lithe college girls enjoying a summer romance with a salad boy. I have met bishops who learned to sail and dig clams when they were in summer camp here at age nine. I remember my own first—and almost fatal—trip by water into Boothbay Harbor.

It was 24 years ago in a tired skiff with an overage outboard. But I was sea-stupid then, still grimed with the dirt and bravado of New York City, and I thought my $70 used skiff and $35 used outboard would carry me and my family safely from Christmas Cove to see the windjammers sail into Boothbay Harbor, only a few miles away. Going there was fine. Getting home was terrifying. A wind and sea had picked up and grew stronger, especially in the open water, from the Ram Island Light up into the Damariscotta River. I remember, 24 years later, how many hours and hours that slow, scary trip seemed to take. We had two children, two adults, a dog and a big picnic cooler aboard. Our freeboard was low. We shipped water from every minor wave. The wheezing old outboard missed, sputtered, but pushed us through the chop at barely three miles an hour. All of us were scared. None of us has forgotten the lesson we learned that day; that a sound boat with a sound engine is the only way to go anywhere, even close-by, even in fair weather.

For more than 20 summers, Steer Clear has been coming into Boothbay Harbor and enjoying the happy circus. Coming east from Casco Bay, I try to time the trip so I cross the mouth of the Kennebec River at slack tide, for the passage can be rough when an outgoing tide meets an incoming wind near Seguin Island. You'll enjoy one story about one of many rough passages, in the following section.

When I have time to spare, I turn up the Sheepscot River, visit Five Islands then push up further, toward Wiscasset and spend a day and night in the lovely quietness of the Oven's Mouth. If I take this course, then I retrace the Sheepscot and turn at Dogfish Head to the Townsend Gut and amble down into Boothbay Harbor through the back door.

Just as often, I make a straight shot from Seguin to outside the Cuckolds and then turn at Fisherman's Island and head into Boothbay Harbor.

By boat or car, you can see it all for yourself.

LONG BEFORE THE PILGRIMS, DAMARISCOVE WAS A PORT OF CALL

DAMARISCOVE ISLAND — We are out among the islands off Boothbay Harbor, where this nation began. It is night now. The wind has dropped; and the sea is so calm where we are anchored that the stars shine back up out of the ocean as well as down from heaven.

The only noises in this cove are the laughing of a loon, the sound of small waves breaking on the rocky shore, and the tide gurgling among boulders.

Lean over the side of the deck, run your hand through the ocean and the sea comes alive with flashes of fire—the phosphorescence miracle. There is a beautiful Italian word for the tiny sea creatures who cause this light to shine in the cold ocean; the name is notilucci. Those dancing lights of the night are as old and primeval as the calls of the loons.

We are anchored at Damariscove Island, a few miles to sea from the center of Boothbay Harbor.

This island is where white man's America began. Long before the Founding Fathers set foot on Plymouth Rock, this island was a flourishing port, the first commercial settlement of consequence in North America.

Today Damariscove is deserted. Even the Coast Guard abandoned its station here in the winter of 1959. Now the Nature Conservancy owns a part of it; only two lobstering shacks and one restored house are here.

Yet here are the roots of America. And very few people realize that.

The Mayflower sailed into Damariscove Harbor before she brought her load of 102 pilgrims to Plymouth. The Pilgrims' own records show that on their momentous voyage they came by Monhegan and Damariscove Islands "to take some coddes before sailing on to Maffachufetts Bay" in 1620.

The year Mayflower sailed to Plymouth Rock, 32 European fishing boats came to load up with salt fish in the Monhegan-Damariscove area. Records show that seven English ships, averaging 180 tons, came into Damariscove Harbor.

Before sunset we rowed ashore on Damariscove to walk along animal paths. The island is two miles long and so narrowwaisted at one point that it nearly becomes two islands. The island is almost barren of trees today, sheep having eaten the vegetation down to the roots and killed it. But years ago, Damariscove was covered with a dense growth of trees. The northern half of the uninhabited island is called Wood End still; but barely a tree grows there today.

We walked south, to open sea, to watch the ocean surge and break ominously over ledges at the harbor entrance. On the chart the waters outside are called, with full justice, "The Motions." Yet this is the harbor where exploreres and early fishing boats from Europe chose to come in under sail to anchor 350 years ago.

Historian Charles K. Bolton in his book, "The Real Founders of New England," wrote about Damariscove Island. "Here was the chief maritime port of New England. Here was the rendezvous for English, French and Dutch ships crossing the Atlantic. Here men bartered with one another and with Indians, drank, gambled, quarreled and sold indentured servants."

This evening the only living things we see are eider ducks, with their flotillas of ducklings, and black-wing gulls above threatening to swoop and eat them. The only buildings are the old Coast Guard station, now restored. But we stand by the harbor and envisage the ships and the men who were here in the 16th and 17th centuries.

To service those fish transports, there had to be wharves, derricks of a kind, salting sheds, houses, stores, taverns and at least a boatyard or two for repairs. Sailors being what they are, they surely found other pleasures too on Damariscove after the long Atlantic crossing.

And nothing of those beginnings of this nation remains except the island itself, although ancient records show that Captain Humphrey Damerill set up the first trading posts here about 1600. To supply those visiting fish transports, scores of fishermen living along the coast from the New Meadows River to the westward and the Georges River to the east, must have brought their catches here to sell. In his diaries of his 1614 voyage hereabouts, Captain John Smith writes about his visit to Damariscove Island.

The roses are in bloom now. And local legend has it that these sweet smelling roses came from France, planted here almost 360 years ago by a French trader. Not far from the old harbor is an inland freshwater pond,

bright with lilies. In the marshy bog of the island we find cranberries growing. The land looks blood-red in the fall, when these berries are ripe and
scarlet.

Long before the Pilgrims stepped ashore from the Mayflower, scores
of British families were settled here and along the nearby coast. They
prospered. And here is the evidence: on their second hard and hungry
winter at Plymouth, 50 of the 102 socalled Founding Fathers, failed to
survive. So Governor Winslow of the Plymouth Colony sailed to Maine's
Damariscove Island to ask its fishermen for food. And those tough,
roistering pioneers of Maine fed the pious, starving Pilgrims for free.

Now, from the deck of Steer Clear, we look at Damariscove Island
where we walked before the stars came out. Nobody else is here tonight,
except the laughing loons and the nesting birds. And, the ghosts of the
men who began these United States.

Down in Plymouth, the promoters are selling thousands of tickets to
gullible Americans to view the rock where the founding Father stepped
ashore.

Balderdash! It all began here.

Mystery—Party Boat Fishing

BOOTHBAY HARBOR — Gail is a ladies hairdresser in
Lewiston and she is crazy about deep sea fishing.

"Gail is on our fishing boat, regular as a clock, every two weeks from
June to September. She just loves to fish. She catches a lot. But the closest
Gail actually gets to a fish is after it is iced, filleted and in a plastic bag,
and she carries it off the boat."

That is Captain Barry Smith talking. He is skipper of "Mystery," a
55-foot party boat built in 1961 for deep sea fishing by famed Lash
Brothers of Friendship, Maine.

I went out on "Mystery" because my own boat was on charter and I
hated being land-bound.

Going on a "party boat" you can have a lot of good fishing and good
cruising for $15.

Fishermen in the Bronx knows this for a fact, maybe better than they
know it in Boothbay. In the Bronx at midnight on Fridays, charter buses
fill with eager fishermen. They drive through the night, arriving at Boothbay before the 8:30 fishing boats depart. They fish off the coast of Maine

all day, then carry their catch home to New York that night.

"We catch 1,500 and 2,000 pounds of fish a day in the good fishing season from mid-June till late July," says Capt. Barry Smith. "Once we get over a school of fish, our decks are lined with 40 fishermen, jigging for cod, pollock, cusk and occasional haddock. That is when the two mates aboard work flat out, helping land the fish, taking them off the hooks for those who want help. Later, on the way in, they clean the fish. All except the biggest are filleted and bagged for the folks to take ashore. Big cod that weigh up to 60 pounds are kept intact. The tourists use up roll after roll of film, getting pictures, standing by their catch."

Barry Smith grew up around Boothbay Harbor. He was mate on a fishing boat for nine years, and has been captain of Mystery for three years. He has his captain's papers for 50 ton vessels. "I love fishing. I even go fishing on my day off. In winter I usually go lobstering. But not this year. I'm a bachelor and girls are scarce in Boothbay in January. So this winter I will go south, to run fishing parties out of Florida."

Barry, neatly bearded, easy-going, says 80 percent of the thousands of people he takes fishing have never before been deep-sea fishing and that 30 percent have never been on a boat. "But they catch on quickly, and most soon get to love it."

In bad weather though, there can be a lot of seasickness. "I hand out only sympathy to cure it" says Barry. The fear of liability and lawsuits prevents party-boat captains from doling out seasickness pills.

Only once in his 12 years on party boats has Barry Smith had a bad scare. "One stormy rough day, the harpoon got to rolling around the bow. I went forward to secure it. A big wave swept me overboard. The boat ran over me, hurting the discs in my back. But they fished me out and I learned my lesson."

Capt. Smith says he takes a week or two in June, when the season begins, to find this year's best fishing spots. A good one has been in 30 to 43 fathoms of water about six miles southeast of Pumpkin Rock. His passengers fish with rod and reel, 40 pound test line and an 8 ounce silver colored jig.

"My fish finder helps locate schools. But some days though the fish are there, they are not feeding. We can tell that quickly because we foul-hook them." This means that the jig hooks the fish in the tail or cheeks— that they are not biting at the bait.

I watched the visitors go ashore. One lady of undetermined years

Victory Chimes, once the queen of Maine windjammers, has departed from Maine waters.

glowed and burbled like a proud young mother "Look at my fish—a 52 pounder!" she cried at the end of a day she will never forget. But among the happy crowd, only a few were from Maine. "Smart Mainers come early in June and take home 75 pounds of fish for the freezer" smiles Capt. Barry Smith. "They know it will taste wonderful in December. And bring back memories too."

SPINNAKERS IN THE FOG

BOOTHBAY HARBOR — My mind boggles still at the sudden sight of half a hundred brilliant spinnakers, flaunting their varied colors like medieval banners against the fog.

The fog had closed in thick around Boothbay Harbor during the Gulf of Maine yacht races.

One moment, we could see a mile. And then, like some huge wet white curtain hung down from heaven, fog blotted out the world.

First to vanish were the Cuckolds, that killer ledge and saintly light just west of the harbor entrance.

As the fog came in on the southwest wind, it swallowed up Fisherman's Passage and Ram Island Light. Then the fog turned into Boothbay Harbor, wiping out the islands, Squirrel, Burnt, Mouse.

By then, the fog was so thick the man at the helm of our boat could not see his lookout on the bow, only 16 feet away. Two disembodied voices cried out questions to each other and floated back answers of cold comfort.

Fifty sailboats were out there bunched together, racing to their mark. But in the fog, they were invisible to their closest rivals, and to Steer Clear.

Fog can play tricks on your mind, as you strain your ears to catch a sound and strain your eyes to catch a glimpse of danger.

Peer long enough into fog and you begin to see a shoreline, a wave breaking, the outline of a buoy, the ghostly shape of a boat.

Listen hard enough and your ears, pricked too fine, will hear a hull cutting through the water, the sound of a lobster boat turning toward you or the warning clang of a bell.

But none of them is there. The fog has you spooked; the non-existent becomes the real.

And the fog creeps into your mind, sowing doubt. Doubt about your reliable compass, doubt about the accuracy of the courses you plotted, doubt about almost everything except those ghosts of noises and boats and shore and ledge which you see or hear when the fog befogs your mind.

There is danger now that you might succumb to the insidious fog and change your course, swayed more by what you think you see than by what you know is there. The sensation is akin to that rapture of the deep which drugs a diver's brain underwater.

Then the thick fog thinned. Not very much, but enough so a pair of eyes could see reality a few hundred feet away.

And there, floating in white empty air, were the spinnakers. Reality or mirage?

The fog still blotted out the hulls, the masts, the other sails of the racing yachts.

But unattached and bodyless, the huge spinnakers billowed out on the ghostly breeze. Incredible envelopes of wind, standing unsupported high in the fog—ghosts of fiery gold, brilliant green, azure blue, blazing red.

The great spinnaker sails are flaunted like the plumes of medieval knights jousting for their ladies. Hard-driving racing skippers who run their yachts like tyrants, will vent all their suppressed desires, vanity and high spirits on buying a brilliant, gaudy, blazing colorful spinnaker, made to their design.

A spinnaker for a 30-foot boat can cost close to $2,000. A winning 43-footer, Scaramouche, has five spinnakers of different sizes, each costing about $1,500. Only a sailor's wife can understand a husband who will stuff $1,500 worth of gorgeous material into a bag in four seconds, pull it out in two, curse it, love it, and sometimes tear it to shreds in a freak accident.

The fog lifted a little more and revealed at last the boats to which the spinnakers belong. But for one glorious mysterious moment half a hundred medieval banners seemed to be ghosts on the fog at Boothbay Harbor.

OARS FOREVER AT REST

BOOTHBAY HARBOR — The simplest words and the plainest symbols are the most moving and eternal.

Millions have watched the state funeral of a president and the most moving sight of all is the empty boots, reversed in the stirrups, on a riderless horse. It is a symbol which spells final departure, irreversible loss, with absolute finality.

Another symbol is the volley of shots fired over the grave of a soldier and the chilling sound of Taps blown on an unseen bugle.

Three short words on a gravestone, "Lost at sea," evoke the loneliness of death, the smallness of man and the immensity of oceans. Walk among headstones of a graveyard in any coastal town of Maine and you see those three small words cut in many a headstone.

See them, too, in the meadows, among the wildflowers, on moss-covered, wind-worn grave markers on a Maine island; those three short words sound with greater majesty than the boom of a giant cathedral organ.

These simple words have a brotherhood with a simple symbol. Oars at rest in an empty dory.

This symbol is not so widely known as the symbol of the empty boots, reversed in the stirrups of a riderless horse. But the families of Maine fishermen have for hundreds of years known this symbol, which signifies death to thousands of loved men, lost at sea in watery graves.

Thanks to the fishermen of the Boothbay Harbor region, more people in Maine and the world now know the symbolism of oars at rest in an empty dory. A lasting monument to men lost at sea has been erected

Our Lady of Peace church is the site of the Fisherman's Memorial, "Oars at Rest" dedicated to fishermen lost at sea.

and blessed near the shore of Boothbay Harbor.

The 20-ton granite block on which the monument rests was moved into place first. Then came the monument—an empty dory, cast in bronze. In it the long oars are forever at rest, crossed, blades pointed to the sky.

The monument sits, overlooking the harbor, on ground given by the Roman Catholic church with the lovely name of Our Lady of Peace.

This is the landmark church known to every seaman making port in Boothbay. At night, the white, floodlit steeple is a beacon signifying home and safety. It is most fitting that this new memorial, this empty dory with crossed oars, will forever be part of this church's homecoming beacon for sailors and fishermen.

The blessing of the Fisherman's Memorial, a dory with oars forever at rest, cast in bronze, at Our Lady of Peace Catholic Church, Boothbay Harbor.

The local Fishermen's Festival—that springtime good-time designed to shake out the cobwebs of winter before shrimping starts—is tapping past and future profits to pay the $30,000 cost of the monument to their lost brothers.

The bronze from which the dory is cast comes from the sea. Fishermen from the Boothbay region and from Monhegan Island, collected more than 1,500 pounds of brass and bronze fittings from wrecks and old boats. John Tourtilotte of Boothbay Harbor melted down the fittings at the J.F. Hodgkins foundry in Randolph, on the banks of the Kennebec River.

That family company, founded 101 years ago to make fittings for boats, cast the dory and the oars-at-rest.

The pattern was made in wood by Sonny Hodgdon, whose family has been building boats at Boothbay Harbor for 150 years. "I had a dory built by Malcolm Brewer, foreman in my father's yard. Malcolm was one of the finest dory builders on the Maine coast," says Hodgdon, "and I used his dory as the reference for building this one."

After the dory was built, it was cut into sections, with each section used as a pattern in pouring the bronze. Then the sections were welded together, sand-blasted and polished to a dull finish. The oars were welded forever at rest. It is a memorial and loving, respectful tribute to Maine fishermen lost at sea as well as a reminder to all of us who make it safely back to port.

HODGDONS: 175 YEARS OF WOODEN BOATS

BOOTHBAY HARBOR — Sonny Hodgdon is half man and half boat, and all Maine coast. He is the sixth generation of Hodgdon boat builders, and his son Timothy is seventh generation boss of the Hodgdon yard now.

Hodgdons have been building wooden boats in East Boothbay since before Maine became a state in 1820. "Most of our records before then have disappeared. But here's a list of Hodgdon-build boats since 1814," says George I. "Sonny" Hodgdon.

I count 285 boats on the list, spanning more than 175 years. Hodgdons were laying keels for the Lena Young and Silver Moon the year the British burned the White House.

A few names in the long roster of her predecessors; the 80-ton pinkie named Union, launched in 1819, the year Spain ceded Florida to the U.S.; the schooner George M. Hodgdon, launched in 1869, the year they drove a golden spike at Promontory Point, Utah, to mark the link-up of the transcontinental railroad; the six Numan schooners, built between 1882 and 1908 for the famed Nunan fishing fleet out of Cape Porpoise.

During the 20th century, America's famous yacht designers kept going to Hodgdon for their boats. The list includes 25 sloops, yawls and schooners designed by George Owen, 34 designed by William Hand and 37 designed by John G. Alden. Still other Hodgdon boats were designed by Herreshoff, Sparkman & Stevens, McInnis, Stadel and Nielson.

Sonny puts away the volumes of old records, which are his heritage. He is more than 60 years old, but his hair is as black as the tar which once went on Hodgdon boats. He is a big man, over 6 feet 4 inches, erect, soft-voiced and slow speaking, forever wearing a khaki shirt and trousers and steel rimmed glasses. He takes quiet pride in his long shipbuilding roots. "East Boothbay once was called Hodgdon Mills. Close to 180 years ago Caleb Hodgdon and his brother Tyler Hodgdon were building wooden boats here. And before the Mayflower, I reckon there were Hodgdons hiding in the wilderness around here."

My mind swings back to picture the men working in the early Hodgdon yard when oxen hauled in the boat timbers and cash was paid for each piece. The record shows the prices; 30 cents for futtocks (the curved rib timbers), 67 cents for floor timbers, 25 cents for white ash top timbers.

Carpenters worked with only the broadax, saw, adz and pod auger. The shipsmith worked his own iron, forging every spike and bolt, mast cap and chain link on his own anvil. The painters cut their own varnish and shellac from the gum, blended their own colors and mixed their own paint. In the 1840s, skilled hands got but $1 a day, helpers 75 cents and the boy who tended the steambox toiled all day for 15 cents. The workday was 12 hours long with a half-hour at 6 a.m. for breakfast and 45 minutes for dinner at noon. The yard owner provided meals at 8 cents each.

If wages were slim, grog was plentiful. To get the men started right on frosty mornings, they were served a tumbler of rum and two glasses of water. Another grog ration was given out again at 11 a.m. and again at 4 p.m. In addition, the cry of "Grog O!" was shouted across the boatyard to celebrate the raising of the sternpost, hanging of the anchor or fastening of the last plank. Free grog at the yard stopped when the temperance movement caught hold in Maine. But the price for a fine Hodgdon-built boat stayed low for a long while.

Take the price of the handsome Imelda, launched in 1939. She was a 91-foot auxilary ketch, biggest motor sailer of her time, built to the design of William Hand. The price was $41,000. Even in 1945, the price of a 28-foot Herreshoff ketch was only $2,500, and in 1946 a 35-foot Alden auxiliary sloop, ready for the sea, cost just $5,200. By comparison, a 43-footer now will cost $175,000 or more.

When Sonny leaves his boatyard for home, he has a walk of 80 feet. Inside the house, with its spectacular ocean views, Sonny is still surrounded by boats. He spends off-hours building beautiful half-models. Ninety of them line the walls—probably the biggest privately-owned, personally-made, collection of half models in the U.S.

His loving skill as a craftsman is in plain view everywhere in his house; in desks, dining tables, highboys and above all in grandfather clocks. "Once we had 15 grandfather clocks chiming the hours. Now we're down to six."

Some of the finest Hodgdon joiner work in recent years went into the refurbishing of the immense schooner America. Sonny and his craftsmen spent several thousand hours transforming her interior to the tastes of Carlos A. Perdomo, the Spanish grandee who owned America.

When America left East Boothbay, Hodgdon presented Perdomo with a specially cast miniature brass cannon. After Perdomo sailed back to Spain, he removed the cannon and placed it on the terrace of his island home on Majorca. The local police forbade him to fire it. But one day the King of Spain visited Perdomo, and so admired the cannon that Perdomo gave it as a gift to his king. The King of Spain mounted the Hodgdon cannon on the battlements of his palace, so he could fire salvos at whomever and whenever he pleased. Such has been the prerogative of kings for centuries.

Recently, Hodgdon received an order for three similar cannons, with barrels are over two feet long. With the order came a check drawn on a Spanish bank in the amount of "tres mils dollars, U.S." A bank in Boothbay Harbor went into a tizzy when Sonny brought it in to cash; at first reading the cashier thought "tres mils dollars" meant three million. Actually, it meant $3,000.

There's a tough side to the five-man crew at Hodgdon's who build these exquisite, polished yachts. One day a 350-ton tugboat broke through the marine railway as she was being hauled out at Sample's yard and sunk deep into the mud below. No one knew how to launch such a monster marooned in mudflats. So they called Hodgdon.

The same crew which had done the delicate joiner work aboard America undertook the job. "Took us 15 days of bull strength and dumb muscle to get stuffing under her, pack her and wedge up her 350 tons. But we got her launched and the broken railway repaired," says Hodgdon with a smile of satisfaction.

Sonny's pride in heritage is evident on his business letterhead. "Fine Yacht Work" it reads, and lists the builders of the last 170 years: "1818 Caleb & Taylor Hodgdon; 1827 Caleb Hodgdon; 1869 C. & J.P. Hodgdon Co; 1918 C. E. & W.A. Hodgdon Co; 1901 Hodgdon Bros; 1970 G. I. Hodgdon Co., Inc."

Makes a sailor feel safe, going to sea in a wooden boat built by a Hodgdon. I owned a second-hand Hodgdon boat years ago, a lobster boat, the Steer Clear I, a 27-footer built in 1948 and still working on the coast of Maine.

PIG COVE

PIG COVE — For a high class address, Pig Cove is hard to beat. I even met the Episcopalian Bishop of Maine here, at All Saints by the Sea, Pig Cove, Southport Island, Maine.

The small church nestles a few yards from the sea. It seems almost to grow out of the rough grey granite ledge on which it stands.

We came to Sunday service here by boat, the way most people came 82 years ago, when the church was first consecrated.

There are moorings to which church-going boats can tie up. There is a dinghy dock for those more hardy souls who choose to row a boat to their salvation. There is even a good size float at which one of the Boothbay Harbor sight-seeing boats drops off passengers and collects them after Sunday services in the summertime.

If you don't come by water, there is a winding path through evergreen woods for those who use cars, and then feet, to go to church.

To find out how All Saints by the Sea began, I contacted Carolyn Joy, whose first-hand knowledge of this charming church can hardly be surpassed.

"I came there in a rowboat when I was two months old, to be christened and baptized," she told me.

Today brides arrive, and depart, by boat, though usually something bigger than a rowboat. "Not only is this more romantic, but it is easier on the bridal train and veil than walking through the woods to the altar," said Carol Joy.

The seaside church had its origins in a picnic held 114 years ago by people from Gardiner to honor their minister John McGrath.

The picnic, in the 1870's, was held on what is today cottage-crowded Capitol Island. It was uninhabited in those days and went by the plainer name of Hog Island. And Hog Island looked across Pig Cove to a mighty handsome point of land. The Rev. John McGrath was much taken by that spit of land. To enjoy it more, he booked himself a room with a view of it at the Gray Homestead, which stood nearby and took in a few boarders.

When McGrath was transferred to another parish in far away Michigan, the vision of Pig Cove went with him. In the 1870's, John McGrath had a prefabricated home, perhaps one of the first in the nation, shipped to Bath from Michigan, then floated downriver to Pig Cove. The minister lived there later on, and held church services under the oak trees by the ocean.

By 1905, the men and women who came to these Sunday services decided they should erect a church. They commissioned the local boat-builder, Charles Gray to build the little church. In 1906 Bishop Codman of Maine came to the shore and consecrated the new church. And every summer since then, All Saints by the Sea has been open for the Lord's business from the last Sunday in June until Labor Day.

On the Sunday we came ashore from Steer Clear to go to church here, Frederick W.B. Wolf, then Bishop of Maine, was there in full regalia of puffed sleeves, bishop's staff and crozier, bishop's giant tourmaline ring, and one of the finest preaching voices in North America, to conduct morning service and deliver the sermon.

The small church was crowded. Along with a dozen others, we chose to sit on the open porch rather than inside. If we glanced over our shoulders, we could see the church-going boats bobbing their bows in prayer. We could look out across Pig Cove to what used to be Hog Island. But the folks from Augusta who came downriver to build summer cottages, wanted a tonier name, and changed the name to Capitol Island, to indicate that they came from Maine's capitol city. We could look out across to Squirrel and Mouse Islands and know the Cuckolds and Ram Island Lights and Fishermans Island lay off to seaward, guarding the great mouth into Boothbay Harbor.

But gazing out to sea seemed a bit inattentive to the Bishop's fine sermon and the hearty hymn singing of the congregation. We changed our gaze from seaward to heavenward. There, above us on the porch, was a full nest of baby birds. As we chorused hymns of praise, the baby birds would raise their scraggly necks in soundless songs of praise. They, unbelievers, wanted worms and grubs for Sunday lunch. Yet the tiny birds were well behaved. After service, the mitered bishop stood directly under their nest. He was in a dangerous target zone. But not one baby bird misbehaved.

We rowed our skiff back to Steer Clear, shed our go-to-meeting clothes, put on swimsuits and swam in Pig Cove. It was a grand way to go to church in Maine.

SPAIN SAILS AGAIN WITH THE LOVELY JESSICA

EAST BOOTHBAY — If a cat may look on a king, as John Heywood wrote way back in 1546, then my little Steer Clear can look at Jessica, the vessel which Vogue called "probably the most beautiful private sailboat in the world."

Recently Steer Clear went to gaze and marvel at Jessica when she was at the Goudy & Stevens yard in East Boothbay.

Jessica is an enormous 203-foot, three-mast topsail schooner. She is steel-hulled and new, built in 1984 in Spain at a reputed cost of about $20 million. The Spanish government agreed to lend 85 percent of the cost price at 5 percent interest for five years, providing this showcase of shipbuilding art was built in Spain. When the magnificent ship came into East Boothbay, a crew of 15 was aboard, with the proud owner Carlos Perdomo in command. To operate the ship costs an estimated $2 million a year.

Perdomo is a businessman in Argentina whose business and pleasure is ships. "I am the representative of the Spanish shipyards in Argentina. My business is with the building of big cargo ships and very big tankers. Spain is the third largest shipbuilder in the world," Perdomo told me when I interviewed him aboard another splendid sailing vessel which he used to own, the America, which was built here.

Jessica is the only sailing ship of its size built in the world in the last 54 years, since the Lawley yard in Boston built the 205-foot Intrepid in 1930. Perdomo says he chose not to build a modern luxury yacht because "I hold more faith in the older, traditional style. Too many times we make mistakes in our rush to go further and faster . . ."

Yet Jessica can sail fast. With 18,726 square feet of working sail available through 11 sails, including topsails and three jibs, Jessica can clip through the sea at an amazing 23 knots in a stiff wind. Her masts reach 135 feet above the waterline. When Jessica sailed in the Statue of Liberty celebration in New York harbor, she made so much speed that her engines had to be turned on in reverse to slow her down to the speed of the rest of the tall ships. Capt. John Bardon, from the Isle of Wight, has 12 professional seamen in his crew, plus electric winches, to set the sails. Even in light winds, Jessica sails at 10 knots.

To build her took three-and-a-half years. The yard which did the exquisite job is Astilloros of Malorca, a yard so long in shipbuilding that it claims links to Christopher Columbus. The steel hull was designed by

South African naval architect Arthur Holgate, who died in a car crash in the United States before the vessel was finished. The interior was designed by Britisher John Munford.

Perdomo roams the world in Jessica, from the icy climes of the Arctic to the heat of the Carribbean. His vessel can make its own climate with total air conditioning and heating throughout, powered by two generators of 25 and 45 kilowatts. She can make her own fresh water at the rate of 18 tons a day. When power is needed, she has a General Motors diesel, 660 horsepower. But there is no TV and no Loran.

The owner's stateroom, with its king-size bed, its bathroom with gold fixtures, its own refrigerator and miniature galley, is far aft for privacy. Three guest staterooms, also with private baths, have queen-size beds. There is a handsome library for reading, writing and business conferences. The main salon is so spacious that 50 people can be entertained for cocktails.

The dining table is specially made and specially gimballed in three directions. Most gimballed tables tilt to the windward or leeward in a rough sea, so people on the windward side get the table in their knees and those on the leeward get it in their chins. But on Jessica 10 guests can dine in comfort at a dining table which stays level even when the vessel is heeling over 20 degrees. Two stewardesses serve them. The chef used to be chef aboard the liner, Queen Elizabeth.

Eye-catchers amid the fine furnishings are eight elephant tusks from one of Perdomo's hunting expeditions in Africa. He also has hunted polar bear and musk ox in the Arctic and shot a 1,200-pound Kodiak bear in the Aleutian Islands. In quieter pursuits, he traveled by plane, jeep, canoe and 400 miles on horseback to be the first man to film the remote Xavantes Indians in Brazil.

Jessica is no sometime-toy for Perdomo. He lives aboard most of the year and conducts much of his worldwide business from the elaborate radio room aboard. He has crossed the Atlantic in this new vessel three times and already logged more than 27,000 miles in one year .

Perdomo was 60 years old when he sailed Jessica into East Boothbay.

His father, who owned a flour business in Argentina, died when Perdomo was 7 years old. Perdomo's education stopped after high school, when he went to work building flour mills throughout South America. Politically, Perdomo opposed the Peron dictatorship in his native Argentina. For this opposition, he was arrested, imprisoned and tortured close

Jessica, built in Spain, with London, England, as her hailing port, is docked at Goudy & Stevens shipyard in East Boothbay.

to death. He escaped to the Brazilian Embassy and was promptly exiled to Brazil.

Perdomo bought his first boat in 1945, a 42-foot ketch. Like most boatsmen, he yearned soon for something bigger and better; graduated to a 64-footer, a near wreck, which he bought for the price of the lead in its keel and then restored. By 1979 he was owner of his sixth boat, the 104-foot schooner America, which he brought to Maine and the Goudy & Stevens yard, where it had been built in 1967, for restoration. Now he has brought his seventh boat, the magnificent Jessica, to Maine.

Jessica is named for an English lady aboard, Norma Jessica. The vessel's home port is also London. But on proud display in the main salon is the launching gift from King Carlos of Spain, a close friend of Perdomo. This is a bronze bell inscribed in Spanish with the words, "Fair Winds, Calm Seas, Bright Stars," signed by King Carlos and embossed with the royal seal.

However the most privileged character aboard, who has full run of the ship night and day, is Pockets, a Staffordshire terrier and Perdomo's inseparable companion.

BRINGING BACK THE ROD (FISHING, THAT IS)

SOUTHPORT — The meeting was triggered by a letter from a stranger, a woman in Boothbay. But I put it aside for 10 days before I made the phone call to Southport Island, near Boothbay Harbor, to set up a meeting with a man called Cecil E. Pierce, as the letter writer had suggested. Cecil Pierce and I met for the first time and talked away an afternoon.

After I'd said goodbye and was driving home, I realized that in Cecil Pierce I'd found one of the world's few truly happy, contented and serene men.

Cecil Pierce was 73 but looked about 60. He is small in height yet sturdy. He wears glasses and what seems to be a perpetual smile. And all the fingers from his left hand are missing.

"I've been a machinist and boat builder all my life," said Cecil, "and about halfway through I got too friendly with a machine and it took off my fingers. Nothing I can do about that, so I ignore it."

We talk inside his house, high on a hill, where Cecil has lived alone since his wife, Lucy, died of cancer. "Nothing I can do about that either, so

I don't moon around feeling lonely. We had a good, long life together, over 50 years, here on Southport Island.''

Cecil Pierce was born in Southport and says he has "never itched to live any place else.''

His two children were born here too, home-delivered by a local doctor. "I remember the doctor charged $10 for the first. When the second one came along, he told me he'd have to raise the price to $15.''

The "kids,'' a son and daughter, are over 50 now and live nearby with their children. "I can throw a baseball to their houses.''

That brings up a story about how Cecil makes the raised rolls for which he's famous on Southport. He smiles. "Mrs. Packard made them first,'' he says. "She was the lady who came to help out when Lucy had the babies. Mrs. Packard got paid not by the day, but by the job. The job with us lasted 10 days. She'd care for Lucy and the baby, clean the house and cook for me. Her price was $25 for the whole job. And she made the raised rolls that I took such a shine to. I got the recipe from Mrs. Packard and I've kept right on making them ever since.''

Roots and memories link Cecil to most people and most places on Southport Island. "The old school house used to be right here, on the site I built this home. I went to school right here. In those days we had about 20 kids and one teacher. I got the job as school janitor and earned 50 cents a week.

"We went to high school only two years in those days. My first job after high school was driving the wagon and tending store for C.E. Pinkham's Grocery, just down the road. I started scared and stayed scared of the horses on that wagon and was glad when summer came and the roads were good enough to use the old truck again.''

In 1926, two years after graduating from high school, Cecil married Lucy Gaudette and they stayed married until Lucy's death.

Cecil's roots run everywhere hereabouts, nourishing his contentment. He served 27 years as a town selectman. "Three of us did all the work. No clerks, no secretary to type.''

The pay was $250 a year, raised to $600 by the time he quit. "We did all the town assessing and set a figure for total town valuation. Now that's up to $5 million. But the population of Southport is still the same, about 400. "Once I knew everyone, and their kids. But when I go down to the post office now, I hardly know 10 percent of the faces.''

In addition to serving as a selectman, Cecil was fire chief for 20 years.

And he knows so much about local history that he became co-author of Southport's bicentennial book, "Historical Gleanings," and was a consultant for the "History of the Boothbay Region, 1906-1960."

But mostly Cecil has worked with his hands. "Right after Lucy and I got married, I needed to make more money than I could at the grocery store. So for 15 years I worked as mechanic in Vance Bell's garage. Then in 1938 I went out on my own as a marine mechanic, mostly fixing engines on fishing boats.

"When World War II began I tooled aircraft parts and had 15 women working in my shop. I installed all the engines in the Navy boats built at Reed's in Boothbay Harbor."

Cecil Pierce also invented and patented a potato-barrel loader that saved the backs of a lot of Aroostook farmers. "But when we'd made and sold 3,000 of those loaders, we had saturated the market."

In the 1950s he started building boats, mostly lobster boats and pleasure craft. He also built a towboat and work barges for Mason Carter, who operated out of Boothbay Harbor and used the boats to put in most of the wharves and pilings along midcoast Maine. "A fine man, Mason. We never had a contract, just a handshake, all the years I built boats for him," says Cecil.

When the Railway Museum at Boothbay needed a full size reproduction of an old passenger car, they came to Cecil Pierce. He studied the old books and original drawings and built the new railroad car in his boat shop.

When the Benedict Arnold Expedition Historical Society needed prototype replicas of the 1775 bateaux, they also turned to Cecil, and he built those too.

When the Maine Department of Marine Resources ruled that all lobster traps should have an escape vent to allow sub-legal size lobsters to escape, it was Cecil Pierce who designed the first model.

Today, retired from boat building, Cecil has become among the world's finest makers of hand-crafted fly rods. I asked him when he started on this and his answer still astonishes me. "As soon as Nixon opened up China."

Cecil explained there is a little area of China, some 15 square miles, back from the Tonkin Gulf, where they grow Tonkin cane, the best source of fine bamboo in the world. "When I could get my hands on that, I began building fly rods."

He buys the bamboo through an importer in New York City and pays $6 for a 12 foot length about two inches in diameter.

He showed me around his workshop, where he has an array of machines he designed, and then made, to thin down the bamboo to his own precise specifications.

Cecil's rods are seven feet long, made in two parts, each from six laminated pieces of bamboo, but they weigh only two ounces. He reinforces the underside of each piece of bamboo with graphite or carbon fibers, made by Rolls Royce in England. "That stuff has 200,000 separate fibers running through it," he says.

The graphite is what helps give his rods their remarkable strength and allows him to work the bamboo thinner and smaller until at the tip the diameter is only 1/32 of an inch.

Cecil assembled one of his rods for me, a featherweight masterpiece of immaculate, painstaking handcraftmanship.

It takes him more than 50 hours to craft one rod. "Then I make all my cork grips and ferrules. I also make my own bags for storing the rods and cases for carrying them. The only things I don't make are the metal guides through which the line runs."

Cecil says he got hooked on fly fishing for trout on the Dead River, near his hunting camp at Eustis, Maine. "When I retired as fire chief, the boys at the fire house pooled their money and bought me an Orvis rod. That's about the best rod made commercially. But I thought I could make a better one. And when Nixon opened up China and I could buy Tonkin cane, I went to work."

Cecil makes most of his rods for himself, a few for special friends, and once in a while he sells one for hundreds of dollars. "It would take out the joy if I went commercial. And I don't want a customer phoning me to ask how his rod is coming along."

Relaxed in his worn, oversize easy chair, Cecil Pierce confesses to a great love for life in Southport, where his ancestors first settled in 1760. "I've enjoyed everything I've done," he says. "I think I'm a rich and happy man."

SMALL IS BEAUTIFUL IN THIS REGATTA

CHRISTMAS COVE — They came down the Damariscotta River, fog swirling around them and the breeze strong on their bows. They paddled handsome canoes, and kayaks, lean and swift as greyhounds; they rowed sturdy Norwegian skiffs and sailed small, classic sailboats; they sculled on sliding seats, with sweeps 10 feet long biting into the water. They came in silence without an engine or motor. Close to 50 small, loved and pampered boats, all less than 20 feet long, ghosted through 12 miles of fog from Damariscotta to Christmas Cove.

"The Damariscotta River looked as it must have looked 500 years ago to Indians paddling the same waters. We could see the hilltops, thick with green pines on either side; but the fog blotted out all sign of houses. The only human sounds were the splash of oars and the whip of sails," said William D. Shew, builder of fine small boats.

This was the small boat regatta held at Christmas Cove, the harbor named in 1614 when Capt. John Smith dropped anchor here on Christmas Day. This regatta is a low-key celebration of the fact that small is beautiful; especially in a boat.

The owners of these small, beautiful boats gather at Mike Mitchell's Coveside Marina here, not to compete, not to party, not to win blue ribbons, but to admire, to compare, to try out and enjoy each other's special loves.

Phineas Sprague Jr. from Cape Elizabeth was here with his rare and special love: a 101-year-old pulling boat from the river Thames in England. The boat is very narrow, pointed sharply at both ends, and has only four inches freeboard. But it rows beautifully. During its golden years on the Thames, lovely ladies lolled languidly and beguilingly on a wicker chair in the stern, protected from the sun, and the eyes of gossips, by parasols.

Loyall Sewall, an Augusta lobbyist, lawyer, lobsterman and stalwart Republican party organizer, brought his 16-foot Whitehall pulling boat, equipped with a sliding seat like those in racing shells. It is christened the Bernard T. Zahn, in honor of his father-in-law, a man very dissimilar in shape to the tiny, wineglass stern of a Whitehall. Sewall also brought his 12-foot Whitehall sailing dinghy which carries another incongruous name—the Solomon S. Curry, the name of a bulky ore carrier once owned by Sen. Charlotte Sewall's grandfather, a mine operator in Minnesota. She is the wife of Loyall.

The beautiful Whitehalls are hand-crafted in South Bristol by William Shew and Cecil Burnham. These are works of art, and cannot be produced cheaply. For example, a 12-foot Whitehall sailing dinghy cost about $2,500 equipped in the 1970s.

Frank Walker sailed his Bullseye, built in 1934 and still a tremendous performer. We raced against her in a squally breeze and a short chop in a Herreshoff 17-footer built by Shew. Near us sailed a 15-foot, double-ender peapod, a beauty built by a student at Dean Puchlaski's school in Newcastle. Rowing his Whitehall, barechested, white hair blowing in the breeze, was Julian Orlandini, a decorative plasterer, who brought his Whitehall all the way from Milwaukee to this regatta in Christmas Cove, where his boat had been built by Shew & Burnham.

In a day of plastic hulls stamped out on factory production lines, it is a rare delight to stand on the dock at Christmas Cove and see 50 gems of small boats, mostly hand-crafted here in Maine.

MAINE OSPREYS ARE THRIVING

DAMARISCOTTA RIVER — The osprey nesting on radar reflector buoy #13 is the bravest osprey on the Damariscotta River. I'm glad to report that ospreys are nesting atop every navigational pylon along 15 miles of this river.

On a Damariscotta River trip in Steer Clear, the sun shone warmly, the skies were azure and the river was an enchantment. The ospreys were enjoying the weather too, sitting atop vast untidy nests, made with a jumble of twigs and sticks, which look like the most uncomfortable and untidiest beds in the world.

White heads would pop up out of each nest as Steer Clear got near. The fish hawks would eye me, first with curiosity, then with alarm. By the time Steer Clear was alongside, alarm would overcome courage, and the ospreys would rise up, and fly off their nests.

All except the osprey atop radar pylon 13. This bird stood its post bravely, guarding the nest, and stared me down until Steer Clear was at a safe distance.

At Ford Island, where Indians crossed the river, the osprey nest is built on the cross bars of the telephone pole at the edge of the mainland, where the wires cross the river. Two ospreys, presumably husband and wife, were sitting together atop this nest.

Cruising slowly down 12 miles of river between Damariscotta and East Boothbay, I counted a dozen osprey nests, all occupied.

To an osprey, living above the river is like living over the diner. No flying off to the store downtown; just one swift dive to the water 12 feet below and there is lunch, breakfast and dinner, waiting only a wing beat away from bed.

Ospreys are almost as big as eagles, about two feet tall and with a wing span of almost six feet. There is enough white on an osprey's head to resemble the bald eagle. They are masters at killing fish, their only food. An osprey hovers over the water, fish spotting. When it sights its next meal, the hunter sets its wings and dives feet first at its prey, hitting the water with a tremendous splash, sometimes going completely under.

Bird experts tell me ospreys have toes of equal length, unjoined by membrane, with curved claws, and underneath the toes are sharp spicules. This is the special apparatus which enables an osprey to grab and then grip a slippery small fish on the flight back to the untidy wooden nest.

The osprey or fish hawk was severely threatened when DDT was widespread as a pesticide. The DDT contaminated fish, the ospreys' primary food supply. In Maine, between 30 and 50 percent of our ospreys were lost in the DDT years. The decimation of these spectacular hunting birds was worse to the south. The 800 pairs of osprey living between New York and Boston were reduced to 90 surviving pairs. By 1987 they were up to more than 230 pairs, and climbing.

Spoiling its way down the food chain, the DDT, widely used to kill mosquitoes and farm pests, got into fish and when the ospreys ate fish infected with DDT, the shells on the osprey eggs became paper thin and broke before the babies hatched.

At last count, Maine had more than 1,200 nesting pairs of ospreys. Judging by the 100 percent occupancy rate of the nests along the Damariscotta River, my guess is that Maine may have over 1,500 pairs of nesting ospreys in 1988.

I've never gone close to those untidy, sprawling nests of twigs. But the experts say they weigh 100 pounds and are actually a close-woven mesh of the debris of civilization, including newspapers, TV antennas, cow dung and plastic bags, as well as large twigs.

Ospreys are legally an endangered species and protected by law. When a game warden arrested a Brunswick man for destroying an osprey nest on Center Island in Quahog Bay and taking a month-old bird to keep as a pet, the culprit was hauled into local court and fined $300.

On Westport Island, near Wiscasset, some sticks from an osprey's nest were detached from the nest during a storm, and made contact with live electric wires below. This caused a power outage in Westport and Wiscasset. Concerned Central Maine Power Co. repairmen removed the nesting materials, while Maine Audubon Society members built a wooden platform atop the CMP utility pole. As soon as some of the old nesting material was placed on the platform, the displaced ospreys went to work and within the hour were rebuilding their new nest site.

But for my money, the bravest osprey of all lives on pylon marker #13 on the Damariscotta River. May all the eggs in that nest hatch brave babies!

TIME TO REJOICE: THE LAUNCHING OF AN O'HARA DRAGGER

ROCKLAND — At christenings, at weddings, perhaps at bar mitzvahs and surely at boat launchings, a special magic transforms the human condition. Stern eyes fill with tears; passionless hearts thump hard against rib cages; and in the throats of emotionless men, Adam's apples begin to bob frantically. Inside all of us lurks a sentimental slob who, thank heaven, comes out of hiding to rejoice at these new beginnings in the human adventure.

I saw this lovely little miracle happen to over 500 people in the Goudy & Stevens shipyard at East Boothbay. As the tide came to full flood at 11 a.m. a two year-old girl, Amy Bryant, and 66 year-old Francis Donahue, jointly swung a champagne bottle to christen the new ship Ranger, and the 120 foot steel trawler raced down the greased ways to begin her life on the ocean.

Most of the 500 were close to the sea, making their livelihoods from boats and fish. They came from Rockland and New Bedford and the Boston waterfronts as well as from this Boothbay peninsular. Many of the men in hardhats and shipyard clothes had helped build Ranger. Some crewed other ships in the O'Hara fishing fleet. Others processed or marketed the catch. All were tough men doing tough work. But when Ranger rushed down the ways and her great keel and heavy steel hull hit the water and the sea exploded in foaming white waves around her, and she came to port astern and finally settled clear and fine and proud on the sea at high flood, all those tough guys were for a few wonderful seconds sentimental softies. Their Adam's apples danced a jig in their throats, and their hands, grease-stained from machine bolts and scorched from welding torches, swiped at unaccustomed, unmanly tears.

Then it was celebration time. The 500 poured into the big boat shed where tables groaned with enormous supplies of food and endless gallons of drink, and celebration music rang out loud and bouncy.

After Eliot Winslow's tugs had nudged Ranger alongside her wharf, and her lines were secured, I went aboard to look over the newest, finest addition to the famed O'Hara fishing fleet.

She's a strong and handsome working ship, beautifully made. The welding which binds together her 200 tons of heavy steel plate is a Maine masterpiece of careful workmanship. I admired the wood in her pilot-house, the cabinets in her galley and mess room, her bunks and storage lockers. You'd be hard put to find carpentry and cabinet work any finer aboard a million-dollar pleasure yacht built by another yard. But that Maine way with wood comes with the package on a Maine-built fishing boat.

Frank O'Hara, the owner, said it all in one classic sentence. After he'd inspected every nook and cranny, he turned to the builders, Jim and Tunk and Joel Stevens, and said: "She might not be perfect. But she's close. Build me another like her, straight off."

The O'Hara fleet, which used to harvest redfish, had to change over to catching groundfish. International politics put the richest redfish grounds off limits to American boats. So O'Hara changed his boats, and his Rockland fish plant, over to fishing for groundfish on Georges Bank and the Gulf of Maine.

Capt. Tim Asbury of Cape Elizabeth became the first skipper of the new Ranger. Her refrigerated hold has room for 300,000 pounds of fish. The fish cutting room is below decks. In foul weather on this trawler, the crew need only be out working on deck for six minutes or so when the nets are set out or hauled back. Below is color TV, stereo music, plush sleeping and washing quarters. A crew member may make over $40,000 a year, and the skipper may earn double. A job on an O'Hara boat is a sought-after berth. But one requirement is that the O'Hara fish boats must be left spotless when the crew leaves after a 100 hour work week at sea. If dirt or fish stain is found anywhere by the O'Hara inspectors, a telephone call goes out telling the crew member responsible to get back from wherever he is and clean up or be fired. Then the second crew takes out the clean ship for another trip after another 300,000 pounds of fish.

ANCIENT PEMAQUID: OLD HISTORY UNCOVERED

ANCIENT PEMAQUID — Tonight, here at the Ancient Pemaquid Restoration, I can reach out and touch Maine's past.

Here is the oldest artifact of its kind ever discovered in America—a Bellarmine stoneware jar, for storing wine or oils. It is dated 1610. It was found in pieces here in the "digs" of Pemaquid and has now been masterfully restored by the Smithsonian Institute. The only jug close to it in age was found at Jamestown, dated 1662. Thus Pemaquid's is older by 52 years.

Close by the jug is a Massachusetts Pine Tree Sixpence, dated 1652. But it could be a forgery. For when King Charles II came to the English throne in 1660 he forbade Massachusetts to issue any more coins. But sly New Englanders kept making currency for another 30 years. They dated all coins 1652, eight years prior to Charles II. Thus the King couldn't prove that they had disobeyed his edict.

Close to the old coins are little curlers for men's wigs. Made of fired clay, the curlers held heat well and were inserted into men's perukes during the night. (People who think wigs are a modern fashion should know that Queen Elizabeth I had 80 heads of fake hair in her wardrobe at the end of the 16th century.)

Hundreds of fascinating 300-year-old relics of early Maine are beautifully displayed in a museum at the site of Ancient Pemaquid.

Amateur archaeologist Helen Camp, of Round Pond, uncovered almost by accident in 1970, the beginnings of the now famous "dig" at Pemaquid.

To house the 25,000 artifacts of America's earliest settlement discovered in the foundations of nine buildings unearthed here, Gordon Van Buskirk started Maine's most fascinating museum of our earliest days.

In it are displayed tools and weapons used by the Wawenock Indians long before the arrival of the first colonists. There are jews harps, scissors, trading beads and axes used in the early 1600's by white men to trade for fish and furs from the Indians. Here are remnants of 3,729 clay pipes smoked by some of the early colonists. In 14 display cases, the early life of Pemaquid is well portrayed. Take those clay pipes, for instance.

Through the Harrington dating formula, the hole in the stem of the pipes is used to tell how old they are. The smaller the hole (8/64 of an inch is the smallest), the earlier the pipe.

This formula ties in precisely with Ancient Pemaquid's history.

For example, only 6.7 percent of the 3,729 pipe stems found are from the period 1620-1650, when the settlement was just getting started.

During the next 30 years, 1650-1680, population increased rapidly. And the number of pipe stems from that period is up sharply to 17 percent of the total. But pipe finds from the next 30 years, 1680-1710, plummet sharply down to a mere 4.8 percent of the total. Reason? Because population in Pemaquid nose-dived. And population nose-dived for the good reason that in 1689 the Indians attacked Fort Charles and burned Pemaquid village.

But after Fort Frederick was built in 1729, peace was restored and people returned to Pemaquid in great numbers. And so the number of pipes dated to 1710-1750 jumps to 1,500 or so, about 50 percent of all the pipes discovered. By this time the hole in the stem had grown from 8/64ths of an inch to 5/64ths.

Walking through the museum, we recalled the hectic exciting afternoon in 1975 when diggers unearthed skeletons, thought to be the bodies of two early Vikings, a mother and her baby. Reporters, cameramen, TV crews descended that afternoon like locusts upon the site. News of the discovery flashed around the world.

The "Vikings," whose bones were rushed to New York for tests by experts, turned out to be an Indian princess and her infant. And she too is on display, amazingly reconstructed, in the museum.

But if the "Vikings" were a false scent, Ancient Pemaquid has indeed been proven and authenticated. The nation's foremost experts now acknowledge Pemaquid as the site of a flourishing colonial village which pre-dates the settlements at Plymouth.

FISHERMEN'S MUSEUM AT PEMAQUID LIGHT

PEMAQUID LIGHT — The famed Pemaquid Lighthouse, built by order of President John Quincy Adams in 1827, began a new life 145 years later as a Fishermens' Museum, created by fishermen and fishermen's wives and widows from nearby harbor towns.

Exhibits, which fill three ground floor rooms of the lightkeeper's house, were all donated by fishermen of the area. They vividly show the history of lobstering, shrimping, clamming, seining and dragging along these shores.

There is a giant pot in which fishermen used to boil tar to preserve the cotton "heads" in the old lobster traps, now made of synthetics. There is an old compass with a candle holder affixed to its side, by which a Round Pond fisherman steered to his homeport in the dark ninety years ago. There are gauges for measuring lobsters, running the gamut of sizes from the time the first size limits were enacted into law in 1879 up to the present double gauge, which sets legal limits on the largest and smallest lobsters which may be kept in Maine.

One prize exhibit is a bright red "make-and-break" engine, the two cycle, three-horsepower motor which first powered lobster boats at the turn of the century. That new-fangled motor was not much trusted by lobstermen then, who always carried oars and often used them to help the engine along. The "make-and-break" engine on exhibit was originally made by H.T. Thurston of Boothbay, and restored by Loring Hanna of Round Pond.

Besides the fishing exhibits, the museum contains the huge lens from Baker Island lighthouse, southwest of Somes Sound.

The Rockland Coast Guard have also loaned a bell buoy and chain, and a whistle buoy.

Whistle buoys, which can be heard in foggy weather as well as seen in clear weather, are operated by the up and down motion of the sea. Air in the whistle tube is compressed down by the movement of the buoy, then expelled through a hole 1/32 of an inch in diameter. When it passes over a bronze disc, the buoy whistles a warning to mariners.

High above the exhibit rooms, Pemaquid Light flashes continuously day and night. That's cheaper than maintaining the apparatus required to turn it on and off. The light is visible 14 miles out to sea.

Pemaquid Light was discontinued in the 1940's as a resident station and the keeper's house was sold by the federal government to the Town of Bristol. For a while thereafter the Vocoline Company used it, installed a furnace to heat it, but removed the old six-over-nine window panes, to its architectural detriment.

Local citizens interested in preserving the fishing history of the area banded together and on July 1, 1972, the Pemaquid Fishermens' Museum was opened to the public. No admission charge is levied, but donations are sought for maintenance.

Pemaquid Point, with its stirring view of the ocean, breaking surf, and Monhegan Island, was visited last year by more than 70,000 people. The Pemaquid Artists Group operates a gallery here, which attracts over seven thousand visitors. No one has even estimated how many photos of Pemaquid Light those visitors have taken, but it may be that half a million photos of this spot are treasured in homes in every American state and scores of foreign countries.

VI
MUSCONGUS BAY

A SLOW CRUISE ACROSS MUSCONGUS BAY WITH
  JIM MCCRACKEN

WATCHING NATURE'S MYSTERIES AT LOUDS ISLAND

NEW HARBOR'S LOBSTER DECKS AND OLDTIME WETSMACKS

FIRST TRIP OUT; FIRST SWIM IN

AUDUBON ON HOG ISLAND: IDEAL MAN IN AN IDEAL JOB

HOW THE PUFFINS CAME BACK TO EASTERN EGG ROCK

NAKED LOBSTER IN HORSESHOE COVE

MONHEGAN ISLAND IN 1605

WHEN WHALES COME VISITING OFF MONHEGAN

THE YOUNGS AT PLEASANT POINT GUT

RESTORING ALLEN ISLAND

ALL HANDS TURN TO FOR FRIENDSHIP SLOOPS

TWO ISLAND AUTHORS: ELIZABETH OGILVIE AND
  DOROTHY SIMPSON

WAITING OUT THE OCEAN'S MEAN SPELLS

ITS HARD TO SPOIL THE MAINE COAST

Pemaquid Light and its reflection in tidal pool. The lighthouse was built first under President John Quincy Adams in 1827 for less than $4,000. In August, 1635, the famous Angel Gabriel struck Pemaquid Ledges with 100 early colonists aboard. Five died.

VI

*Here in Muscongus Bay are my truly home waters. Here in New
Harbor was the home mooring for Steer Clear for more than 15 years.
The hailing port on her stern still is New Harbor. My first cruising
boat, the predecessor to Steer Clear II, was a very used lobster boat.
She had her mooring just up Muscongus Bay in Round Pond harbor.
So as far as boating on the Maine coast is concerned, I grew up on
Muscongus Bay and its islands, and these will always be my home
waters.*

*Muscongus Bay is the body of water between Pemaquid and
Monhegan, and within it lies a happy concentration of the beauty, the
glory and the history of the Maine coast. Yet it is unsung and unvisit-
ed compared to Casco Bay and Penobscot Bay. Meet Muscongus Bay
and enjoy it.*

*Begin with New Harbor, narrow, secure, crowded, historic, and one
of the most beautiful fishing harbors in Maine—especially the tucked-
away Back Cove.*

*Merritt Brackett was the indispensable man for many years to
scores of lobstering and fishing boats of New Harbor. He was a doctor to sick boats and he made house calls, day or night, to heal them.
For years Steer Clear, and almost every boat in the harbor, put in a
call to Merritt when anything mechanical went wrong.*

*Merritt fixed boats here for 50 years, until arthritis crippled his
huge hands. When he was doctoring an ailment in Steer Clear's Palmer engines, he'd recall similar ailments on engines of other boats.
"Harry had the same kind of trouble two boats back. And Percy
down in Round Pond had trouble with an oil leak between his engine*

block and reverse gear, just the way you do. We'll try the same remedy on you." Merritt, big, grey-haired, quiet-talking, slow-moving, knew every engine here by its first name. He was an able, kindly, reliable friend to boats and fishermen all along mid-coast Maine. I doubt if ever again there will be a boat doctor to equal Merritt Brackett.

Manley Gilbert was "Mister New Harbor" for all the years Steer Clear home-ported there. He ran Gilbert's wharf and his wife Vi ran and made heavenly fresh raspberry pies for their little restaurant. His father and grandfather fished from New Harbor before him. Manley's light blue eyes were always twinkling, his face was forever smiling and he was one of the gentlest and polite men walking the world. He tells a story in this section about his father who at 14 years old sailed the coast in a lobster-smack and at 15 was captain of a 60-footer.

New Harbor hardly seems the right name for this history-steeped shelter. More than 381 years ago, a local Indian named Skidwarres led Raleigh Gilbert, nephew of Queen Elizabeth's famous sea captain Sir Walter Raleigh, into New Harbor. In mid summer of 1607 Gilbert had anchored his vessel, the Mary and John, eight miles across the bay in Georges Harbor on Allen Island. Gilbert and his partner, Captain George Popham aboard the Gift of God, were leading the first 120 settlers from England to establish the first white settlement at what is now called Popham, at the mouth of the Kennebec River.

Before they tried to establish the first white settlement, Gilbert wanted to make contact with the native Indians. And aboard his ship was Skidwarres, an Indian from Pemaquid, who had been kidnapped two years earlier by explorer Capt. George Weymouth and taken to England as a prize exhibit. Skidwarres was now being returned to his native land and would act as the link between the new English settlers and Indians.

According to an account written in the early 1600s, Gilbert lowered a small boat at Georges Harbor and a few sailors rowed Gilbert and Skidwarres "past many gallant islands" across the eight miles of Muscongus Bay into New Harbor. Once ashore, Skidwarres led Gilbert three miles across the peninsular to Pemaquid, where the Indian chief Nahanta had an encampment. There, Nahanta and Gilbert held a two-hour meeting. But according to records written on the voyage by James Davis, their meeting did not go well. The next day, Gilbert sailed out of Muscongus Bay for the Kennebec River, where he and

George Popham founded the ill-fated Popham colony, 13 years before the Pilgrims landed at Plymouth.

Monhegan Island was an even earlier landmark for explorers. Some believe that Vikings about 1,000 A.D. carved the rune stones near the old Coast Guard station on little Manana Island, next to Monhegan. Others tell the legendary tale that about 564 A.D. the wandering Irish monk Saint Brendan roasted a lamb here. Others say John Cabot was the first white man to set foot on Monhegan in 1494. However, written records of the voyages of Verranzano in the ship La Dauphine indicate he was at Monhegan in 1524. Martin Pring in his ships Discovery and Speedwell dropped anchor here in 1603. Captain John Smith of Pocahantas fame was here in April, 1614, and wrote such glowing descriptions of "the ile of Monahigan" and its fine fishing and hunting that eight ships from London came here in 1616.

By 1618, Monhegan had a year-round settlement. But after war between England and France spread to the North American colonies, the French Baron Castine, down the Maine coast at Castine, attacked the Monhegan settlers from a frigate and, with Indians doing most of his dirty work, he burned and laid waste the first white settlement on the island.

Baron Castine's attack on Monhegan was especially ferocious because he was settling a personal score as well as striking a blow for France against England. John Palmer of Monhegan had seized a ship carrying a cargo of wine for the baron. The missing cargo consisted of 70 'pipes' of Malaga wine (one pipe equals 126 gallons), one pipe of brandy, two pipes of oil, and 17 barrels of fruit. So the Baron's revenge was fierce. The island families fled by boat to Massachusetts, and Monhegan was abandoned.

In 1749, Monhegan was bought for a mere ten pounds, thirteen shillings, by a tinsmith from Boston named Shem Drowne, the artist who made the golden grasshopper still seen today atop Faneuil Hall in Boston. Maine paid 200 pounds to buy Monhegan back from Massachusetts.

Artists are on Monhegan today. The trek of painters to this island began 85 years ago, when Robert Henri did glorious work here. Henri sent his wild, young pupil Rockwell Kent here in 1905. Kent so loved it that he stayed, working as sternman on a lobster boat, womanizing, fighting and painting some of his best work. Then, just before World

War I, George Bellows painted here for three years, followed much later by Joseph de Martini, Leo Meissner, Reuben Tam and Jamie Wyeth, who has a house on the island.

Monhegan is a summer mecca for tourists now, with tour boats and mail boats delivering hundreds of visitors daily. Yet Monhegan protects its land and shore and fishing by strict regulations, self-imposed. Monhegan lobstermen work their traps in the bitter Atlantic only from January till June. Monhegan men fish in the toughest weather when thousands of lobstermen do no go out to sea. For the other six months, Monhegan lobsters multiply in safety. No one except year-round Monhegan islanders is allowed to lobster within three miles of the island.

Monhegan's land is protected too. Half the island is preserved forever wild, thanks to a fund set up by the heirs of Thomas Edison. On the rest of the island, limited sources of fresh water, further enforced by building codes, virtually prohibit the building of more houses. An island regulation forbids overnight camping; and a mooring in the harbor is seldom available. The simplest way to visit Monhegan is on a mail boat from Port Clyde or tour boat from Boothbay Harbor, and spend the day enjoying Monhegan with its silent Cathedral Woods, its galaxy of wild flowers, its cliffs towering 163 feet over the crashing surf of the Atlantic Ocean.

There are dozens of enticing islands in Muscongus Bay. The one I visit most often is Louds Island because of its quiet coves and sweeping, empty beaches. The island is named for William Loud, a retired English naval officer who settled here in 1750, after buying the island, then called Muscongus Island, from Shem Drowne, the same Boston tinsmith who paid ten pounds for Monhegan. Louds inhabitants turned obstinate, and Democratic to boot, in President Lincoln's time. Their Democratic leaning hugely upset the staunch Republicans in the mainland Town of Bristol, where Louds islanders voted and paid taxes. Bristol took their money, but would not accept their votes for a Democrat and tossed the island's ballots into the fire. Nevertheless, Bristol demanded the island furnish nine men for the Union Army, as part of the 45 man quota for the whole district. The islanders, in fury because their votes had been burned, refused to go. The Union Army dispatched an army officer bristling with authority to collect the draftees. All the men were out lobstering when the officer came

ashore. No sooner had he stated his business that an island wife,
cooking dinner, bombarded him with hot roast potatoes. The major
fled. The island men never went to fight in the Civil War.

The places and pleasures of Muscongus Bay are so many and so
varied they'd fill two dozen summers. Here is a smattering of the joys
I found aboard Steer Clear in Muscongus Bay.

A SLOW CRUISE ACROSS MUSCONGUS BAY WITH JIM MCCRACKEN

MUSCONGUS BAY — The best place in the world to begin to know a man and build a friendship is at sea on a small boat.

This is how I began to know Jim McCracken who came back home to Maine after 26 years as an editor of the Reader's Digest. He was a white-haired man with eyes as blue as Galway Bay and a tongue blessed with the story-telling magic of an Irish leprechaun. He died as 1988 began.

One peacock day in June, McCracken came cruising with me among the islands of Muscongus Bay. Jim and I ran the boat from "the poor man's flying bridge," the simplest, cheapest and most practicable contrivance for getting the benefits of a flying bridge without top heaviness.

McCracken and I sat up there, basking in the sun, doing a relaxed five knots, as we cruised out of New Harbor, past uninhabited Haddock and Ross Islands. Gulls soared up from Haddock where they nest by the hundreds and raise fluffy fledglings, which, when disturbed, sit motionless and marvelously camouflaged to match the speckled granite ledges where they first taste life. On Ross, there are no trees, no bushes. Long ago, sheep pastured on this small island, ate every blessed thing, roots and all. To this day, little grows on Ross.

Threading our slow course through hundreds of lobster buoys and toggles, we ease along the channel between Louds and Marsh Islands, past barren-looking Killick Stone, where wild iris grow in sea-sprayed secrecy and bloom to richer blues and deeper purples than their mainland cousins. On past tiny Indian Island, where the great Indian chief Samoset is buried, according to its owners, Judy and Mac MacKenzie. Off to the east we see Wreck Island where herons by the hundreds nest high in the dark evergreens. But in 20 years, their droppings will likely kill these trees. Wreck leads into the weirdly named Jones' Sea Garden, and a bit seaward lies that blob named Eastern Egg Rock, where the puffins are coming back to nest again. Then comes lovely Georges Harbor, with a stone cross to mark the spot where Captain George Weymouth landed and held the first Protestant service in the new world on a Sunday in 1605.

Between these history-haunted islands, McCracken tells the 20th century story of his frantic days as one of the unknown breed of bread-and-butter writers, the prolific pounders who turned out millions of words for radio serials.

"I sat here in Maine and pounded out three half-hour shows a week for The Cisco Kid, rival of The Lone Ranger, all about cowboys, sheriffs and the wild west. But I'd never been west of the Ohio River. Got paid the great sum of $50 a show to start. Then I wrote a private eye radio serial—Boston Blackie—though I had no firsthand knowledge of cops and crime, or even of Boston. For two years, I pounded out all those cliffhangers of the wild west and big city detective work from a farm in Jefferson, Maine, where my wife's people had a summer camp. I finally dried up, burned out after a million words or so. So I slammed shut the typewriter and switched from grinding out radio dramas to editing. Went to the Reader's Digest and stayed 26 years."

We turned and cruised back west again across Muscongus Bay, and dropped anchor off a sandy beach on Louds Island, ate a lazy lunch and reminisced, amazed at how often our paths had crossed.

We climbed into the dinghy and went ashore to explore Louds Island. A mile down the beach, we turned inland to meadows where farms, long abandoned, had once flourished. I led Jim to the island cemetery.

No more than two dozen headstones stand in this remote spot of sacred ground, protected still by an ancient wall, built from rocks taken from the meadow, and shaded and sheltered by a single oak tree. We mourn for a moment over the tender, tiny grave of an infant one year and 10 months old, buried here more than 100 years ago. Nearby are the lichen-yellowed headstones of ship captains and their wives who lived to be over 80. And then, there are newer headstones, fresh carved in 1969, to the Polands who sailed and fished off these islands for generations. Near the shade tree is the newest grave. Flying over it is a fading blue and white pennant with the legend "In Memoriam . . . Portland Police Department." It is the grave of Frank D. Ellsworth who owned this part of Louds Island and drowned here in May 1978. We had known Frank, and stand at his grave, looking out across the water to the islands he had loved.

Overhead two ospreys soar, in search of food for young in the nearby nest they have used for years. Tide is going out and a great grey heron stalks the flats on delicate, spindly legs. Offshore a pair of seals are playing. Standing on a ledge, looking out at some of the most lovely scenery in the world, we count 19 islands; and we feel the long, imperishable continuity of Maine history and people.

The Ice Age swept through here 10,000 years ago, leaving the granite ledge on which we stand. Samoset and the Abenaki Indians he led fished these waters and farmed this island land. Alexander Gould in 1650 was probably the first white settler to walk this beach. William Loud, once an officer in the English navy, built his home here 248 years ago.

Back aboard Steer Clear, we head home to New Harbor. We pass the Japanese style cottages on Marsh Island, built for William Sloane Coffin, when he was the controversial chaplain at Yale during the Vietnam war protests. It is sunset now and in the sky we hear the drone of a spotter plane, twisting, banking, swooping low among the ageless islands. The pilot is searching for the same species of fish which brought tough men in small boats across the Atlantic in 1610 to fish here. Tonight the pilot will radio a steel-hulled, diesel-powered seiner that he had spotted a big school and to get out here and set nets.

Men and their machines change. But the islands and the fish remain the same.

WATCHING NATURE'S MYSTERIES

LOUDS ISLAND — Something was moving in the sea oats. No breeze blew, but beyond the tide mark on the empty beach the high green grasses of the sea oats were swaying.

Curious, I reached to the navigator's table on Steer Clear and picked up the binoculars and focused on the swaying sea oats. I was able to see a light brown blur moving among the top of the stalks. Maybe some seabird, feeding at daybreak, I thought, though the blur did not move like a bird.

Just then, the grasses parted a little and revealed the head of a grazing deer. A second later, its mate moved into view. I called to my shipmate sleeping below in the cabin, who came quickly on deck, carrying another pair of binoculars. "Over there, behind the sea oats! Look quickly!"

Quiet though we were, our whispers carried across the 100 feet of water and 50 feet of beach loudly enough to alert the two deer. Now their heads raised up above the high sea oats, and they gazed intently to where Steer Clear was anchored.

We lowered our voices. But those long ears of the deer pricked up, and their heads swung slowly left to right, sweeping like the antenna of radar, trying to pinpoint the human sound on the silent air of daybreak over a Maine island.

For moments, both sides stood transfixed. Two humans on the boat eyeing two deer on the shore. Two deer on the island, standing motionless, their ears straining for a sound from us. The skiff ripped the silent tension. Some tidal current beneath the surface of the sea suddenly nudged the skiff and it banged on the hull of Steer Clear.

The deer fled.

We put down the binoculars, happy to have shared this silent moment with two delicate deer, grazing at dawn on an island shore.

The sea around us was smooth, empty, silent at daybreak. No sound of a lobster boat, no sight of sail. No breeze to ruffle the flat silverness of the sea. It was not yet 5 a.m., and we sat in the cockpit, waiting for the new day to begin.

A lonely loon laughed, breaking the stillness with its eerie sound. Not many loons sleep the night on the ocean. Most are inland on the lakes, raising their young. We hear a whirring over us. A great blue heron from the island shore is moving out on the first flight of the day, huge wings noisy on the dew-soaked air as it gains speed and altitude. Now, on the seaward side, we hear a clumsy splashing and thrashing in the water. A shag, a cormorant, is taking off.

Shags have a terrible time getting airborne when they take off from the sea. They simply cannot get up the necessary airspeed as quickly as gulls or ducks. Shags bounce and splash across the water, legs and webbed feet beating the surface noisily and clumsily, working hard as an overloaded, underpowered plane wobbling down a runway for take-off.

Finally, as it seems about to crash, the shag gets airborne. Then a magical grace and daring skill climbs into its cockpit, and the wide-winged bird skims the waves, the downward beat of its wings brushing the ocean in a brilliant display of low flying.

Steer Clear swings slowly on her anchor, moving a few degrees, stopping, moving a few more degrees. This is the best way to see the wondrous world of an island shore, a kind of slice-by-slice tunnel vision, which focuses your eyes on one slice of a cove at a time. This way you see far more than by taking in the full sweep all at once.

There is a new blow-down, a spruce uprooted in a violent storm last winter, its weird maze of underground roots exposed to human eye, a network of miracles. Spanish moss is killing its neighbors, in an endearing, misty green but murderous embrace. Looking lovely and innocent, the moss is silently throttling to death a hundred trees.

Yet the birds sing unperturbed by the sweet strangulation. Yellow warblers flash their brilliant beauty among lush bushes of sea-scented wild roses.

Hungry fish crows, dressed in witches' black, caw raucously as they swoop to devour. An osprey circles her untidy nest, clutching a still-wriggling small fish in her talons; and then, sweet mother, she feeds it to her baby.

The morning breeze freshens. It is 7 a.m. and the sun is high enough now to disturb the stillness, and quickly the breeze picks up to five, to 10 and then to 15 miles an hour by 7:30 a.m.

Steer Clear swings farther, this time to reveal three big mother eider ducks shepherding a dozen furry babies around the cove. A black-wing gull swoops on the hunt, and the mothers unite to drive off the predator. Then there is one short, sharp squeal. The loon, submerged like a submarine, seizes a baby eider from below.

The world and its creatures are about their daily business. The deer have long gone and that movement among the wild sea oats now is nothing but the wind, blowing in from Monhegan.

NEW HARBOR'S LOBSTER DECKS AND OLDTIME WET-SMACKS

NEW HARBOR — Free with every lobster here, you get a million-dollar view—a view that will live in you memory's eye long after your digestive tract has forgotten Homarus Americanus. Lobster-eating here delights the eyes as much as the taste buds.

Lobster lofts are giant-sized decks, built high above the water of New Harbor. They are open to the sky, to the sunset, to the ocean breezes— and the ocean fogs. They are open also to dive-bombing attacks by voracious seagulls, who sometimes swoop down, seize and fly off with a lobster claw snatched from the table. On a clear day from the lobster lofts

New Harbor—This was home to Steer Clear for 15 years, and is still the hailing port on her stern. This is one of the prettiest working har-

at New Harbor, you can see forever. And what a sight it is.

Close-in are the working boats almost under your table. Look down and you see lobstermen coming alongside the wharf to sell the lobsters you'll eat tomorrow. Look across the lovely, narrow harbor and you'll see draggers coming home after hard work at sea; you'll see men on the seine boats preparing to leave at sundown, guided by a spotting plane overhead to a fish-crowded cove where they will set their nets.

Out at the harbor entrance you'll see the big marker buoy ride the swells rolling up Muscongus Bay from Pemaquid Point and the Atlantic beyond.

First off-shore island your eye spots is Haddock, the nearby island inhabited only by gulls, and whose meadow is filled with wild iris and whose shores brim with driftwood, salt-cured and sun-bleached. Beyond is Wreck Island, nesting place for herons; to the north is Louds Island which once seceded from the United States. And everywhere, bobbing brightly on a summer sea, are myriads of brilliant lobster-trap buoys.

bors on the Maine Coast. But it is narrower in fact than it looks in this wide angle picture.

Stretch you eyesight to reach 10 miles and you'll see the steep cliffs of famed Monhegan Island.

The tall lonely lighthouse almost due east is Franklin Light. South from Franklin, but hidden, lies Friendship, home of the famous Friendship sloops. Up the bay as you look outward from New Harbor lies Hog Island, run by the National Audubon Society; behind you are the archaeological diggings at Pemaquid, where white settlers were doing business before Pilgrims arrived.

This is the million dollar view which comes free with the lobsters on the old Gilbert dock in New Harbor.

Gilberts have been "in lobster" at New Harbor for 150 years.

Grandfather Gilbert wet-smacked lobsters—20,000 lobsters at a clip across the Bay of Fundy—for the Willard-Daggett Fish Company in Portland.

"My father," Manley Gilbert once told me on the old Gilbert wharf, "skippered his first schooner when he was 14. One stormy night he was forced to lay-over out at Monhegan. In the bad storm, his schooner was wrecked, and my dad felt his sea-going career was over at age 14. The owners, Wilson-Daggett, ordered him down to Portland, and he went. Caught the train out of Damariscotta, carrying his money satchel, his ship's log and his papers, expecting to be fired.

"Instead they gave him a 60-foot steam vessel and sent him out again as skipper, aged 15 by then. He was still wet-smacking the coast 40 years later, when I was a boy old enough to go with him."

A wet-smack is a vessel with a double bottom. Below the "false" firm deck, lies the wet hold, punctured so sea water can flow constantly through it. Into that wet hold went over 20,000 lobsters, taken downeast, to be brought live to market in Portland.

Ashore in those days, when lobsters were 10 cents each, and long before lobster lofts were dreamed of, another Gilbert brother ran a store and a small machine shop in New Harbor. By the 1930's a little restaurant was opened by the Gilberts.

But not everybody you'll see eating lobster at New Harbor is a native or an ordinary tourist. Look around you. Maybe the bean pole man in red shirt and shorts at the next table will be the famous baby doctor Benjamin Spock, ashore from his 23-foot sail boat. Or maybe you'll recognize that haughty looking fellow at the table behind, off a far bigger, more splendid yacht. That's William Buckley, the forked-tongued political wit from TV's "Firing Line."

Celebrities by the dozen and ordinary folk by the thousands flock to eat the lobster and enjoy the view from New Harbor's lobster lofts.

One way to spot celebrities from the cities is to look for the people who don't know how to eat a lobster without a knife. Here you use your hands to break soft shells or borrow a hammer for hard shells. But if a man or woman asks for a knife, they are from away.

First trip out; first swim in

NEW HARBOR — The waters of Muscongus Bay and the passage between Haddock and Ross, close-in islands, seem strangely naked in early May. The lobster buoys are missing. The sea looks forlorn without them.

Water temperature is the reason no traps are here. The lobsters have

New Harbor—The old pogie factory astern of Steer Clear's mooring for many years.

not yet crawled the long journey inshore to their summer feeding grounds. The water is still too cold in May.

But their migration is starting. Lobsters and summer visitors migrate to Maine and depart on the same temperature clock. When the cold of winter comes to Maine, lobsters and summer folk leave for warmer temperatures.

Summer people wing it to Florida or the Virgin Islands, hopping onto planes.

Lobsters do it more slowly. The crawl out to deeper water, miles off shore. Out there, the cold of winter does not penetrate so severely down into the deep water crevices where lobsters spend their winters.

But it is tougher on the fishermen and boats which must go offshore in winter to catch them. This is why the number of lobster boats out hauling traps decreases dramatically by Christmas, and why the prices for lobster go higher.

By June, the water inshore is slowly getting warmer and soon the lobsters will be swimming and crawling closer to the coast, the islands and shallow water, as the sun warms it.

But now, in May, the inshore water temperature is bone-chilling. I know. I had to go swimming in it.

Thank heaven for wet suits. I have learned to stow my wet suit aboard as soon as my boat is launched. Steer Clear was launched April 28th. I got my comeuppance, for rushing the season. It poured rain for the next three weeks, and we were able to go out in the boat only twice.

But by the end of May, the weather turned glorious. We rushed to Steer Clear and loaded her with gear, clothing and galley supplies.

We headed for the islands of Muscongus Bay which I had not seen for seven long months. We circled Haddock, went down the passage between Marsh and Louds Islands, cut east by Killick Stone, past Thief Island, went inside Wreck Island and Harbor Island, paid a quick obeisance to George's Harbor, Banner and Allen Islands, waved to the Monhegan boat coming out from Port Clyde, crept past a favorite cove on Burnt Island, turned by Old Man and Old Lady Ledges to come down toward Eastern Egg Rock, where the puffins will soon be winging home.

At the nasty breaking seas over the Devil's Elbow, we put the glasses on Wreck Island to check on the huge untidy nests where herons raise their young. I turned again, putting up large flights of sea ducks all the way. The male eiders are still inshore, with the mousy-feathered females. Soon those males will leave to spend summer at sea, while the females raise their young and stand guard over those feathery rafts of babies. We drifted down toward Jones' Sea Garden.

My navigator watched, amused as I made the rounds of my favorite islands. "You are like a dog, getting back to his old haunts. Making the rounds of his territory, leaving his mark on every fence post," observed the navigator.

Then came the icy swim.

It was then that we picked up yards of submerged fish net. A dragger, whose nets had been ripped on sharp rocks on the ocean bottom, had thrown overboard those parts of the net beyond repair. In two miserable seconds, that net was wound tight around Steer Clear's rudders and propellers.

That's when I found out the water temperature was 49 degrees.

I dropped anchor and climbed into my wet suit, found the long sharp fish knife in the ditty box and peeled back the black tape which protects the cutting edge. On my thumb, it felt razor sharp. I slid the knife's string collar over my wrist, so as not to lose it in the ocean. Then, I made a rescue line fast to a stern cleat and drifted it overboard, so it would be in easy reach when I was in the ocean.

The moment had come to go overboard. There was no minor chore left to postpone this action. Wearing a false smile, I clambered down the boarding ladder, stuck one foot into the water.

Lord, that ocean was cold! "If its too cold for a lobster, why the devil am I getting into it?" I muttered.

That first instant when the icy ocean trickled inside my wet suit was bad, yet not quite so bad as the anticipation. I dove down under the hull, slashing at the net entwined around the propellers. With each handful I cut free, I'd surface and throw the stuff up into the cockpit. The job went well until the last few feet of net. That was wound in so tightly that it was hard to get a knife to cut through it.

These final moments of cutting are the ones I dread. Curled up in a fetal position under the hull, cold, hurrying, slashing with a razor-sharp knife at twine. That's when I recall a girl at Harbor Island who slashed her own toes with her knife, doing the same job. Yet she never felt the wound due to the cold. Until she stood bleeding on deck, with toes half off, she never knew she had butchered herself.

Finally, the last of the net was cut out. I got safely back on deck, blue with cold. There is nothing more stupid-looking than a shivering man trying to get out of a wet suit which simply will not peel off. This second skin clings and clings, despite the weirdest contortions to be shed of it. At last I'm free and stark naked, towelling hard to get the cold blood flowing. That is the moment when a lobsterman friend comes slowly astern, cuts engines, looks me over and says "Swimmin' a bit early ain't yer, Bill?"

Audubon on Hog Island: Ideal Man in an Ideal Job

HOG ISLAND — It happens too seldom. But when a man and his work, his home, his wife and his island all fit together in happy harmony, there is a rightness to the world.

More than 50 people from dozens of states, Canada and Germany find this rightness and more when they set foot on Hog Island in Muscongus Bay.

Hog Island is the oldest National Audubon camp in the nation. The island's most permanent fixture is John Johansen, the boatsman-warden who began his work here year-round in 1973.

Johansen, a retired Coast Guardsman, had already worked 20 years among the islands of Maine, repairing and painting remote lighthouses, laying cables to offshore lights, building ramps and railways for lifeboats.

One day in Camden soon after his retirement, Johansen heard that the Audubon camp on Hog Island was looking for a chief boatsman and caretaker. He got the job. The man and the island have been ideally matched ever since.

"Take the mooring closest to the island shore and lie on it overnight," Johansen shouted from Hog Island wharf. We tied Steer Clear to the mooring and rowed ashore to talk with Johansen.

The 333-acre Todd Wildlife Sanctuary on Hog Island was established in 1936 as the first of four Audubon camps for adults in the United States. From the end of June until Labor Day adult campers arrive on Hog Island for a two-week experience they are likely to treasure for the rest of their lives.

Each summer, four two-week sessions are conducted on Hog Island. More than 200 men and women aged from 17 to 70, come from across the nation and several foreign countries to enjoy an intensive living-and-learning experience on one of the loveliest islands along the Maine coast.

Each day begins with the ringing of a great ship's bell on the island shore at 6:30 a.m. After breakfast, the campers divide into small groups and the day's activities get under way. They will last until 10 at night.

Classrooms are the spruce forests, the island shores, the ocean itself, the tidal mudflats, the great blue heron colony on nearby Wreck Island, the puffin colony on Eastern Egg Rock, the harbor seals sunning on the ledges.

The instructors are enthusiastic, experienced experts in specialized fields. Steve Kress, a Ph.D. from Cornell University, has been teaching here for 20 years. Kress started the puffin project on Eastern Egg Rock, an uninhabited small island halfway between Hog Island and Monhegan. Kress began his project to bring puffins back to Eastern Egg Rock in 1974. Since then dozens of young puffins have been fledged there.

National Audubon camp on Hog Island, Muscongus Bay, looking from Bremen, on the mainland.

Traveling aboard Osprey and Puffin, the two large boats belonging to the Audubon Society, campers go to other islands in Muscongus Bay. Anchoring offshore, they climb into the dories towed behind Osprey and Puffin and land, for example, on Wreck Island to see great blue herons nesting and raising their young on this uninhabited island.

Every class gets its turn setting a drag off the stern of Osprey, under the guidance of a marine biologist. Classes bring their assorted catch of marine life back to the lab on Hog Island to study the various species under microscopes at night.

While some classes are away on the boats, others are working with instructors in the spruce forests, the meadows and the shoreline of Hog Island. Peter Salmansohn, a teacher from Rhode Island, may be explaining the geology of rocks. Or Grace Bomarito, a botanist from Detroit, may be opening fascinating new worlds to her students as they examine scores of different island plants and flowers.

The staff is chosen, in part, because each has a strong personal attachment to Maine islands in addition to a needed technical skill. Many return summer after summer.

Johansen is Mr. Hog Island, the only person working here year-round. "Hog Island belongs to me alone 10 months a year. I share it with others two months a year," he says. "I love this place and this job." Johansen and his wife Mary live year round in an old farmhouse on the mainland at Bremen, a short row across Hockamock Channel from Hog Island. From their porch, they look across a big sloping meadow to Hog and 19 other islands in Muscongus Bay.

"A millionaire could afford this place; but could never find it," he says standing on his wharf. His year-round duty is to maintain the Audubon buildings on Hog, on the mainland, the three wharfs, the half-dozen boats and all the attendant machinery.

"I enjoy doing all that. But what I love is what the island does to the people who come here from their city jobs. "When I take them off after two weeks on the island, on the water, on the mudflats, they can't bear to say goodbye to this place and this way of life. They're very quiet on that last boat trip. You could cut the emotion with a knife, it's so thick."

How the puffins came back to Eastern Egg Rock

EASTERN EGG ROCK — In bigger numbers than ever before, the puffins stand on Eastern Egg Rock, white chests thrown boldly out, motionless, facing the Atlantic.

We steered east from Pemaquid Point then bore down to the low-lying ledge called Eastern Egg Rock, in Muscongus Bay, a couple of miles from Monhegan.

No sign of puffins as we approached. Slowly, feeling disappointment, we rounded the tip of Egg Rock, dodging lobster buoys, and suddenly there stood the puffins. They looked as preposterous yet as dignified, as comic yet as endearing, as they do on picture postcards.

Being helmsman at a moment like this is a tantalizing job. There, only a few yards to port, stand the bewitching puffins. But a few yards closer are lobster buoys, toggles and the pot warp which loves to wrap around propellers. Look too long at the puffins and pay the price of pot warp in the propellers, and then the penalty of diving overboard, knife in hand, and swimming under the boat to cut the pot warp which has entangled

Puffins on Eastern Egg Rock, between Pemaquid and Monhegan. Efforts are being made by the National Audubon to establish a puffin colony here.

you, and then retie the severed ends so the lobsterman has no trouble locating his trap.

As helmsman, I remember this. I keep my eye on the pots, resist the temptation to gawk at the puffins and resolutely pay attention to duty, while the ardent birdwatcher on board shrieks her excitement at what she sees.

After 10 minutes of such discipline, I make her spell me at the helm, take the fieldglasses and climb out on the bow for a look myself.

Puffins are penguin-like birds, with sad clown eyes and outsize red, blue and yellow beaks. Their primary home on the Atlantic seaboard is in Witless Bay, Newfoundland. Once they were plentiful here on Eastern Egg Rock too. But about 100 years ago, when it was fashionable for ladies to wear puffin plumes in their hats, hunters came to Eastern Egg Rock and spread huge fish nets over the little island. When the puffins emerged from their burrows, they were trapped and killed by the thousands. In the end, the puffin colonies died out in Maine, except for colonies on Matinicus Rock, far out to sea, and Machias Seal Island, far down east on the water border with Canada.

No puffins had nested here on Eastern Egg Rock since 1895. Then in 1973 a young, tenacious ornithinologist named Dr. Stephen Kress, from Cornell University, came to Muscongus Bay as an instructor at the National Audubon camp on nearby Hog Island. Kress decided to try to woo the puffins back to Eastern Egg Rock.

Kress, armed with a dozen permits from Maine, U.S. and Canadian governments, began small, with fewer than a dozen chicks transplanted from Witless Bay when they were ten days old.

Every year since, Kress and his happy band of puffin helpers, have brought more puffins, usually 100 at a time, from other nesting places to Eastern Egg Rock. He catches them, puts them into empty 42-ounce fruit juice cans, packs the cans into special cases, then carries them onto a charter plane for the flight from Newfoundland to Wiscasset. From there he rushes them by truck and then by boat to burrows on Eastern Egg Rock. In less than 20 hours, the transplanted puffins are in their new home in Muscongus Bay.

And year after year Kress and company wait. Wait and hope. They hope that the puffins they hand-fed until that crucial night when the baby puffin "fledged," and flew off to some unknown part of the ocean, will survive. They hope that four or five years later that same bird will return to breed on Eastern Egg Rock.

Edie Weinstein was a puffin helper at Eastern Egg Rock for four years. At 29, she held the record for continuous living on this barren ledge among the puffins and the terns—three weeks on end. It is far from an easy life out here, day and night, in fair and foul weather, living in a wooden shack, feeding off supplies of tinned food and water. But to her, it was a busy and exciting life.

Busy because the baby puffins brought here must be hand fed. Twice a day at each burrow, Edie laid out 14 small frozen smelts, which she had unfrozen by dipping in sea water. Here there are no mother birds to catch fish for the young. A good working mother puffin carries half a dozen small fish in her mouth, holding each there while she catches yet another. Then she lays her hoard of food near the entrance to the burrow for her one small chick to eat. Those chicks grow fast, and must be fed about 28 fish, two or three inches long, each day. A mother cannot possibly work hard enough to feed more than one baby.

This is one reason it is such a slow, risky, painstaking business to re-establish a puffin colony. Only one egg is raised. Then the fledgling flies off when it is 40 to 45 days old and lives at sea for three years—if it survives. Then, maybe, that puffin will return to Eastern Egg Rock, where it was fledged, finding this tiny ledge in the magical way certain birds return to their birthplace.

"Last night" Edie told me in August 1981, "our first fledgling flew away. I put a little wooden stick in front of each burrow and watch each morning to see if the stick has been knocked down. When it's knocked down, that is a sign that the baby puffin has come out of its burrow to exercise its wings and muscles in the night. This had been happening for seven nights at this particular burrow. Then this morning, the 14 small smelts I had left there for food were untouched. I reached down into the four foot long burrow to see if the chick was there. It was not. It had jumped off the cliff and flown into the night, out to the ocean. That is the first flight a puffin makes."

It is of course a wrench to see the babies vanish. But that wrench has its own exciting compensations. Each fledgling is banded, so it can be identified. Identifying a returning bird is rare excitement and huge and motherly satisfaction.

"This year I was out on Egg Rock when a bird I had raised three years before flew back home and landed where it had fledged. I saw it. I recognized it. Sure, it wore its identifying band too. Bird Number 27. It was mine, the baby I had fed, and it had come back to Eastern Egg Rock. So did bird 16," reported Edie.

The young puffins have their enemies who eat them, notably black-backed gulls, which have multiplied hugely, from 11,000 pairs to 35,000 pairs.

To scare off this enemy, the Audubon Society introduced a large colony of Arctic and Common terns onto Egg Rock. The agile, aggressive terns act as a kind of air umbrella over the baby puffins, making the predator gulls keep their distance. To inveigle terns to Eastern Egg Rock, the Audubon Society plays tape recordings of the siren songs of other terns.

Today Leach's petrels also share this scarred, weathered island ledge with the puffins. Petrels, like puffins, make their nests underground or in rock crevices.

The puffin colony on Eastern Egg Rock is still small; its long term future is still in doubt. But the outlook for success grows more promising. On the day we circled the island in Steer Clear, we counted 27 puffins standing on the rocks. "Our highest count ever was 31," says Edie. "And I'm sure there were others we could not see." Furthermore, female puffins have returned to lay eggs in burrows on the island. If they raise their single egg, then puffins will again be breeding on Eastern Egg Rock, for the first time in almost 100 years.

But the puffins will not multiply quickly. First, they do not mate until they are almost five years old. Second, they lay only one egg, in June, which hatches 45 days later. Therefore it is vital that this embryo colony being re-established on Eastern Egg Rock be protected.

As I maneuvered Steer Clear for a last, loving look at the puffins, I understood why the first explorers, with so much else on their minds, were so taken by these wonderous birds that they made special mention of them in their logbooks. Samuel de Champlain, in his map dated 1607, named Machias Seal Island "Puffin Island." Eastern Egg Rock may one day be re-christened Puffin Island of Muscongus Bay.

NAKED LOBSTER IN HORSESHOE COVE

CRANBERRY ISLAND — The dark-haired young man in yellow oilskin pants was standing in his skiff when he drew alongside Steer Clear, anchored in the narrow Horseshoe Cove on Cranberry Island where we had spent the night.

"I've got a lobster here which just shedded in my boat," he said. "Won't live till I get in. No good wasting it. Would you want to cook it right now for breakfast?"

He handed across a lobster without a trace of shell at all. Just soft, naked flesh. Then he held up the shell the lobster had shed a few moments ago, put his outboard in gear and sped off. We immediately cooked the shell-less lobster, steaming it very briefly because there was no shell for the heat to penetrate. The flesh quickly turned scarlet, far brighter red than the shell of cooked lobster. We ate fresh lobster omelet for breakfast, a more festive start to the day than a millionaire gourmet can buy.

Two summers had passed since we last spent a day and night in this narrow cove, where there is barely room for one small boat to swing. To get inside, you must run a tricky obstacle course between a hundred closely set traps. The gaudy, freshly-painted lobster buoys are spectacular splashes of brilliance, with dayglow colors of orange, green, blue and yellow bobbing on a flat sea. But they are a minefield of a kind. Beyond the last trap at the cove's entrance, there is only five feet of water at dead low tide. At low water, the ledges surrounding the cove turn into miniature mountains hemming in Steer Clear. But the low-tide reward is a sandy beach, edged by wild blue iris, giant yellow mullion, pink and white morning glories, tall sea dandelions and masses of beach peas with their two-toned purple flowers.

As the tide turns, the cove changes. The ledges surrounding Steer Clear shrink from 14 feet high to a mere five feet. The sandy beach disappears. The depth finder shows the water under the hull has deepened from five to 14 feet at full high.

The previous afternoon a different lobsterman had come hauling close to Horseshoe Cove. We had just climbed back aboard Steer Clear after many swims and miles of beachcombing. The idea of fresh lobsters for dinner was enticing. So, not knowing we'd be given lobster for breakfast next morning, my dog and I jumped into the dinghy and rowed out to do a little business. Wayne Havener, a fine, gray-haired lobster-catcher from Friendship aboard his Stephanie G., sold us three soft-shells. As the sun went down, hot and huge, we sat on the open deck eating some of the sweetest lobster in the world. After chewing a claw or a tail, we'd toss the shell overboard, back to the sea which nurtured it. Quickly, the boat was surrounded by schools of harbor pollack, jumping ravenously for the remnants, devouring them before gulls came swarming in to scavenge. The lonely cove was the most handsome, seabreeze-cooled restaurant possible; and the pollack staged a splendid floor show.

But even harbor pollack have their likes and dislikes. We found they dislike snails cooked in garlic butter. We had picked up three dozen snails along the beach and enjoyed most of them as appetizers. But the pollack swam away in disgust when we offered them what was left of our snails in garlic.

A sailor's pastime at night is to eavesdrop on conversations over the marine radio. We tune in on Channel 26, used by cruising boats to place phone calls through the Camden Marine operators to all parts of the U.S. and once in a while to foreign countries. Of course, eavesdropping is nosey; but there is something companionable about overhearing these snippets of other sailors' lives and loves and work. Everybody does it.

The operators at Camden Marine are swamped on summer nights with calls from cruising yachts. All boats must give their names—a delicious dictionary of sea dreams—and their call letters. This is followed by an indigestible concoction of numerical and alphabet soup, the area codes and numbers they are phoning plus the cacophony of credit card numerals. Placing a ship-to-shore call is a complex business. But the conversations, which other boats can overhear, are a delight of love and whimsy, sometimes sadly spiced with minor tragedies. These are innocent peeks at family lives usually hidden from strangers by sealed envelopes, closed doors and private phones.

One young boy, left at home far away, took a call from his father aboard a boat off the Maine coast. The father was exuberant, happy to hear his son's voice. Not so with the boy, who had never before had a call from a boat. Finally the lad said, "This doesn't sound like my Dad. Who is this?" The father could not satisfy his son's doubts that it was indeed him. So out of the blue, the boy asked: "What's my birthday?" The flabbergasted father stumbled over the date, then got the year wrong; and lost credibility. "Here son, I will put your mother on the microphone." The boy told his mother he wanted to know who that man was, because he didn't sound a bit like Dad.

Another call was to a bright, laughing daughter at home who had just taken some grueling exams, but refused to forecast to her cruising parents how well she had done. But she told the world that in studious preparation for the exams she had not had a beer for three weeks, and now was on her way to celebrate and make up for lost time. Her embarrassed mother on the boat urged more discretion "because every boat in Maine may be listening in."

One call from boat to home triggered a detailed inch-by-inch description from grandfather of an operation just performed on his big toe. Grandfather sang the praises of his toe doctor to all ships at sea.

We heard the start, but alas, not the conclusion of imminent violence at sea. A fishing vessel called the Coast Guard on emergency Channel 16 to report a suspicious boat circling him. He gave its name and description. The Coast Guard contacted the named vessel, finally raised an answer. And that skipper said: "I'm scared to death out here. That fishing boat is tailing me. He says he has a shotgun ready." Then the fishing vessel came back on the air to complain that the other vessel had deliberately cut his trawl nets. The young Coast Guard voice urged both men to cool it. "Stay calm. Take no action against each other. I'm dispatching a boat out to you now. This needs jurisdiction, a referee. Cool it, both of you. We are on the way. And a Marine Warden is on his way, too.''

I cut off the marine radio telephone, and turn on the depth finder, worrying about how much more the tide will drop in Horseshoe Cove.

When the tide is running out at night and the water under your anchored boat is getting shallow enough to bring on worry as to how much more will drain out, there is a rule of thumb worth remembering. According to this rule, the tide rises and falls 1/12th of its range during the first and sixth hours after high and low water slack; 2/12ths during the second and fifth hours; 3/12ths during the third and fourth hours.

At dark of midnight, as you look off the bow, wondering how much more the tide will drop during the final hour, it is comforting to know that 11/12ths of the water has gone; and you are likely to get by without trouble in the next few minutes.

Thunderstorms have been clobbering parts of inland Maine, according to the NOAA weather reports on the radio. The heat and stickiness even out here among the islands is threatening thunder to come. There is haze, milkiness, and some fog. When we get caught in a thunderstorm at sea, the dog is terrified and I only pretend to be calm.

Once, in Blue Hill, we had been caught on anchor in a very severe and scary thunder and lightning storm. We huddled in fright as the lightning struck around us. Then one bolt hit Steer Clear through the radio antenna. For a moment we felt the fear of sudden death. Then the storm stopped as suddenly as it had started, and the moon and stars came out, bringing the amazing grace of peace after frenzy.

This time the thunderstorm passes to the west and misses us, thank heaven.

We tune back to emergency Channel 16. We hear a boat farther down east in trouble, calling for help. The storm has not caused their trouble. But a bee has. Someone aboard was badly stung on a remote island, and has begun to suffer a severe reaction. The boat is racing for harbor. The Coast Guard promises them an ambulance and medics will be waiting at the dock.

We are snug and blessedly safe from storm and bee stings. We switch off the radio and the troubles of the world. We put Beethoven's Seventh Symphony on the tape deck, turn the volume up to full. The majesty of his music rings out gloriously across the sea.

Monhegan Island in 1605

MONHEGAN ISLAND — Begin on May 17, 1605, when the little English ship Archangel first sighted Monhegan Island, nine miles out from our coast. With 29 men aboard, Archangel had sailed from England on Easter morning, heading across the North Atlantic. The passage had gone well until Tuesday, May 14, when Capt. George Weymouth and his crew got the hell scared out of them. The mate was out in front, in a rowboat, taking depth soundings, when he suddenly warned that there were huge rocks and barely six feet of water under him. In a mad rush, Archangel tacked, swung about and headed for deeper, safer water. She and her crew had barely escaped shipwreck on the Rose and Crown Shoal, off Nantucket. To get away from those dangers, they steered downeast for three days and nights.

Aboard Archangel as the journalist-historian of the voyage, was James Rosier, who told the story of sighting and landing at Monhegan in a book called "A True Relation of the Most Prosperous Voyage and Exploration in the Year 1605."

"On Friday the 17th of May about sixe a clocke at night we descried land," wrote Rosier. "But because it blewe a great gale and the sea was very high, it was not fit to come upon an unknown coast. We stoode off until two in the morning; then standing in with it againe, we descried by eight in the morning an Iland some six miles in compasse." The island was Monhegan.

"About two a clocke in the afternoon our Captaine with twelve men rowed in his boat to shore," Rosier continued. "This Iland is woody, grouen with fir, Birch, Oke, Beech . . . On the shore grow Gooseberries, Strawberries, wild pease and Wild rose bushes; and much wilde fowle of divers kindes breed upon the rocks and shore . . . Our men with a few hooks got above thirty great cods and Haddocks, which gave us a taste of the great plenty of fishes which we found afterward wherever we went upon this coaste . . . Toward night we drew with a small net and got about thirty very good and great Lobsters, many rockfish, well fed, fat and sweet in taste."

Rosier goes on to tell of spectacular gardening results, far better than gardemers ever get in Maine or on Monhegan today. He wrote; "We digged a plot of ground wherein we sowed peaze and barley, which with-

Monhegan—One of the first islands in Maine to be discovered, charted and described in narrative detail, Monhegan was a landmark to Europe-an explorers before 1600. This photo, from about 1950, shows the island before the buildings of last 30 years. A halt to new homes took effect in the mid 1980's. About 20 families live year-round on Monhegan, but in July and August, hundreds of day-visitors come by passenger boats from Portland and Boothbay Harbor.

in sixteen days grew eight inches; and so continued growing every day halfe an inch.'' Rosier made greedy readers in England drool with thoughts of wealth as well as food when he described catching mussels. ''We found a great abundance of mussels; and in one were fourteen Pearles of prety bignesse; in another above fifte small Pearles.''

For a month, from mid May until mid June, 1605, Weymouth and his crew explored Monhegan, the islands of Muscongus Bay and went far up the Georges River. They made friends and traded with Indians. They took five Indians captive and carried them back to England when they sailed away from Maine on June 16. The Archangel made harbor in England safely on July 18, and to all who would listen Weymouth and Rosier sang praises of Monhegan and the coast of Maine.

WHEN WHALES COME VISITING OFF MONHEGAN

MONHEGAN ISLAND — The first whale surfaced 200 feet off the starboard bow of Steer Clear. Within a minute, two more broke out of the ocean. For 10 minutes the three whales surfaced and sounded, circled, disappeared, and came back.

Mostly they stayed about 200 feet from Steer Clear. But the biggest surfaced so close I felt he might be heading for the boat. The boat seemed to fascinate him as much as he fascinated us. He stayed on the surface, huge head above water, holding his position by pumping his enormous tail slowly up and down.

He had one glittering eye fixed on us. Somehow, he didn't look threatening but only intensely curious. Then he inhaled with a whistling noise, arched his back and dove, slapping the water into foam with his giant flukes.

We had been cruising slowly toward Monhegan Island, when we heard a noise like the W-H-O-O-S-H of air pouring from a puncture in a big tire. I thought it might be a leak from a foghorn aboard, or—much worse—a leak in the propane tank on deck. Then, 200 feet ahead on the starboard bow, we spotted a cloud of white air, rising out of the flat gray sea. Below the cloud was the gray-black head of a whale.

I pulled the throttles back to slow and crept ahead to where we had seen the spout. I ran to the stern and shortened the dinghy line, so we could stop or reverse without danger of getting slack line in the propellers. As I turned to run back to the helm, I could smell the whale's breath.

The spout a whale makes when it surfaces is the air it blows out its enormous lungs. This was the whitish cloud we'd seen, stale air being exhaled through the blowhole on top of its head. The cloud rose 15 feet and began drifting downwind to Steer Clear. The stale breath had the rank odor of rotten eggs. Whales suffer from halitosis.

But when we reached the spot, we could see no sign of the whale. Then some 300 feet away, we spotted two more whales.

These were not "black fish," a species of minor whales. They were swimming faster than baleen whales, and were smaller, about 25 feet long. They were toothed whales, erroneously called "killer whales," since there is no documentation of a whale ever deliberately killing a man.

Perhaps Steer Clear should have headed away from them, for safety's sake. But strangely I felt little fear. I'd had eye contact with that first whale, and he had seemed friendly and inquisitive. Had these been sharks, I'd have been in full flight, pouring the coals to Steer Clear to get away fast.

To me, sharks are evil, malevolent and vicious. I hate even their baby cousins, dogfish. But with whales, I feel a bond, perhaps because they too are warmblooded mammals like humans, with social customs and a language. About 100 million years ago whales were land creatures too.

Toothed whales are not seen in Maine waters as often as baleen whales. Toothed whales, pilot whales and orcas (the misnamed "killer whales") eat fish. They have rows of teeth and are fast swimmers so they can catch their dinners.

Baleen whales, though much bigger—up to 100 feet long—have no teeth and are slow swimmers. They are vegetarians, who eat enormous meals consisting only of minute plankton or krill.

A baleen whale can take in 5,000 gallons of sea water in a gulp, strain it through its jaws and then expel the water while retaining the plankton. These minute vegetables and minerals of the ocean have enormous nutritional value; a full grown baleen eats about eight tons of plankton every day.

The females produce babies which measure 23 feet long and weigh two tons at birth. These enormous babies suck their mothers' rich, thick milk for seven months, gaining weight at the rate of seven pounds an hour.

Whales don't have external ears like other mammals but, thanks to a special inner-ear, they have extraordinarily acute hearing. Whales can hear sounds across vast distances, perhaps as far as 60 miles.

Whales have a language for communicating over these distances. Their "voices" emit sonic and ultrasonic waves. The lowest of their noises produce sound waves of 20 cycles per second, and these are easily heard by man.

I have listened to them, and they sound like an oil-starved, creaking door, or a nail being pulled out of a plank. But at the high end of a whale's voice register, the ultrasonic noises reach up to 256,000 cycles per second. People cannot hear these noises, since our ears cannot detect sounds at frequencies higher than 20,000 cycles per second. But whales can hear them miles away. Their high-frequency sounds travel 62 miles in 60 seconds.

However whales cannot see as well as humans, because their eyeballs are fixed in their sockets. To change its angle of sight, a whale must move its entire body.

But whales—especially toothed whales—possess a marvelous mechanism which allows them to dive down thousands of feet, endure the enormous pressure down there, and then race to the ocean surface without suffering "the bends." Such changes in pressure would crush and kill a human, but whales are never bothered by it. Perhaps the two feet of blubber fat in which they are wrapped offers some protection.

Whales seem to enjoy their yearly trips to Maine waters, perhaps because they were never much hunted here. Native Indians hunted whales in a crude way, and James Rosier in the early 1600s described how they did it.

"The whale," he wrote, "bloweth up the water and its body is 12 fathoms long. The Indians go in company with their king in a multitude of their boats and strike him with a bone fastened to a rope made of the bark of trees. Then all their boats come about him, and as he riseth above the water, with their arrows they shoot him to death."

The wondrous whales which we saw near Monhegan have probably swum more than 10,000 miles since they were in Maine last summer. With luck you may see some this summer and be awed, yet feel an uncanny kinship to these friendly giants.

The Youngs at Pleasant Point Gut

PLEASANT POINT GUT — Walt Young had run the lobster dock in Pleasant Point Gut at the mouth of the St. Georges River for a good many years. He'd been at it a long while 20 years ago, when we first anchored in the Gut, in our first little lobster boat.

I was new at these little fishing harbors in those days and came on too fast, jumping ashore, a stranger, trying to make a friend of Walt (I didn't know his name then) with a torrent of talk.

I remember he didn't speak a word in reply that day. I filled up with gas, paid him and when I pulled out from his dock with effusive good-byes, he barely waggled his wrist.

More than 30 visits later, Walt Young had become a good friend. So when I saw him drive down to his wharf, I rowed the dinghy ashore from Steer Clear to see him for the first time since he'd been taken sick.

Walt seemed fine again. The same gentle voice, slow smile, same small bones, same dry humor. He said he'd come down to the dock this Sunday morning, expecting a truckload of bait for his lobstermen. Then he got a message that the bait wouldn't be in for two days. He took the bad news without a word or even a change in expression. "I can't do a thing to change it," he shrugged. And we sat, looking at the little snug harbor and its moored boats.

"Got one barrel of pogies left. We'll make do with that. Lobstering has been poor all spring. They are just beginning to come now," he said.

The redfish bait preferred by many lobstermen is trucked down from Canada. Price is up to $45 a barrel or more. It was $26 a few years back.

We watch the terns dive. They are the most beautiful of seabirds, with their graceful, sharply curved wings. The harbor is filled with them today.

"Krill, baby herring, are in the harbor. That brings 'em." Walt tells me he'd just seen a tern dive on a fish, catch it and fly up. "It wouldn't slide down. Guess he must have had it backwards in his mouth. So he dropped it from 30 feet. Dove back on it, caught it again the right way and swallowed it. Some fast dive that was."

The diving terns hover 30 or 40 feet up in the air, spot their tiny prey, then plummet down in a fast dive-bombing attack. A tern's body is not much longer than the length of a man's hand. For them, diving from 30 feet must be the equivalent of a man diving from 300 feet. I imagine the terror a young tern must feel doing it for the first time.

"Ever seen a seal catch a mackerel?" asks Walt. He tells me that he was on the wharf one day at low tide, watching a seal, when a mackerel swam by about five feet under the seal. "That seal turned about like greased lightning and in a split second he'd caught that mackerel. First time I'd seen it happen that way."

Since there would be no bait truck to unload, Walt said he'd head on home. I whistled up Piper, my Dalmatian, who'd been off enjoying land smells, rowed the dinghy out to Steer Clear and was getting ready to haul up the anchor and leave Pleasant Point Gut, when I saw Dennis Young, Walt's grandson, sculling his punt out for a visit.

I watched that effortless twist of his wrist and envied the knack by which, using one oar off the stern, Maine fishermen propel their punts so swiftly and easily across the harbor. I've tried and get nowhere. It is a knack you must learn before you are 10 years old.

Dennis, a strapping, handsome young man in his early 20s, used to go as sternman on a big lobsterboat which fished about 700 wire supertraps. "A sternman can make good money, $125 on a good day, with no overhead. As sternman you get 20 percent share," he told me. For a while, Dennis thought that kind of highline fishing was the way he wanted to go. But he had now found it was a mad race with the bank.

"A big 40-foot boat with diesel electronics, radar and depthfinder would cost me $100,000," says Dennis. "And the wire supertraps cost $50 each, rigged, and I'd want 700. That puts the investment stake up around $135,000. Add another $125 a day for fuel and bait. Plus what I'd be paying a sternman. I'd be racing the bank every day."

To meet his bank payments, operating overhead, and 20 percent for the sternman, would mean going far offshore in winter and worrying everyday of the year. So Dennis lowered his sights and chose to lobster from a 30-foot wooden boat, 36 years old, inshore and alone.

He is happier, he says, but wonders if lobstering from June to December can ever support a young man and his family these days. So come Thanksgiving, Dennis will go to Florida again to work all winter as a bellman in a hotel where the lowest priced room is $150 a day.

"I don't like it much, even though I can get to the beach and swim most afternoons. I prefer Cushing, Maine."

Dennis climbs off Steer Clear and sculls his punt with that wondrous wrist motion on a single stern oar, over to his 36-year old wooden boat and I watch him cast off. There are 8,000 licensed lobstermen along

Maine's coast now. The full-timers own big fiberglass boats, with big, superwire traps, with radar and electronics. Yet the Maine lobster catch still hovers around the same old level of 20 million pounds a year. The price per pound is higher, but like Dennis, I wonder if a few years from now there will still be a good life and fair living for a young man in a small boat, fishing 300 traps alone in Maine.

RESTORING ALLEN ISLAND

ALLEN ISLAND — Betsy Wyeth has been working to bring Allen Island back to vigorous, practical life. And trying to do it in a way that the rejuvenation of Allen could become a how-to-do-it example for other privately-owned Maine islands.

But there is more to the Betsy Wyeth story which makes it important to Maine and the nation. For it was at Allen Island that Capt. George Weymouth dropped anchor in May 1605. A cross of granite marks the site where the first Protestant church service in North America was celebrated. The tattered crew, 3,000 miles from home, gave thanks for safe arrival on the edge of an unknown land. This ancient anchorage is called Georges Harbor on the charts.

Weymouth and his crew rested, repaired their ship, traded with Indians—even kidnapping five of them to take back to England. Two years later the first white settlers aboard the Gift of God and the Mary and John, put into Allen Island on their way to start the first, ill-fated colony at Popham. With them was the Indian Chief Skidwarres, one of the five kidnapped by Weymouth two years earlier. So the early roots of our nation are at Allen Island.

"When I bought Allen Island," says Mrs. Wyeth, my husband (Andrew) and my son (Jamie) and I studied copies of the old Neptune charts made by the English Admiralty before the Revolutionary War. It showed a farm and wharf on Allen Island before 1776. We found that John Allen left his island to fight in the Revolution."

Allen Island, 450 acres in size, lies between Port Clyde and Monhegan Island, across from Burnt Island, the one-time Coast Guard station now owned by Jamie Wyeth. The mail-and-passenger vessel to Monhegan passes close by Allen Island on its run to Monhegan. Passengers aboard have seen, and sometimes criticized, the clearing done since Betsy bought the island.

Andrew Wyeth was among the first to urge his wife to clear the timber which had overgrown the one-time meadows which had helped feed livestock kept by erstwhile farm-and-fishing families on Allen Island. Weather had ruined the old island buildings and wharf.

"The first essential was rebuilding the wharf, so we could land men and equipment," Mrs. Wyeth says. Once the new wharf was built, Earl Norwood, a logger from Union, barged his equipment out to Allen. Dougie Boynton, a fisherman from Monhegan, got the work crew together. Philip Conkling from the Island Institute of Maine planned the overall operation.

In three months, close to 50 acres had been cleared and reseeded to meadows. A home-made sawmill produced 60,000 board feet of lumber. Dan Whittet, a young builder from Cushing, built a handsome two-story farmhouse, post and beam, on Allen. Solar power was harnessed to make electricity. Nineteen sheep were brought from Metinic Island, a breed of island sheep so hardy they have survived more than 100 years of island winters.

Where will all this work lead? Betsy Wyeth says she sometimes sits beside the granite cross where Weymouth and his tattered crew landed on 1605, and thinks of what lies ahead for Allen Island . "There are living quarters now for at least three fishermen, a good wharf for their boats. They can live and fish from here and make the island a working home for eight months a year. Why own something so wonderful as Allen and not have it used?"

I asked her the blunt question. "Fine as the work you've done may be, is it only a hobby for the well-to-do?" She answered frankly: "I had a hardheaded, outside appraiser come here to answer that very question," she said. "He estimated that I'd get every dollar spent on the wharf, the land clearing and the house, back and show a profit—if I ever sold Allen. Which I never will."

ALL HANDS TURN TO FOR FRIENDSHIP SLOOPS

FRIENDSHIP — Friendship lives up to its name. And its name originates from the fact this spot was chosen by Indians and whites to end years of war between them with a "Hatchet Burying Ceremony." The cove still is called Hatchet cove.

The islands off Friendship, stretching into Muscongus Bay, once held

Friendship sloops racing in light breeze on Muscongus Bay, close to the town and harbor of Friendship where the sloops began 100 years ago.

thriving granite quarries. Today, Friendship's only business is lobstering. More than 170 lobstering licenses are held among Friendship's 800 men, women and children.

In Friendship's lovely harbor, sheltered from Atlantic storms by a fan of tree-crested little islands, seven lobster wharves buy the catch and tend to the needs of the local lobster fleet. In a year, these seven wharves handle a million pounds of lobster.

The Friendship sloop, now one of the most sought-after "family yachts," was designed and built for lobstering by Friendship men long before Maine fishermen dreamed of power boats with gasoline engines. The earliest Friendships sold for $400 almost 100 years ago.

Today, a Friendship sloop sells for up to $160,000. Regardless of the material used, fiberglass included, all are built along the same basic design set by Wilbur Morse. He constructed the first Friendship sloop, a little 19-footer, on Bremen Long Island in the winter of 1874, when he was 21.

Morse built between 400 and 500 Friendship sloops, some of which have sailed the seven seas. A traveler found one in Hawaii, and fishermen off Italy, after a severe storm, found a trailboard (part of the prow) with Morse's twined ivy trademark hand-carved on it, along with his signature.

Another Morse-built Friendship was wrecked off the Netherlands. The story is that murder suspects had stolen her and sailed across the Atlantic to escape arrest. But until the 1920's, when lobstermen took to marine engines, most Friendships remained true to their original purpose— lobstering off the Maine coast.

The Friendship Sloop Society is a close-knit authority on these blue-blooded boats. To be admitted to the inner circle of the Society, an owner must have a sloop that possesses the original Morse lines; distinctive hard bilges, a deep-sloping keel running full length, hollow garboards, a sharp clipper bow and an overhanging stern with elliptical transom.

Some of the original Friendships are sailing still, but lobstering no more. James R. Wiggins, once editor of the Washington Post and now owner of the Ellsworth American, has restored Amity, a 30-foot sloop built in 1900 by Wilbur Morse.

Jarvis Newman of Southwest Harbor sails Dictator, built in 1904 by Robert McLain. Roger Duncan, who wrote that bible "Cruising Guide to New England," has long sailed Eastward, built by James Chadwick. The beautiful Chrissy, built by Charles Morse in 1913, is sailed by Ernst Wiegleb of Pleasant Point. A big 35-foot beauty named Sazerac, built by Wilbur Morse in 1913, spent winters at Newcastle next to Steer Clear for many years.

Today these old beauties are far outnumbered by the new Friendships, many made of fiberglass. But the hauntingly lovely and simple lines of the first Friendships are still the hallowed hallmark in the newest versions.

Two Island Authors: Elizabeth Ogilvie and Dorothy Simpson

GAY ISLAND — Two wonderful and unusual women, Elizabeth Oglivie and Dorothy Simpson, live in a 110-year-old house called Tide's Way, here on Gay Island. Between them they have written more than a million words in dozens of books, most with settings on Maine islands.

We secured Steer Clear to Al Elliot's mooring in Pleasant Point Gut, across the mouth of the Georges River from Port Clyde, and rowed to Gay Island for our yearly visit. The two writers have been getting ready to move off the island for the winter. This is an easy move; just a two-minute ride in their outboard to their winter house on the mainland at Cushing. If anything has been overlooked, they can get in the boat and fetch it in a few minutes. "That makes a good excuse to keep going back to the island on any bright winter's day," Dorothy Simpson says. In April, the process is reversed.

These two writing women bought their house and 33 spectacular acres on Gay Island 45 years ago. The price they paid was a pittance by today's standards. And for it, they got the old white farmhouse, wharf, fishhouse, miles of ocean and island views, great ledges for sunbathing, fine flats for clamming and crabbing, and some of the best lobstering and musseling water. They also got plenty of quiet and privacy, though there are now a few other island neighbors.

Their long friendship is rare. Miss Ogilvie is past 65 and Mrs. Simpson is over 75, although both look and act far younger, perhaps because of all the island-living chores they have done together.

They first met on another island, Criehaven, when they were girls. Mrs. Simpson's family had lived and lobstered from Criehaven for years; the Ogilvies came as summerfolk from their home in Quincy, Mass. Criehaven, 25 miles offshore from Rockland, is a tightly-knit lobstering community, with about 11 boats going out from there.

But it's a far softer life today than when Mrs. Simpson grew up on the island. Now the families no longer winter out there. Mrs. Simpson's brothers—she is the oldest of 11 children—have been lobstermen. She married a lobsterman. "Until recent years," she says, "I never lived anywhere but on Maine islands—Criehaven, Wooden Ball, Matinicus and now Gay Island."

Between them, these two wonderful women have about 100 years of island living. And between them, they have written close to 50 books. Mrs. Simpson wrote that essential reference book and history, "The Maine Islands," plus a series of juveniles which featured Janie Marshall, an island girl.

Miss Ogilvie has published more than 30 novels, many of them set on Maine islands, plus 11 juveniles and uncounted poems, essays and articles. Her productivity is immense. Every year, when I go ashore for a visit, she seems to have a new novel just off the press and another new one ready to send to her publisher.

Her writing day begins at dawn. "I can't sleep much after 4 a.m. So I get up and write, usually for about five hours at a stretch. By 10 a.m. I can go out with a clear conscience and pick berries or catch mackerel if I feel like it. I feel smug. I've got a day's writing down on paper." Her quota is a minimum of 1,000 words a day.

Her first novels, "High Tide at Noon," "Ebb Tide" and "Storm Tide," all written before she was 30, were set on Criehaven and featured the Bennett family. "But," she warns "writing a series about the same characters is likely to create a laziness in the author."

So her novels often go far afield. The two writers spent six months in Scotland, much of it in the islands of the Outer Hebrides, and in tracing Miss Ogilvie's Scottish ancestors.

Out of all this research and notetaking Elizabeth Ogilvie made a novel about a Scottish family on the verge of setting out to the New World and Maine. More books are likely about their family's first years of settling in the United States. She keeps in touch by letter with authorities in Scotland to authenticate details, as for instance, which police authorities were involved in arresting a man for murder at Stornaway.

"I've done the historical, hysterical costume novels. I'm not too good at the bodice-snatching of the wenches by the brawling nobles, but I learned the knack of that, too," she says.

First and foremost, she is a storyteller, a romantic entertainer, with a remarkable eye for lively detail. "I worried when I finished this last book. It was in a new vein for me. I worried my publishers might turn it down. I know friends who have been writing for the same publisher for many years and have seen that turndown come out of the blue. And it hurt them a lot." But that load is off her mind. Her newest is on its way toward the printers. And the next is in her typewriter. Book number 33; or is it number 35?

Waiting out the Ocean's Mean Spells

MAPLEJUICE COVE — A good way to outfox bad weather at sea is to tuck up inside Maine's bays and rivers. This way you can still enjoy a cruise, when boats offshore are fighting fog, rain squalls and nine-foot seas.

We are tucked nicely up inside, as I write this on a battered, sea-going typewriter in the stern of Steer Clear. I feel a close bond to this old typewriter. It has done a lot of traveling to very odd places with me.

We've worked together, got stranded together, in jungles and airports, in pup tents and exotic hotels. I bought this Smith Corona portable in 1952, to cover Eisenhower's first campaign for president.

It is small and light enough to use in a plane seat. But it is tough, and lives inside a thin, metal case. The case was a handsome gray 35 years ago. Now it is chipped, scarred and dented from travels on five continents. Now it lives aboard the boat from May to November and the salt water is taking its toll. The letter "c" skips, and the ribbon sticks. But, all in all, it has survived the past 35 years better than the man who pounds it.

We are tucked this morning inside a cove up the St. George River, deep inside Muscongus Bay.

Early this morning, two whale boats from Outward Bound on Hurricane Island, 12 miles to sea from Rockland, came into the cove. On the two small boats there were a total of 23 men and women, 16 years old to 37.

One woman came from California, one man came from North Dakota. The 23 had been living together on these 20-foot open whaleboats day and night for a week. Sleeping under tarpaulins, rolled up in sleeping bags; eating out of mess-kits from food they carried.

They started their morning at 5 a.m. by going ashore for a five-mile run and a dip in the ocean. "I'm getting used to it now, but the first week was awful!" said a woman who is a computer programmer in New York City.

An hour later, the two whale boats were off. They left under oar-power, a dozen students manning one oar each in each boat.

Once out into the breeze, the sails would be hoisted. Next week, they would be dropped off at uninhabited islands and each student would begin his or her survival test—three days and nights alone on a small island, with only a ground sheet, some matches, a little fresh water and piece of line and a fishhook.

At the end of 23 days, they will all go back to different jobs, places and backgrounds, taking with them an imperishable bond to each other, their whaleboat and the Maine coast.

These 23 will also be remembered in Friendship. Yesterday, they went ashore in Friendship and in one day painted a small church, as part of their community service.

No sooner had the whaleboats left our cove than an outboard with three clam diggers pulled in to work the flats around us at low tide. The youngest—a lad about 12—ran the outboard between the minefield of lobster trap buoys. As each bent over to dig in the oozing mud, trousers and shirt separated at the small of their backs. You can spot a clam digger by the patch of dark sunburn six inches square at the small of his back.

We bought half a peck to eat at supper tonight. At this moment, the clams are hanging off the stern in a string bag, being washed clean by the tide. There is plenty of company in this cove this morning. Our next visitors were two lobster boats, in to haul half a dozen traps close by Steer Clear. One man had two small children with him, a boy about eight and a girl about six.

"Giving the wife a break," he shouted to us. "We got company coming for the holiday and she is cleaning house and getting a big dinner. So I got the kids as helpers this morning."

On shore, you don't get so many interesting visitors before 10 a.m.

I turn on the VHF radio for the latest marine weather reports. Small craft warnings for heavy seas. Gale warnings and 20-foot seas out on the Banks. But tucked away far up the bay, it is calm, sunny and clear.

It's hard to spoil the Maine coast

ROUND POND — Take fish oil, if you want an example of how hard it can be to spoil the coast of Maine.

Making fish oil is about the smelliest, nastiest process you can imagine, especially the way it was made in local fish factories 100 years ago.

They cooked the fish—menhaden—by steam. They then squeezed the oil out by hydraulic pressure.

And then they took what was left of the fish to the fertilizer factory next door and made some of the strongest smelling "good stuff" ever spread on a field.

The beautiful coastal villages of Maine thrived on the fish oil and fish fertilizer business. It paid for handsome homes and churches.

Today, nobody could get a license from the Maine Environmental Protection Department to make fish oil and fish fertilizer in coastal towns.

But the records show that in 1876, the coastal towns of Lincoln County produced over 2,000,000 gallons of fish oil; and then ground up what was left to produce 21,414 tons of fertilizer.

The smell must have been awful. But the records don't complain about the smell. They do, however, talk about money. Fish oil fetched as high as $1.25 a gallon during the Civil War.

At that price, two million gallons of it brought in $2 1/2 million to the fish towns of Lincoln County. Add in the money made from fish guts as fertilizer, and the local 'take' exceeded $3 million a year. And $3 million then was equivalent of $30 million today.

The fish factories and their smell and gruesome gurry have long since gone. And there is no trace of permanent damage to harbors.

If fish oil smells bad, ship building is messier. Yet every town in Maine with a waterfront once built ships.

In the single year of 1873, Maine yards launched 353 ships, almost one every day of the entire year. In the 30 years between 1851 and 1881, Maine boat yards built over 6,320 ships. To man these sea-going ships, more than 11,375 Maine men were "shipping out" in the year 1860. And 759 of them were masters of ships sailing the seven seas. In the 1880's, every tenth master of full rigged ships in the American merchant marine came from Searsport, Maine.

Maine was the nation's biggest shipper of lumber, ice, lime, granite, as well as the biggest maker of ships, catcher of fish and producer of fish oil and fertilizer.

Far from being 'quaint, last outposts of unspoiled and unsophisticated America,' as some writers like to portray the coast of Maine, these coastal towns were rich and cosmopolitan long before the world had ever heard of Los Angeles and before Chicago was more than a cow town.

More than a century ago, seacoast households in Maine served Canton ginger in syrup brought home from China, and tea from India. Silks from Paris and screens from Japan, camphorwood desks from the East Indies, and rum from the West Indies were gracing homes along the coast of Maine when Custer made his last stand at Little Big Horn. Maine newspapers 100 years ago carried pages of foreign news, because foreign news was of prime local importance in Maine. A revolution in South

America could mean the loss of Maine ships and the deaths of Maine men.

Maine's local grammar schools had an international flavor 100 years ago. Maine ship captains would bring the sons of foreign friends to be educated here in Maine. The records of one small coastal school in 1883 list five boys from Cuba, three from Liberia, two from New Orleans and one from Mobile as students.

Those "unspoiled, quaint, unsophisticated" Maine fishing villages knew the best and the worst of the wide world long before the rest of the U.S.A.

*Another delightful summer scene, sailboats in the famed Monhegan Is-
land race.*

Fort William Henry at Pemaquid Harbor has flown the flags of three na-
tions in its history. The English and the French flags flew here before the
American Revolution.

VII
ROCKLAND
& CAMDEN

246

A sailor's friend—The lonely lighthouse that guides you safely through the storms back to haven in a port.

VII

The shortest run Steer Clear makes regularly is from a mooring in Pleasant Point Gut to an anchor in the Caldwell Islands, at the mouth of the St. George River, just west of Port Clyde. Distance under two miles.

First, the name enticed me to Big and Little Caldwell Islands. Later, a Rockland real estate agent suggested I should buy them. "The price is $30,000 for both," he said in 1969. I told him it was outrageous. He called again in 1975 to say the Caldwell Islands were on the market once more, price $60,000. "That price is ridiculous," I said. He sweetly reminded me I'd said that when the price had been $30,000. By now the price may top $200,000.

But I still poke in there partly to kick myself and partly to relish the beauty of the special place where the two Caldwell islands join at low water. Wild iris and wild white roses grow there, and in mid-summer lush wild raspberries tempt man and bird. There is now one house on each island.

From the Caldwell Islands, we run into nearby Port Clyde, the eastward end of Muscongus Bay.

Port Clyde is a small town with character and muscle; serious fish boats, working and pleasure wharves, tourists, the mail boat to Monhegan, a fine waterfront store for ship supplies, a restaurant on the dock with hot home baked pies, a small hospitable inn, and a handsome lighthouse. Port Clyde stays plain, unpretentious and focused on fishing, no matter how many tourists invade it to catch the Monhegan boat.

We top our water and gas tanks and restock the food supplies before heading east to Rockland and Camden. When Steer Clear rounds Mosquito Island and sets course to Muscle Ridge Channel, I feel the exhilaration that signals the start of a cruise. We are not in our back yard of Muscongus Bay any longer; we are starting on a cruise.

The word "cruise" chokes in my throat a little. It implies luxury and sunbathing on an afterdeck. There is not much of either on Steer Clear. "Cruise" also connotes scheduled destinations, set arrivals and departures. Aboard Steer Clear, we leave such stuff on shore.

On Steer Clear's "cruises," we amble and gunkhole and overnight in island coves or small fishing harbors. We don't make beelines, as some cruising boats and yachts do, from one major "yachting" port to the next. We go into these to gawk at luxury yachts, to stock food lockers or fill fresh water tanks. There's often no fresh water at the lobster dock in small Maine fishing harbors. I know many boats which cruise the Maine coast, going from Portland to Boothbay, to Camden, to Bar Harbor and finally to the beautiful beach at Roque Island, far downeast. They do it on a schedule, and make it there and back in 10 days or two weeks.

But not Steer Clear. We take two months. When we run out of cruising days, we leave the boat on a morning along the way, bum a ride or take a bus back to work in Portland for a week; and then come back next Friday night to board the boat and amble and gunkhole some more on weekends until summer is almost over. Then we head home to Buttermilk Cove in September.

Thus we seldom make it even from Port Clyde to Rockland or Camden in a day, although a direct run is only a few hours. On some trips we'll turn in at Southern Island Light, where Andrew and Betsy Wyeth may be summering, and pick up a mooring in Tenants Harbor and go ashore for dinner with old friends who live here or with new acquaintances from other visiting boats. But most often we go half way along the Muscle Ridge Channel, then turn to sea and anchor among the blessed trio of lovely islands—Dix, High and Birch. And there we stay one, two or even three days. (I'll include some pages from Steer Clear's logbook about the beauties and strange histories of these island jewels.)

The Muscle Ridge run from Whitehead Light to Ash Island gong and from there to Owls Head Light and into Rockland Harbor takes

*three hours if you resist gunkholing. But this passage is so filled with
memories that we amble, enjoying the recall of previous trips . . . I recall one tense, scary afternoon when sudden, dense fog cut visibility to
zero. Seven boats were all converging at almost the same time on the
Ash Island gong, some heading east, some west, some planning to cut
out through Fisherman's Passage. All seven began blasting foghorns.
The blasts came from all directions. Fearful of collision, most boats
either went dead in the water or circled at a snail's pace, with look-
outs posted to spot a ghost ship closing down on them. It was a tense
game of blindman's bluff. We could hear horns, engines, voices, all
too close, but we could seldom see another boat. Suddenly the fog
scaled up, and all seven boats saw each other revealed in bright sunshine. Too tensed to even swap waves with each other, the boats
moved off in different directions, thanking God there had been no col-
lisions.*

*I recall the crazy day we landed a helicopter on Two Bush Island,
setting down on the foundation slab where the lightkeeper's house
once stood. We were flying in a luxurious Bell jet helicopter, well
sound-proofed, equipped with fine deep leather chairs. The pilot flew
us very low and slow, and then hovered, backed and filled, above the
islands of Muscle Ridge which we knew so well from the decks of
Steer Clear. But from the helicopter, seeing all sides of each island at
once, old friends looked strange, almost unrecognizable. Seals, which
we'd seen from the boat a few at a time, ledge by ledge, we now saw
from the air, and they lay by the dozens around the entire perimeters
of islands, looking as ugly as old cigar butts washed up close to island
shores.*

*The Light at Owls Head, built in 1825, towers high above at the
eastern end of Muscle Ridge Channel. We alter course to head down
into Rockland harbor, named as The Great Landing Place by the
Indians.*

HEAVENLY TRIANGLE: DIX, HIGH, BIRCH ISLANDS

ABOARD STEER CLEAR — The anchor will be hard
to haul, it is dug in so deep. We have been lying on it three days and two
nights, tucked in between Dix and Birch, with High Island astern. Steer

Clear is alone here now, but half a dozen cruising boats have come in to anchor near us each evening and left each morning. A lobsterman who has been fishing these waters daily comes by this morning, throttles down and drifts alongside. "Something wrong?" he asks. "You've been here so long."

But every stopover in this heavenly triangle of islands seems short. These islands always seem incredible in present quiet beauty and their raucous industrial past.

It seems incredible that the U.S. Treasury building in Washington, D.C. and the mammoth New York and Philadelphia Post Offices are made from granite quarried here on Dix Island. So are hundreds of big city buildings across the U.S.A.

We walked around Dix again yesterday, looking for the cellar holes of the Shamrock and the Aberdeen, two enormous hotel-barracks which housed a thousand men on Dix, quarry workers from Ireland and Scotland, Italy and Sweden. Only wildflowers bloom and meadow larks sing where these 500-room bachelor barracks once stood. The roads where men, horses, oxen, steam engines and machines hauled mammoth blocks of granite to the quays, are gone, overgrown with high grass and brush.

I walked on to the northwest point of Dix, to see what is left of the mansion which granite-king Horace Beals had built. He had built a sumptuous 26-room mansion for a young wife who left him, married three more times and became the Duchess of Tomajo. Gone, totally gone.

A few new summer houses have been built, unpretentious vacation spots for five families. Along the shore there are a few fishing shanties for storing gear, and maybe a cot, a kettle and a burner. It seems incredible that a thousand men filled this peaceful island with noise, dust, shouts, curses and songs and, all too often, with tragic, bloody accidents in the quarries and occasional murderous brawls outside the Shamrock.

Did those sweat-stained men, I wonder, row across the little cut to swim on beautiful Birch Island? This low, small island has one of the finest white sand beaches in Maine, a handsome, safe-and-shallow-water picnic place at low tide. Just above the sand beach is the high ground of the island—one vast grass-and-wildflower meadow. Stand atop it and you see dozens more islands, ledges and sea channels too small and too complicated to navigate except by the lobstermen who work this water and the occasional clamdigger in an outboard. Sit atop the high ledge of granite facing Dix and watch sunset over the Camden Hills, and then moonrise over the Atlantic. Be at peace, and think about the ghosts on the other island in this heavenly triangle—High Island.

On High Island, the great granite business leaps out to grab attention even today. Jutting high and wide out into the water is an enormous stone wharf, built of huge blocks of granite quarried from High Island. Schooners up to 100 feet long tied up here. Some days three schooners loaded at once, one on each side of the wharf and one at the front.

Ghosts of the great granite era are waiting now on the granite pier. Rusted iron eyes set in rusted gigantic bolts wait still for the dock lines. Great thick strands of rusted wire cable are ghostly remnants of the hoisting machinery used to lift granite blocks into the schooners.

The ghosts persist inland. Beside the overgrown road which leads up to the great quarry, there lie piles of cut granite blocks, waiting half a century for shipment. They were cut to become cornerstones in some huge federal building. Hundreds of small blocks lie on the ground, trimmed to become paving blocks in some distant city street. They have been waiting 60, 70 and 80 years and more. It feels as though all work in the quarry had suddenly stopped, as though a calamity or plague had hit one mid-day.

Scramble through underbrush and over chunks of hewn granite to the top of High Island and you may get the wits scared out of you by the weirdest, ghostliest noise.

Suddenly you break out of the underbrush and are on the brink of a cliff dropping sheer down into a deep green lake. Your foot breaks a branch, or sends a rock pebble careening down. At the sound, the dark green lake below churns to panic. Your skin prickles, your ears resound with shock at a loud but eerie noise.

It is the noise of hundreds of ducks taking off in fright from the algae-covered lake below. A thousand wing beats echo, the noise magnified by the quarry walls. Flights of birds zoom up, then fly out to sea.

The fresh water from which they rose in sudden fright, is the accumulation of rain, falling over the years and being trapped in the abandoned granite quarry. Slimy green algae and other vegetation multiplies in the stagnant water, which now provides rich food and secure shelter for hungry and storm-tossed birds.

Once immigrants from Italy, Ireland, Scotland, Sweden hammered and set dynamite charges to explode the quarry walls. Now the quarry is silent sanctuary for seabirds.

As Steer Clear leaves this heavenly triangle of islands, the ghosts of schooners and quarrymen seem to wave goodbye from the great granite pier on High Island.

MAINE'S ICE AGE COMES UP WITH THE ANCHOR

BIRCH ISLAND — We spent the night anchored among islands off the Muscle Ridge Channel, between Tenants Harbor and Rockland.

When we hauled anchor in the morning, it came up coated in black, gooey, thick, smelly mud. Wonderful holding ground. And very ripe; 10,000 years old.

Mud from the Ice Age blackens the decks of Steer Clear, sticks to hands and shoes and gives an indescribable stink of history to the foredeck, histroy which makes a man feel as short-lived as breath on a mirror.

A day ago we moored in Pulpit Harbor on North Haven to see again the unmatchable, unforgettable sight of sunset over the Camden Hills; and then watch the moon climb over the island trees and shine on the dark quiet waters of Pulpit Harbor. The Camden Hills are miraculous to view day or night from Penobscot Bay.

There is a close tie between the black, smelly mud on my anchor chain and those glorious Camden Hills. The tie is Maine's Ice Age. The Ice Age covered those Camden Hills. The Ice Age buried Mount Desert. The Ice Age made the white sand on Birch Island where we swam.

The end of Maine's last Ice Age came about 10,000 years ago, and its retreat is what made these islands and the rocky, rugged coast of Maine and made the great bays called Casco, Muscongus, Penobscot, Frenchman and Fundy.

Cruising in a small boat among these islands year after year, and gunkholing among the coves and up Maine's rivers, rouses your curiosity about the past. You wonder how these unique and lovely gems of the Maine coast were made; about the men and women who first discovered these places and the lives they led—and the Indians before them—over the hundreds of past years.

Back on shore, there never is time to find out half of what you'd like to know. The geological textbooks are often too technical for this layman. The ideal answer would be to have aboard a geologist who can explain the story behind the rocks and ledges and mud. The crux of the story is the Ice Age, the years when ice thousands of feet thick covered all the land where now are Bangor, Bucksport, Belfast, Camden, Rockland, Boothbay, Bath, Brunswick and Portland.

When the ice melted, the sea level rose, until the ocean covered Maine at least 100 miles inland from where the coastline is today. The evidence is there to see and smell.

Go inland 100 miles today and in places 200 feet above sea level, you can find the same kind of ice age mud, with the same strange stink and the same fossil, rock and clam shell ingredients as the mud on the anchor, which I hauled up from the ocean bottom in Penobscot Bay.

The retreat of the ice began about 8,000 B.C., passing through West Virginia. By 7,000 B.C., the great melt had reached north to Connecticut. By 6,000 B.C., it was shifting to southern Minnesota and by 4,000 B.C. the last ice was retreating from northern Maine. The great melt flooded Maine to make our rocky coast, our bays and islands.

There is a lot of ice left still in Greenland and Antarctica. If that ever melts away, as the ice of the Camden Hills and Mount Desert melted away, the ocean may rise again—high enough to drown Boston, New York, Washington and London.

It makes a man feel his breed is very, very young when he hauls up an anchor caked in mud made by the Ice Age 10,000 years ago.

SEA DOG WINS AGAIN

ABOARD STEER CLEAR — I am trying to make a sea-dog out of Piper, my young Dalmatian. This may be a mistake. Piper has already survived strychnine poisoning and being hit by a car. But making a sea-dog out of her may be the death of both of us.

Piper is on her first cruise on Steer Clear. At dawn this morning I swore it would be her last. Everything that happened at 5 a.m. this day is proof that while a blue-eyed Dalmatian pup is as pretty to watch as a racehorse, she can be a pain aboard a small boat.

Piper loves to chew soft things. Last night she did. While I slept blissfully in the forward cabin, Piper had a party aft. During the nighttime, she climbed up onto the navigator's table and helped herself to a big box of soft tissues and a big bunch of soft, lush grapes.

Piper demolished both in a private orgy. When I awoke at dawn, the afterdeck looked like a street cleaner's nightmare. My immaculate deck was ankle deep in shredded Kleenex. A slippery mess of grape skins was glued to the woodwork. And sprinkled like pepper over it all were remnants of my softest socks, which Piper had ripped off a clothes line and shredded.

By dawn's early light, this long-suffering man went to work with broom and dustpan, bucket and mop, the clean-up guy for dog. The dog lay luxuriously on the boat cushions, tail wagging in delight at the sight. She gave small barks of encouragement at me. I snarled back at her.

That chore done, I poured a steaming cup of coffee from the galley and took it forward to the bow. In splendid isolation from the dog, I could sit sipping coffee; and watch the sun come up, burning haze off the glassy sea and lifting the fog curtain yard by lovely yard to reveal an island shore 300 feet away. This is a boatman's treasured joy; total removal from man's world, brief, frenetic and bickering, and total immersion in nature's world, everlasting, orderly and peaceful. A man can hear the music of the planets as he sips coffee alone with the sunrise over the ocean.

Then came the havoc, the split seconds of catastrophe caused by a Dalmatian dog. A wet black nose suddenly is thrust under my elbow; scalding coffee is spilled over this pajamaed man; man yells like a fiend; scared dog leaps backward, falls overboard from the bow into the icy ocean; and panic-struck dog seems to sink. Idiot owner impulsively dives to rescue dog.

Icy ocean shock submerges owner. Spluttering and shivering, the owner surfaces. Excited dog thinks she's discovered new game. Barks joyously, circling owner playfully. Infuriated owner reaches out to grab crazy dog. Dog swims off. Owner swims after dog. Dog accelerates. Dog's paddle outdistances owner's crawl stroke.

Man's brain begins to operate. He abandons fruitless swim chase after dog and heads for dinghy. Scrambles over gunwale, scraping belly painfully on oarlock. All frozen thumbs now, owner unties dinghy from boat and slams thumb as he puts oars into oarlocks. Dog swimming merrily straight out to sea, full speed ahead for Spain.

Wringing wet owner rows in hot pursuit. Finally catches up with dog. Tries hauling animal aboard. Tricky. Comes close to capsizing twice. Rescues ungrateful beast from sea. Beast proud and happy after first long swim in ocean. Owner unhappy. Heads back to boat, swearing at dog.

New noise. Noise of shipmate laughing heart out, on deck, bent double with laughter at sight.

"Is Piper alright?" she asks as this man, gasping and blue, grabs the handrail. "I'll get a towel for Piper. The poor dog must be half frozen!"

With a snarl, I hand up the soaking wet beast. The animal, safely back on board, shakes herself wildly, drenching my new boat cushions, dripping all over my immaculate decks.

Ignored after my ordeal, I clamber aboard, freezing cold and sopping wet in pajamas.

"Strip right there!" orders my shipmate "before you mess up the boat. I'll get you a towel as soon as I have dried Piper!" Naked, alone and goose-pimpled, I stand. Dawn at sea no longer rouses the poet in me.

"Next cruise, that dog stays on shore!" I growl.

I glare at the dog. The dog turns her blue eyes up to me. And wags her tail.

And—curse it—I reach down and pat her. The wet tail speeds up, thumping out a drum of joy on the deck.

Dog wins again!

ROCKLAND—BEAUTY AND THE BEAST

ROCKLAND — Beauty and the Beast lie down together in this seaport city.

Here is the ugliest and the loveliest; the oldest and the newest. Here the past, the present and the future are jumbled together along the waterfront. A stinking fish waste factory is next to lovely windjammers. Great art is near a snow plow factory. A handsome, huge harbor has the Maine State Prison, nearby. A stirring history and a rowdy present are hallmarks of Rockland.

Rockland-built sailing ships began setting world speed records 135 years ago. Deacon George Thomas built the fast and famous clipper Red Jacket here in 1853, launched her from where Jordan's Market stands in the North End of Rockland.

Red Jacket was the biggest ship ever built in Maine at the time of her launching. She weighed 2,306 tons, stretched 251 feet overall, had a beam of 44 feet and drew 31 feet of water. She was a masterpiece and, for those days, a luxury ship.

The clipper's figurehead was a life-sized likeness of the Indian Chief Sagoyewatha, who fought for the British in the Revolution and was given a red jacket by them, hence the ship's name; later however, in the War of 1812, he fought with the Americans against the British.

Many touches of luxury added glamour to Red Jacket's speed. Her huge after-cabin was finished in rosewood, mahogany, satinwood and zebra wood. In addition to the officers' cabins, Red Jacket boasted 14 luxurious staterooms and a forward house with hammocks for a crew of 62 men.

When Red Jacket was launched Nov. 2, 1853, hundreds of guests from Boston and New York flocked to Rockland. Local schools were let out, and townspeople crowded the boat yard for the occasion.

The ways were greased with beef tallow and soap, and then sprinkled with flax seeds, to help launch the huge sailing ship into the water.

Some two months later, on Jan. 10, 1854, Red Jacket sailed from New York for Liverpool burdened with every kind of handicap.

Her hull was uncoppered, her crew was untried, she ran into hail, snow or rain almost every day of the crossing. Yet she smashed every record. Her lapsed time, dock to dock, was 13 days, one hour and 25 minutes, a record for sailing ships of her size that still stands today.

Captain Asa Eldridge was a showman. He sailed his great vessel past the two tugs sent to meet her off Liverpool and swept her up the Mersey River under full sail.

Then he performed the kind of feat few skippers ever attempt, let alone with a ship on her maiden voyage. He sailed Red Jacket within yards of the pier, only then deigning to throw her yards back while making a 180 degree turn to lay her up to the pierhead with a precision that drew cheers from onlookers.

Red Jacket never returned to the United States under an American flag. The British White Star line immediately chartered her for round-the-world voyages.

Walking along Rockland's waterfront today the flavor of the city's greatness as a port is still faintly in the air. In the steamboat era, 30 ships sailed out of Rockland, taking passengers to ports from Bar Harbor to Boston. But to truly sense Rockland as a busy port, you must swing your mind back in time.

From Rockland and neighboring Thomaston and Warren, Maine men have launched more than 3,000 ships, from the little pinnaces built by early settlers through the eras of clipper ships and minesweepers up to the lovely schooners of today.

Men became millionaires in Rockland. Enormous fortunes were made in Rockland lime, Rockland fishing fleets, Rockland boat building. Life boomed in high style in Rockland.

And in low style, too. In the heyday of sail, thousands of ships sailed into and out of Rockland harbor every year. With all those sailors in town, the Rockland waterfront had as many saloons and whorehouses as the wildest boom town in the Wild West.

They say that the liveliest street of sin in Maine was Sea Street in Rockland, where bars and girls flourished. The name has changed to Tillson Avenue now, and only the oldest have memories of Sea Street. But a gleam lights up in the eyes of a few hearty grandfathers at the mention of "The Spanish Villa" or "The Point". Rockland still has a special, untamed masculine vigor.

Lime built Rockland's wealth. In the 1850's, coastal schooners were hauling upwards of 1.5 million casks of lime out of Rockland Harbor yearly to cities along the Atlantic coast. Rockland lime helped to build many of those cities. It also built the Lime Rock Bank, the Lime Rock Railroad and the Lime Rock Gazette in Rockland.

Every working day more than 140 wagons made a thousand trips between the limestone quarries and the Rockland waterfront. They frequently had to struggle axle deep through the mud, causing traffic snarls so terrible that they led to the building of the amazing Lime Rock Railroad in 1891.

Along this unique railorad track, 12½ miles long, four engines pulled 500 small dumping-cars, filled with lime rock. Small as the railroad was, the loads it moved were huge. Records for 1919 show it hauled 33,166 tons of coal, 16,042 tons of soil from the quarries, 144,627 tons of cement and brick, and 130,779 tons of lime. The last equipment of the railroad was sold in 1942.

More than 25 million tons of lime were shipped out of Rockland. Lime, however, was one of the most dangerous cargoes a ship could carry, and because Rockland harbor handled 1.5 million casks of lime a year, Rockland had more than its share of ship fires.

Whenever water seeped into a lime cask, fire resulted. There was no way to put out such a fire except by suffocation. The burning vessel was towed to a remote part of the harbor. There, all hatches, vents or holes letting air into the cargo hold were plugged tight shut. Months later the fire might die from lack of oxygen. If it didn't, the ship was scuttled.

But Rockland has a vigorous culture, too.

Here is the Farnsworth Museum, one of America's fine small museums, with close ties to N.C. Wyeth, Andrew Wyeth and James Wyeth. Here is the birthplace of poet Edna St. Vincent Millay and the home of Maxine Elliot, once the toast of Broadway and Paris; Maine's greatest photographer Kosti Ruohomaa, was born, worked and died here too young, at age 47; and the greatest Maine composer, Walter Piston, was born here and died in 1976. Louise Nevelson, the world-famous sculptress, grew up here as Louise Berliawsky.

According to Rockland records, in 1605 Capt. George Weymouth of England sailed up the St. George River in his ship Archangel. While Weymouth and 17 of his crew explored the site where Thomaston now stands, James Rosier, the historian of the expedition, led nine men to the place where, 383 years later, Rockland today stands.

But it was not until 1765 that the first settler came here, Isaiah Tolman, from Stoughton, Mass. By 1770, 11 families had settled in Shore village, the first name of Rockland.

And 10 of those 11 first families appear to have prospered, multiplied and stayed in Rockland. I went back to the records of Shore village, so I would know the names of the first families of Rockland and treat their descendants with due respect. And then I checked the phone book. I'm happy to report there are 27 Tolmans, the name of the first settler in 1765, in the Rockland-Belfast phone book today.

All the original 11 names are listed except one. Hugh Killsa, came here in 1770 from New Hampshire, married Lois Robbins and had nine children. But no one by that name is listed in Rockland's phone book today.

However, Rockland's other first families multiplied in Biblical style.

The Spear family multiplied most, with 45 names in today's phone book. It was 1796 when Capt. Jonathan Spear began the clan here. I count 30 Crocketts—and the original Jonathan Crockett came to Shore Village from Portland in 1769. The others who made up the 11 families in 1770 follow, with brackets telling how many by the same name are listed in today's phone book 278 years later: Barrows (4); Blackington (7); Fales (13); Jameson (25); Keene (13); Lindsey (10); and Rankin (7).

There's continuity plus fertility in Rockland.

Victory Chimes, three masted 100-year old schooner, passes Steer Clear, anchored at Butter Island, Penobscot Bay.

WINDJAMMERS AND THE BUILDING OF HERITAGE

ROCKLAND — One of the special pleasures of Penobscot Bay is seeing the windjammer schooners under full, majestic sail. Fourteen of these beauties, some more than a century old, sail on week-long cruises out of their homeports in Rockland and Camden. Most of their captains know Steer Clear because, over the years, we have shared the same coves or harbors for overnight anchorage. When they invite us to come aboard for a visit, we always go.

We go for two reasons. First because of the beauty, history and workmanship in these boats. Second because of the infectious joy of their passengers.

Each summer 5,000 passengers go cruising in Maine waters aboard these handsome schooners. They come from all across the nation, and abroad. They are of all ages, from seven to 70. For a great many, this cruise may be their first voyage at sea, their first time on a sailing ship, and their first experience of the coast of Maine. When those "firsts" are mixed into an office worker from Detroit, or a young bride and groom from Duluth, the result is usually bubbling happiness and excited wonder. They can seldom get enough of the islands, the coves, the seabirds, the quiet, the stars and the surf. They enjoy talking about their new joys. Many come back, year after year. "For $500 we get six days and nights of sailing the Maine coast. What other vacation could set us up so well for another year of living and working in a city?" said the honeymooners from Duluth.

The owners and crews of Maine windjammers are a special breed of seamen and women and often wonderful craftsmen to boot. Here, as an example of them, is the story of one couple—Douglas and Linda Lee, young owner-builders of the windjammer-schooner "Heritage," and the day they launched her in Rockland harbor. They invited us to the launching. The handsome invitation from the Lees and their partner John Foss didn't show the sweat of four years of work, nor the big gamble of every cent they owned and every dollar they could borrow. Their invitation read:

"Coastal Schooner Heritage Launching.

The Heritage will be launched on the High Tide at Noon on Saturday, April 14, 1983, at the North End Shipyard, Rockland, Maine."

Five years later, I remember the day well. This was the first launching of a commercial coastal schooner in Rockland since the Brinkman went down the ways of the old Snow yard 65 years ago. For 100 years before that Rockland had been the hub of schooners. So thousands of Rocklanders came to cheer this rebirth of Rockland history on the day Heritage met the sea.

Heritage is 94 feet long, 24 feet wide, draws 8 feet of water and 18 feet when its centerboard is down. It is the spitting image of the best of those two-masted coastal schooners which made Maine the king, queen and crown prince of boats and boat builders 100 years ago.

Take, for example, its centerboard well to see what makes Heritage such a special vessel in modern boat building. It is made from oak, 12 inches thick, 19 inches wide, 31 feet long. It was sawn here in the North End Shipyard by young craftsmen. The decks are 5,000 board feet of pine, three inches thick and four inches wide, all of it cut on a four-sided planer built in 1902 which, rejuvenated by Douglas Lee, did the whole job in five hours.

Heritage has been carrying 33 passengers on week-long voyages along the coast of Maine every summer since 1983.

Douglas and Linda Lee and partner John Foss hold captain's papers and licenses as Masters of Sailing Vessels. Lee, from West Bath, went to Morse High School in Bath, took a master's degree in mechanical engineering at the Pratt Institute in New York City. "My Dad had a Maine coastal schooner, the Richard Robbins Sr.," he says. "I crewed on his boat, went as cook, then mate, finally captain until I was into my 20s.''

Doug and Linda met at the Pratt Institute, where Linda took her degree in fashion merchandising, and worked later as an assistant buyer in a huge New York department store. "I married her," says Doug, "and took her to Maine and aboard the Richard Robbins for our honeymoon. I worked as cook and Linda was my cookee."

Rebuilding and sailing old commercial vessels has been their life since marriage. When they were in their early 20s, they bought for $5,000 an old oyster dragger. It was the 65-foot Isaac H. Evans, which had been built in 1886 in Mauricetown, N.J. They sailed it from New Jersey to the historic Percy and Small shipyard on the Kennebec. Two years later, after spending $50,000 cash and thousands of hours of their own hard work, they launched the Isaac H. Evans for the second time in its long life. Ever since, the Issac H. Evans, 102 years old, has been sailing as a successful cruise ship on Penobscot Bay.

Next, with partner Foss, a Bowdoin graduate and former Coast Guard officer, they spent three long winters rebuilding and rejuvenating an even older schooner, the Lewis French, built in South Bristol in 1871. This vessel has been a cruise ship in Maine waters since 1976. It is the oldest commercial vessel still sailing in the United States, aged 117 years. (The Isaac H. Evans is the fourth oldest.)

By 1979, the Lees and Foss had turned 30 years old. They had rejuvenated old vessels, and captained them successfully as cruise ship windjammers. With the money they earned, the three bought a broken-down shipyard on the Rockland waterfront, bought and restored two condemned houses to live in, also on the waterfront. Looking for a new challenge, they began research to build a completely new sailing coastal schooner as coastal schooners were built more than 100 years ago.

During the four years they worked building Heritage, Linda had two babies. The oldest, Clara, seven years old in 1988, and Rachel, five, are veteran sailors, who help with lines, and in the galley aboard Heritage.

Doug Lee takes me aboard his vessel, shows me the quarters where the four Lees live below the huge, handsome wheel. He shows the enormous cookstove where Linda makes fish chowders and Sunday roast beef for 33 passengers. He shows the donkey engine on the foredeck—a jewel built in 1917 and perfectly restored by Lee—which works the bilge pumps and anchor windlass. He shows the cabinet work in the guest staterooms, cramped, yet elegant, and the spacious after cabin where guests and crew gather after the anchor is set.

Lee is proud of the work. "We built every inch of her right here. Even forged her metal. We did it in the cold of winter, when we were not out sailing the other boats."

Lee says he put Heritage into the water after spending about $350,000 on building it, and $100,000 more after launch. That is less than half the price it would cost to duplicate Heritage in a regular shipyard. Even so, getting financing was hard. A bank in Rockland decided to say "No" to Lee and Heritage. He took out a large mortgage from the Merrill Trust Co. of Bangor, but still needed more money. He got private loans, often from customers who had sailed with him and Linda and Foss aboard the Isaac H. Evans or the Lewis French.

Heritage is a lovely, nostalgic vessel. But more than the strength or the beauty is the fact that the skills needed to build it are alive, well and flourishing in Maine.

Young hands are doing these old jobs as well as they were ever done before. Despite the moaning and groaning that "the old skills are lost forever," you can see these skills in the North End Shipyard at Rockland. The young craftsmen sometimes use tools and machines that are three and four times as old as they are.

Together the young workers and the old tools make a good sight for skeptical eyes.

OUTWARD BOUND ON HURRICANE ISLAND

HURRICANE ISLAND — One of the great success stories of the Maine coast is the rugged Outward Bound School on Hurricane Island, a long hour's boat ride into Penobscot Bay from Rockland.

More than 6,000 people a year are experiencing Outward Bound. Since it began in a tiny way in 1966, more than 40,000 men and women of all ages and backgrounds have been through Outward Bound on this granite island, or its satellites in Bethel, Maine, and the Florida Keys.

I first knew Outward Bound in its infant days. My son John went there the second summer it was in operation, in 1967, between his graduation from Lincoln Academy and his enlistment in the U.S. Navy for the Vietnam War. There were 200 youngsters, all males, during that entire summer compared to many thousands of men and women this year. The fee for a three week course in 1967 was $400, and there were 20 part-time instructors on the island and six people in the Rockland headquarters. Now there are 300 instructors, 50 people in the administrative office on shore, and the yearly revenues are $7 million. Hurricane Island has within 25 years grown into the biggest of the five Outward Bound operations in the United States.

Hurricane Island whaleboats and their crews are familiar and welcome sights among the midcoast islands and coastal towns, where they sometimes paint a church or meeting hall in a day, as a goodwill gesture. They sail open wooden boats, based on a ketch design of the 1880s. Whaleboats look deucedly uncomfortable and spartan for the dozen young men and women who sail, row, eat, and sleep aboard them, totally exposed to wind, rain, fog and stormy seas for seven days and nights. But these boats are strong, simple and seaworthy. Those are vital qualities when rank amateurs are the crew, under the command of two experienced instructors.

Hurricane Island boats are unmistakable. Unmistakable at a distance because of their uniquely shaped white sails; unmistakable on windless days because no other boats on the Maine coast are rowed with twelve people at the oars; unmistakable at night, because on no other boats will you see twelve people huddled together, trying to sleep out on the open deck; unmistakable at dawn, because only on a Hurricane Island boat will you see twelve men and women diving overboard before 6 a.m. to swim in icy Maine water.

The basic three-week course at Hurricane Island Outward Bound is a rugged, rigorous experience for body, spirit and mind, designed to discover unknown abilities and to stretch self-reliance and team work to the limit. For example, in a new kind of mutual dependence required in a whaleboat, you may find a girl from a wealthy Atlanta family rowing beside a black boy from Detroit, a college kid from Yale pulling beside a high school drop-out from Montana. Regardless of birth or background, a dozen young people who have never before been to sea, find themselves together in an open boat for a week, dependent upon each other, having to live, eat, sail, sleep, go to the bathroom, in front of each other. They quickly learn they must respect and trust each other.

But they have been intensively prepared on Hurricane Island. Before this week in an open boat, they have endured and shared many hitherto undreamed of challenges. For example, every morning at 6 a.m. they have run five miles around the rough terrain of Hurricane Island; and at the end of the run, each has jumped from a 20 foot high cliff into the icy

Outward Bound: practice drill in recovering from a capsize in a Hurricane Island whaleboat.

ocean, regardless of whether they have ever before been a runner or a swimmer. Working together as teams, they have rappelled 100 foot high vertical rock faces, conquered obstacle courses, washed other people's dinner dishes and stood watches in the wee hours at the island's emergency radio sets.

During three weeks of complete interdependency, they also experience a test of self-dependency which few men and women ever face in their lives. Each is put ashore alone for three days and nights on an uninhabited island. Each is provided only with a ground sheet to sleep upon, a few matches to start the fire which they keep burning for warmth, company, food. They have a small supply of water, a fish hook, a small ration of food. But nothing to divert them from themselves—no book or magazine, no radio. The rules forbid a Hurricane Islander from even talking to passing boats. Lucky ones may be blessed with days and nights of fine weather during their solo. Others may be alone in thick fog or drenching rain. They get to know themselves as never before. They get to know they can survive alone. They acquire new confidence in their bodies, minds, souls by pushing all three to hitherto unknown limits and coming through the experience in good shape.

Outward Bound may sound like a grueling, outdoor challenge only welcomed by environmentalists and exercise freaks. But Maine's Hurricane Island School does far more. For example, Outward Bound has been running a special "Youth-at-Risk" program in Florida, mostly for street gang kids, in serious trouble because of crimes and drug and alcohol abuse.

Florida has a contract with the Hurricane Island Outward Bound school to put 550 youngsters-at-risk through a grueling 28-day program each year. It is an alternate which the youngsters can choose instead of going to jail or reform school. Outward Bound teaches them a new kind of self-reliance, self-esteem, self-worth. For four weeks, they live and work together, traveling in canoes, camping on riverbanks, experiencing and surviving strains, challenges and stress they never knew they could meet successfully.

Results? Far better than achieved by keeping the same kind of at-risk youngsters in state institutions. And the expense to tax-payers is less.

Records show the recidivism rate, the tendency to return to criminal habits, of "graduates" from the Outward Bound special program has dropped to 19 percent compared to 40 percent and higher in other programs at jails and reform schools.

Maine, after watching the success rate in Florida for 10 years, opted to launch a similar program in 1988-9 to use Outward Bound for Maine "Youth at Risk".

In a different direction, Outward Bound is educating educators in its special fields. "We now have three college semester programs, each 90 days, for which participating colleges grant 15 credits," says Outward Bound.

One course, running from September to December, is called the Maine Experience. It begins with a sailing expedition among Maine's islands in 30-foot pulling boats, progresses to a series of natural history studies on board the 55-foot motor vessel Hurricane or the schooner Bowdoin, and winds up with cross-country skiing in December.

From January to April, another course is run at the school's bases in the Florida Keys and Everglades, with studies in tropical marine life, ornithology and environmental issues.

Atop Hurricane Island, Outward Bound students get a course in climbing a rock face.

Between March and May, another 15-credit college course begins with mountaineering and winter camping skills in the White Mountains, New Hampshire; then moves with the season to rock-climbing and canoeing, balanced with studies in natural history and community service.

In 1988, Outward Bound began Elderhostel programs for men and women 55 and over, in ice-rock climbing in winter and open boat sailing in summer.

Outward Bound originated at the preparatory school in Scotland attended by Prince Philip and others in the royal family as a hands-on experience supplemental to traditional classroom education.

The influence of Outward Bound at Hurricane Island has spread throughout a spectrum of American life. Major corporations send teams of young executives for training. There are special programs for inner-city minorities, for educators, for women, for alcoholics, for senior citizens, for young law-breakers.

As the horizons of Outward Bound have widened, so have its facilities. The school now has satellite bases all along the Maine coast, inland to Bethel, at the Dartmouth College campus, in Chesapeake Bay, and in the Florida Keys and Everglades.

That rough, long-abandoned granite island off Rockland, where thousands of immigrants from Italy and Ireland once quarried Hurricane

Whaleboats from Outward Bound on Hurricane Island, clip in a stiff breeze on Penobscot Bay.

granite for great bridges and federal buildings in Washington, New York, Boston and Philadelphia, is again influencing America. Today it is influencing minds and philosophies more than edifices.

COASTAL ART ON A STORMY DAY

CAMDEN — Poor Billie Clark was, the records show, a town drunk who imbibed vanilla extract when he could not afford anything better. When he died alone in 1938, he was buried in a pauper's grave. But today his magnificent ship goes sailing on. I found his masterpiece when foul weather kept Steer Clear in Camden.

Today, you can marvel at Billie Clark's masterpiece, the Minnie Gurney, which stands in the place of honor at the art gallery of the Camden-Rockport Museum and Historical Society. It is a detailed model 9 feet long, 4 feet high, of a full-rigged ship of the 1880s under full sail.

Clark's ship carries 31 cloth sails, all bellied out in a spanking breeze, seeming to send the magical sounds of wind, sail and ship humming through the timbers of four tall masts.

Cringles, reef points and roping are worked into each perfectly stitched sail. The detail of the rigging is precise and expertly made.

Clark labored long and alone, hand-carving from hardwood 230 miniature blocks, each pierced and grooved and still in working order. The records show he spent 20 years working, destroying and remaking his Minnie Gurney.

Below decks, Clark furnished his loved ship finely. He decorated the captain's quarters with hand-carved, miniature furniture, complete to lamps, chairs, beds, even miniature books on the miniature bookshelves.

He named his four-master ship the Minnie Gurney. But no ship of that name exists in old shipping registers. Speculation is that Minnie Gurney may have been the name of a girl treasured in Clark's dreams. If so, he paid her the enormous tribute of painstaking work done over 20 years.

A notation in a half-forgotten folder on Clark, which the museum curator found for me, says ''Billie Clark was addicted to vanilla extract and when under its influence, he would smash up the Minnie Gurney in anger. Then when he sobered up, he would rebuild his ship.''

Clark, the town drunk buried in a pauper's grave, would be astonished to see his Minnie Gurney occupying the place of honor in the Camden-Rockport Historical Society.

No one is willing to set a dollar value on this remarkable ship model. But I found a letter which values it at the cost of a pauper's funeral. In the thin folder on Clark, is a letter written 50 years ago by Mrs. Percy Good, local undertaker, protesting she had not been paid by the town for the pauper's burial she had given Clark.

She said Camden had been paying $95 for paupers' funerals, then had dropped the price to $75. But she had never been paid a cent for Clark. She wrote that on the morning she removed Clark's body from his dilapidated house, the model of the Minnie Gurney had been there. But when she returned after the funeral, the model was gone.

She thought that Alton French, a local storekeeper, had taken it for unpaid bills. She thought the model was worth more than the $75 she asked for funeral expenses. (French later donated the model to the historical society.)

On the day I went ashore from Steer Clear and discovered Billie Clark, the Cramer Museum and the Camden-Rockport Historical Society was also featuring the work of three native painters. The men's lives caught my fancy.

Hanging on the wall were paintings of local scenes by E.H. Bramhall, a boat builder who was born in Belfast in 1846 and died in Camden in 1906. Standing out boldly among his art work is Bramhall's outsized business card:

E.H. BRAMHALL
Boat builder
Steam Yachts and Launches
Rowboats and Sailing Yachts

Close by the illustrated business card is Bramhall's handwritten, one-page last will and testament:

"I, Ezra Hall Bramhall, bequeath one dollar to my eldest son, Louis E. Bramhall, and nothing else. To my son, Howard E. Bramhall, I bequeath one dollar also and all of my materials for woodworking, drawing and painting. All the rest of my property I bequeath to my sisters."

This self-taught painter and boat builder who disinherited his two sons was, at the age of 19, captain of a United States troop transport during the last year of the Civil War. When Bramhall was 40, he quit building boats for a while so he could construct a pontoon bridge in his boatyard at Camden for a distant and foreign island. When it was finished in 1888, he shipped it out in pieces, went with it and rebuilt and installed his pontoon bridge on Curacao Island in the Netherlands Antilles.

Painter William S. Barrett, 1853-1927, was born and died in Rockport. He too began as a local boat builder, but he turned into a better and more prolific painter than Bramhall.

Barrett went away, first to New York and then to Paris, to study painting, but returned to Rockport for the last 20 years of his life. While he lived in New York, an exhibition of his work was handsomely praised in the New York Times and New York Herald. At his death in 1927, Barrett left 400 paintings.

In 1972, when Barrett's work was shown in El Paso, Texas, the seascapes of this Rockport boat builder were compared to the great paintings of Turner. When they were shown in Chicago in 1975, critics likened Barrett's talents to the talents of Whistler and of Turner.

When he lived in Rockport, Barrett lived in solitude as a recluse. But at sea, he was gregarious. Barrett moored his yacht, The Whim, in Rockport harbor and cruised in it with such famed Monhegan painters as Rockwell Kent, George Bellows, A.T. Bircher and Paul Dougherty.

The third local artist in the show was Willis E. Carleton, who was born in Rockport in 1854 and died here in 1945. His specialty was designing and painting magnificent stage scenery for lavish Broadway shows and for grand opera—an esoteric career for a boy raised in Rockport 130 years ago. Scale models of Carleton's lavish sets were displayed, next to pauper Billie Clark's full-rigged four-masted sailing ship.

Another fascinating look into the roots of Rockport and the heritage of Camden is the home of Rockport's first white settler, Robert Thorndike, built before the American Revolution.

Thorndike, who lived for 104 years and fathered 12 children, built his small frontier home in 1770. His eldest son was born in it in 1773, the first male white child born in Goose River, as Rockport was called then, and he lived in it until 1825. Frederick Conway bought the house in 1826, and generations of Conways lived in it until 1916.

Over the centuries, additions were built on. A special charm is that the furnishings of each period are still in place. vivid testimony to the progression in comfort and cash.

In the original small sleeping cha...ber above the living room-kitchen, a visitor can see how the roof timbers were fastened by tree-nails (trunnels) and see the marks of the adze and broadaxe on the beams. The barn holds a collection of old sleighs, carriages, farm implements, ice-cutting saws and a hand weaving loom. The Thorndike house is an intimate close-up look at more than 200 years of living and working by Maine pioneers and their farming descendants.

HELEN AND MARGE: THE MAINE CONNECTIONS AT CAMDEN

CAMDEN — Helen Andrews and Marge Knight surely have more male admirers than any two women in Maine.

They have them by the thousands. Their admirers come from as far as Japan, Holland, Spain, Greece, Norway—and from as close as their own Camden Harbor.

But not ten admirers in a thousand would recognize Helen Andrews or Marge Knight by sight. They know their voices, two of the friendliest, most helpful and cheerful voices along the coast of Maine.

Helen and Marge are year-round operators of Camden Marine Radio Telephone, the link between boats at sea and home and business on shore.

The variety of their customers is staggering. Fishermen far out on Georges Bank talk every day and night to Helen or Marge, and through them reach their fish plants along the New England coast to work out schedules on when and where to land their catch. They call their wives, telling them when to be at the dock.

Psychiatrists aboard sailing yachts may use Helen and Marge to link them with distressed patients in midtown Manhattan.

The skipper of a Japanese freighter may ask Helen or Marge to connect him to his home office in Tokyo; a Boston-based banker will arrange fuel delivery to his Maine island by calling Camden Marine.

In a summer month, the log at Camden Marine shows 12,000 contacts with ships at sea off the coast of Maine. From about 4 p.m. until close-down at 11 p.m. during July and August, a barrage of radiophone calls to Camden Marine pours in from the cruising boats.

Parents are calling home, all across the nation, to see if the kids are behaving. Businessmen, on a sea-going holiday, cannot resist calling the office and impressing land-bound colleagues and secretaries with a radiotelephone call from a boat at sea.

All this private business is done in public. A pastime after dinner at sea is to listen to other people's phone calls. Fascinating trivia for the most part, sometimes spiced with tragedy, tantrums, and ruthless-sounding money deals.

This eavesdropping is legal. All ship-to-shore conversations can be heard by anyone with a VHF radio.

The names of the calling vessels can be an enchantment. Who would not be titillated to overhear Wings of the Morning calling Laguna Beach, Calif.? Or the cruise ship Caribe arranging visas and plane tickets for three Pakistani stewards and a pastry chef from Greece?

But it is the personal touch and warmth of Helen Andrews and Marge Knight which make Camden Marine a part of the family, in the way the operators of old-time switchboards used to be in small towns.

I remember with glee Camden Marine's voice going out to sea one night saying "Aphrodite, Aphrodite, it sounds like you've got laryngitis tonight. You should spray your throat and gargle before you turn in."

I remember with delight the night a vessel in Camden Harbor needed to borrow a guitar and a banjo and asked Marge to help. She made calls all around Camden for hours on behalf of this music-starved crew.

Marge is a key figure in birthdays and births and sometimes sudden deaths. She is everyone's helpful friend-on-shore.

Camden Marine is not part of the telephone company. It was started by Penobscot Bay pilots, and it is run with the rare combination of efficiency and person-to-person friendliness which the computerized New England Telephone Company can never match.

LILIAN BERLIAWSKY: FROM HIGH FASHION TO USED BOOKS

CAMDEN— Never be surprised at who is doing what in Maine. A dignified bishop points his backside to heaven once a day as he digs a bushel of clams on low tide. A former "madam" in New Orleans does a flourishing mail order business in rope ladders. A former top researcher in psychiatric disorders quit his big city hospital, came to Maine and now finds happiness in making beautiful stained glass. A former Ph.D quit the scholar's life to become a happy collector of garbage in a small midcoast town.

Wonderful transformations abound in Maine and one of the nicest is at the used bookstore on Bay View Street, Camden. I found it when fog days and cabin fever drove me ashore.

I tied the dinghy at the town dock and walked one block to the sign "A B C D E Books," where up to 30,000 precious volumes are stocked. There I met Lillian Berliawsky, once a highly successful jewelry-and-handbag buyer from Saks Fifth Avenue and Bergdorf Goodman. The "used books" lady of Camden was one of Manhattan's top fashion buyers.

In Maine, Lillian Berliawsky, seller of second hand books, is a delightful magnet to collectors from around the nation and across the ocean. To the fashion merchants of Fifth Avenue, she was the bright and beautiful young Lillian Mildwoff, who married Nathan Berliawsky of Rockland in a ceremony performed in 1948 by the Chief Naval Chaplain. That ceremony was followed with a Manhattan reception at the Pierre Hotel.

"If you can buy jewelry, you can buy books. If you are a good buyer, then you are a good buyer—of anything" smiles Lillian Berliawsky. She stands barely five feet tall, brown eyes brilliant when the talk turns to books or painting. Her sister-in-law was the famous artist, Lousie Nevelson. "Once my office was on the 74th floor of the Empire State building," she says. "I was in it that summer day when a plane crashed through the 76th floor. Camden is better."

Her husband Nathan Berliawsky, formerly owner of Rockland's Thorndike Hotel, and brother to sculptress Louise Nevelson, brought Lillian to Maine in 1948. (He had been brought to Rockland from Russia, in 1903, at the age of two.) "I was into books by 1962. Then in 1967 I lost my lease in Rockland and moved into these two adjoining stores here in Camden."

Books are everywhere. Labyrinthine paths run between shelves piled with books higher than a man. Book browsers wander to their favorite pastures. A baffled newcomer is lost. But ask Lillian for a title and her smile lights up the room and she marches you unerringly to the very spot where your heart's desire is waiting for you to buy it and take it home to live with you. The variety is staggering. Cookbooks in all languages and from many centuries. Art volumes which are priceless. Books on Chinese Emperors and African explorers. A library in itself of World War I, another of the Civil War. Biographies galore. Choice old magazines. Inside locked areas, very special rarities are shown to avid and loving collectors.

"No. I don't specialize. Everyone who walks through the door has a special field they cherish. Who am I to turn up my nose at books in the field they love? If the books are good, I buy."

The passing parade of tastes is fascinating to watch. While I was in the store one lady bought a choice copy of the Chinese Tales of Genji; a man from Boston came searching for a rare monograph by Bernard Berenson; a student bought paperbacks on economics; another man came in to buy guide books to Africa; a professor came to find Clarkson's "History of Russia"; another buyer found a first edition of a Gladys Hasty Carroll novel and another bought a first edition of a children's book by Nathaniel Hawthorne. Then I saw the most touching buy of the day . . . A choirmaster came back, this time with money in hand and a lot of it, to buy a very early edition of Handel's Messiah with Handel's alterations in his own hand. He leaves, happy, clutching his cherished prize.

"Now Handel will have the home he deserves. It makes me happy too" says Lillian. "There is emotion in this business the long, hard search; the unexpected find; then the sale to just the right buyer." Some of her books fetch thousands of dollars. "Of course, a good sale is a joy. But selling to the right buyer, creating the happiness—this is as important as the money."

Lillian showed me through her special world. I ask her why the odd name of "The A B C D E" for her used books shop. She tells me "Those letters are the beginning of all knowledge, all literature and much happiness."

IF IT MOVES, YOU'LL SEE IT AT OWLS HEAD TRANSPORTATION MUSEUM

OWLS HEAD — Jim Rockefeller came alongside Steer Clear in a harbor launch on a foggy morning in Camden Harbor and asked: "Have you ever been to the Transportation Museum at Owls Head?" We had not. And we all agreed that for sailors stuck in Camden Harbor for another fog day, a visit to the Owls Head Transportation Museum might be just the ticket.

Jim Rockefeller, chairman of the museum, round-faced, balding, forever cheerful, said he would be back at 1 o'clock with a car at the dock. Bob and Midge Archibald, guidance teachers vacationing on the sailboat Piper from Hingham, Mass., had shared a raft mooring with us for three fog-filled days and nights, and they were glad to leave a cramped cockpit to visit the transportation museum with us.

Owls Head Transportation Museum, Rockland, displays a fascinating variety of fine old cars, planes and even steam rollers. Top picture shows Mrs. Harvey Gamage, South Bristol, in her 1908 Sears Roebuck Motor Buggy.

Don't be turned off by the words "transportation museum," though two duller words could not be joined together. This is a trip of high romance and nostalgia and delightful fun of a rare kind. But if you are hair-shirted about unadulterated enjoyment, then you can adulterate the enjoyment by saying the trip is educational, a study in history, in engineering, in the development of the American economy and lifestyle—and in the history of air war.

You'll see and hear, touch and possibly even drive, antique cars, fly old aeroplanes, run one of America's first steamrollers and first one-lung farm tractors. You'll be amazed at the beauty of ancient engines turning heavy fly wheels.

Every plane here flies, every car here runs, every engine here can be fired up and put to work.

You'll thrill at the sight of the blazing red Stanley Steamer racer, with its sleek lines and gleaming brass headlights, hinged windshield and shiny brass horn. Lift up the hood, and there is no engine; instead a white asbestos firebox. It takes 20 minutes to fire up this beauty's boiler and get her steam going. Then she'll do 100 mph.

An historic touring car 1914 Benz from the collection at Owls Head Transportation Museum near Camden.

Bottom picture is of a Spitfire, (R.A.F.) which helped with the Battle of Britain in World War II. This plane is owned and flown by Thomas J. Watson Jr. of North Haven, Maine.

Only 19 cars like her were ever built, 90 years ago. Only three like her are in the world today. The Stanley twins who built her came from Kingfield, Maine, Sugarloaf ski country now. They summered at Squirrel Island in Boothbay Harbor. Famed for their Stanley Steamers, first built at Mechanic Falls in 1897, the Stanley twins were geniuses of such diverse talents that they also invented the dry plate battery and were expert violin makers.

But because the steamers took 20 minutes to fire up and the Model T Ford took only 30 seconds to start, the Stanleys went out of business by 1923.

At Owls Head you'll see also the first "horseless carriages," built in 1903 and earlier. You'll see the 1907 Cadillac Model K, and the Model T Ford of 1913. What's better, you'll see these classics running up and down the runway of the old airfield where the museum is located, a few miles out of Rockland. The Model S and Model A Fords are here, too.

In the mood for nostalgia of the bootleg-gangster-flapper era of the Roaring Twenties? Then you'll relish the sight of the enormous luxury of a 16-cylinder—yes, Virginia, 16-cylinder—Cadillac, first built in 1927.

For elegance unmatched today, look at the lines and the interior of the old Pierce Arrow touring car, the brute muscle of a rare 1930 Bentley Speed Six, or a 1939 Super 8 Packard with a body custom built by Brunn.

If dignity and restrained richness are your taste, try the classic Rolls Royces which may be bought—price on request.

Here, too, is the greatest fighter plane of all time, the Spitfire Mark 9 of the Battle of Britain, the plane that held off Hitler. This is one of only eight in the world still flying.

Going back to World War I, here is the replica of the Fokker Tri-plane, flown by the Red Baron. Beside that heroic plane are the Allied planes which finally beat it—The Spad, flown by Ace Eddie Rickenbacher; and the Neuport, made in France.

Jim Rockefeller crashed the precious 1912 Curtiss Pusher. A young girl repaired the torn wings, which are made of cotton.

On a foggy day in Camden, visit this museum at Owls Head, and you'll enjoy a treasure trove of Americana.

CAMDEN: MIDCOAST JEWEL

CAMDEN HARBOR — Thank God and His Ice Age for the Camden Hills; thank Mary Louise Bok for the open park at the head of the harbor; and thank James Richards for being the first settler to land here by boat May 8, 1769. The end result is Camden, midcoast jewel of Maine.

But whom do we thank for docking windjammers in the heart of town? Were there hot debates in town council when the schooners first wended through the crowded harbor to discharge and embark their weekly load of cruise passengers just off Main Street? Today these windjammers are a hallmark of Camden. The schooners crowded into the harbor in the very center of town is what makes Camden the place "where the mountains meet the sea."

If the throngs of summer seem too much today, picture the crowd of 10,000 which came to Camden Harbor in 1900 to see the launching of the largest schooner in the world, the six master George W. Wells, 325 feet long. To celebrate the day, the battleships Kearsage and Indiana dropped anchor here and sent officers and crew ashore to the gala dance in the Opera House.

If, in midsummer today, it is almost impossible for a visiting boat to find a mooring or swinging room to anchor, it was worse 82 years ago. On August 30, 1906 seven battleships and four destroyers plus armadas of schooners, yachts, fishing boats crowded into Camden harbor to honor Camden's own naval hero, William Conway. He was the man who refused the order to haul down the flag at Pensacola Navy Yard in 1861 in the Civil War.

But it is the Camden Hills as much as the harbor which have pulled people here for centuries. In the early 1600s, James Rosier wrote admiringly of the "great mountains". In 1614 Captain John Smith wrote about "the high mountains against whose feet doth beat the sea." Thoreau, Edna St. Vincent Millay, Hodding Carter and a hundred other writers have praised the beauty of the Camden Hills.

Highest of the Camden Hills is Mount Megunticook (1,380 feet), followed by Ragged Mountain (1,300 feet) and Bald Mountain (1,272 feet). Rising up almost out of downtown Camden is 800-foot Mount Battie with its spectacular, unforgettable panoramic views across the islands of Penobscot Bay, and the convenience of a summer road to the summit.

Camden Harbor—Tall masted windjammers with the Mary Day in foreground.

When I see parents trying to stop their children from careening down the steep inclines of Mt. Battie, I'm reminded of the wild ride of man and bear around Mt. Battie more than 200 years ago.

In the winter of 1783, the first settler in Camden, James Richards, went bear hunting with two newly arrived friends, Leonard Metcalf and a man named Webber. Richards had the only gun, and he stalked and shot a big bear on Mt. Battie. Webber and Metcalf meanwhile smoked out the den. Two large cubs raced out. Metcalf seized one by the ears, but Webber was too scared to help wrestle the bear cub to the ground. So Metcalf jumped astride the bear cub, and off the man and bear went, tearing around the mountain. Metcalf tried to lean down to slit the bear's throat, but his knife kept closing.

Metcalf, his face, hands, clothes ripped to ribbons by the wild ride through forest and thorn bushes, was done in. The bear cub collapsed from exhaustion. Whereupon cowardly Webber finally arrived on the scene with his hatchet and finished off the prostrate bear.

First settler James Richards was reputedly the greatest hunter of his time and is credited with killing 30 bear and 70 moose around Camden. Megunticook, meaning Harbor of the High Mountain, was the original Indian name of Camden when Richards sailed into harbor from Dover, New Hampshire. On watch in the bow was a black man, the deckhand and mate. He and Richards shouted in admiration at the first sight of Camden harbor, the wooded shore, the mountains.

"There!" shouted the black man, pointing at the lovely little island at the harbor entrance. "There! That's my island! That's the place I want!" Richards said "It's yours!"

Thus it became Nigger Island in 1769. And that was its name on U.S. government charts for over 150 years. Finally, the island was bought by the publisher of the Saturday Evening Post and Ladies Home Journal, Cyrus K. Curtis, who kept a huge house and yacht in Camden. Curtis gave the island to the town. The town changed the name from Nigger to Curtis Island, and so it is called on current charts. The lighthouse, built in 1825, still guides ships into Camden.

By 1790, the population of Camden, including settlements at Goose River (Rockport now) and Clam Cove, was 331 persons. The inhabitants joined forces to petition the court of Massachusetts to upgrade their "plantation" into a town. On February 17, 1791, Camden became Maine's 22nd incorporated town, under a deed signed by John Hancock, governor, and Samuel Adams, lieutenant governor. They first wanted to call the town Adams. But the court changed the name to Camden, to honor an English politician. Charles Pratt, later the Earl of Camden, was a bright and liberal member of Parliament in London who had risen to become Lord Chancellor of England. But his outspoken support for the

Camden Harbor—Looking in.

American Revolution cost him his high post as Chancellor. He had, however been raised to the peerage as first Earl of Camden. To do him honor for his help to the American Revolution, Camden, Maine, Camden, New Jersey, and Camden, South Carolina, are named in his memory.

Camden is a good town for a sailor to be fogbound, particularly if you get a mooring in the inner harbor. Steer Clear has many times lay alongside one of those sensible rafts in the inner harbor, where two boats can tie in the space it takes one boat to swing. On fog days, we tied the dinghy at the town dock and explored everything from Camden's many good shops, that will flatten a wallet quickly, to good restaurants, good marine supply stores, and a fine library. The architecture of many of the big old homes built by wealthy ship captains is superb. The state park at Mt. Battie, 5,000 acres in all, including mountains and shore, is a spectacular hiking area. In the harbor, there are million-dollar yachts to gawk at. But beware the outer harbor, which is choppy sleeping and noisy with boat traffic.

When Steer Clear leaves Camden, she goes out a better boat than she came in. On one foggy stayover, we put new plexiglass windscreens around the poor man's flying bridge; on another recarpeted the cabins; on a third, we bought a new outboard for the skiff; on a fourth, the top mechanics and boat carpenters at Wayfarer Marina gave us a tune-up and a facelift. The hospitable, unswanky, old-fashioned Camden Yacht Club does well what too few yacht clubs do at all—which is help and befriend visiting boats and boatmen.

Camden is a fine harbor to enter; but an even better to leave, for ahead lies the paradise of Penobscot Bay and the myriad islands of Penobscot Bay.

Islesboro Island and Penobscot Bay from our plane.

VIII
PENOBSCOT BAY;
NORTH HAVEN &
VINALHAVEN

Fox Island thorofare: the lovely link

Capt. Tom has found paradise

Seabird count from a plane

The dog days of cruising

A terrifying adventure; overboard in the basin

Matinicus Rock: and the Buchheisters

Finding shelter in a storm

Timberwind: through a nightmare to a dream

Tension comes in loud and clear

Piecing together the 'defence' 200 years later

Penobscot River is quiet now

Terror boarded Steer Clear with fire at sea

Charles Lindbergh used to land on this meadow on North Haven, when flying in to visit Anne Morrow.

VIII

Coming out from Camden Harbor, my shipmate asks "Where are we going today?" I enjoy rolling out the answer. "Drunkard, Fiddler and Sugar Loaves."

We'll pass these marks with meaty names ten miles to sea, when we make our turn at Browns Head Light into the Fox Islands Thorofare, between North Haven and Vinalhaven.

Deciding between islands in Penobscot Bay is like choosing between rubies and sapphires. These are the loveliest cruising waters in the world. Here lie scores of island jewels, each with its own magic. They are special gifts of God and the Ice Age, scattered like random necklaces in a cold, clear patch of ocean only about 12 miles long and 12 miles across, from the west side of the Fox Islands to the east side of Deer Isle.

Each year I cruise Penobscot Bay, I ask "Why go anywhere else—ever?" In the bright sun and clean salt air of my 'poor-man's' flying bridge, I look out at the islands across the bay. A film plays through my memory's eye, showing the islands of summers past and the islands of days and nights to come. Salt-caked names with the sound of breaking seas . . . Pulpit Rock, Cradle Cove, Duck Harbor, Pig and Sows, Widow-Island, Eagle, Eggemoggin Reach, Grog Island, Lazygut, St. Helena, Murder Rock, Brimstone, Folly Ledge, James and Willies Ledge, Ragged Arse, Pretty Marsh.

My head brims with anticipation of sheltered coves, solitude, diving for scallops, digging clams, harvesting mussels for supper; walks through island meadows sweet with wildflowers, where you can feel the roll of the ocean, hear the sound and smell the salt of the sea, yet cannot see it, barely 200 yards away. My head fills with memories too—of island graves with lichen-yellowed headstones to men lost at sea and to babies who died before they were three months old, so many of those babies. I remember cellar holes from the earliest stone houses; and nights on deck under a canopy of bright stars shining from a dark velvet sky; and long sleep in a gently rocking boat with the lap of waves at my ear.

"Steer Clear! Calling Steer Clear! Are you there, Bill?" The radio squawks me back from daydreams of the bay. Coming up from my stern is lobster-dealer Jim Brown on his way back to his pound in North Haven after selling lobsters on the mainland. We wave for the first time since last year. "I'll see you in a bit, Jim. Be in to your dock later," I answer on the radio.

Drunkard's Ledge, the Fiddler and the Monument are coming up, ahead to port. I point them out on the chart spread on the cabin roof between my shipmate and me. "We'll turn at the buoy and go into the Thorofare between Sugar Loaves and Browns Head Light." Surge of happiness.

FOX ISLAND THOROFARE: THE LOVELY LINK

FOX ISLAND THOROFARE — Martin Pring of Bristol, England, might be the most surprised sailor in heaven that the passage between North Haven and Vinalhaven is still called the Fox Island Thorofare. That was the name Pring gave it 385 years ago when he dropped anchor here.

Pring, in his 50-ton ship Speedwell, with a crew of 30 men and boys, and his smaller vessel Discoverer, 26 tons with a crew of 13 men and one boy, dropped anchor here on a July evening, 1603, long before any colonist set foot in Jamestown or any Pilgrim landed at Plymouth Rock. Pring wrote lavish praises of the fishing and the woods in this thorofare. He was especially taken by the "great silver foxes" he saw loping along both shores. So he marked the islands on his chart with the name "The Fox Islands." And that was their name for 186 years, until in 1789 John Vinal lobbied the Massachusetts legislature to change it from the Fox Islands to Vinal Haven. Vinal Haven was the name for both islands until North Haven separated from Vinalhaven in 1846.

Today, both islands are served by car ferries to and from Rockland several times a day, summer and winter. Consequently there's year-round commuting to the mainland, to visit friends, take trips, see doctors and dentists, do major shopping—or just to get off the island for a break. In summer, the traffic is heavy and constant, partly because both islands are lovely, partly because both North Haven and Vinalhaven have many rich and famous summer people with houses filled with guests, and partly because taking the ferry is an easy way for tourists to enjoy the Maine coast and islands without the bother and cost of a boat. The ferry ride to Carver's Harbor on Vinalhaven is longer, but especially beautiful because it goes through Leadbetter Narrows and up Hurricane Sound.

Three Windjammer Cruise Schooners on a glassy sea in Penobscot Bay. Tabor Boy is in foreground.

Ferries are a splendid way to see the Maine coast from a wholly different perspective than you can get from a car on land. Using ferries you can cover much of the coast.

Visitors can begin with island-seeing and whale-watching trips from Portsmouth and go to the Isles of Shoals. Then they can drive to Portland and go to sea again among the scores of islands in Casco Bay, aboard five sightseeing vessels as Longfellow II and Buccaneer or ride the Casco Bay ferries. Further downeast, sight-seeing boats run morning, noon and night from Boothbay Harbor out to the nearby islands and daily to Monhegan. Another ride is from Port Clyde, where the mail boat leaves winter and summer to Monhegan Island. Some day excursion trips run out to Penobscot Bay from Rockland and Camden. Both these ports specialize in week-long Windjammer cruises. Maine Audubon runs trips to bird islands several times a year. A State of Maine ferry runs from Lincolnville Beach to Islesboro, and another leaves from Bass Harbor on Mt. Desert to Swans Island. Longer distance ferries, which are as big and luxurious as cruise ships, run from Portland and from Bar Harbor to Yarmouth, Nova Scotia.

In the Fox Islands Thorofare you'll see every kind of boat, from the ferries to elegant sailing yachts, to lobster boats, to sculling skiffs and kayaks, to the fast unswerving big sardine carriers, loaded with fish for Rockland, Portland, Gloucester or Boston.

Handsome sentinels of the Thorofare are the two lighthouses—Browns Head Light at the western end and Goose Rock Light at the eastern end.

Browns Head Light is one of the very few "manned" lights left in Maine. It is so enticing a house and view—and it is on land, accessible by car—that Browns Head Light has always been a first choice station for a qualified Coast Guard family. The light was first built in 1832, by order of President Jackson, and then rebuilt in 1857 under President Buchanan. The orginal 1,000 pound fog bell is on display at the Vinalhaven Historical Society, a small museum well worth visiting.

Fog may be the one drawback to living at Browns Head Light. Even when the weather inside the Thorofare is clear, it can suddenly turn thick fog at Browns Head and stay almost impenetrable across the bay to Owls Head or into Rockland. Browns Head is not a good place to wait for a scale-up. I've waited there, and been scared. The North Haven ferry makes the run without hesitation and comes bustling through the fog, horns blowing, but ship invisible. Sardine carriers bear down fast, horns blaring, wasting no time on fog in the rush to get their perishable cargo to harbor. Small boats like Steer Clear are likely to dawdle between Browns Head and the Sugar Loaves, hoping for a scale-up that will give 50 yards or even 50 feet of visibility. All blow their horns. Sitting out the fog, it seems the sounds of all the horns bounce back and echo, intermingling with the deafening sound of the great diaphone off Browns Light. After 10 minutes of perilous dawdling, Steer Clear usually turns tail and returns to quiet anchor in Perry's Creek, midway down the Thorofare.

Goose Rock Light at the eastern end is the total opposite of the comfortable homestead at Browns Head Light. It is a caisson light, a cylinder sticking up out of the water, with a beacon on top and without an inch of ground around it. When the bachelor keeper arrived on station, in the days when Goose Rock was still a manned station, he would haul his dory up behind him, tieing it high above the water to the caisson. Once inside the cylinder, the only place for the keeper to get fresh air or exercise was on the little iron walkway encircling the light. A woman whose husband-to-be was once the bachelor keeper at Goose Rock told me that he had to walk eighty-eight times around that cat walk to get a mile of exercise. Goose Rock Light was built in 1890, and keepers worked, lived, walked and slept inside this caisson for 73 years, until it was automated in 1963.

Yet those bachelor keepers had one place nearby to interest them—Widows Island, only about 100 yards away. A large institution was built in 1888 on the island and stood there almost 50 years, most of the time unused, until demolished in the 1930s by the WPA. But, alas poor light keepers, it was not an institution for widows—the name Widows Island comes from the fact that a widow, Penelope Kent Winslow, lived on the island, from 1770 to 1820. The U.S. government bought the island in 1850 with the intent of putting a lighthouse on it, but instead built the caisson light at Goose Rock. "Just the spot" thought the U.S. Navy "to build a quarantine hospital." Sailors back from duty in Panama and the Caribbean were coming home after exposure to the dreaded yellow fever, and the Navy needed more isolated places in which to quarantine the men. In 1855 the navy built temporary quarantine quarters on Widows Island. After 33 years of temporary building, the navy built a permanent quarantine station to house 50 patients plus medical and housekeeping staffs. But, in the way government has, no sooner was the permanent quarantine hospital built than the government realized that the dreaded yellow fever was not transmitted by sailors but by mosquitoes. No one was ever quarantined and the giant building stood empty until in 1905 when ownership was transferred to the State of Maine. The state made Widows Island into a summer holiday camp for the "convalescent insane" from the state mental hospitals.

Apparently the state made a good job of it. They installed a swimming pool, built a wharf and provided a schooner, the General Knox, on which inmates went sailing. One month, Widows Island was for female patients only; and the next month for males only.

But after ten years, the state abandoned this summer holiday island as a resort for the "convalescent insane", and once more the buildings stood empty, until torn down in the 1930s. After which there was nothing and no one on Widows Island to interest the bachelor keepers across the water on Goose Rock Light.

There are two almost legendary stories about animals which met death and disaster in the Fox Island Thorofare—one about a whale, the other about an entire menagerie.

The whale story involves Granny Robbins, daughter of a first settler on the Fox Islands, a Revolutionary War soldier named John Newbury. Over the years, Granny Robbins became the most respected midwife on the Fox Islands and reputedly delivered more than a thousand babies. In her later years, Granny Robbins was taking a walk along the shore when she came upon the carcass of a big whale, a wonderful gift of God which she saw as a free source of expensive whale oil which lit the lamps in her home. To mark the whale as her undisputed property, Granny Robbins pulled off and unravelled one of her woolen stockings. She wound the yarn around the great beast as best she could manage, and tied one end around the trunk of a tree. With the prize whale properly identified as belonging to her, Granny Robbins strode home to get strong men with sharp knives to cut up her whale for oil and blubber.

Now for the tale of more exotic animals. In the fall of 1836, "Royal Tar", a sidewheeler launched six months earlier in New Brunswick, caught fire, as she sought shelter under Bluff Head, North Haven. Aboard were 72 passengers, 20 in crew and a menagerie of circus animals, all bound for Portland and Boston. No one is certain exactly what caused the fire. One story says the weight of an elephant was so great that it bent the wooden deck until it touched a hot boiler below and the wood caught fire. Soon the entire ship was ablaze. Only 29 out of 72 passengers were saved, for a loss of 43 lives, including eleven out of twelve children, and twelve of the sixteen women passengers. By comparison only three out of twenty in the male crew were drowned. All the animals aboard, including camels, zebras, a leopard, a tiger, two lions, an elephant and other species were drowned. The carcass of the elephant, which would not jump overboard until its hide was on fire, was washed up on Brimstone Island, down the bay. Its discovery caused consternation at the time, and the legend of elephants in Penobscot Bay persists today, 152 years later.

Downtown North Haven, a single street with about a dozen buildings, abuts one shore of the Thorofare. Steer Clear motors slowly by its Casino, a weathered shingled yacht club with wide porches, wicker chairs and plenty of dock space, past the ferry slip where the North Haven boat lives. (All island ferries in Maine must overnight at the island they serve, for use in emergency.) Past Waterman's, one of the best known meat and grocery stores along the Maine coast, and then we turn in to make a "must-stop" at the dock at J.O. Brown & Son, boat builder and lobster dealer.

We have to "lie off" and wait out in the channel, waiting for space at Brown's dock. This is the only place on the Thorofare and all of North Haven to get gas, sell and buy lobsters and get boat work done. So there's a constant flow of outboards, sailboats, cruisers and lobster boats to both sides of his single dock. On the big lobster car float just off the dock is the hut where lobsters are bought from and bait sold to fishermen.

We wait amid the traffic happily. For Jim Brown's is a 'must-stop' for Steer Clear twice every year, coming and going out of the Fox Islands. It's been that way for 20 years. Finally a boat leaves and we nose in to tie alongside.

Jim Brown comes striding down the ramp to greet us. He is a slender man, erect, very quiet spoken, wears steel-rimmed glasses and a sweet smile. He is in demand somewhere every minute, yet has the knack of never seeming to be in a hurry, never too swamped to spend a few minutes greeting us, swapping news on the dock while we fill our tanks.

Four generations of Browns have run this dock and boat yard and have been the good friends, teachers, boat builders, advisors, guardians of a kind to hundreds of North Haven families for close to 100 years. And the dock, the ramp, the boathouse, the rickety office where Jim sells paint, shackles and rope—none of these seem to have changed very much, except for the gas pumps, in the eyes of most people alive today.

But the Browns have seen North Haven change enormously, from a quiet lobstering and farming island into a colony of summer homes for the rich and famous. Yet the change hasn't changed the Browns.

The original North Haven dinghy was built here in 1880 by J.O. Brown for the original summer person on North Haven, Dr. Weld of Boston. Dr. Weld and a boatload of his yachting friends from Boston were cruising through the Thorofare in 1880, on their way downeast. They liked the island so much, they went ashore, stayed over. Dr. Weld bought land and hired a carpenter to build the first summer place. Thus began the summer flood of visitors.

After Weld came back the next summer, he wanted a sailing dinghy for poking around the island coves and designed one. Brown built it. That became the famed North Haven dinghy. About seventy five like it have been built since, but the originals are treasured heirlooms in the families where elderly sailors teach grandsons to sail in the dinghy on which they first learned to sail.

Jim Brown and his son also build fine, heavy-timbered, offshore lobsterboats, tough enough to fish safely in the Atlantic in winter. But they build only one every two or three years.

We leave Steer Clear at Brown's dock to make a quick visit to another "must-see" friend and a lasting fixture of North Haven, Franklin Waterman of Waterman's store. This longtime family grocery and meat market is fondly known from Bar Harbor to Boston and has served all the islanders and summer people as the only grocery on the island. For years, Waterman's carried a bigger line of S.S. Pierce products than any store in Maine, a brand of foodstuffs the Boston summer people could barely live without.

Franklin has been butcher in the family store for longer than the 20 years I've been going in for our chats and supplies for the food lockers on Steer Clear.

The rest of downtown North Haven consists of the ferry slip and office, a book and gift store, a small library, the politest post office in the U.S., a few homes, the Casino—and that is about all.

Only the Internal Revenue Service could (but won't) hazard a guess at the enormous wealth represented by all the blue-blood, old money families with summer places on the Fox Islands. Certainly it is far, far beyond the wildest dreams of treasure which ever crossed the imagination of Martin Pring when he dropped his anchor here in 1603.

The land on the island has changed hands. Most is now owned by peo-

Hauling in Penobscot Bay, off Deer Isle. Note the furled staysail, used to keep the bow pointed into the wind.

ple "from away". Today off-islanders own 90 percent of the shorefront and about 75 percent of all the inland acreage on North Haven. It is a tribute to them and to the native families that these islands still stay a quiet, lovely and happy haven for so many different kinds of people.

But to keep this wealth and the huge cottages in perspective, I like to remember the story told me by Isidor Gordon, a famous junk dealer and political fixture in Rockland. "During the Depression, 1,500 acres of island land came into my possession," he said. "They couldn't give waterfront away then. I didn't pay much for it and I couldn't sell it for much either. Island land was almost worthless in the 1930s and 1940s. After the crash of 1929, they tried to sell me a beautiful waterfront estate, 45 acres, with a fine house on it. I didn't want it at any price. But finally they got me to take a look. I offered to buy it for the last year's taxes. So I got the fine house and the 45 acres on the waterfront for $700."

At the store, Franklin Waterman finishes packing loads of groceries for the Cabots at Pulpit Rock and the IBM Watson farm, then hands me the little box for Steer Clear. We shake goodbye, and I carry the stuff back to Jim Brown's dock, next door. "Where you headin' this trip?" asks Jim, as he casts off my docking lines. That's the question to answer when you are cruising Penobscot Bay.

"Don't know just yet. Probably go across to Perry's Creek and worry about it overnight . . ." We wave goodbye.

CAPT. TOM HAS FOUND PARADISE

PERRY'S CREEK — Capt. Tom Curry of South Portland is one of the most unusual sailors cruising the coast of Maine. Fittingly, we met him in an unusual way.

On a foggy day, anchored in Perry's Creek, off the Fox Thorofare, I was startled by a thumping on the hull of Steer Clear.

A big, burly man in a tiny plastic dinghy was there, and he handed me a plastic container, the kind used to store food in a refrigerator. "Creme caramel with rum," he said. "For your dessert at dinner tonight. I just made them for you."

He said his name was Capt. Tom Curry. He came aboard for a visit. And that is how I met one of the most unusual sailors on the coast.

Six months of the year, Capt. Tom Curry is captain of a huge container-cargo ship named Green Harbor, a vessel as long as three football fields, which sails from New Orleans to Singapore, via Europe, the Mediterranean and the Indian Ocean.

The other six months of the year, Curry is on vacation in Maine. Here he is captain of a 29-foot sailboat which he sails alone.

"My wife likes the boat well enough. But she can't sleep aboard. Sleeping in the little cabin gives her claustrophobia. So I cruise alone for three weeks at a stretch. Then, she drives to a port along the coast and we meet for dinner together."

Dinner is a major event in Capt. Tom Curry's sailboat. For he is a gourmet cook and a connoisseur of wines. He is compiling a special cookbook of his own recipes, made in his own galley.

"I plan my menus long in advance for every dinner on each cruise. And lay in a stock of all the ingredients and wines I will need before I leave my homeport."

Each morning on his solo cruises, Curry gets under way by 5:30 a.m. "I like to arrive at my destination, usually an island cove, by noon. This gives me the entire afternoon for my hobbies."

One of these is painting. Another is music. A third is cooking.

Before six o'clock in the evening, the elaborate preparations for his gourmet dinner are finished. This night he tells me he will be dining, solo, off chicken breast marsala, broccoli with hollandaise, and for dessert he'll eat English trifle. To enhance his sailor's meal, he will drink vintage white burgundy wine.

An overnight friend and neighbor to Steer Clear in a favorite spot, Perry Creek, North Haven.

"I keep my wines chilled in the forward bilge, within inches of the cold ocean," he confides. At 6 p.m. sharp, Capt. Curry sits in solo comfort on his deck, listens to music and sips two dry martinis before going below for dinner.

Curry, who left Ireland when he was five years old, is a graduate of the Maine Maritime Academy, class of '43. He calls his sailboat Bon Temps.

"The old French explorer Samuel de Champlain founded the order of Bon Temps. It means 'Good Cheer.' And I interpret that to mean good food, good wine and good company."

When winds are too light for sailing, Curry pushes the Bon Temps along with a 12-horsepower motor. "On my other boat, Green Harbor, we have a 32,000-horsepower engine."

When Curry is on leave, his co-captain commands Green Harbor to Singapore and back. "He's Jim Komlosy, and he lives on Chebeague Island, just 10 miles from me."

I can report from first-hand knowledge that Capt. Tom Curry serves a marvelous creme caramel au rhum, in Perry's Creek, Vinalhaven.

THE DOG DAYS OF CRUISING

CALDERWOOD ISLAND — Nighttime fog refuses to budge when the sun comes up. So the two cruising boats in the lee of Calderwood Island are still lying out on anchors, waiting for visibility. This hour or two of fog—enforced idleness is a good chance to take Piper, our Dalmatian, ashore for a walk.

As Piper and I start out in the dinghy, another man and dog in the other boat have exactly the same idea. We reach the shore about the same moment. He eyes me. His dog eyes my dog. And vice-versa.

Would the two dogs fight? Or be friends? Male or female? His dog is a big, handsome golden retriever. "Too big an animal for the little sailboat they came from," I murmured to myself. "Too big by far for my light-boned, light-furred Dalmatian."

So I take Piper walking down the beach in the opposite direction from the big retriever.

Dogs, of course, know better. Piper, the little female flirt, knew immediately that the handsome retriever was a male. And he knew that the good-looking Dalmatian was a female, more enticing than anything else on the rocky shore.

The dogs abandon their so-called masters and race toward each other. They play. They gambol. They flirt outrageously in the fog.

And with a helpless shrug of our shoulders, the other man and I walk toward each other. We do not play or gambol or flirt in the fog. But we talk. We talk about boats. Then about cruising. Finally about dogs. Then narrow it down to what makes a good cruising dog.

"It is not size or breed," says my new friend. "My dog is too big for my boat. Worse, he likes to swim, then climb aboard and shake, spraying everything and everyone."

I share confidences with him about my cruising dog. "Even my Dalmatian is too big for the boat. She sheds, and those white hairs are everywhere. At night, she'll sneak her way into my bunk and hog the sleeping bag until I'm scrunched into one corner."

He nodded wisely. Lit his pipe. "I know. Same trouble. But none of those things really matter." His pipe was going well now. "I will tell you what makes the difference between a good cruising dog and a bad one. Bladder. How long can a cruising dog hold water?"

We stood on the beach in the fog and we talked in dead seriousness about dog's bladders.

"That golden retriever of mine crossed his legs for 30 hours once. We got becalmed sailing from Cutler to Boothbay, across the Gulf of Maine. Slow trip. And that dog lasted 30 hours. How long can your Dalmatian last?"

That was not a calculation I had at my fingertips. But I remembered spells when we couldn't get ashore and Piper had simply curled up and slept, uncomplaining. "About 18 hours. She's lasted a full 18 hours; she might go longer," I replied.

'DOC GREG': ISLAND DOCTOR

CARVER'S HARBOR — Will "Doc Greg" be allowed to stay on as the beloved physician of Vinalhaven Island, an hour-and-a-half by boat from the nearest mainland hospital? Or will the Washington bureaucracy, in the form of the National Health Service, abide by the rule book and force a 36-year-old doctor to abandon life-and-blood medicine in order to shuffle papers behind a desk in Washington, D.C.?

The plot is a real-life soap opera. Newspapers and TV shows have been trying incessantly to make contact with the real-life Dr. Gregory O'Keefe. He and his surgical-nurse wife finally took their phone off the hook. And that led to yet another episode in the soap opera saga which was making news across the nation.

Secretary of Health and Human Services Margaret Heckler, boss of tens of thousands of employees, tried to phone O'Keefe but could not get through, because all phone lines to the island were constantly busy. She asked Sen. William S. Cohen of Maine for help. The senator's office reached an island policeman, who tracked down O'Keefe with the urgent message he should call his boss, Secretary Heckler.

After the island doctor and the Cabinet officer had their phone talk, Mrs. Heckler said she would resolve the dilemma before the island doctor was pressured further to leave the expectant island mothers who are his immediate concern, and head to a Washington desk job, at a salary increase from his present $50,000-a-year post at the Island Community Clinic.

Happily for me, I know Vinalhaven. I've moored my boat in Carver's Harbor, gassed up, bought ice and food, wandered the island roads, picked the wild berries and—best of all—spent many an hour in the Vinalhaven Community Clinic with O'Keefe's predecessor, the forever loved Dr. Ralph Earle.

And this medical situation on Vinalhaven is no soap opera. It is about as real, plain, honest and meaningful as a bond can ever be between a community and its doctor.

The National Health Service made a fine appointment eight years ago when it named the young O'Keefe to serve the medical needs of this island community of about 1,400 people in winter and around 4,500 in summer.

O'Keefe was only 28 years old when he moved to Vinalhaven, in 1975, fresh from Dartmouth College Medical School. The young doctor arrived to try to fill the shoes of Dr. Ralph Earle, an island medical legend, who had died in harness. Earle had first set foot on the island as a boy, while vacationing with his father. In 1937, after graduating from Hahneman Medical School, he came back to Vinalhaven as the island's only doctor.

For the next 35 years the name of Dr. Ralph Earle was on the birth certificate of every child born on Vinalhaven, except for the years in World War II when he was away in the armed forces.

Earle began the island clinic. He pioneered the research and the treatment of widespread hereditary diabetes among island families. He developed preventive medicine on the island, at a time when it was a fad word in metropolitan cities.

The island clinic pioneered prenatal care for expectant mothers. By 1970 islanders were making 3,000 visits a year to the clinic, including everyone from tots to grandmothers. Earle was doctor and friend to them all. Then he grew ill and died in 1975.

Before Earle died, he persuaded the NHS to provide a doctor to follow him. He helped train summer interns, O'Keefe among them. When Earle died, it was the young O'Keefe who was assigned to Vinalhaven Island.

Filling Earle's shoes was a hard job, especially for a young doctor from away and fresh out of medical school. But O'Keefe managed to fill those big shoes, and more. He and his wife and son have grown deep roots in this special island community. He has won the trust, love, gratitude and friendship of his tight-knit family of patients.

On the island, Greg O'Keefe provides all medical service, around the clock, seven days and nights every week, at homes or in the clinic. He has become adept at home deliveries and at emergency trauma care. The number of patient visits to the clinic has climbed from 3,000 in Earle's day to more than 5,000 today.

Low tide at Carvers Harbor, Vinalhaven—Huge granite quarries on Vinal-haven once employed 1,000 men. In 1899, a granite shaft 64 feet long, weighing 310 tons in the rough was cut here. North Haven and Vinalhaven were first mapped by Martin Pring, from Bristol, England, on a voyage in 1603. More than 100 years ago, Carvers Harbor in 1878 cured 22 million pounds of fish.

This is a special kind of medical practice, requiring a special kind of doctor. O'Keefe drives the ambulance, runs his own laboratory tests and takes his own X-rays. He tends the newborn and the old. One patient wrote to Washington protesting the threatened transfer of Dr. O'Keefe: ''I am 60, my husband is 62, my Dad is 78, my Mother is 76, and my grandmother is 96. We all live on Vinalhaven, and we all depend on Dr. O'Keefe.''

Dr. A.J. Lantinene, president of the Knox County Medical Society, which includes Vinalhaven wrote Senator Cohen saying: ''The logic of rupturing this relationship and sending a uniquely effective physician to Washington to shuffle papers is not comprehensible to members of this Society. If the true purpose of the Public Health Service is to provide excellent health care to isolated communities, this could best be done by leaving Dr. O'Keefe on Vinalhaven.''

Vinalhaven is where O'Keefe and his family want to work and live. Yet to do so, O'Keefe has been forced to resign from the NHS.

"We are making ends meet. The clinic is flourishing, thanks to the islanders and summer folk. Our big need now is to get a dentist out here two days a week," O'Keefe told me.

SEABIRD COUNT FROM A PLANE

CESSNA SKYMASTER — "Can you fly a seabird count with us at noon tomorrow?" asked Alan E. Hutchinson, wildlife biologist with the Maine Inland Fisheries and Wildlife Department. I said "Yes" and left Steer Clear in Pulpit Harbor. At noon the next day I'm waiting to join the plane at Owls Head airport.

Weather, plane and pilot are all nearly perfect for flying a seabird count over the Maine islands. The ducks are still out there in mid-October, especially the eiders. In the next three hours, we see more than 15,000 of them.

The day is one of those special early fall days unique to Maine; crystal clear, so that over Monhegan you can look out from the plane and see Cadillac Mountain on Mount Desert to the east, the Presidential Range far to the west and the rolling glories of the Camden Hills just inshore. The sun is bright, so the white feathers of male eiders shine brilliantly as they ride the sea swells. From our altitude of less than 500 feet, I can see deep down into the clear, clean ocean. For the first time, I see the submerged lines of pot warp running from lobster buoys to their toggles and then on down to the traps on the ocean bottom.

Our plane is a twin engine, six-seat Cessna Skymaster. This high-wing aircraft is ideal for bird-spotting and island-viewing. There is no lower wing to obscure the view and the propellors of the engines, one fore, and the other aft, are outside the line of vision.

At the controls is Andy Stinson, one of those wise pilots with graying hair, a veteran of 21 years of flying small planes as a Maine game warden and before that as one of the pilots flying with the legendary Dick Folsom out of Greenville, on Moosehead Lake. He has logged more than 15,000 hours flying small planes over Maine forests, rivers and islands.

Alan Hutchinson, the wildlife biologist, rides in the co-pilot's seat. He is making the count. From long experience together, he and Stinson have developed a technique for making an accurate estimate of seabirds which congregate in flocks of a few hundred to as many as 6,000 in coves or

Outside Carvers Harbor, Vinalhaven. Setting a lobster trap from dory.

by ledges in the open sea where the feeding is good. Hutchinson dictates his seabird count into a recording machine at each ledge and each island we fly over. We usually make a lazy figure-eight flight pattern, with our right wing far down over each target. In this way we not only get a thorough look, but we put the sun at every angle so that it shines on the harder-to-spot neutral brown feathers of the female eider ducks.

This is a costly business. All told, it costs taxpayers $65,000 a year to keep track of the migratory seabirds on Maine's coast and Maine islands.

For instance it costs $140 an hour to charter this Skymaster plane in which we are flying today. The plane, with Stinson at the controls, left its base at Lincoln early this morning, picked up Hutchinson at Bangor a few minutes later and then flew to Pemaquid Light, where they started today's bird count.

By noon, Hutchinson and Stinson had made the count along the midcoast islands from Pemaquid through Muscongus Bay as far as Port Clyde, and stopped for a lunch snack and to pick me up at Owls Head airport. We then flew from Owls Head down the Georges River, out to Monhegan Island and then east, circling in lazy eights over every island and ledge to Vinalhaven.

We covered scores of islands and ledges and estuaries. By the time Stinson landed at home base in Lincoln, the Skymaster had logged about eight hours flying time. That bill alone amounts to $1,120 for this one day of bird counting. And to keep track of the migratory seabirds through the year, a flight like this one is made every 30 days.

Where does the money come from? As usual, it comes from a mix of state and federal money: $16,250 from the state and $48,750 from federal government.

Much of the federal money comes from the tax on firearms ammunition used in part by hunters of seabirds. And much of the state money comes from the Maine tax levied on oil transport at sea.

Maine now has a multi-million dollar reserve on hand to clean up oil spills, collected from a 1-cent-a-barrel tax on oil transported across Maine waters. In recent years, some $10,000 from this fund has helped finance this flying inventory of seabirds and seals, whose lives and habitats might be endangered by an oil spill.

Experts at the Maine Department of Environmental Protection use this inventory information to decide whether to move wildlife from an area threatened by an oil spill and to assess damage done to wildlife by a spill, damages which would be charged to those responsible for the spill.

One surprise on this low-level, intense inspection of the islands and ledges is seeing how different islands look from the air than from my boat.

From a boat, I see only one small segment of an island at a time. From the air I see the entire island at once. I can see all of its shorelines and all of its surrounding ledges, whose perils cannot be fully seen from the deck of a boat. It is a scary sight for a boatman.

Islands which I thought I knew well from my boat are almost unrecognizable from 500 feet in the air. Monhegan, which I know well from the harbor and from cruising alongside its shorelines, looks totally different when you look down and see the entire island at once. The relationship between Big Green and Little Green, between Matinicus and Criehaven, are wholly different flying over them at 140 knots than cruising between them at 10 knots.

Wooden Ball Island which seems forbidding enough from a boat, seems infinitely more so looking down on it from 500 feet. I marvel at how Dorothy Simpson, a Maine-bred writer, and her clan managed to live there year round, many years ago. From the air, I see the remnants of two caved-in buildings and the rugged cove where islanders, somehow, moored their boats. The barren island is criss-crossed with the remnants of stone walls which once marked sheep pastures.

Nearby Seal Island is long, totally deserted. Once it was used by the

Navy as a target and from the air we can see the debris of exploded shells glinting in the sun, strange marks upon the tortured red rock.

On the last leg of the flight, we fly up the Muscle Ridge Channel, circling each island and each ledge between Whitehead Light and Owls Head Light. Here are favorite basking ledges for seals. From the boat I had been excited by seeing six or a dozen seals at once. From the air at low tide, I see a hundred or more. But from the air, the seals have no beguiling charm or beauty. They look like cigar butts thrown into the clear water.

A TERRIFYING ADVENTURE: OVERBOARD IN THE BASIN

THE BASIN, VINALHAVEN — Never take a dinghy into The Basin at Vinalhaven on a running tide. We made that mistake. And in the next few minutes we came close to death by drowning. This, our 18th cruise among the blessed, beautiful islands of Penobscot Bay, memorable for two weeks of almost perfect weather, will now stay forever unforgotten and unforgettable.

The morning dawned brimming with promises over Long Cove, where we'd anchored for the night. An azure sky, a calm sea; stiff-legged, long-necked herons stalking the low tide mudflats for their breakfast; graceful terns swooping and shrieking over the mussel beds; the climbing sun already warming long grey ledges enough to blunt the chill of the water from Hurricane Sound. Inviting enough for a quick trip ashore with the dog and a fast dip for Piper and me before breakfast.

By 9 a.m. Sheila and Tom Donaldson, our cruising companions aboard their boat Mark East, signalled they were ready to up anchor. On Steer Clear we led them out of Long Cove toward Leadbetter Island and turned east toward the famous Basin. We anchored the two boats outside the narrow entrance and climbed into two dinghies to go into the Basin.

One of the special pleasures in cruising is to show friends treasured places they have never seen. And The Basin at Vinalhaven is a fantastic spot, long treasured. At low tide, The Basin looks like a weird moonscape of a million years ago; a mysterious, eerie body of water where prehistoric gods seem to have hurled gigantic boulders. We were eager, too eager, to show this spectacle to the Donaldsons.

They climbed into their large metal dinghy, powered by a powerful outboard. My shipmate, Piper, the Dalmatian, and I climbed into our smaller dinghy, a Fiberglas job with a three horse kicker. We carried the usual paraphenalia for this kind of expedition; field glasses and camera, mask and snorkel, and two life jackets. Midships in our dinghy was a large wooden lobster crate to be returned to Raymond Beveridge, a North Haven fisherman who'd sold us a batch of his lobsters in it, all eaten the night before. And a half filled plastic gas tank. That wooden crate and that plastic gas tank proved to be the most valuable life preservers aboard.

In our little dinghy, we led the way through the modest rip at the narrow entrance to The Basin. The turning tide was flowing swiftly but, it seemed as we approached, relatively calmly over the boulders at the entrance. We beckoned to the Donaldsons, 100 feet behind, to follow our track. We were in the narrow entrance to The Basin now.

Then suddenly, dead ahead, I saw rough, white water as the running tide gathered force, rushing over and down a series of boulders at the throat of The Basin. My shipmate, perched atop the lobster crate amidships, had her back to it. "Get down into the boat!" I shouted to her. "Rough water ahead!"

In the next few seconds, I knew that vicious, swirling turbulence ahead was more than our dinghy could survive.

I swung the little outboard to steer us hard left, to the nearest shore not 50 feet away. We closed on it to within 15 feet.

Then a whirlpool grabbed the light dinghy and spun us back toward midstream. There the rushing water pushed us closer to the fearsome turbulence ahead. Again I tried to head over to shore, and the little boat strove hard under full throttle to alter direction. Her bow turned. As it did, another whirlpool grabbed the stern where I sat and spun us right into the edge of the violent white water. The force of it threw the motor halfway off its bracket. We lost all freeboard. Water poured in and I yelled, "We're sinking! We're going under!" Before the words were out, the boat was gone from under us. Gone from sight.

All three of us, woman, man and dog were thrashing close together in the white, choppy, swirling torrent, fighting to hold our own against the rip. The lobster crate—bless it—was floating, bobbing there, between us. My shipmate had a fist-like hold on the rope handle at one end, until the dog tried to scramble to safety aboard it and thereby pried the crate out of her grasp. I brutally knocked Piper off and tried to swing the crate back to within my friend's reach. Her head kept vanishing under the racing whitecaps. She could not or would not grab back the rope handle at her end. Then in a flashing mini-second I saw why. Both her arms were wrapped around that big plastic container half filled with gasoline. She clutched it for dear life. It was buoyant and kept her from going under.

She had always been a very strong, able swimmer. The ledge of an island shore and quieter water was less than 50 feet away. Surely she could make it. She was gaining, foot by foot toward it, fighting the current. But the waves kept sloshing over her head, and momentarily she'd vanish. I tried swimming as hard as every muscle in me could, trying to bring the crate closer to her side. But the damn, lovable dog kept trying to climb on it, and I would lose a few feet of hard-won distance. Again and again I had to knock Piper off. The crate was buoyant, but the rip tide racing through its slats exerted such force that it seemed to weigh a dead-weight ton, pulling hard against my one-arm stroke and two frantically kicking legs.

Out of the violent chop at last; into still water, a backwash. My shipmate, waterlogged by all she'd swallowed, at last had her head in the air. "Swim hard!" I yelled. "Can't breathe! No strength!" she answered. But inch by inch, foot by foot, she was getting nearer the ledge.

"Get your legs down! I think you can touch bottom now!" I urged her. But she could neither get her legs down nor touch bottom. A rushing current beneath the surface prevented her. I felt firm rock bottom under my feet. I reached out with my swimming arm, helped her to make headway, and used my other arm to maneuver some of the lobster crate under one of her shoulders.

The ledge at last. She flopped her head and shoulders on to it, too totally spent to haul the rest of her body out of the sea. A few minutes rest and working together, we got her completely up onto the ledge and stretched out on high, dry rock and drained much of the swallowed ocean out of her. Then I dragged Piper in.

With all of us safe, I looked up to see Tom Donaldson coming at a run from the other side of the small, rock island. "Thank God you're both alive and safe. We saw your boat spin out of control and then vanish. Next sight was your heads in the drink. Sheila threw life jackets out. No way we could go after you."

As soon as Donaldson had seen what had happened to us in our fiberglass dinghy, he managed to turn his heavier, bigger boat and make for the safety of another adjoining ledge. Then he came racing to find us. "I'll run back and tell Sheila you're both alive. And Piper too." He patted the wringing wet dog and raced off.

Now my own reaction began; a bout of severe shivering from head to toe. This thin frame of mine is not well padded against the chill of a long, unplanned swim in the Maine ocean. I stripped and lay on the sun-hot ledge till the shivering decreased. Looking down at the turbulence where we'd capsized, I cursed my stupidity for getting us into so dangerous a mess. Yet the white water could not be seen from the entrance; and once the turbulence was in view, it had been impossible to avert the catastrophe with so light a boat and so little power. I thanked God for getting us out alive. And for keeping the Donaldsons from following us into the same fearsome trap. And I cursed my idiocy for not double checking the tide tables instead of being misled by the relatively quiet flow of tide at the entrance to The Basin.

We waited in silence, each with our thoughts. Nothing we could do until The Basin filled and slack water arrived. I tried to interest the Donaldsons in at least looking at the weird moonscape scenery of The Basin we'd come to see. They were not interested.

Still no sign of the lost dinghy. At slack water we saw a big lobster dory come through the entrance. He headed our way and brought his boat alongside the ledge where this shipwrecked foursome stood. A quiet, courtly man in his oilskins, he introduced himself formally. "My name is Arthur A. Warren." I told him my name and sheepishly explained what had happened. Arthur A. Warren, with infinite politeness, made no comment. "I know you," he said. "A couple of years ago I came aboard your boat when you were anchored in Long Cove and drank coffee with you. I'll go haul my traps in The Basin now. And when I'm done, I'll come and tow you out to your boats." In 40 minutes he was back, reporting no sight of the dinghy, but bringing back the lifejackets thrown us by Sheila Donaldson.

Over many months since then, Warren searched for the lost dinghy, even using grappling hooks, trying to locate it on the bottom. But he found no trace.

The sea was merciful this time, taking the dinghy but sparing the lives.

When, later, I told the story to a fellow boatman, Russell Wiggins, the wise editor of The Ellsworth American, he shook his head philosophically and said "Its lucky we seldom pay full price for stupid mistakes."

Amen, amen.

Three years went by. Then one August morning we got word that Arthur J. Warren had found the drowned dinghy in the Deep Hole.

For three years that miserable, tippy, fiberglas dinghy had lain in the cold, murky depths. At low tide and high tide, in summer warmth and bitter winter chill, that poor lost boat had been beneath the sea.

Then three years after the accident, Arthur J. Warren was hauling traps in the Basin. One trap would barely budge. Warren hauled till his back bent and his "slave" ran hot. Finally the trap broke loose from the bottom. When it bobbed to the surface, a yellow nylon line was wrapped around the slats of the lobster trap. And at the end of the line hung my dinghy, loaded with bottom mud and barnacles.

Astonished at his find, Arthur J. Warren marvelled again at the strange ways of the sea. He towed the beat-up dinghy to shallow water, dumped encrusted mud from it, and tied it to a lobster buoy. At home that night, Warren relayed the news to our mutual friend Jim Brown of J.O. Brown's boatyard on North Haven, who then sent me a postcard with the news of this resurrection of my dinghy, three years after it had drowned.

That dinghy was recovered from 111 feet of water, out of the Deep Hole in the Basin.

I made the four hour sea trip from New Harbor back to Vinalhaven, collected the resurrected dinghy and then towed her behind Steer Clear from North Haven to New Harbor, a five hour run. Then I lugged her up over the wharf to a station wagon and hauled her home.

She was stained filthy brown, encrusted with barnacles. But her seats were intact; her tow line was still attached; even her name and numbers were legible. Her motor was gone; but her oarlocks were still in place.

I have now learned why the fatted calf was killed and cooked to celebrate the return of the prodigal son. For during all the years that dinghy was bobbing obediently behind Steer Clear, I treated her meanly. But after the lost dinghy came home, I spent a week scrubbing her down, restoring her sheen, pampering the lost dinghy, raised from the dead and the deep after three years by Arthur J. Warren.

MATINICUS ROCK AND THE BUCHHEISTERS

MATINICUS ROCK — Carl and Harriet Buchheister between them had been enjoying God's good earth for over 140 years, when they told me about The Rock. Between them, this husband-and-wife team knew more about Maine birds and flowers than any couple in the world. This life-long pursuit had left its mark upon each of them;

a rare glow of inner happiness, so warm and so vibrant it shone brightly even at a first meeting.

I first met the Buchheisters in a motel room in Waldoboro. They were in Maine from their home in North Carolina to attend an annual meeting of the president's council of the National Audubon Society.

Carl Buchheister was president of the National Audubon Society during the 1960s and 1970s. The year we met, the president's council was convening on Hog Island in Muscongus Bay, a sanctuary island run as a summer study camp by the National Audubon since 1936.

This Audubon council meeting coincided with close to 100 years of combined Maine memories of Matinicus Rock cherished by Carl and Harriet, memories wheeling upon puffins and phalaropes, petrels and herons, arctic terns and a hundred species of wildflowers.

Their motel room was filled with boxes of files. Brown envelopes bulging with clippings, notes and references were spread out on the twin beds. They contain the reason for our meeting; Buchheister memories of Matinicus Rock.

Harriet's special passion in life has long been a 32-acre volcanic outcrop, more than 22 miles out to sea, called Matinicus Rock Light. It is not an easy place to land even today. Fifty years ago, when Carl and Harriet first braved it out to the Rock, landing was most difficult.

Yet it was a far more difficult place to get to and live upon 155 years ago, when President John Quincy Adams appointed Capt. John A. Shaw as the first keeper of the Matinicus Rock Light at a salary of $450 a year.

"For 155 years men and women, even girls like Abby Burgess, have kept that light burning," said Harriet. "But before I die, there must be a book written, a tribute paid to all the keepers of Matinicus Rock. And that's what these masses of papers are all about."

Harriet was a small, almost fragile woman dwarfed by her huge, suntanned, handsome husband in that motel room. But she ordered him about to find each special paper she was looking for, and he willingly found it. She was a bit crippled physically, but moved about agilely with the aid of two canes.

"Two years ago," she told me, "I went into the hospital for a hip operation, a replacement. Mighty expensive it was. But free of charge, they gave me hepatitis too. Filled me with blood with the hepatitis bug in it. And that gave me this other darned thing—what name do the doctors call it, Carl? osteo-something. Sure, it hurts. But I'm allergic to painkillers. So I use my mind to manage the pain. But I know the medicine that will cure me quick. Another trip out to my Rock. They'd have to land me in a bosun's chair, haul me over the surf and the ledges. I'm game. But those doctors are inclined to be stuffy about the idea.''

Harriet's brown, almost black, eyes shone with her will and enthusiasm as she talked about the Rock, its keepers, its birds and flowers. ''Carl is the bird expert. He knew every bird out there by its first name. So in self-defense, I took to flowers, way back in the 1930s. Makes me mad when people write about the Rock as barren. No trees grow there. But it is far from barren; it's a wonderful garden. I collected, cataloged, and researched 53 different kinds of flowers and grasses growing out there. All my reports are in the National Arboretum now. Wonderful strong colors in those flowers. Most came from England as seeds, hundreds of years ago.''

Together the Buchheisters remembered a summer night more than 40 years ago. ''The assistant keeper woke us up at 2 a.m. yelling for us to come down out from the loft. 'Don't dress,' he said. 'Come as you are, stark naked or in pajamas.' We rushed out. By the light of the moon shining through misty fog we saw thousands of terns diving and devouring flying moths in the moonlight.''

Carl talked with admiration about the courage and stamina of those arctic terns. ''They are only 17 inches long, with delicate red feet and red bills. But those little birds are world champions in long distance flying. Each year they fly close to 24,000 miles. From The Rock they fly north to the arctic, make their passage via Iceland to Ireland, down the coast of Europe, down the coast of Africa, across the South Atlantic, past the Falkland Islands into the Antarctic. Then in June, they fly back 12,000 miles to Matinicus Rock. Mate here. Lay and hatch their eggs in August. Then off they go again to fly another 24,000 before they arrive back to the Rock the next May 17.''

Carl was writing a history of the National Audubon Society. ''The National Audubon Society was born on the Maine islands,'' he said. ''In the 1890s a New York insurance executive named William Dichter came up here to try to stop the slaughter of terns and other birds, which were being massacred by the tens of thousands to make plumes for ladies' hats.

''He paid lighthouse keepers $50 to keep the gunners off the nesting islands. He asked help from the American Ornithological Society but they were cold scientists, not bird lovers. So Dichter and an artist friend raised

$12,000 to pay part-time wardens. The birds, almost killed to extinction, got some protection. And from that beginning, in 1896 the National Audubon Society was started, mostly to protect colonies of migrant birds nesting on New England islands.''

Today, Matinicus Rock is a bird sanctuary and a favorite nesting place for puffins as well as terns and petrels. But before Carl could tell me more about puffins, Harriet was singing the praises of the lighthouse keepers.

She had tape recorded conversations with old Maine people whose relatives once kept the light on Matinicus Rock. She had collected old records and letters which described family life on the Rock and the perils of keeping the light, in the days before boats had engines and when keepers had to sail or row dories to buy groceries in Rockland, 25 miles each way.

She recalled the story of 14-year-old Abby Burgess, who came to the Rock in 1853, when her father was named keeper. Her mother soon became bedridden, and Abbie took care of her two younger sisters while she also learned how to tend the light. In January 1856, her father rowed to Rockland for food supplies. But, caught in a series of bad storms, he couldn't get back to the Rock for a month.

Teenager Abbie manned the light alone, and also cared for her bedridden mother and young sisters. Later, Abbie married a keeper of the Rock, bore four children on Matinicus Rock and buried her infant daughter Bessie among its granite ledges. Some 20 years ago, Harriet Buchheister found two-year old Bessie's grave and set out a carved headstone to mark it.

The keeper whom Abbie Burgess married was Isaac H. Grant. Three generations of Grants worked as keepers of the light, the oldest living on the Rock until he was 90.

The story of hardship and heroism through storms which smashed lights and keepers' homes are incredible to hear in this day when helicopters ferry food, medicines, and fresh crews to the Rock. ''Those keepers and their families are a glorious, indelible part of Maine history. That's why I've spent years gathering all this material about them. They merit a book,'' cried Harriet, stomping the floor with her canes. Her love affair with the Rock began 50 years ago and has burned like a torch ever since. Matinicus Rock Light is automatic now. No keepers of the light live on the Rock.

FINDING SHELTER IN A STORM

HOLBROOKE ISLAND — We'd been warned by marine weather forecasts that Hurricane Dennis might produce 12 foot seas during the night at the offshore islands where we were headed. So we changed plans and decided to anchor in the shelter of Holbrooke Island, between Castine and Cape Rosier. There we should find quiet waters.

Years ago, when Kenneth Curtis was governor, I cruised to Holbrooke Island with him on a happy, pioneering occasion. Miss Holbrooke, a sweet, erect grey-haired lady, whose family had long owned this handsome island, was deeding it to the state of Maine.

This was one of the earliest, if not the first, times an island owner chose this course to safeguard and preserve the future of a treasured island. Since Miss Holbrooke took this action to preserve her island, more than 120 island and seashore properties have been safeguarded in similar fashion by their owners, through the Maine Coast Heritage Trust and the Nature Conservancy. But I remember Miss Holbrooke standing proud before the fireplace in her island living room, handing over official papers to Governor Curtis in a simple, short ceremony.

So, to stay away from Hurricane Dennis, we cruised by the bell buoy off Dice Head Light, came past the black can at Nautilus Rock and then crept along between Holbrooke and Ram Islands to find a cove near Goose Falls, sheltered in the lee of Backwood Mountain. It was an hour before sunset, the tide was ebbing fast, and off Ram Island two large ledges began to uncover.

At first glance, they did not look like ledges from where we anchored, though they were marked on the chart. They looked instead like driftwood logs. I put the binoculars on them, and saw the logs were seals.

As the tide dropped and the ledge uncovered more, a dozen more seals began to gather, and to clamber onto the seaweed covered ledge. Soon 20 seals lay there, drying and snoozing in the rays of the setting sun. Young seals, with their skins still furry white rather than sleek gray, frolicked in the water nearby, playing tag with each other, plunging, turning, leaping like porpoises out of water, gallivanting in puppy-like antics. Finally, tired out, they too clambered up to sleep on the ledges.

By now the ledge was totally covered with the seal colony. Plump, lazy, spread-eagled in happy innocence, the seals stretched out on backs, on bellies, some with flippers up in the air, piled in careless, comfortable abandon on each other. Behind Holbrooke Island, the giant orange ball of the setting sun dropped fast. The tips of spruce trees seemed to lace the sun's surface—a weird and lovely picture of dark green branches silhouetted against a vivid orange sun.

A black-hulled Hinckley sailboat, Cimbia from Castine, came in to drop anchor for the night, 100 yards from us. The seals, enjoying the last warmth of the sun, did not raise a head in curiosity. As darkness crept over East Penobscot Bay, the breeze dropped, the sea became velvet black and wholly calm. The seals and their ledge vanished from sight as the light failed. We put away the binoculars and began long-delayed preparations for dinner. Hurricane Dennis was far away.

A red light came slowly toward us across the velvet black water. The green light showed, then the white hull of another sailboat, creeping very slowly into the cove. The light stopped moving. We heard the anchor chain clatter as it was paid out by a figure on the bow; the sharp noisy spurt as another figure at the helm put the engine in reverse; then a faceless voice from the bow calling out "OK. The anchor is set firm! Cut the engine!"

Silence fell over the cove. We could see the cabin lights shining as other cruising people set about making their meal or lay reading in their bunks.

Aboard Steer Clear, I turned on the ship-to-shore radio telephone. We could hear other cruising boats up and down the Maine coast placing calls to their families and offices across America, creating envy in Pittsburgh and Detroit, Boston and Washington as they described where they were anchored.

Listening over this ocean party line, and sometimes placing a call or two, is part of the evening recreation. Most conversations are happy ones and concerned with reports of the day's sail and inquiries about who is taking care of the pets left at home.

But sometimes the torments and frailties of the human condition cast their painful shadow across these radio links between ships to shore. Last night we heard a distraught mother, voice carefully controlled, calling a doctor and a hospital, frantic for news of her college-age daughter.

The young girl had been taken by police to a New England hospital after they found her in "disoriented condition," wandering lost inside an empty house.

The youngster had been due to join her family aboard their boat in

Maine the next day. Now she was in a hospital room somewhere, zonked out by drugs, and her mother was helpless at sea, unable to talk to her. "Just tell her that I love her deeply. Tell her that, please, doctor." That was the only message she could relay.

I went on deck for a moment to savor the silent night in the quiet cove. The only noise was the eerie hoot of an owl high in the trees off our stern and the echo of that mother's cry of worried love.

TIMBERWIND: THROUGH A NIGHTMARE TO A DREAM

PENOBSCOT BAY — Some 26 vacationers from big cities are enjoying a special kind of heaven-in-Maine as they sail in Timberwind among the islands of Penobscot Bay.

They loll on deck. They feel the ocean breezes blowing over their sun-baked flesh and see the wind bellying out 2,300 square feet of white canvas sails. In their nostrils is the tantalizing smell of fish chowder, cooking in the galley, a deep sea change from the auto exhaust stench of their city streets.

Tonight they will rock to sleep in their bunks or drag a mattress on deck and watch shooting stars falling from a clear, clean sky, scintillating with a million other stars.

The memories of this day and night will live on like an oasis in their minds, when these same people are herded into subways or strap-hang on rush-hour buses in New York, Detroit, Chicago and other bread-winning purgatories.

To them, the decks of the two-masted cruise schooner Timberwind will always remain a special kind of heaven. But they'll never know what a frozen hell of fear and death these same decks were to Capt. Theodore Langzettel, who sailed Timberwind single-handed through ice and raging seas for 23 hours. He had lost his crew.

This was in Timberwind's other life.

In its first life, Timberwind was Portland's pilot boat. It was built by Victor Cole and launched in 1931 at Brown's wharf on the Portland waterfront. The wooden-hulled, two masted schooner had two engines as well as sail. For 38 years, from 1931 until 1969, it carried Portland Harbor pilots out to the old Portland Lightship, near which the pilots boarded incoming ships and navigated them safely into harbor. Today Timberwind is 57 years old, spiffy, immaculate and sea-safe.

A Maine sailor and his wife own and operate Timberwind, taking paying passengers on week-long cruises among Maine islands. Bill Alexander
is a teacher of physics and chemistry in Waterville; his wife, Julie, is a
registered nurse. They bought the old Portland pilot boat in 1969, spent
two years converting it, and are now in their 17th summer of windjammer cruising out of Rockport.

The peril and pain of Timberwind's first life as the Portland pilot boat
show no scars on the timbers visible today. But deep within is wood which
groans at the memory of one dreadful night in mid-February 1958.

Capt. Langzettel was skipper of Timberwind then. He was color-blind
and so could not quality for a pilot's license himself. (Later, he was lost
at sea aboard his own vessel.) Aboard with Langzettel, then 45 years old,
was Portland Harbor pilot Paul L. Litchfield, 52, of Cape Elizabeth and
two crewmen, Joseph H. Murray, 27, of Portland and Frederick E. Kennedy, 28, of Cape Elizabeth.

With a gale of wind blowing 50 mph from the northeast, the temperature at zero, seas running 20 feet high, and heavy ice forming, they headed
to meet the Norwegian tanker Siranda beyond the Portland Lightship.
The 500-foot Siranda was hours late arriving, so the pilot boat rode the
gale and blizzard far beyond the 7:45 a.m. estimated time of arrival of
Siranda.

The skipper of the Norwegian tanker, Capt. Haakon Osnes, had been
on duty on the bridge for 36 hours when Langzettel was close enough
to launch his dory with pilot Litchfield aboard and two crewmen at the
oars. They made it through the blizzard and raging seas to Siranda and
were ready to send the pilot clambering up the rope ladder.

At this moment, Siranda rolled down and picked up a big sea from its
windward side; then rolled back hard to leeward and dropped that load
of water into the dory. A Niagara Falls poured down on the dory and sank
it immediately.

Litchfield and the two oarsmen were hurled into the freezing, raging
seas. All three grabbed for the rope ladder. Litchfield was washed back
into the sea and never seen again. Norwegian sailors hoisted the two frozen oarsmen aboard. But Langzettel kept searching for his missing man
and dory, circling in ice and vapor as he stood in the open at the helm
of his pilot boat.

He lost sight of the Lightship and the tanker. He was soaked, freezing, alone at the helm of the 65-foot schooner, and lost. To stay alive he

Steer Clear in a quiet moment.

had to duck below for shelter every few minutes. At 11 a.m. he radioed for help. Another tanker, the Rincon, heard him and picked him up on radar and steamed toward him.

In the lee shelter of the tanker, Langzettel was guided toward the Lightship, where he waited for the storm to moderate. A Coast Guard lifeboat and the cutter Cowslip tried to rescue him but could not because of the storm. After 24 hours alone, wet and frozen at the helm, Langzettel finally brought his vessel safely home.

This summer day, that vessel, now Schooner Timberwind, has 26 people aboard enjoying heaven-in-Maine.

DAYS OF THE 25-POUND LOBSTER

ABOARD STEER CLEAR — It is long past Labor Day. Last night we anchored and slept off a small island in Penboscot Bay. Mid-September until early October can be the best time for cruising the Maine coast. The days sparkle, fog is short lived, the air has a nip. You have most islands and coves to yourself. There is wine in the sea breeze. You can see forever across Penobscot Bay. And most cruising boats are gone.

In August, these waters were a kaleidoscope of sail and power; the coves a nighttime rendezvous to coveys of cruising vacationers. Last night we were alone. Or almost.

Ken and his family came out to their summer shack. Ken is one of the few lobstermen who move out to live on and lobster from the islands in the summer. The summer shacks are simple, basic shelter and the youngsters grow brown and strong before returning home to the mainland by Labor Day for school.

Last night, as Ken's lobsterboat came chugging in, we waved, shouted greetings and watched them unload. They carried empty boxes up the grassy path to the shack. The kerosene lamp was soon sending out its golden yellow glow.

"We're here just to clean her out for winter," Ken said as he sculled in with a single oar off the stern of his dinghy. "We'll batten down, close up and go ashore for good tomorrow."

After a while, the kerosene light in the kitchen goes out. Briefly another goes on in the bedroom, the only other room in Ken's summer place. Then that goes dark.

It is now almost 10 p.m. The wind is down to a soft breeze, southwesterly, just enough to ripple the moon's sheen on the empty ocean. I go on deck. There is no sound here. No birds make night noises on the little island. The only sound is the lap of waves kissing our hull, and the gurgle of the tide running in and out through the rocks of Ken's wharf. I can see the lights of draggers working out beyond Hurricane.

I go down to the cockpit and turn on a lamp to read a pamphlet about Maine lobstering 107 years ago. I found it recently in that treasure house of old books—L. Berliawsky of Camden. Mrs. Berliawsky has reprinted from Scribner's Monthly Magazine of 1881 an article called "The Lobster at Home in Maine Waters," written by W. H. Bishop, and illustrated with a dozen wonderful woodcuts.

According to Bishop, the traps and the lobsters were both bigger and heavier than they are today.

"The traps have the appearance of mammoth bird cages. Each structure is four feet long, two feet wide and two feet high," wrote Bishop in 1881. "The bait used is is cod's head or a row of cunners arranged on perpendicular hooks within. The lobsterman has 150 such traps covering a circuit five or six miles in extent . . . A lobsterman with his dory filled with a pile of these curious cages ventures far out to sea, often at no little personal risk.''

I look over at Ken's 36-foot diesel-powered boat with its hydraulic gear for bringing in traps that are smaller and lighter than those described by Bishop. I think of those Maine lobstermen in dories and sloops, hand-hauling heavy traps, traps that were weighed down with rocks, and heavy lobsters.

According to Bishop, writing in 1881, "A mature lobster should measure without the claws from one to two feet long and weigh from 2 to 15 pounds . . . Lobster have been taken as heavy as 25 pounds. At South Saint George, below Rockland, hangs the claw of a lobster which in life weighed 43 pounds.''

Bishop in his Scribner's article reports the gripes of lobstermen of Maine 107 years ago. They sound like the same gripes you hear today. "It is claimed," writes Bishop "that the size of lobsters and profit of the lobster business are being diminished steadily by the industry with which the pursuit has been lately followed.'' The gripe today is the same—too many part-time lobstermen.

Bishop reports another gripe of 1881: "The shores teem with traps and the competition is so fierce that whereas a lobsterman once made four or five dollars a day, he now regards himself as lucky if he makes but one dollar.''

A hundred years ago, lobster smacks under sail travelled from cove to cove and harbor to harbor, buying lobsters. One smack came to buy the bigger lobsters, bound to market in New York and Boston mostly. Another smack-buyer came from the nearby lobster-canning factory to buy "smalls." Canned lobsters were a huge Maine business then. One canning company alone had 23 canning plants along the coast. Bishop describes some of their operations:

"The canning factory opens at one end to the sea and the wharf. Two men bring in squirming loads of lobster on a stretcher and dump the mass into coppers for boiling. Dense clouds of steam arise, through which we catch vistas of men, women and children at work. The boiled lobsters are thrown into carving tables. Men with knives separate them into constituent parts and then the meat is put into cans. The first girl puts in a suitable selection of parts. The next weighs it. The next forces down the contents with a stamp invented for the purpose. The next puts on a tin cover with blows of a little hammer. These are carried to the solderers who seal them tight . . . then they are plunged into bath cauldrons and boiled . . .''

Solderers made top money, says Bishop, being paid $12 to $15 a week. The girls got no more than $3.50 a week. "Yet even at this wage, a respectable class of female labor is engaged. This is not so remarkable when the wages of school-keeping have been reduced to $2 a week.''

Nine-tenths of the canned lobster were sold to foreign markets.

A law in Maine of that time prohibited the canning of lobsters except between the first of March and the first of August. Some said this was to safeguard the lobsters. Others said it was to safeguard the lobster-eaters from possible poisoning. Still others said it was to benefit the owners of canning factories.

As soon as lobster-canning stopped, the canning of sweet corn started. The corn-factories and the lobster-factories were owned largely by the same companies. Some felt the owners of the canneries got the lobster-canning season law passed so they could have a ready supply of solderers for cans of corn. Bishop quotes a local informant as saying: "It ain't in the interest of the lobster, nor yet of the public. The factory owners wants the sawderers down to Freeport and Gorham for cannin' the corn—that's how it is; and they don't want no one else a-goin' on with cannin' lobsters when they ain't at it.''

TENSION COMES IN LOUD AND CLEAR

DOGFISH ISLAND — We picked up the first scene of a search-and-rescue drama on our ship's radio at 4 p.m., and stayed with it for five tense hours till the final curtain at 9 p.m.

"This is Serendib," we heard. "We are lost. In dense fog. Surrounded by ledges and little islands. Think we hear the foghorn on the Fox Island Thorofare at Vinalhaven. Can you help us?''

Serendib was calling the Rockland Coast Guard over the VHF emergency channel 16. The voice from the Serendib was calm on the surface. But beneath the controlled calm you could hear the fear, the worry, the plea for help, the prayer for an answer.

"This is the Serendib. Can you read me? Serendib in emergency, calling Rockland Coast Guard. Come in please.''

Now the Coast Guard came back, loud and clear, firm, comforting, a reassuring link to help. "Serendib. This is Coast Guard, Rockland. Switch to channel 22."

Aboard Steer Clear, we were safe and secure, lying on anchor off Dogfish Island, Vinalhaven. Fog had driven us in.

Other boats also sought safe refuge, in coves and small harbors all along midcoast Maine. Dense fog enshrouded east and west Penobscot Bay. Our hearts went out to the Serendib, lost and encircled by unknown islands and threatening ledges, only a few short miles from our safe sanctuary.

I switched to channel 22, but heard only static. Then came the voice again. "This is Serendib . . ." Back came the Coast Guard, asking more information. Serendib gave the number of people aboard her and a description of the vessel. She said she was a 34-foot Webb Cove lobster boat converted to a pleasure boat. That she had been trying to find the entrance to Fox Island Thorofare from the east. That she thought her position was somewhere off Calderwood Point on the east side of Vinalhaven.

I unrolled my chart of the area. And saw the water off Calderwood Point was a fearsome maze of rocks, ledges, shallows, puzzling for a stranger to navigate even in clear daylight. In this dense fog, I knew how terrifying it must be out there for those on the lost boat, seeing only ledges, hearing only waves breaking on granite that could rip out her bottom.

The skipper of the Serendib identified himself: Francis X. McAffrey of 115 Cannongate, Nashua, N.H. The Coast Guard at Rockland called by radio to their 41-foot boat, No. 416. By happy coincidence 416 was returning from Heron Neck Light on the southern end of Vinalhaven. She was equipped with radar and radio direction finding gear. The Coast Guard base at Rockland diverted 416 to search for the lost Serendib.

Serendib voiced relief that the Coast Guard was not far away and would be searching for them. Serendib said she would anchor.

"Give me a slow count, so I can get a radio fix on your position," ordered the coxswain aboard 416, Bos'un Mate 2nd class Brian Pisz, from Massachusetts.

The voice of Serendib came back, controlled and calm, but brimming with eagerness to cooperate 500 percent with this helping hand outreached to find him. He began his count, slow and measured . . . "Serendib one, Serendib two, Serendib three . . ." and thus up to 10 and back from 10 through all the numerals to one.

"We read you loud and clear, Serendib. Stand by while I plot our radio fix on you . . .

"Serendib, this is 416. We have a fix on you now. You are between Griffin Ledge and Halibut Ledge, quite a piece from your estimated position of the entrance to Fox Island Thorofare. We will start moving toward you. Stay on that anchor and keep listening on channel 22."

Time dragged slowly by. We hung by the radio, wishing comfort to those of Serendib, wishing luck to 416, creeping through fog between wicked ledges, hunting for the lost boat.

"Serendib, this is 416. We're heading to you. I think we have you on radar now. But I want another radio direction finder fix on you. This time, give me a short count—up to five and back."

Serendib acknowledged and began her slow count.

"Serendib, this is 416. Yes, we have you. We are getting close. Do you have a horn?"

"416, this is Serendib. Yes, we have a horn. We have a bell."

"Serendib, this is 416. Sound your horn. Ring your bell. We have our foghorn blasting every two minutes."

"416, this is Serendib. I hear you. I hear your horn."

"Serendib. Roger from 416. We hear you now too. We are closing slowly. You should have us in sight in a moment."

"416. This is Serendib. We see you. We hear you and see you!" On Steer Clear we laughed and shouted, sharing the joy there must have been aboard the Serendib and 416.

It was close to 7 p.m. The search had lasted close to three long, tense hours.

"Rockland Coast Guard, this is 416. We have made contact with Serendib. We will escort them to North Haven. Visibility zero. It will be slow."

Now there was silence. Serendib and 416 were under way. Rescued and rescuer creeping along the same track through dense fog, dodging islands and ledges that were blimps on 416's radar screen, but invisible to the human eye.

Two more hours and the radio came to life again; 416 reported they had Serendib in the anchorage at North Haven. Other vessels cut in to say that Serendib was in the channel. They shone spotlights on her. But the fog was so thick, it was barely possible for boats in the same anchorage to see each other.

On the radio, Serendib and another vessel gave thanks and commendation to 416.

That cold, anonymous name of 416 will long be engraved in the memory of Serendib, and all who heard the rescue, word by clipped staccato word. Well done, Coast Guard!

DIVING FOR SUNKEN HISTORY

STOCKTON HARBOR — Divers surface from the murky, muddy waters off Sears Island. They are exploring the wreck of the 85-foot "Defence," a 16 cannon privateer scuttled by her American crew in 1779 to prevent capture by the British.

Divers in black wet suits, black helmets, masks, breathing apparatus, flipper feet and oxygen tanks, clamber out of the water onto the floating platform that is working headquarters for the archaeological exploration of the gunship from the American Revolution lying on the bottom. The tall diver nearest me offloads the heavy oxygen tank; peels off the scalp-tight, black helmet and to my amazement long blonde hair tumbles down. A sweep of the arms and the black clinging wet suit is peeled off. There, in a vivid blue bikini stands Cynthia Orr, 22, team leader of five divers and a graduate in anthropology from the University of Pennsylvania.

The water is cold down where the Defence has been lying in her muddy bed for almost 210 years. Cynthia Orr takes a mug of hot chocolate and goes into consultation with Avery Stone and Betty Seiffert. They are in halters and shorts, and their academic qualifications, too, are awesome. Miss Stone is the official Recorder for the American Institute of Naval Archaeology. In this capacity, she keeps a meticulous journal which details every operation connected with Project Heritage Restored. She and Cynthia Orr bend over the diagram of the sunken ship and plot on its grid system exactly the time, place and nature of the artifacts which Cynthia brought to the surface.

Next, Cynthia Orr talks with Betty Seiffert from the Maine State Museum. From a steel card-index file, Betty takes a large blank card. First, she sketches on it the handle of a pottery jug, just recovered by Cynthia; gives it a catalogue number; measures and records all its dimensions and notes the precise location on the wreck where it was found. Betty repeats the whole process with each find. She now has catalogued a total of 391 pieces recovered; 29 metal artifacts such as spoons, cannonballs, grape shot; 52 pottery and glass items, such as jugs for oil and bottles for ale; 55 items of bones and textiles. Among these are barrels marked "pork" and "beef." They each contained 32 big pieces of meat. The bones are still in good shape, after two centuries.

"The reason the artifacts are so well preserved is the cold and the mud" explains Betty Seiffert. "For more than 200 years the water down there has been very cold. And the wreck has been covered in thick mud. The mud cover stopped oxygen getting to the ship. So no underwater life such as worms or fungus have eaten away at the ship and her contents. Everything we cannot recover this season, we bury again in a mud and sand mixture to preserve it till the diving begins again."

Cynthia Orr refills her mug with hot chocolate and takes hold of a yellow line at the end of which is a diver on her team, working on the Defence below us. She jerks the line sharply. "One jerk means 'Are you OK?' The reply is a quick jerk on the line from below, meaning 'OK, thanks.'" Two jerks from below means "Give me more slack so I can go down further." Three jerks means "I want to come up slowly. Five or more quick jerks spells "Trouble."

Cynthia Orr says this is her third year diving on "Defence."

"My first two years here I was a student. Now I am paid staff—a team leader. Another girl from the University of Pennsylvania is here diving this summer, Nancy Orton." She points to a girl in a white bikini out on a raft monitoring the air hose.

"Nancy is a graduate student. Her specialty is Middle American archaeology from pre-historic times. Mine is anthropology. Nautical archaeology fascinates me. When I finish here, I fly to Italy to join another expedition partly sponsored by AINA (American Institute of Nautical Archaeology). We will be diving in the Lipari Islands where the volcano Stromboli is. The dive will be on wrecks of Greek ships from the 4th century . . . And later this fall I will work in Greece on classical archaeological digs for a year . . ." There are three quick jerks on the yellow line from the diver below and Cynthia lets out more line.

"That is Sheila Matthews, down there. She is assistant director of this entire project. She is a graduate student in Underwater Archaeology from Texas A&M."

Director of this project is David C. Switzer. He sits in swimming trunks on the rail of the support vessel from the Maine Maritime Academy at Castine, which is a major force in this underwater probe of a vessel sunk in the American Revolution. Switzer is Professor of History at the University of New Hampshire and director of this project.

The ship we are diving on, was part of the Penobscot Expedition—probably the worst fiasco in military operations of the Revolutionary War.

In 1779, the British had established a naval base at Castine. To drive them out, Massachusetts sent a naval force of 40 ships transporting over 1,000 troops in July, 1779.

Admiral Richard Saltonstall was in command overall; and commanding the militia troops were General Solomon Lovell and General Peleg Wadsworth. The artillery was under the command of Major Paul Revere. But Saltonstall turned out to be a timid and inept commander. He had the British vastly outnumbered; but instead of attacking, he stalled for a month. In those weeks, British reinforcements sailed on into Castine.

The sight of six British warships scared the daylights out of Saltonstall. He panicked. His fleet and soldiers fled up the Penobscot and Bagaduce Rivers. But the privateer gunboat "Defence" tried running for safety into Stockton Harbor. The British pursued. The crew then blew up the powder magazine and that explosion sank the ship in the 15 feet of water where she has lain ever since. The defeated Saltonstall was court martialed and stripped of the right to ever command forces again.

Paul Revere, the artillery commander, walked home to Boston. The routed American troops fled through the wilderness, back to Massachusetts.

"The tremendous importance of this sunken vessel named Defence," says Switzer, "lies in the fact that this is the only known war vessel of the Revolutionary War that is still almost intact. It is this which has led MIT, the AINA, the National Geographic, as well as the Maine State Museum and the Maine Maritime Academy, to sponsor this archaeological work. Our ultimate goal is to raise all or a very large section of Defence.

Defence was built in Beverly, Mass. Her first, and last voyage, was to Castine. There were 16 cannon aboard which shot six pound cannonballs. Each cannon weighted over 1000 pounds. Two of these cannon have been raised from the Defence. These are on loan from Maine to the U.S. Naval History Museum in Washington.

Switzer shows detailed drawings of the ship and the artifacts recovered.

"The huge size of the cookstove is astonishing," says Switzer. "It is made of brick, and measures four and one half feet wide, four and one half feet deep and almost five feet high. It weighs a ton. In its center is a big cavity, into which a huge copper cauldron fitted. That cauldron is 32 inches long, and 32 inches across and almost two feet deep.

"The Defence carried 100 in crew, a huge crew for a ship only 85 feet long and 22 feet in the beam. But as a privateer, she carried extra men to take charge of the prize vessels she captured."

Switzer shows what has been recovered. Among the items are cannon wadding, shoes, a sailmaker's palm, which is a kind of glove for a left-handed sailmaker, clay pipes, tool handles, pewter spoons, wine jugs, ale bottles, a silk hair-ribbon still tied in a knot, barrel staves, and wooden mess kits for troops.

PENOBSCOT RIVER IS QUIET NOW

PENOBSCOT RIVER — I've just made a 100-mile trip with the Coast Guard from Rockland up the Penobscot River to Bangor and back.

I hope to sail up all the great rivers of Maine. I now have done the Penobscot, the St. Georges River, the Damariscotta, the Sheepscot, the New Meadows, the Royal River, the Medomak, the Kennebec and others. The great rivers of Maine brim with beauty, history and ghosts. Up these rivers sailed the Indians, the Vikings perhaps, the first explorers, first settlers and first traders. The earliest Red Paint men travelled the rivers and feasted on their banks, mostly on oysters.

On the Damariscotta River is the world's biggest oyster shell heap, 31 feet deep in oyster shells. Indians were the third and most recent of the oyster eaters along the Damariscotta. Scientists say that the oldest oyster shells beside the banks of the river date back to 2900 B.C. and that the heap of shells really got big 1,500 years ago and grew since then to become the biggest oyster shell heap in the world.

But the banks of the Penobscot seemed bare this November. All the leaves were gone. Through tree skeletons, you could see the true contours of the high ground beside the river, where American Revolutionary troops were routed in defeat, including Major Paul Revere.

Standing in the stern, watching the brown river water churned by propellors, there was a sweet sadness, a nostalgic melancholy to making the trip on a river empty of traffic. In better days, traffic on the Penobscot River was busier than on Route 1 today.

The only vessels we saw this trip were oil tankers or oil barges tied up in Bucksport and Bangor, discharging. No vessel except ours was moving.

Bangor used to be the world's biggest, busiest lumber port. The river swarmed with ships. In the single year of 1860, there were 3,375 ship arrivals in Bangor. In the 50 years from 1838 to 1888, more than eight billion—repeat billion—feet of lumber were shipped out of Bangor.

We tied up for the night alongside an abandoned, rotting set of pilings in the middle of downtown Bangor. We were the only vessel there. But 100 years ago, ships were so thick here that a man could walk across their decks from Bangor to Brewer. When the lumber ships went down river, they would go 36 at a time, rafted three abreast and 12 rows deep loaded with timber to the gunwales.

Bangor boomed, a wild town, filled with saloons and whore houses, catering to thousands of sailors from the sea and to log drivers and lumberjacks hitting town after months in the Maine woods. But the night we went ashore, Bangor was a dull and proper town. The only red light glowing near the waterfront was from a lantern in the railroad shunting yard. Not a sailor, a lumberjack, a riverman or a roistering brawl anywhere on the Bangor waterfront. No fun anywhere!

But in 1988, Bangor is beginning to bring new life to one old, wonderful waterfront.

TERROR BOARDED STEER CLEAR WITH FIRE AT SEA

VINALHAVEN — Fire at sea. Three terrifying words. Add a fourth, and the spasm of terror multiplies. Fire at sea alone. I know. Because it happened to me aboard Steer Clear. But nature works a mysterious cure for terror. It wipes out, almost, the memory of vivid terror. And that shocks me almost as much as the fire did.

To write about the barely-remembered fire at sea, I reread my ship's log, weeks after I'd made the entries.

Suddenly I was reading about the fire. It was like reading about something which had never happened to me. I then realized that I had told no one about it, and that nature had wiped that swift spasm of terror from my memory's active file. So I'll write about it here, in the hope the account may stop somebody else from making the idiotic, stupid mistake I made. I'll simply transfer the rough words written in the log of Steer Clear soon after the flames were dead.

"Off Vinalhaven Island, Tuesday night, July 22, 1987 on anchor. Flash

fire aboard! A wall of flame for two seconds, 3 feet high, 3 feet wide. Huge, terrifying—and then died out. Scared hell out of me. Idiot mistake. I poured a handful of water onto hot oil in the fry pan—and whoosh! firestorm!

"I was in the galley making dinner. Heating cooking oil in skillet for frying up a chicken. Handy on the next burner sat a kettle of cold water. I poured a little water from there because that was easier than getting a few drops from the sink pump to test whether the oil was yet hot enough for frying. Tossed probably a tablespoon of cold water onto hot oil— and a wall of fire exploded instantly. Flames filled the whole galley. Orange and yellow terror, from wall to wall and up to the ceiling.

"For a split second, I saw the whole boat afire and then exploding. Then just as quickly the whole blaze died out completely. I was still alive and Steer Clear was too! I don't like to write it down, even in the log. It brings back the awful scare and makes me mad at myself for being such an idiot. But I'm writing it down, so the mistake will stay always in the front of my head.

"Lesson to be remembered always: No water on hot oil or fat. Until now, I never understood that old saying, 'Oil and water never mix!' But I never knew the combination explodes like a bomb.

"Second lesson: Why didn't I automatically grab the fire extinguisher in the galley? Because the flames died out so quickly? Because the fire explosion was such a shock? Or because I have never had to use a fire extinguisher—and had done no drills?"

That's the end of the log entry about the fire, except for an account of scrubbing up the mess, a job which took four hours.

I've been cooking on the Steer Clear galley for 20 years, and never had a fire before. I hope—never again.

The rest of the log for the same day is happier reading. It had been an idyllic day, alone in a small boat in a secluded cove on a lovely Maine island miles out to sea. I was taking a "lay-by-and-rest-up" day in an inlet where seals and herons play and where fat mussels abound for a luscious meal. Suddenly I had a surprise encounter with an old friend, not seen in four years.

Years ago, Big Dennis had crewed on fish boats out of New Harbor, Monhegan and Port Clyde, and our paths had crossed often. This time it was the mussels which brought us together again.

Three dories motored into the silent cove, followed by a lobster boat with a mussel-cleaning cage in the stern. The men in each dory worked a long rake to haul in mussels from ledges in shallow water. When they had 50 to 70 bushels of mussels aboard, they took them for cleaning to the lobster boat. One man in one of the skiffs yelled out "Bill!" I waved and he came alongside. For a moment I didn't recognize him in this setting. But it was Big Dennis, now in the mussel business, and he hung onto my rail, all 260 pounds of him, as we talked away a happy half-hour.

He lives aboard his "yacht," moored in the Fox Thorofare. It is an old 36-foot, black-hulled Egg Harbor cruising boat with a flying bridge, converted to a work boat. In it, Big Dennis hauls 150 to 200 bushels of mussels to market in Rockland. They fetch about $3.50 a bushel these days, were even up near $5 at times this year. Some change. A few years ago, few people in Maine would eat mussels, let alone harvest them as a cash crop.

Twelve years ago, when I was picking a bucket of mussels for dinners on Steer Clear, lobstermen laughed and held their noses at the idea of eating them. Now mussels are a gourmet dish here, as they have long been in Europe. Mussels have become a million dollar a year business for Maine.

Three hours after saying goodbye to Big Dennis I splashed that tablespoon of cold water into a skillet with hot oil in it. And inside a split second, came too close to saying my last goodbye. But, thanks to a God who looks after fools, here I am telling the story.

Merchants Row—An abandoned lobster crate on an island field. Scores of islands, many uninhabited, and with small coves for anchoring, digging clams or picnicking, make an enticing week of cruising the waters between Vinalhaven, Isle au Haut and Swans Island.

IX
DEER ISLE

Cliffs and surf at Isle au Haut, near Duck Harbor.

IX

*Which way to Deer Isle, the long way or the short, the front door
or the back door?*

*The short way is through the front door—a straight run across the
bay from Vinalhaven to Mark Island Light and into Stonington. No
more than an hour's run in Steer Clear. The long way is to head
north, up the bay among the dozen blessed islands and then come
down through Eggemoggin Reach, and then to Stonington by the back
door. This can take from seven hours to seven days, depending upon
how many times we succumb to temptation spots along the way—
Eagle Island, Butter Island, the Barred Islands, Great Spruce Head Is-
land, Beach Island, Bradbury Island, Pickering Island with a side trip
into favorite swimming places at Hog and Pond Islands, and whether
we overnight in Bucks Harbor, or visit friends along the Eggemoggin
Reach.*

*I choose the long way. On this trip, I'm solo; no shipmate, no dog,
nobody else's timetable to keep. It's freedom; but at a price. The biggest price to pay for being alone on cruises is not being able to share
the sights and pleasures. Sharing doesn't divide the joy—it doubles it.*

*To compensate, memories of earlier trips among these islands come
flooding back in nostalgic waves. I recall not only other trips in Steer
Clear, but remember stories of a century or two centuries ago about
families and hermits, loves and tragedies on these islands. The islands
seem uninhabited now or used only part of the summer by only one
family, compared to the hundreds of people who used to live all year
long on the islands.*

The Light atop Eagle Island is always a magnet to my mind and eyes, even after 20 years of seeing it. Today I slow down Steer Clear after I get within a mile of Eagle Island, then alter course to come closer and closer until I'm directly under the cliff on which the Light is perched, 106 feet up. It peeks out handsomely from among the spruce which grow green around its gleaming white tower.

The light was first built in 1839 to help guide thousands of sailing ships from the ocean to the Penobscot river on their way to load cargoes of lumber at Bangor, the biggest lumber port in the world. More than 3,000 ships a year loaded in Bangor. Eagle Island Light guided them from the ocean over Hardhead Shoals, toward Dice Head Light at Castine, which passed them on to Fort Point Light, at the entrance to the Penobscot River and Bangor.

Penobscot Bay is almost empty of boats today. But I imagine the days when hundreds of schooners under full sail pointed to Eagle Light. The first lightkeepers, in the days when Van Buren was president, were paid $100 a month. They had to supply their own uniforms, their own food, even their own boat. They used to hang lanterns in the light tower. The oil in the lanterns was fish oil or whale oil, lugged up in drums from the beach, 106 feet below.

Quinn—there is an Eagle Island name with continuity! Quinns lived on Eagle Island for more than 130 years. Samuel Quinn bought the island and all the sheep on it, plus nearby Fling Island, in 1844 and paid $1,500 for the whole 270 acres.

Standing at the helm alone today, I recollect the day we went ashore and swam at Lighthouse Cove and then walked to the old island cemetery and counted the headstones of 22 Quinns, seven "unknowns," and five Howards. I went looking that day for traces of where 30 or more "rusticators" from Boston and New York spent summers in the famed Quinn House. But I found none. Even the old keeper's house was burned by the Coast Guard, in 1964, after the light had been automated.

Steer Clear drifts below the automated light. I try to picture Marion "Aunt Elva" Howard, the last relative of the Quinns to live year-round on Eagle Island.

This remarkable woman had strong roots in Eagle Island which storm nor winter nor age nor isolation could wither. She had been

*born on Eagle Island before the 20th century and was graduated in
1912 from the one-time Eagle Island school. Two years later she went
to live and work on nearby North Haven as a telephone operator,
then moved to Camden as a taxi-dispatcher, and finally returned to
her beloved Eagle Island in 1953. She lived alone here until she was 80
years old. I blow a kiss from a stranger to "Aunt Elva" Howard and
ease Steer Clear into forward gear and move on to the lovely beaches
and woods and hilltops of beautiful Butter Island, only minutes away.*

*Attached to a tree near the beaches of Butter Island is a small metal
band which stays forever in my mind because it symbolizes one of the
loveliest, quietest memorials of the world. The band simply states
these woods are the Alvida forest, a memorial to Alvida Cabot, and
urges visitors to enjoy them and protect them. The bands were put
there at the direction of Thomas D. Cabot of Boston, who bought
Butter Island in the late 1940s. Thanks to Cabot, the island has been
preserved wild, uninhabited, unspoiled in its natural glory.*

*A winding path leads from the woods on the shore, through the Al-
vida forest, up the hillside to the peak. Stand at the peak and 40 islands in Penobscot Bay surround you. In the distances are Cadillac
Mountain, Blue Hill and the Camden Hills. And miles of blue water,
with the gleam of white sails catching the sun. Few sights in the world
bring such a sense of joy at being alive, atop an island in Maine. Or
such a sense of the minuteness of man in time and space. Among the
islands of Penobscot Bay, all the struggles, the wars, the plantings, the
harvestings, the building of ships, the drowning of sailors, the birth of
infants, the feuds of families, the failures of farms and the fortunes in
shipping, lumber and granite—few have left much of a lasting mark
on these enduring islands.*

*After we climbed to the top of Butter, we walked for miles across
the island, looking for cellar holes of the farms which had been here
since before the Revolution. No traces. We searched especially to find
traces of the incredible Dirigo project which had briefly flourished on
Butter Island, rising from dreams in 1896, peaking from 1900 to 1914
and dropping to abandonment by 1916. But for almost 20 years the
Dirigo project soared.*

*The Dirigo project was an early housing development. An Arab
tent city on Butter Island, with 497 family tent sites, was laid out by
the bachelor Harriman brothers, Boston architects who bought Butter*

in 1895. They renamed the island "Dirigo," after the Maine state motto "I lead," and emblazoned the new name in huge white letters on the hillside.

These Harriman brothers advertised their "New England Tent Club" to the "yuppies" of their time, promoting it as the ideal club for "young club men of good social standing." At Dirigo, they could become landowners in an exclusive Maine island community which emphasized clean outdoor living.

The Arab tent city never materialized. But instead, the Harrimans built a hotel, a casino, and other "summer paradise" buildings for 100 guests. Ferries ran frequently from Rockland to Dirigo. Better still, the round trip from Boston by steamer cost only $5.50. The steamer left Boston at 5 p.m. and arrived at the new wharf on Dirigo at 7 a.m.

World War I ended Dirigo. The guests stopped coming. The ferries and steamers stopped running. By the 1920s, the empty, grandiose buildings had been vandalized and winter weather collapsed what was left.

Most islands in the bay hold memories for Steer Clear, some of hairy times in foul weather, but more of splendid times in fair weather. The memories pile up after 20 summers of meandering through these lovely waters and blessed islands. Often in the winters, I'd read books about some of the islands as they used to be. Almost 200 years ago, most of these islands were farmed, or used for raising sheep, salting fish, logging and somehow making a living for generations. Of course, almost every island has its own stories and legends. Usually the tragic or macabre ones last longest.

Pickering Island, which lies between Butter and the Eggemoggin Reach, is the setting for one of the more macabre stories of recent vintage.

The island, which had been settled in 1775 by Samuel Pickering, was sold in 1885 to Dr. Stacy B. Collins of New York for $2,000. He turned the island, which had been farmed for 110 years, into his summer residence. Dr. Collins built a strange house, high, with a curious square turret at one end. The shingled house was curious in another way. It had no windows on the lower floor, except for a couple of slits. All windows on the upper floor were barred, strange for the only house on an island in 1885. Soon the story circulated that the house was dark and heavily barred because inside it Dr. Collins kept his mad wife, or his lunatic mother-in-law, or patients from insane asylums on whom the doctor was conducting medical and other experiments. One story circulated that the doctor kept simple-minded barmaids from the city locked up inside to amuse him through his summers on his private island.

To guard against intruders into his privacy, Dr. Collins is reputed to have kept packs of fierce dogs to patrol the shores and attack anyone who tried to land. How true? How much rumor? Some people show old photos of the strangely barred and weirdly designed fortress of a house to confirm the stories. Others say they were only nasty rumors, spread by a drunken clam digger who had been viciously chased off the island by the dogs and owner. Dr. Collins' house stood weird and empty for many years after his death. It was burned as a hazard in the 1950s. Yet there is still an eerie sense of the macabre when you stand at evening on the cove of Pickering Island near where Dr. Collins once lived behind bars.

Steer Clear heads to Pumpkin Light. Pumpkin Island Light, built in 1854 at the time of the Mexican War, flashed for a century and was sold at auction in 1934. The Light is now a private house, and marks the entrance into the shelter of the Eggemoggin Reach. Ahead is the most beautiful suspension bridge in Maine, spanning the Reach from Sedgwick on the mainland to Deer Isle. Out come my cameras. Every time we go under this bridge, I make more pictures of it. The pictures are almost all the same. Yet the bridge so awes me by its beauty and its engineering, that I keep trying to make photos which will capture these qualities. The photos never do. From a small boat, the Deer Isle bridge is one of the special beauties of the Eggemoggin Reach.

For those who like to know the nuts-and-bolts behind the beauty, here are a few facts about the bridge.

The 50-year-old bridge was built for just under a million dollars in 1938, financed by the State of Maine and the federal Public Works Administration. Before 1938, a ferry, able to carry four cars, was Deer Isle's only link across Eggemoggin Reach to the mainland. The twin towers of the suspension span soar 185 feet. Total length of the bridge is almost a half mile. The lovely center span is over a thousand feet long, between towers. Each main cable is 7½ inches in diameter, made of 19 strands of half-inch galvanized steel.

On Memorial Day weekend 1978, when the bridge was turning 40 years old, she went a bit wild in a high wind and warm weather. "It began waving up and down like a rope when you whip it" said state trooper Bruce Setler, who was so alarmed that he had the bridge closed to all traffic. The bridge was undulating three to five feet, according to eye-witnesses. Joan Mondale, wife of vice president Walter Mondale, was spending a long Memorial Day weekend on Deer Isle at the time. Mrs. Mondale was stranded until the swaying Deer Isle bridge stopped dancing the hula, and was declared safe again for traffic. Engineers said the wild swaying was probably triggered by a rare combination of rising temperature plus gusting high winds, and that this devilish duo stretched the steel cables and this allowed the suspension bridge to dance a jig. For a few hours, rumors flew across Deer Isle that the bridge was about to collapse and isolate the island from the onrush of summer traffic.

But the beautiful bridge has never danced the same weird way again.

Steer Clear ambles slowly along the Eggemoggin Reach, enjoying the shelter and the scenery. Passages along the Reach or the Thorofares at the Fox Islands and Deer Isle, are not, in our log book at least, a link to get you from here to there in a hurry. For us there is always a relaxing gentleness to the Reach, with the rolling meadows and headlands of Sedgewick, Sargentville, Surry, the Benjamin River. Often we make a detour to visit old friend Russell Wiggins, who used to edit the Washington Post and was ambassador to the United Nations. Now he runs the Ellsworth American, one of the best weeklies in America, and sails his Friendship sloop Amity. Like Wiggins, his boat is also a classic. Both have weathered fair and foul for more than 80 years and still go splendidly and joyously.

At Center Harbor, midway along the Reach, we detour again to visit Joel and Allene White. Joel, son of E.B. White, is a fine boat builder and marine architect who established a great reputation at his boatyard here. Allene is a food columnist for the Maine Sunday Telegram. Often in years past, Steer Clear would tie up to the boatyard dock and I'd walk to see E.B. White on his farm in Brookline, in the years when he was still sailing his little sloop.

Temptations surround a boatman approaching the end of the

Reach. On the Deer Isle side are islands and coves and anchorages which wind in and around each other and are heaven to explore. There's always a snug spot to spend a night in calm water and silence, alone. Seldom is there another cruising boat anchored overnight in these hideaways. But, fair warning; it is hard to leave next morning. Sometimes we haven't. Instead we've laid on anchor for another day, or two, and taken the skiff for slow, close-up discovery of low water coves, mussel beds, heron nests, clam flats and total peace.

Few boats take more time than Steer Clear to circumnavigate Deer Isle; once it took 15 days.

THE AMERICA'S CUP: WON BY DEER ISLE MEN

DEER ISLE — The America's Cup has no bottom. So it is useless as a cup. It has not much value either. The original price of the ornate Victorian silver cup was 100 guineas, less than $300 today.

To racing sailors, however, the America's Cup is the foremost event in their world. It ranks with a World Series, Super Bowl or the Kentucky Derby. What's more, it is the oldest international event in sports history. And perhaps the only one where the money is all outgo and no income. Many millions of dollars are spent on trying to win it, but there is not a nickel in gate receipts. International pride and prestige are hugely involved, but the America's Cup is in fact a race between two private yacht clubs: most often over the years between the New York Yacht Club, as defender of the Cup, and the yacht club of the challenger.

It is unlikely, but true: Deer Isle men played the key role in winning America's Cup races almost from the start. Deer Isle men sailed the boat. In the first races for the America's Cup, the entire crew of the American victors came from Maine.

In 1895 the entire 33-man crew of the 130-foot winner Defender, came from Deer Isle. Their skipper was white-bearded Capt. "Hank" Haff. He and his Deer Isle crew trounced the English Earl of Dunraven's Valkyrie III, which carried more sail and managed to crash into Defender and carry off its topmast shroud. After firing off vividly worded protests, the angry Lord Dunraven packed up and went back to England and his Royal Yacht Squadron.

Next to challenge for the America's Cup was a man who had been blackballed from membership in the Royal Yacht Squadron because he had no aristocratic blood in his veins and had made his money from, of all dastardly occupations, trade. He was Sir Thomas Lipton, who made his fortune by selling tea, Lipton's tea.

In 1898 tea-magnate Lipton issued his challenge from Ireland and the Royal Ulster Yacht Club of Belfast. This one-time grocery clerk was to dominate the America's Cup races for the next 30 years, building up a public image as one of the most gallant losers in the world of sport, and in the process making Lipton's tea a household word. In 1899 he sent over the first of his challengers, the 130-foot Shamrock.

To defend the America's Cup, a syndicate headed by J. P. Morgan commissioned Nathaniel Herreshoff to build Columbia. Once again the American yacht was crewed entirely by 22 men from Deer Isle. Their pay was $60 a month for the officers and $45 for the seamen. For each race sailed, all hands got a $5 bonus.

Once again a 100-percent Maine crew won the America's Cup. Once again the inhabitants of Deer Isle uproariously celebrated the victory by their seamen. But this time there was an accident. The old cannon they fired as a signal of triumph, a relic from the war of 1812, discharged prematurely and broke and lacerated the right forearm of Fred Beck. After emergency treatment on Deer Isle, Beck was sent off on the next boat to Portland for further repairs. The last professional crew defended the cup in 1903. When amateurs took over, Deer Isle men were no longer signed on to man the huge 130-foot racing yachts.

Maine, however, came back into the forefront of the America's Cup races. In 1937 Bath Iron Works built Ranger, one of the most successful racing yachts of all time.

The nation was wallowing in the depths of the Depression when one of America's wealthiest yachtsmen arrived in Bath to talk boats and money with William S. "Pete" Newell, head of BIW. He was Harold S. Vanderbilt.

Glumly, Vanderbilt told Newell that because of the Depression, he had failed to raise even half the cost of building Ranger from his millionaire-yachtsmen pals at the New York Yacht club. If the boat was to be built, said Vanderbilt, he would have to foot the entire cost out of his own pocket.

"How much will it cost me?" Vanderbilt asked. Newell said he had no idea. He had never built such a boat. But since Vanderbilt had already paid for two America's Cup winners, Rainbow and Enterprise, Newell

Deer Isle Bridge from Eggemoggin Reach. Our skiff is astern. This is the most graceful suspension bridge in Maine.

said that Vanderbilt ought to have a price in mind. Vanderbilt grunted that times had changed since then. So Newell made him a sporting offer. At a time when families along the Kennebec were hard up for a dime, Newell told Vanderbilt: "I'll build Ranger for cost, with a ceiling of $130,000, and add 50 percent of the labor cost to cover my overhead."

The sporting offer made Vanderbilt happier. "Done," he said. And that was that. There was no written contract. Newell and BIW began work in December 1936 and launched Ranger in May 1937. BIW's Ranger went on to win the America's Cup, beating Endeavour II, the challenger owned by English aircraft tycoon T.O.M. Sopwith of Sopwith Camel fame, in every race. Ranger won every race it entered throughout its career. This Maine-built boat was hailed as the supreme example of America's yacht-building art.

Still another Maine link to the America's Cup came in 1970, when Goudy & Stevens of East Boothbay built a replica of America, the schooner which in 1851 triggered the first of the America's Cup races.

The first America, 101 feet, 9 inches long, with a 23-foot beam, was built along the lines of the swift pilot schooners which raced out of American ports to meet incoming vessels and be the first to put a pilot aboard and collect the pilot fee.

The owner of the original America was John Cox Stevens, first commodore of the New York Yacht Club. He sailed it to Le Havre, France, in 20 days. In France, he outfitted it with racing sails and added a gleaming new paint job before crossing the Channel to Cowes, England. There he hoped to win back the money he'd spent building the boat by betting that his America would beat the best of England's racing yachts.

But when the sporting English aristocracy saw America's turn of speed, they suddenly turned not so sporting and refused to bet. Finally America was permitted to enter a 50-mile Royal Yacht Squadron race around the Isle of Wight for the 100 guinea Cup on August 22, 1851.

The start was at anchor. America was the last boat to up anchor and get underway. But it finished first by a whopping 18 minutes. It was like a Little League team winning the World Series to have a pip-squeak boat from "the colonies" invade Cowes, the world capital of yachting, and thrash the best of Britain's boats.

America carried home to the United States the "Holy Grail" of the sailing world, now called the America's Cup. The New York Yacht club invited the Royal Yacht Squadron to come over and win it back. But the Civil War held up yacht racing for a few years, and it was not until 1870 that the English came across the Atlantic to try to win back the cup.

They failed, miserably. As the years went by, more nations competed. Expenses for building the 130-foot J-class boats became too great. The rules were changed to permit the 12-meter class, boats less than half the size. The crews, which had numbered up to 33 men when the Deer Isle boys triumphed, are smaller, and computers aboard are evidence the sport has become a science.

BILLINGS MARINE: WHERE FISH BOATS MEET YACHTS

STONINGTON — Dick Billings fitted his big, solid frame into a chair aboard Steer Clear and said "Size of the boat doesn't matter a damn. This little 30 footer of yours is just as important to you as that 68 foot, two million dollar yacht over there is to her owner. Maybe more."

Dick Billings is the grand old man of Billings Diesel and Marine Service Inc., on Moose Island, Stonington. His father and uncles began the Billings Yard here in 1929. His son, Harlan, runs the yard now, and Dick pretends he is retired. But long before the Billings Yard came to Moose Island, earlier generations of Billings had been boat builders on Little Deer Isle.

There is nothing smart and fancy about the Billings Yard. This is a no-frills place. But behind the drab array of huge metal buildings, of four

Richard Billings, of Billings Diesel, Deer Isle, aboard Steer Clear. The Billings family have been on Deer Isle for two hundred years. Billings Marine, on the Thorofare, is among the most complete shipyards between Halifax and Boston.

marine railways which can handle boats 125 feet long, draft of 11 feet and weight of 300 tons, besides storage for 150 boats, besides Travel-lifts which can put straps around a 30-ton boat and lift it bodily out of the water, besides six substantial docks, behind acres of boats and messes that spell 'boatyard', lies this heavy fact: Billings is the biggest full-service yard between Halifax and Boston. The workers here are geniuses with engines, especially big diesels; and Billings Marine stocks a mammoth supply of parts. "No commercial fisherman, no yatchsman on a cruise, wants to hang on the dock, waiting for a part to be freighted in. So I've got it; or else I'll make it," says Dick Billings.

Sitting in the stern of Steer Clear, talking boats with Dick Billings, is a rare lesson in history and sea lore. "My father, Sheridan, and his three brothers, George, Cecil and Edward, began this yard in 1929. They all had been yacht captains for the money men of New York. Worked for Sonny Whitney and that crowd, skippering their yachts in summer, taking the business moguls such as Cornelius Vanderbilt from their estates on Long Island Sound to Wall Street in the fanciest of steam yachts. Those fellows would not commute by train. Then in winter, they'd bring the yachts to Maine for overhaul and take 'em down to New York come spring."

When World War II came, the yachting stopped, and Billings turned to building boats for the navy. "We had 450 people working when we built boats up to 150 feet for the government. Everything from T-boats to boats for the Arctic, with an inch of armor plate over six inches of green heart oak."

By 1967 the Billings Brothers who had begun the yard in 1929 were dead. "Then I bought it, from the Bar Harbor Bank," says Dick. "My father let me go fishing as a young man. I was captain of my own 54-foot seine boat when I was 18. But my dad insisted I learn a land trade, too. So I studied engines, mostly diesels, since I was a kid. I knew fishermen and fishing boats—draggers, seiners, sardine carriers. So, I swung the yard toward servicing the commercial fleet. Today we are 75 percent commercial, 25 percent yachts."

Before Dick Billings bought the yard from the bank in 1967, after sickness then death of his father and brothers had put the yard on failing times, he had been a fisherman and flier for 18 years. "In 1949, I went down to Port Clyde and met Hugo Leihtinen, who was a pioneer fish spotter from planes down there. He wanted me to go flying with him in the worst way. I said, "No way. I'm scared. I'll get sick." But finally Dick went up with Hugo. "Out by the Muscle Ridge Shoals, I saw herring. Grabbed the stick and headed home for my boat. Hugo was dumbfounded. He didn't know I'd been a flier for years. I told him that if we got those fish, I'd make it right with him. We got the fish; 43,000 bushels in 10 days, and Hugo ended up with eight $100 bills for that little ride in his plane."

Dick Billing's first-hand experience with every kind of fishing boat has built a special kind of confidence and communication-without-words between Dick Billings and the commercial fish boat skippers who come to Billings when they need repairs.

"Best spotting I ever had was over at Gun Point. We found over 100,000 bushel of fish. Didn't take 'em all, of course. But we got a goodly share before the school broke and scattered."

Today Dick Billings, surrounded by boats of every size and every price, keeps only a beat-up 20 foot cabin cruiser for himself. He lives in a fine old home with magnificent water views, close to the boat yard. There in a cove he keeps moorings for his friends.

"My son Harlan runs the business now. I've been mighty proud of him and the way he runs the place. My daughter Larna Gray lives over in Blue Hill. So its just my wife Stella and me. And I kind of slack off. We go to Florida in winter, and I travel around down there, bidding on business for the yard up here."

Harlan, like his father, is a walking encyclopedia about marine diesels. He is one of the few "Super-master Machinists" in the field and is backed by two more diesel experts in the enormous machine shop at Billings. The great 385 horsepower G.M., Detroit and Caterpillar diesels which power the commercial boats and some big yachts, have a price tag of $50,000 and up.

"We get 'em all. The big fishing boats and the plush yachts. I think the biggest yacht that comes here is Black Hawk, a 123 Fedship belonging to Charles Wertz, who owns the Chicago Black Hawks."

Customers from my little 30-footer to the $2 million yacht to the fishing boat with trouble in its engine shaft, all get the same treatment from Dick and Harlan Billings. Unless you know them, it is easy to mistake Harlan or his father for one of the yard hands working on the dock. Fish boats and pleasure yachts know that Harlan can be a guardian angel to a boat in trouble along the Maine coast. Somehow he gets to it, tows it in and fixes it.

Maybe this genius with boats is born in the Billings bloodstream. More than 250 years ago, before America had her independence, Billings men were building and tending boats on Little Deer Isle. This is one reason why Steer Clear puts into Billings at Stonington for a visit almost every year. It is no fancy marina, but it is a gold mine of good Maine men and fine Maine ways with a boat.

CRADLE ENCOUNTERS

DEER ISLE — I sat on a makeshift cradle in Billings Marine, where Steer Clear had been hauled for a day of refastening of her quarter rails. There I enjoyed two chance encounters, thanks to the quick camaraderie which springs up between patients waiting for their boat doctor.

The first encounter was scary in the opening seconds. As I walked across the boatyard, a booming voice called out, "Are you Bill Caldwell?" I turned to see a giant fisherman towering over me, 6 feet, 6 inches tall and 250 pounds of mass and muscle. "You wrote a column about me years ago. My name is Steve Robbins."

I quaked, wondering what I'd written as my memory raced through hundreds of old columns. Then came relief as he explained: "I'm the Maine fisherman whose boat was seized by Canadian authorities a quarter-mile into Canadian waters, they said. The U.S. and Canada were still having a dispute over the sea borders. You heard about the seizure somehow, and got hold of my wife. Then you reached me by phone when I was being held in Canada. The Canadians had impounded my $135,000 boat. I was facing a $25,000 fine and six years in jail. It was Labor Day weekend, 1978. The American consulates and embassy were closed and I could get no help. Somehow you got through to a duty officer in the State department in Washington and then roused a bunch of officials in Maine government and reached the authorities in Canada and wrote a column the next day. That column helped me a lot. And I've always wanted to thank you for it."

Relief went through my body as I looked up at the giant towering over me. I remembered that international incident when our government bureaucracy seemed to cold-shoulder a Maine fisherman seized at sea by a foreign government and a Maine fisherman felt helpless and alone in a foreign port, his vessel and gear impounded. It had been one of those stories when the newspaper had helped to focus the spotlight on a citizen snarled between governments.

Thus, years afterwards, two voices known to each other only over the telephone met in a boatyard where we were both getting repairs. Robbins showed me his fine new steel-hulled dragger, the Stacie Vea, in for sand blasting and repainting of the hull. And he loaned us his new truck to drive into town to buy supplies. It was a fine encounter.

The next close encounter came as I was lying under the makeshift cradle, attaching new zincs to the rudders of Steer Clear, while Billings carpenters refastened the quarter rails. "Hello! I'm Anson Norton," said a voice above me. "You knew my father. He ran the boatyard on Isleboro and then had the trawler Nord which you went aboard in Camden Harbor."

A tall, dark-haired man of about 33, dressed in immaculate jeans and fresh-pressed shirt, he handed a wrench to me as I tightened the new zincs. Then we visited for a while and that night Norton came aboard Steer Clear for a steak dinner. His boat West Wind had come in for engine adjustments. But when his boat was only a few yards from the dock, he had entangled three feet of heavy rope around his cage and propeller, damaging both.

Over steak that night, Norton said he is one of only 11 fishermen working out of Criehaven Island and living there from April until December. Criehaven is 23 miles offshore from Rockland. Just beyond Criehaven is Ragged Island, last ledge with trees between Maine and Spain. Indians called it Raketash, which white men long pronounced Ragged Arse. But our government, unwilling to print such words on a chart, now labels it Ragged Island.

Criehaven used to be a year-round settlement, with a church, a school, a post office, a store and a mailboat to Rockland. None of these exist today. No one now lives year-round on Criehaven. By long tradition, if not by law, no one may lobster from Criehaven except the 11 fishermen who hold land or rights on the harbor inside the breakwater.

"But the fishermens' families who live on the island from spring till fall love it out there," says Norton. He tells us there are four summer families from away. And there are young families with school-age kids who fish from Criehaven. "We had a community supper before Labor Day. With visitors and kids, 50 of us sat down to eat together." The little airstrip on Criehaven is overgrown now, but Herb Jones' flying service links Matinicus Island, close by, to Rockland. Three people can fly to the mainland for about $40.

The largest landowner on Criehaven is, strangely, Richard Kremetz, a jewelry manufacturer from New York City, who intends to keep the land undeveloped, unspoiled and clean. "Life out there is so beautiful and clean," says Mrs. Norton, a Brewer-born girl, "that when we take the boat over to the store on Matinicus Island, it seems dirty and littered."

It was past 10 p.m. when Norton climbed down the ladder from Steer Clear and walked across the boatyard to sleep aboard West Wind. And as I turned into my bunk on Steer Clear, I felt thankful for two close encounters made from Steer Clear's cradle.

CROTCH ISLAND GRANITE

CROTCH ISLAND — Visitors in Maine waters are first puzzled by the strange sight, then incredulous. They see gaunt skeletons of huge cranes and guy wires etched against the sky, rising from atop an island in East Penobscot Bay.

Their eyes are telling lies, they think. But no, this is Crotch Island, at the western entrance to the Deer Isle Thorofare. This 400-acre island is solid granite, topped by spruce trees. Granite quarrying started here 118 years ago, begun by Job Goss, a stonecutter from Massachusetts in 1870.

Goss quarried Crotch Island granite for the Mount Holyoke dam and bridges in Providence and New York. As orders grew larger, more capital was needed to buy more sophisticated equipment. Goss sold out to construction companies from New York and Connecticut, who brought in pneumatic drills, built a compressed air plant to operate them, and cranes to lift the gigantic granite blocks.

By 1901, hundreds of stonecutters, imported from England, Scandinavia and especially Italy, were working on Crotch Island for $20 a week. On Saturday nights, this small army of lonely foreigners slaked their thirst and quenched their other bodily needs across the water in nearby Stonington, then a small fishing village of dirt streets, wooden sidewalks and few inhabitants.

Soon Stonington gained a wild reputation for illegal liquor (Maine was dry), flagrant prostitution, open gambling and unsolved murders. On weekdays, Crotch Island men quarried granite to build the Boston Museum of Fine Arts and the Triborough Bridge in New York.

But by 1914, the granite boom burst and the quarries were sold back to the local John L. Goss Co. They cut the famous "Rockefeller Bowl" for the Rockefeller fountain at the family estate in Tarrytown, N.Y. That slab of granite weighed 225 tons, was 22 feet square and five feet thick when cut in a single piece. After being shaped and polished, it weighed only 50 tons when shipped to Tarrytown.

But work petered out to a trickle of small jobs after the 1920s. After

Crotch Island Granite Quarry, off Stonington, in Penobscot Bay. Little Crotch Island, at the western entrance to Deer Isle Thorofare, has been quarried for a century and there are still millions of tons of granite. The granite in President Kennedy's gravesite at Arlington, Va. came from here.

President Kennedy's assassination, Crotch Island granite briefly flared into prominence again. Because Kennedy had loved to sail Penobscot Bay, 1,500 pieces of "Sherwood pink" granite from Crotch Island were ordered for his grave in Arlington National Cemetery. Thereafter Crotch Island was again abandoned. Its cranes long stood idle and rusting, etched against the skyline, incongruous sentries looming over a devastated little island.

But the quarry became active again. Tony Ramos, once a sculptor of granite monuments, bought most of the island, and his New England Stone Industries of Smithfield, R.I., quarried Crotch Island granite once more.

The spectacular skeletons of the cranes mostly stand weird, gaunt and idle against the sky. But below them there sometimes explodes on the silence of the sea, the jet-like roar of torches, 12-foot-long monsters which, at 2,400 degrees, burn through granite, cutting it into 40-ton chunks for shipment to the Ramos plant in Rhode Island.

I went ashore on Crotch Island and talked with Jim Ashworth, the foreman who began work here in 1980, cleaning up the mess left when the quarries had been abandoned. He was driving through two new roads and rebuilding two piers. He had a gang of men, two mobile cranes, one able to lift 40 tons, the other 80 tons, and two enormous dump tractors able to carry 40-ton blocks to the two wharves.

"None of the old quarrymen were left," says 35-year old Ashworth "so we trained younger men to the work. We hire only local people from Deer Isle and bring them back and forth by boat."

It is heavy work. The granite on this island weighs 138 pounds per cubic foot. With torches blazing at 2,400 degrees, with sledge hammers and iron wedges, with the help of some rather gentle black powder explosive, the crew quarries granite in 400-ton blocks, then subdivides these into transportable blocks of 20 to 40 tons.

Many years ago, granite was used 12 inches thick or more in the construction of office buildings. "Today," says Ashworth "architects are using granite as a veneer, only two and sometimes only one-inch thick, to face steel structures. Men at our plant in Rhode Island do this veneer cutting with special wire saws, then polish and finish the surface. It can be three years between the time we get an order for a job and the time the granite is actually used on the building site."

When the quarry is working, the noise is deafening. Workers wear pro-

Granite Quarry on Crotch Island. The mess left behind in a granite quarry. The sight is common on islands in Penobscot Bay.

tective earphones, steel-toed boots, hard hats, goggles. In the weird moonscape of this huge quarry far out to sea, they look like men from a planet in outer space.

Little Crotch Island has been producing granite for scores of American city buildings for over 100 years. I asked Ashworth how much more granite could be quarried from this 400-acre island. "We are still working only the face of the quarry," he said. "Even after 100 years, an unlimited amount remains."

A ROBIN FLOURISHES AMONG THE FISHERMEN

STONINGTON — Robin Peters is one of the most unlikely and delightful success stories in Maine. She's the publisher and editor of Commercial Fisheries News, New England's fishing newspaper, a monthly.

On the face of it, it is incongruous that the foremost spokesman and technical journalist about Maine and New England fisheries is a young woman. Her avid readers are the macho men who man draggers, trawlers, scallopers and the tough fishing vessels which endure the fogs and gales of Georges and the Grand Banks.

Robin Peters was a mere 22 years old when she had the gall and the gumption to start her newspaper on a shoestring in 1973.

"I was crazy then. I had no qualms that my idea of a special newspaper for Maine fisheries might not work. So I started it," says Peters.

Today, she's issuing a 76-page paper, and 10,000 experts in the fishing industry are paying $15 a year to buy a subscription.

I moored my boat in Stonington and went ashore to meet Robin Peters in her Commercial Fisheries office on Main Street. Stonington was a strange place for a 22-year-old woman from Massachusetts to land with stars in her eyes about the two quirkiest businesses in the world, fishing and newspapering.

But Stonington is also the right place. Here, on Deer Isle, they brag there are more fishing boats than anywhere else in Maine. Here, on the small, handsome islands between Stonington and Isle au Haut, a few miles further to sea, hardy men quarried massive granite for some of the best known buildings and monuments in the United States.

Stonington is where millionaire yachtsmen used to recruit the skippers and crews for America's Cup racing yachts, in the era when those boats were 130 feet long and crewed by 33 sailors rather than computers. Until 1930, the main street in Stonington was not paved. Traffic was mostly horsedrawn, leaving a trail of pollution, so plankwood sidewalks ran through town. The oldest business on the waterfront is the historic S. Freedman & Co., a clothing store for work clothes, first started by an itinerant peddler. Yet Stonington was the scene of Maine's biggest drug smuggling bust and is a summer haven of vacationers from across the nation.

Peters has the most spectacular business office in town. A great semi-circle window commands the harbor and the water thoroughfare which fishing boats and fish carriers travel incessantly. When she looks up from galleys of the next edition of Commercial Fisheries, Peters can count two dozen islands stretching out to the beautiful heights of Isle au Haut.

A word battle she witnessed between Spence Apolloinio, then commissioner of the Department of Marine Resources, and a fisherman, Ralph Norwood of New Harbor, triggered Peters into her adventure in publishing. "I determined that two opposite views should both be expressed. But there was no medium then for an exchange between practical fishermen and white-coated marine scientists. The scientists seemed to regard fishermen as ignorant. Fishermen distrusted the Ph.D's who didn't have boat paint on their shirts. That gulf had to be bridged and I wanted to build that bridge with a newspaper," she says.

She got help at the start from another success story—Nathaniel W. Barrows, who had bought the Island Ad-Vantages, Deer Isle's weekly paper, when he too was 22. And out came the first tentative issue of Maine Commercial Fisheries, a thin, under-financed giveaway.

Today, Peters has nine full-timers on the staff, and draws on a stable of freelance experts to write important articles on new problems, solutions and experiments in the fishing industry, ranging from catching through selling of fish.

In recent years, Commercial Fisheries has won two national design awards. Its circulation is booming, despite moving from a giveaway to a subscription of $15. Ms. Peters has been a Maine representative on the New England Fisheries Council, a policy-making body which decides the fishing quotas and regulations for five New England states.

"The fishing industry is a closed world, hard to know well enough to write well about it," she says. "But the more we cover it, the more space we need to report its complex news. We run a 76-page paper. But we could print 300 pages and still not carry all the news."

Peters is 36 now and an admired respected voice, bridging the gaps between fishing fleets, bankers and research scientists. She says, "Thank heaven I didn't know at 22 what I know now. If I had, I would never have had the nerve to launch this paper."

A DRUG BUST ON THE MAINE COAST

DEER ISLE — Drug smugglers, like booze smugglers in Prohibition days, do big business in small coves along Maine's 2,500 mile coast. A 42-foot lobster boat, crewed by three fishermen, can make $55,000 to $90,000 in a single night, ferrying drugs from a mother ship from Columbia to trucks waiting beside a remote harbor. Here is the story of one of Maine's first big drug busts, the one in Cat Cove in the Oceanville section of Deer Isle, where Steer Clear often spent a night.

I've got a few things in common with those smugglers and pot-runners who got nabbed in Deer Isle, landing 34 tons of marijuana, street value $20 million.

I've often used the same dock they did. And I used to stay at the house they later bought in Cat Cove. My boat and Jubilee, the big pot ship, traveled the same winding, tricky course to get to the same waterfront estate; but not on the same night.

My friend Ralph MacKinnon, who used to be a banker in New York, bought the 20-acre property back in 1960. When we were cruising off Deer Isle, we used to poke our way in Steer Clear out of Jericho Bay, past the wonderfully named Lazygut Islands, through a couple of shallow spots and swing in a wide arc to Ralph MacKinnon's dock at Cat Cove.

It was a most happy house then, with Ralph and his late wife, a former newspaper reporter on the White Plains, N.Y., paper, cooking huge meals and putting us up in their guest house for a night's sleep ashore and the luxury of a hot bath.

In March 1979, Ralph MacKinnon sold the place for $225,000. Ralph and his second wife were off vacationing in Hawaii, when a Tom Ryan stopped in at a real estate firm and asked about secluded property with deep-water anchorage. Ryan inspected the MacKinnon place once—and bought it. The transaction was handled by attorney Paul Sherwood of Stonington, acting for MacKinnon, and Frank Walker of Ellsworth, acting for the buyer.

Sherwood saw no buyer. He was given the purchase papers and a certified check for $125,000 as down payment by the buyer's attorney. The remaining $100,000 of the purchase price was to be paid over several years.

Tom Ryan, however, was not the new owner of record. That was a woman by the name of Paula Leurs, whom no one hereabouts has ever seen.

But Ryan was certainly the go-between and the man-in-residence and the man who paid the $125,000 down payment with a series of bank checks on a series of out-of-state banks. MacKinnon's suspicions were aroused by those checks, and the anonymity of the new owner. He talked to police.

After the local and state police became suspicious of the too quiet strangers, the estate and its new occupants were put under around-the-clock surveillance. Plainclothesmen from state and federal agencies, using night scopes, kept watch day and night throughout the summer and fall from a cottage they rented across the cove.

About mid-October, these law officers saw 30 to 40 people working around the waterfront and the half-dozen buildings on the estate.

Jim Greenlaw, a local caretaker, told the new occupants it was time to take in the big float and put away the dock for the winter. The newcomers were surprised they could not keep the dock in all winter. But they told

Greenlaw to leave it in the water until after the first of November.

Police then got a tip that a boatload of marijuana from Columbia was headed to Maine and would be unloaded at the Cat Cove dock on the night of Oct. 19-20.

Late on the night of Oct. 19, police laid their trap. A 21-foot patrol boat from the Department of Marine Resources was positioned behind Lazygut Islands. Two 42-foot Coast Guard patrol boats were put on alert in Jericho Bay. Two Hancock County deputy sheriffs readied a roadblock on the Deer Isle bridge. Stonington and State police established another roadblock at the Oceanville Bridge, the only road exit from Oceanville and Cat Cove.

More than 20 officers, armed with shotguns and rifles were in place by 3 a.m. Oct. 20. One was armed with cyanide pellets and protective clothing in case of attack by guard dogs. Even the K-9 state police dogs were in hiding. The moon was setting. The trap was about to be sprung.

At 3 a.m. Oct. 20, 1980, State Police Sergeant Harry Bailey cut through two heavy wire cables stretched across the driveway entrance to the former MacKinnon place at Cat Cove. Two police cruisers, blue lights flashing, sped through the opening and led the raid which culminated seven months of undercover surveillance and resulted in the seizure of 34 tons of Columbian marijuana at quiet Cat Cove.

Some 20 of the alleged smugglers who had just finished unloading 1,263 bales fled as the trap was sprung. Nine men, two women and three children were quickly captured. One man leapt into the water, pursued by a police dog, and was captured by a police officer in a small boat.

By first light of dawn, tracking dogs and police captured four more in the woods and behind the little Oceanville church. Late Monday night still another man was captured when he hitched a ride in a car which turned out to be an unmarked police cruiser.

But four others escaped aboard the mother ship, a 71-foot trawler named Jubilee. Gunning its 440 horsepower engine to full power, the Jubilee fled for the open sea; and for eight hours Jubilee was chased by Coast Guard vessels and helicopters.

Finally, the 82-foot Coast Guard cutter Point Hannon, out of Jonesport, cut across Jubilee's bow, training .50-caliber machine guns on her. Jubilee heaved to, was boarded, the four men aboard were arrested, the ship was seized and taken into Southwest Harbor.

By the time the roundup was over, police had seized more than $20 million of marijuana (street value), seven boats, 13 new motor vehicles, two camper trailers, five outboard motors, quantities of shortwave radios, police scanners and electronic equipment, a farm tractor, $25,000 in cash and had arrested 23 people.

"The drug smugglers were stupid from the start," Ralph MacKinnon told me.

"The first mistake was their stand-offish secrecy. In a tiny, friendly remote community like Oceanville, Ryan strung cables across the driveway. He and the others living in my old house never went to local stores or the post office. They hid away. Refused visitors. That behavior aroused suspicions. Soon the place was under 24-hour surveillance by police."

MacKinnon continued: "Then they got my old caretaker, Valmore "Jim" Greenlaw, to put more flotation under the big float, so it could hold a lot more weight. Why? Then they had a lot of small rubber boats brought in. Why? Finally in the dead of night, the smugglers came steaming up that quiet, seldom-travelled waterway in a strange 71-foot steel trawler named Jubilee.

"Everybody living along that shore knows the sound of each engine of the few fishing boats which come by. So a strange boat in the nighttime poking through a tricky channel alerted them all to an oddity. Those smugglers didn't understand a darn thing about how to fit into smalltown Maine." MacKinnon shakes his head, wondering how a New York banker who retired to the coast of Maine ended up in the thick of dope runners.

WOODENBOAT

EGGEMOGGIN REACH — Success on your own terms; doing what you like best; and doing it in the place you like most. Then, finally taking in $2 million a year. Sound good?

It's happening beside Eggemoggin Reach to Jonathan Wilson, the man who, on a shoestring, began the magazine called WoodenBoat.

When I first met Wilson in 1976 he was 30 years old, and living in a one room cabin in the woods near Brooksville. It had no electricity and no running water. Heat came from a wood stove, and he cut the wood. He and his wife at that time, Susie, built the cabin. They shared it with two small sons. And on the floor, often by kerosene lamp light, Wilson and his helper, Mary Page, pasted up every page of the early issues of WoodenBoat.

Six years later, while cruising up the Eggemoggin Reach beside Deer Isle, I paid another visit to WoodenBoat. This time, Jon Wilson's office was in a 30-room mansion set on a 61-acre waterfront estate, which he bought for $220,000 in 1980.

WoodenBoat, a handsome, glossy, four-color magazine, now sells close to 100,000 copies at a cover price of $3.50. About 8,000 copies circulate oceans away going to WoodenBoat readers in Japan, Australia, England and Europe.

When I first met Wilson, he was soliciting advertising over a telephone attached to a tree. He could not afford to pay for poles to bring telephone wires from the road to the cabin. This year WoodenBoat will carry more than half-a-million dollars worth of advertising in six issues, none of it solicited from a phone on a tree.

To get money to put out the first issue in 1973, Wilson sold his soul, almost. He sold his 35-foot Alden ketch, a wooden boat, got $11,000 for it and spent $10,000 to print 12,000 copies of the first issue. He had only two advance subscribers. For weeks he hawked single copies of his first issue and sold subscriptions from the back of his car. He sold 200 subscriptions at that year's boat show in Newport, Rhode Island. Several years later, Wilson returned to the Newport boat show in style, taking most of the 30-person staff of WoodenBoat with him, and putting them up at an inn, which WoodenBoat now rents for the occasion. The magazine now hosts a massive party for exhibitors at the Newport boat show, the very people to whom Wilson hawked his first issue a few years back. That first issue has already been reprinted several times and is still a collector's item. Incidentally, Wilson has bought another wooden boat for himself, a 33-foot Concordia named Free Spirit, a 40-year-old classic.

Wilson is a native of Kingston, R.I. As a boy, when his parents were getting divorced, he found comfort messing around in boats at the Thimble Islands of Connecticut.

After a brief stab at a business administration degree, he left college to work in a boatyard, learning the wood trade. He and Susie came to Maine and spent the winter of 1970 on Hurricane Island, repairing wooden boats for Outward Bound. It was the first time in 50 years, since the granite quarries shut down, anyone had lived all winter on Hurricane Island. From there, they moved to Pembroke, near Eastport, the only place he could buy a bit of waterfront land at a price he could then afford. There he built a few peapods.

"As a wooden boat builder alone in Pembroke, I was isolated," he says. "I knew that other wooden boat builders knew shortcuts and better ways of doing things than I did. But we were isolated from each other, and each kept his trade secrets close to his chest."

To reach out, to interchange, Wilson thought of starting a newsletter. But there were too few wooden boat builders. What about a magazine which would reach not only wooden boat builders, owners, designers but, above all, those who just dreamed of wooden boats and loved them? This idea set his heart and brain afire. He sailed his Alden ketch to Bucks Harbor, sold it, and began WoodenBoat magazine without knowing a thing about magazine publishing.

He almost foundered during the eight months it took him to peddle the 12,000 copies he had printed of his first issue. But once readers had the magazine, wooden boat enthusiasts loved it. Over 1,000 subscription orders came in the mail. He kept on. In the second year, a fire burned him and his new magazine out. The next issues were put together in rented premises, sitting on packing cases in Brooksville. Then a fire destroyed his office.

Salvaged from the fire was the file containing 75 manuscripts. They often came in unsolicited, but written by experts, although the young magazine could afford to pay only four cents a word. "We paid only $5 for pictures, but some of the best marine photogaphers in the world sent us their work."

Wilson had hit upon a wonderful formula. He was turning out a highly specialized magazine which answered an unmet need; a magazine which loved, revered and professionally knew about wood and the building of wooden boats. Circulation climbed. Readers wrote devotedly and fanatically from all over the U.S., from Fiji, Japan, Australia, Europe. This was the adrenalin Wilson needed to keep going upstream. He began to hire a staff—an art director, a business and circulation manager, a copyreader, a secretary. By 1976, at its third anniversary, circulation was 17,000; by the sixth year it was 35,000; by the ninth year it was 85,000. By the twelfth year, close to 100,000.

A sign of permanence and prosperity is the 30-room mansion and its 61 spectacular acres overlooking the Eggemoggin Reach, which now houses WoodenBoat and its staff. Until a few years ago Wilson took out as salary only $100 a week, and paid others $150. That has changed. To celebrate their move to such handsome quarters, WoodenBoat gave an open house party. More than 500 people came by car, plane and wooden boat. When the magazine hosted a National Wooden Boat Regatta, wooden boats filled every anchorage for miles.

This Maine enterprise, which began with a phone nailed to a tree, now has computers and a massive research library. It has branched out from the magazine to publish specialized books, to make and sell boat-building kits (for $150 and up) to print and market boat plans ($200). It issues a glossy catalog in four colors which sells by mail 34 pages of WoodenBoat products from painters' caps to T-shirts to half models. It has a flourishing WoodenBoat School, which runs for 16 summer weeks. Experts teach hands-on courses in boatbuilding, sailmaking, professional boat survey-ing. There are 17 courses in all, each taught by a well-known expert, each lasting from one to three weeks and ranging in cost from $200 to over $600. Soon after it opened, 270 students were enrolled, many from overseas.

Jon Wilson was 27, married, clean-shaven, poor and boatless when he began WoodenBoat. At this writing, he is in his mid forties, he is beard-ed, and unmarried. He has had to turn over the job of editing his maga-zine to others, so he can concentrate on bigger business planning. He has made a unique and howling success in a field to which he came as an im-poverished amateur. And he has had the good judgment to keep Wood-enBoat in the same isolated part of lovely Eggemoggin Reach where it was born.

TOWING THE MAYFLOWER II HOME

DEER ISLE — "Thank God we weren't Pilgrims cross-ing the Atlantic aboard the Mayflower."

That was the gut reaction of all five of us who towed Mayflower II from Deer Isle, where it had been undergoing repairs, back to its home port in Plymouth, Mass.

This was not the romantic feeling we expected to have toward a ship so prominent in our nation's history. But after seeing how Mayflower II rolls and pitches, we knew that crossing the Atlantic in 1620 aboard it must have been brutal, dangerous, wet, smelly and downright miserable for the 102 men, women and children crowded into the ungainly ship for 66 days and nights.

We towed the Mayflower with the tug Argonaut. Argonaut was skippered by Greg Hartley, who once worked on oil drilling ships in tropical waters off Africa, Thailand, Singapore and in the stormy, icy waters of the Labrador Sea.

John Brando, Argonaut's engineer, spent six years installing and repairing Detroit diesels on fishing boats. He was also chief engineer aboard America, the reproduction of the schooner which won the first America's Cup. Chuck Cheney, cook and mate, and Dana Hodgdon, able seaman, both in their early 20s, rounded out the Argonaut crew.

It was a young but experienced crew, carefully selected because they would be towing a national monument; Mayflower II is a one-of-a-kind ship, insured for $1 million.

Weather postponed the Mayflower's departure because the wind was blowing too hard. Her insurance policy forbids Mayflower II being at sea when the wind is more than 20 miles an hour. So we waited. It was winter dark by the time Argonaut came alongside Mayflower II to tow her out of Billings Marine, Stonington.

There, through the gray dusk and a driving snowstorm, we see Mayflower II. She's a sight to make hearts thump and eyes water with pride of country, as Mayflower brings a wave of schoolroom history flooding up.

Her pointed high stern towers 40 feet above the keel and dwarfs the fishing vessels nearby. Hartley cautiously brings Argonaut close alongside, and the two boats are lashed together.

Hartley clambers aboard Mayflower II and goes into a huddle with its four-man crew. They decide on the maneuvers to get Mayflower off the wharf and under tow. While the crews pass towing lines and secure them with huge shackles, I grab the chance to prowl Mayflower II from stem to stern.

The ship is black, dour, small, clumsy, and cramped. The only spaciousness aboard is in the master's cabin, high aft, and in the great cabin, in the deck below, where in the original Mayflower, the Pilgrim leaders berthed. Mayflower's passengers—28 children among them—lived and slept between decks, squeezed into miniscule berths. Here, between decks, is where they cowered when gales pounded them, and their ship hove to for days, while huge seas poured down on them from the upper deck. The only cooking space was up and forward in the fo'c'sle, an open brick fireplace with sand in the bottom.

By 6 p.m. the crews have rigged the towing bridle. The docking lines are cast off. Hartley eases Argonaut's two 350 h.p. diesel engines into slow forward. Harlan Billings, in a workboat, pulls Mayflower II's stern off the wharf and keeps it on a taut line to ensure it will not swing. "She's vulnerable now, if that wind grabs her broadside," Hartley says.

At the start, Hartley uses a short 50-foot tow line. We head slowly into the darkness, with visibility cut further by driving snow. Close behind us, the Mayflower see-saws. First she runs to port, then crosses to starboard, then runs up on us, the long, high bowsprit looming dangerously close astern and towering high above our tug. Making less than three knots, with our precious Mayflower II in tight tow, we slowly thread our way out to more open water.

These are tense minutes. Hartley is cool, but uses every aid in the pilot-house. He checks the computer readouts on the Loran C against the maze of blimps on his radar screen, and against his dead reckoning compass course. He also keeps a watchful eye on the depth finder. Every few seconds Hartley peers aft to watch the silhouette and running lights of Mayflower II as she saws left, then right, then rolls and bucks in the chop and seems to be running down on us. But he is satisfied that he has his precious tow under control.

Once in open water, the crew slowly pays out more line, until there are 250 feet out. We increase speed to six knots and Mayflower II settles down and rides nicely. On the black sea, the only glow is from the portable running lights we rigged on Mayflower II. Once in a while Hartley turns on a spotlight to get a visual fix on an unlighted buoy which he is tracking on radar.

Time now for a delayed roast beef dinner, eaten in shifts. It is past 9:30 p.m., and two of us turn in for a couple of hours sleep. Moments later, it seems, I feel a hand on my shoulder and a flashlight shining in my eyes; "Bill, we're coming up on Monhegan. It's 11:45 p.m." In another hour, a fishing boat will meet us and take me off near Ram Island, outside Boothbay Harbor.

The winds and weather are better than predicted. I grab a cup of coffee and join the others in the pilot house. Off to port, in the darkness, lies Damariscove Island. The first Mayflower is said to have stopped there in 1620 to load up with cod on her way to Massachusetts Bay. This Maine island was a flourishing fishing station long before the first Mayflower crossed the Atlantic.

Later, when the pilgrims were starving at Plymouth during their second winter, they sent a boat to Damariscove Island to get supplies. The records show the fishermen at Damariscove and at Pemaquid freely gave the Pilgrims grain to keep them from starvation.

At 2 a.m. we spot the lights of the lobster boat waiting for us. Harold Simmons looms out of the dark night and draws alongside as Argonaut briefly slows down. We cannot stop dead in the water lest the tow line go slack. I make the jump from Argonaut to the lobster boat.

Argonaut's deep-throated diesels rev up and Mayflower II comes obediently, silently taut on the towline. The odd couple head on for Plymouth, 24 hours away. The loud horn from Argonaut blasts a farewell. We watch the vanishing lights of Mayflower II and wonder how those Pilgrims ever made it. In the black night above us a satellite is racing through space.

ISLE AU HAUT

ISLE AU HAUT — Go to Isle au Haut. Don't miss it or you'll go to the grave cheated. There is no place in the world to match it. And you can get there without a boat, though it is six miles to sea out of Stonington. If you are landbased, simply park your car and take the excursion boat from Stonington town wharf, which makes the run to and fro several times daily in summer. You'll pack more beauty into a day than you could in a year elsewhere. The boat takes you among the heavenly small islands between Stonington and Isle au Haut. When you land, be prepared to walk. The island is six miles north to south and two miles east to west, with a forested mountain spine, topped by Mount Champlain, 554 high, soaring from the ocean.

On Steer Clear, we have come into Isle au Haut from all four directions. The approach I like best is from the south, coming in from the Gulf of Maine, so you see towering Isle au Haut (High Island) before you see the coast of Maine. Then you understand why in the 1520s, Giovanni da Verranzano, an Italian with one eye on beauty and the other on politics, named Isle au Haut, Mount Desert and Monhegan, ''The Princesses of Navarre.'' His patron, King Henry of Navarre, had three teenage daughters whom he believed to be the most beautiful princesses in all Europe. So his courtier-sailor-explorer Verranzano named Maine's three most beautiful, most conspicuous islands ''The Princesses of Navarre.''

Running in to Isle au Haut from the open sea on a fine morning, Steer

Clear first puts into deserted Head Harbor, the first anchorage facing the Atlantic. Once this was a busy fishing community. Now there is only an abandoned wharf, one blue-hulled sailboat and one herring dory at their moorings. Only seven houses are left among the meadows, most restored from abandonment by summer people. But a gnarled and independent islander clung on and lived year round in the house where he was born, until he was almost 90 years old. Only at that age, and after his wife had died, did the wonderful, stubborn Gooden Grant let friends persuade him that it was time for him to give up Head Harbor. He reluctantly moved to the mainland. Just for the winters. In summertime, Grant came home to Head Harbor after he was well past 95.

Stone walls, older than Gooden Grant, are tumbled down now. For half a century the walls have no longer done the job they were built to do by patient, back-weary island farmers—to pen sheep and cattle. The farms, pastures and farmers are gone. The once-plowed and planted fields, the meadows which pastured sheep and cows rest, filled now with songbirds, long grasses, wildflowers and bees gathering their nectar. There is wildness here, loneliness, an eerie sense of the long-dead farming-fishing families who once called Head Harbor home, year round.

Gooden Grant was a Head Harbor man for close to a century, and his father was a Head Harbor man before him. The father, David Grant, an inland Mainer with a college education at the time Maine won statehood, moved onto Isle au Haut in the 1840s. He paid fifteen dollars to buy a hundred-acre farm, and on it he grazed five hundred sheep. By 1860, more than a thousand sheep grazed on Isle au Haut.

His son Gooden Grant, born in Head Harbor in 1876, when his father was fifty-two, said his family never had to buy a pound of meat. Father David also ran one of the three stores which sold everything to the twenty families of Head Harbor, who had little contact with the islanders who lived down on the Thorofare, five miles away over the dirt track.

By the time Gooden Grant was ten, he and his brother Les were fishing for pogies from a rowboat and squeezing the oil out of them, to be used in making paint. The brothers pressed 100 pogies to get a gallon of oil and sold it for one dollar. By the time he was 14, Gooden was lobstering on his own, hand hauling from a peapod. He was already a huge man, weighing 205 pounds, with shoulders broad as a lobster trap lathe (thirty-six inches). He and his brother used to harness all their combined muscle to the job of hauling kerosene to Head Harbor. On "kerosene day," the brothers would row eleven miles to the mainland, to load their pea-pod with big drums of kerosene, then row eleven miles back with their cargo. They'd beach the boat half a mile away, so they wouldn't have to row the last awful leg around Eastern Head. The boys, topping four hundred pounds between them, would roll those fifty-five gallon drums the last half mile down the track to Head Harbor. Both lived well past 90 years.

When he was 35, Gooden married Madelaine, a schoolteacher from another island, and brought her to Head Harbor to help run the family store. In 1911 Gooden built a house for his new bride. In 1914, his father David M. Grant, died at the age of 90 and the family store was sold. Brother Les died at age 92. Gooden was 97 at this writing, and still coming to Head Harbor in the summer.

Head Harbor is too wide open to the roll and the winds coming right in from the Atlantic to suit this cautious boatman. Roaring Bull Ledge, by the entrance, didn't get its name for nothing. The bull's roar is still the sound of the great combers from the Atlantic, breaking on their way into Head Harbor. So Steer Clear moves out, down the western shore and pokes into Duck Harbor. Seldom do cruising boats come in here, for the approach is not enticing, and the harbor is narrow. But the great hump of Duck Mountain gives snug protection. The name of the harbor and mountain is Duck, because this is where Indians drove sea ducks into nets across the narrow entrance and caught them by the thousand. They smoked the ducks over fires at the water's edge and in October they took thousands of smoked island ducks to their mainland settlement to feed the tribe through long winters.

Between Duck Harbor and Head Harbor, rise up the great high cliffs of Isle au Haut. We row the skiff ashore and find the hidden trail, scrambling up through rock and brush to the stormbeaten magnificence of Western Head. Stand atop Western Head on a summer day and be intoxicated by the smells of bayberry, juniper and spruce. On a calm day, step out on a granite ledge and look far down to the ocean, gaudy with bright bobbing lobster traps.

But clamber on these ledges when the wind howls and watch in fear as the Atlantic pounds in over Roaring Bull Ledge to vent its fury against the cliffs, and hurl blowing spray fifty feet skyward. Then your heart will wring with fear for any fisherman out in a small boat.

Out from Duck Harbor, past the fish weirs in Moore Harbor, Steer

Clear points for one of the youngest and prettiest lighthouses along the coast—Robinson Point Light, built in 1907, the only lighthouse built in the 20th century in Maine. After the light had been automated in 1934, the keeper's house was put up for auction and was happily bought by Charles H. Robinson, an Isle au Haut man. He later made it into a lovely small inn. It marks the entrance to Isle au Haut's Thorofare.

We idle through the Thoroughfare between Isle au Haut and Kimball Island, a restful, sheltered stretch of water, with safe anchorage for cruising boats.

Ashore in the little village, there's a cellar hole to remind you of the island's early, fecund settler from Boothbay, a man with the splendid name of Peletiah Barter. He came ashore here in 1792, fathered ten children here and died in 1832. By then almost 100 people were living in farms on the island. By the 1860s, islanders had a lobster cannery which shipped its product 3,000 miles to Crosse & Blackwell, specialty grocers in London. Wet-smacks from Isle au Haut carried 1,500 live lobsters on weekly trips to Boston in the 1870s. Population in 1880 was up to 274, compared to about 24 year-rounders now.

A Boston landscape gardener, Ernest Bowditch, was the man who first made Isle au Haut a mecca for summer people. All the U.S., owes him and his family an everlasting debt. The Bowditch family and their friends bought and gave to the Park Service 4,000 acres of the island to be preserved wild forever as a national park. Today most of the island is owned, cared for and run by the Acadia National Park, on Mount Desert.

In 1879, Ernest Bowditch, grandson of the famed Bowditch who wrote the bible of navigation, sailed a rented boat out from Stonington, landed at Isle au Haut. He loved the island, stayed and boarded for a while with Captain William Turner on the Thoroughfare.

When Bowditch got home to Boston, he raved to his friends about the island he had "discovered." They formed the Point Look Out Club, bought land, built eight cottages, and adopted three basic club rules: No children; No dogs; No women.

But before long, many of the original Point Look Out bachelors got married. That ended their rules about no women, no children, no dogs. Land on the island was cheap. The Bowditches and friends at Point Look Out bought so much land that by 1946, the Bowditch family owned over half the island—then gave it all away to make it a National Park. Thus, Maine is the only state to have national parks, on Mount Desert and Isle au Haut, which were gifts to the nation, and not land bought by the government.

Walk east on the only island road and on the right stands "Miss Lizzie's house," long the post office and home of Isle au Haut's best known and longest-admired woman. Lizzie Rich was born here, at Rick's Cove, in 1893, delivered by a midwife who charged three dollars. In 1909, at sixteen, she began work in the island post office. In 1927, Miss Lizzie, aged 30, was named island postmaster. She held that job until she reached 70. Then the federal government insisted that Miss Lizzie, like all other postmasters in the U.S., had to retire. Reluctantly Miss Lizzie retired as postmaster. The next day she carried on the same duties with the new title Clerk in Charge, which had no mandatory retirement age. The island postoffice kept doing business in the same corner of Miss Lizzie's living room. Eight years later, there was a brief interruption one March evening, when Miss Lizzie was 78 and alone in her house.

"My hips just plumb cracked in the kitchen," she later told me. "I fell to the floor. Inch by inch, I pulled myself across the floor until I could reach my walkie-talkie. I called Stanley Dodge. He and some helpers came right over. They lifted me up, strapped me in a rocker, carried me, rocker and all, into the back of his truck and drove me to the town landing, where they had a boat waiting. They carried me and the rocker into the boat, wedged us tight in the cockpit and off we went across six miles of open water to Stonington. I'd busted my hips at 5 p.m. By 8 p.m. I was all fixed up in my bed at Blue Hill Hospital . . . Now that's some service," she said.

Miss Lizzie was soon back on the job at the post office, using a walker. And, using that walker, she still fetched pails of water from the well out back of her house. She used the walker to get to church—the church up the hill which she'd been attending for 75 years. "It took me 15 minutes instead of two to get there," she told me. She still handled the mail in the post office she'd run for more than 65 years.

We rowed the skiff over to Jack Crowell's dock, a hundred yards across the Thoroughfare on Kimball Island. Jack and his wife Alice and I had met first years before at South Bristol, where he was overseeing the building of Hero, at the Harvey Gamage shipyard. Jack's job there was to draw upon his expert knowledge to make sure this wooden vessel was strong enough to withstand the crush of Arctic ice. We had sat around his kitchen table back then, as he told me about his days in the frozen far north. Since then, Steer Clear has put into Kimball Island, where Jack and Alice live in the only house on the island.

By now, I should be used to finding people living on Maine islands or in Maine harbor towns, who have seen and done masterful things in remote corners of the globe. One is foolishly apt to think islanders are islanders only and small town Mainers are rooted permanently to the community where they were born and raised. The evidence is vastly different. Never more different than with Jack and Alice Crowell.

Alice looked and behaved like a bright and beautiful and gay international beauty, flitting around her island dressed in brilliant sarong-like dresses. In fact she was born on nearby Burnt Island, in a house built about 1825 and still there, basically unchanged. Her father was a fishing boat captain and farmer. She was a true island woman. But she travelled wherever her husband Jack Crowell went, which is almost everywhere, but especially the Arctic.

Jack Crowell of Kimball Island began going to the Arctic in the rugged early days of Arctic living. Between 1926 and 1938, Crowell made seven trips there with MacMillan, as master of the supply ships on those expeditions. In 1941, the U.S. government sent him to Thule, Greenland, to take charge of the landing strip there, a vital link to Russia at the early stage of World War II. Later he held high positions with the Strategic Air Command, and the National Science Foundation. When he finally retired, he and Alice fulfilled the dream they had cherished. They came home to live on Kimball Island.

Waiting out the fog, Bucks Harbor.

FOGBOUND: PURGATORY OR PARADISE?

BUCKS HARBOR — Ambling in a boat alone among the Maine islands at the speed of a slow bicycle rider; living, cooking, sleeping, working, day-dreaming for 14 days and nights, six of them in thick, wet fog, and doing it all in a confined space 30 feet long and 10 feet wide. Is that purgatory? Or is it paradise?

Shore-side recollection tends to paint it all as paradise, because that's the way we wish it were. But it is purgatory at times.

Bad is a three letter word. So is fog. Put them together and you get a six letter word—dismal. Put six days and nights of dense fog back-to-back and you get a nine-letter word—purgatory. My dictionary defines purgatory as "a place of punishment."

My place of punishment on one cruise was Bucks Harbor, at the head of the Eggemoggin Reach. The patron saint of sailors was whispering good advice into my ear the evening the fog came down. He told me to push on across the last of West Penobscot Bay and go into Bucks Harbor instead of anchoring for the night alone out in the Barred Islands. In Bucks Harbor I stayed, socked-in for six foggy days and six foggier, wetter nights. I got one more lesson in accepting one more thing I cannot change—fog.

I also made these discoveries: There can be pleasure in purgatory, when purgatory is Bucks Harbor; that 144 hours of fog can be the perfect time to look up old friends, especially ones with hot water, showers and flush toilets. I discovered that an "Establishment" yacht club can be kindly to a fog-locked stranger; that in the tiny post office in South Brooksville, a sweet postmistress gives used paperback books to sailors who've run out of reading material; that Bucks Harbor Market used to sell Maine snowballs (kept in the freezer since winter) for $5 a bag in July to visiting yachtsmen to cool their sundowner drinks. This same little market supplied ice cream to F.D.R. after he and Winston Churchill signed the Atlantic charter at sea.

Add in Condon's garage, the yarn store and the Golden Stairs gift shop, and there you have the total of commerce in South Brooksville. To someone on dry land, with wheels and dry bed, these high spots may sound dull. But to a sailor locked in by fog, visits to these oases became the hubs and joys of a socked-in day. Granville "Granny" Henthorne and his wife Priscilla, at the Bucks Harbor Marine, were pillars of help and laughter

Fog and more fog. This is in Bucks Harbor near the Eggemoggin Reach, but could be almost any Maine harbor on an August cruising day.

to a sailor fog-locked for six days in their harbor.

On fogbound days and nights, I watched $160,000 yachts come creeping out of the dismal murk into Buck's Harbor, radars and Lorans working overtime, crewed by vacationing sailors, male and female, who were drenched, cold and eyestrained. "Are people who cruise the coast of Maine sunny optimists or oil-skinned masochists?" I asked myself. And refused to answer.

Such were the minor pleasures of purgatory in the fog.

Then the sun came back and paradise returned. On a crystal-clear early morning, Steer Clear leaped away from her mooring and headed past Pumpkin Light and down the Eggemoggin Reach and under the Deer Isle Bridge.

Before noon, I was cruising past Grog Island into the eastern entrance of Deer Isle Thorofare, where I cut out to sea a further six miles to Isle au Haut. Its high point, named Mount Champlain for the French explorer, shoulders up 554 feet, towers over Penobscot Bay, Merchants Row and the myriad island jewels at its feet.

Here is the loveliest cruising, swimming, sunning and exploring water in the world. Freed from fog at last, I tore up my schedule to head west to get back to work ashore. Instead I decided to treat myself to 24 hours of heaven, wandering crooked courses among two dozen of these blessed islands between Deer Isle and Isle au Haut.

At deep of night, stars by the millions bedazzle the heavens and reflect back from the still dark ocean. At dawn the sun rises up out of the Atlantic to kiss these islands first of any land in America. And out here I hear no sound except the eerie bleating of unseen sheep and the throb of a distant dragger, its great diesel thrumping out from Stonington.

So here, in deep, unsheltered but calm waters, I stop, shut down the engines and drift silently and in solitude. I eat supper, as the tide rocks and drifts Steer Clear gently as a baby on its way to sleep. Stars are bright and scintillating when I start engines again, find my island cove and secure my anchor for another night.

The big moon will not be overhead till 2 a.m. I set the ship's bell to ring loudly then, so I can be out on deck to witness the moon's glory shining across the ocean.

This stay-over means a long run west tomorrow and an early start. So by 4 a.m., I've drunk coffee, eaten peaches and hauled up the anchor line. By 5 a.m. I'm across the bay, through Fox Island Thorofare. By six, I'm across Penobscot Bay and passing the Owls Head Light, waving to lobstermen hauling along Muscle Ridge Channel.

After passing Southern Island Light, where Andrew and Betsy Wyeth have restored the old lightkeeper's house, I get a lovely impulse to put in for a visit to Matinicus. But my gauges say its time for fuel. So I go down past Mosquito Island into Port Clyde for fuel and supplies.

It turns out to be a great stop. Al, a sunburned friend from Thomaston, is repairing gas pumps on the dock. Brown-eyed Tracy Baldwin, who runs the waterfront store, is balm to a solo sailor's eyes and helps me replenish my ship's stores.

It's hours since breakfast and time for a break for lunch. I head out to sea once more, toward Monhegan, and drop a lunch anchor by the granite cross on Allen's Island, where Weymouth held the first Christian service in 1607. Too soon, its time to make the long haul across Muscongus Bay, leaving Pemaquid Light two miles to starboard, heading on down to Seguin, as the sun starts down. It is dark by the time I've come past Cundy's Harbor and up the New Meadows River to pick up Steer Clear's home mooring in Buttermilk Cove. It's been a long hard run. I'm tired. I decide to sleep on board one more night. When I switch off the reading light over my bunk, I think back over this solo trip. As I go to sleep, there is no doubt in my mind. Cruising Penobscot Bay is paradise, spiced with a pinch of purgatory.

Fisherman's home and fishhouse.

X
MT. DESERT
AND DOWNEAST

ABRAHAM SOMES, FIRST WHITE SETTLER

LIGHTNING TERROR IN SOUTHWEST HARBOR

JACKSON LAB—SCIENCE ON THE MT. DESERT

GHOST FROM GERMANY IN BAR HARBOR

WORKING THE MUD FOR MONEY: CLAMS

FIGHT AT PETIT MANAN: GULLS VERSUS TERNS

ON ANCHOR AT IRONBOUND: DEPENDING ON THE INVISIBLE

GOODBYE TO PIPER

BLUE HILL AND JONATHAN FISHER EPILOGUE

PLACENTIA ISLAND

Far, far, far away from city noise.

X

The surest way for Steer Clear to get to Mount Desert is to make a beeline for it, in one straight run. Otherwise we fall prey to temptations along the way. Too often we make a lunch stop at Dix Island in the Muscle Ridge Channel and find it too lovely to leave. Then we stop at St. Helena or McGlathery Islands off Stonington and laze away another day. Blue Hill Bay inveigles us; or we stay over at Bartlett, Swans Island or Little Gott. And then, we say, there is so little time left to enjoy all Mount Desert offers; so we have to turn for home, bypass this glory of Mount Desert on the grounds that no slice is better than only half a loaf.

Finally we bit the Bar Harbor bullet. One mid-September, ten days after Labor Day and the summer crowds, we made a straight run from Boothbay Harbor to Great Harbor at Mount Desert. There we headed up Somes Sound, and found a new enchantment. Ever since then, Somes Sound has been a magnet.

First, Somes Sound is sheltered, beautiful and surprisingly empty of all boats, from little outboards to rich Hinckleys and Concordias. Ambling up the Sound gives a happily enclosed feeling, like the protection of a fjord after a long run on open ocean.

There is a sweetness to the name Jesuit Springs, our first stopping place. We poke Steer Clear into Fernald Cove, close to the entrance into Somes Sound, to rediscover the fresh water spring from which Jesuit missionaries drew water in the 1600s, when two Jesuit priests, Father Briand and Father Masse, tried to settle here. At half tide, you can find the same spring today, as they did in 1613. You can still draw sweet, clear fresh water from it, although at high tide the salt ocean covers it.

We anchored and rowed ashore in Fernald Cove to fill water jugs, more because we wanted this historic water aboard than because our fresh water tanks were low. As we bent at the spring to fill our jugs, I remembered there had been bitter fighting on this spot. The two Catholic priests, with 25 sailors and 35 French colonists, had encamped on the high ground above Fernald Cove 375 years ago. They had christened the high ground Saint Sauveur. The Jesuits spent a happy summer here, trying to convert Indians. But the smoke from their campfires roused the hunting instincts of an English naval patrol, whose mission was to drive out the French, coming down from French Canada, from the island England claimed as their territory. The English Captain Samuel Argall headed his 14-gun frigate toward the smoke.

Argall was a tough sea dog who had helped establish the English colony at Jamestown, Virginia. He sailed his man 'o war stealthily into the cove and he went after these French intruders hammer-and-tong. He captured their vessel, ill-named Jonas, stormed their camp, burned it, captured the priests and settlers. Then Argall erected a Protestant cross atop Saint Sauveur mountain and erected a marker claiming the region for the King of England. From then on, English and French were locked in a long series of fights for ownership of Mount Desert. So many warring ships filled their casks at Jesuit Springs that it is still often called "Man 'o War Brook."

The views of the mountains surrounding Somes Sound are spectacular from a small, slow moving boat. Some believe that Mount Desert, 16 miles long and 12 miles wide, is the most beautiful island in the world. In 1604, the French explorer Samuel de Champlain had sailed in here and written in his log, "This island is very high, and cleft into seven or eight mountains, all in a line. The summits are bare and deserted. I named it Isle des Monts-deserts."

Today those mountains are meccas for millions. Acadia National Park on Isle des Monts-deserts is the second most visited national park in the United States. Each year, the number of visitors to Mount Desert increases. By the year 2,000, more than six million visitors are expected to stand atop Cadillac Mountain, according to projections by

*Harvard University made for the National Park Service. Five times as
many people visit Mount Desert in one summer as live in all of
Maine.*

*Cadillac, highest mountain on the Atlantic coast, towers 1,532 feet
above the sea. From Steer Clear on a mid-September day, we look up
to the mountains and see no one. If cars and crowds are there, they
are as invisible as ants, moving across granite 400 million years old. Its
a healthy perspective in a self-important, short-sighted world.*

*Relics from 4,000 B.C. have been discovered here. The Red Paint
People and three successive Indian cultures were here before the first
white men set foot here 400 years ago.*

*A man feels minuscule, and yet blessed, to take his boat up waters
surrounded by such beauty and antiquity. The concept is too much to
handle, so I focus on one man—the first white settler, Abraham
Somes who sailed up Somes Sound in the summer of 1761.*

ABRAHAM SOMES, FIRST WHITE SETTLER

SOMES SOUND — Abraham Somes sailed his sloop up
the Mount Desert River, as Somes Sound was called in 1755, one of the
first refugees from Massachusetts to head for the better life on Mount
Desert. He pioneered the way for much later Massachusetts refugees, such
as the president of Harvard, Charles W. Eliot and New York's J. Pier-
pont Morgan and John D. Rockefeller. I wish I knew more about Somes,
the man who decided to head downeast from Gloucester. He was one of
the first men from Massachusetts to hornswoggle a whale of a bargain,
buying lovely land in Maine from a native.

Somes bought Greenings Island at the entrance to the Sound. He paid
a gallon of rum to an Indian summering there. How much further he
sailed up the Sound that year, we don't know. But Somes loved the place
and must have spoken well and loudly back in Massachusetts about what
he found in Maine.

For in 1761, Francis Bernard, who was the royal governor of England's
Massachusetts Bay colony, with a wife and ten children to support in Boston, gave himself deeds of ownership to much of Mount Desert. But he
needed to entice settlers if his land was to attain cash value. So he offered
free land to Abraham Somes, who already knew the region, if he'd leave

Gloucester and move up to Mount Desert as a settler. Somes grabbed the offer and in 1761 he headed back to sail up the Sound again, still called Mount Desert River. This time he had a partner aboard with him, James Richardson, love child from a colorful romance in the Old Country.

As I piece the story together, Somes did not tell his wife he was intending to upstake from the civilization of Gloucester and remove his family to the wilds of Mount Desert. He told his wife that he was headed to Mount Desert River again to cut barrel staves. To me, and maybe to her, that sounds suspicious, for it's a long, long sail from Gloucester to Mount Desert just to cut barrel staves. But Somes and his friend Richardson set sail downeast, supposedly to cut a cargo of barrel staves.

Soon after they reached the head of the Mount Desert River, Somes and Richardson so loved the pretty and sheltered country that they decided this was the spot to live. They named the spot Somesville, settled in for the winter and cut wood. The next spring they sailed back to Gloucester to tell their wives. They closed up home and shop in Gloucester, and filled the boats with their families, food and furniture and set sail to begin new lives in Somesville.

Somes's companion, James Richardson, had been born in Scotland. His father had been head gardener on the estate of a Scottish nobleman. The gardener and the nobleman's daughter, Lady Jane Montgomery, developed a secret love affair. Braving the fury of her aristocratic parents, the young lady married the gardener. They eloped to America. Their son, James Richardson, became the partner of Abraham Somes. Together Richardson, Somes and their families became the pioneer white settlers of Somesville. The Mount Desert River was later renamed Somes Sound. The Richardsons got left out of the new geography.

Their lives were good enough to tempt others to join them. A chart of 1772 shows six homes at Bar Harbor and Hull Cove, four at Somesville, two at Southwest Harbor, four more on the Cranberry Isles and one at Bartlett's Island. By March 1776, the year of the Revolution, there were enough men living here to hold a town meeting in Stephen Richardson's house. That night, according to records in the historical society, the men decided to pool their muscles and tools and build a road.

Somesville is still a small and lovely village. We tie Steer Clear to the town dock, where there is four feet of water at low tide, and walk across a meadow to the road and into the town's friendly grocery store. At night, we move out to a small cove behind Bar Island and anchor there alone, with the backdrop of a finely designed modern house. This cove is one of the loveliest hideaways on Mount Desert, and we bless old Abraham Somes first for finding it, and, then for settling here more than 227 years ago.

There is a lively record of life in Somesville 134 years ago which few boatmen know about. It comes from the minutes of the meetings of the Ladies Home Sewing Circle of Somesville, founded on a windy March day 1854, almost 100 years after Abraham Somes first sailed on his early bachelor trip into the Sound in 1755.

On a windy March day 1854, the local Somesville ladies adjusted their bustles, smoothed their gimps, left their husbands and families to their own devices, and fared forth to set up the Sewing Circle. They had high intentions—and lived up to them for more than the next 100 years. The organizing papers say ''The Circle is organized for cultivating social habits, making intellectual and moral improvements and giving aid where needed.''

That is a transcript of the spidery handwriting in the old record of their first meeting. The Ladies Sewing Circle hewed to their intentions, especially in giving aid where needed. For example, they raised money to build a boardwalk over Somesville's muddy main street, bought a bell for the village church, built an iron fence around the village cemetery.

Other Sewing Circles in other towns may have done much the same. But the Somesville Sewing Circle has a distinction, a peculiar badge of a special breed of practical-minded woman. They bought a hearse. They earned the money to buy the hearse by selling fancy needlework and home-baked cakes. The new hearse added dignity to the burial of friends and neighbors, who had hitherto gone to their resting place on a cart.

And the ladies' hearse was a good investment. For more than 60 years, the Sewing Circle rented their hearse out for funerals at $1 for Somesville's dead and departed, $2 for funerals over in Hull Cove and Bar Harbor. The hearse helped carry the dead to their final resting place for 66 years. Then in 1926, the ladies sold it for $5, finally surrendering to the motorized competition to their horse-drawn hearse.

The records of the Sewing Circle proves that foul weather never deterred the ladies. An entry of New Year's Day 1861, reads ''The Circle met with Mrs. George B. Somes, three ladies present, it being very unpleasant.'' Entries through the hard winters of the 1880s show Somesville women were a hardy breed, undeterred by snow and sleet. But in the 20th century they grew more tender. A blunt entry of April 11, 1918 reads "Some members seemed to be cold, or thought they were, but we will excuse the hostess, Mrs. A.C. Fernald, as it is war time and we must save fuel."

Newspapers in the 1980s headlined debates over the admittance of women into traditionally men's organizations; and of men into women's militant groups. But Somesville was more than a century ahead of such bickering. The Ladies Sewing Circle solved the sexist problem in open-minded fashion.

Article 10 of the bylaws of 1854 says "Any lady may become a member of this society by paying the sum of 25 cents and signing the constitution. Any lady or gentleman may become an honorary member by paying 50 cents." Two gentlemen became honorary charter members of the Ladies Sewing Circle of Somesville in March 1854—Timothy Mason, and J. Follensbee. Stout-hearted males. Are there male members of Ladies Sewing Circles anywhere in Maine in 1988?

The Sewing Circle raised money by offering good bargains. The record of the first annual fair in 1855 lists the sale of two shirts, 50 cents; one bonnet, 25 cents; two yards of hair cloth 31 cents; a collar, 15 cents; 20 horse blankets for Mr. Follansbee, 50 cents; one paper of needles, 40 cents; 20 quilts for Capt. Sargent at $1 each . . ."

My heart leapt at an entry on their 100th anniversary in 1954. It states "Mrs. George L. Somes, 83, is the oldest living member of the Ladies Sewing Circle, and a descendant of the village's first settler Abraham Somes."

It makes very good sense to stay put in a spot like Somesville.

LIGHTNING TERROR IN SOUTHWEST HARBOR

SOUTHWEST HARBOR — Lightning fascinates me. And terrifies me.

The latest terror came during a lightning storm when we were in Steer Clear, lying on anchor in a boat-crowded harbor.

The hot, muggy night turned suddenly chill. Then came the cloudburst and our little world was awash in a torrential downpour. Then came a deafening roar of thunder and suddenly a burst of blinding light lit up the whole black harbor.

Bolt after bolt of lightning shattered the night, renting the black skies, turning black water to weird brilliance.

For a few moments the two of us watched in awe and amazement. But fear escalated into terror as lightning bolts exploded so close to the boat that they seemed to be striking us. The boat seemed to shake like a drenched dog.

The terrorizing fear seemed to rush simultaneously into both our minds. Steer Clear has tall radio masts towering above it. Inside the cabin, there's a concentration of VHF and CB radio gear and electronic depth finders. And forward, near the bow, a heavy metal anchor chain ties the boat to the metal anchor, 15 feet below. How much conductivity? Danger?

We dared not voice our thoughts. Would the antennae or the anchor chain attract the next lightning bolts directly into the boat?

The storm lasted two hours, which seemed like twenty-four. We waited it out, sitting together on a bunk in the cabin, hands clasped, half in prayer, half in comfort.

Next morning, we installed knife switches so that the radios and other electronics can be grounded outside the boat. After those safety precautions were operating, I rowed ashore again and purchased books about lightning to find out more about the phenomenon which had first fascinated me, and finally terrorized me.

Now I wish I had not read them. Ignorance can be more comfortable than a little knowledge.

I've found out that in the blinding instant it takes for a lightning bolt to strike, its electricity heats the surrounding air to a scorching 30,000 degrees centigrade. That is five times as hot as the surface of the sun, says my book.

I found out that lightning races through the air at 90,000 miles per second. Each year, lightning kills 180 Americans. Four out of five victims are men. The electric current in the lightning bolt is so powerful it paralyzes the heart. The current is 10,000 times more than the amount used in the electric chair for executions. Thank you, helpful book.

There is altogether too much lightning around. More than 100 lightning bolts strike somewhere in the world every second. That is more than eight million a day. And they hit the Earth's atmosphere with more than twice the voltage put out by all the generators in the U.S.A. combined.

But in Maine, even lightning has, excuse the pun, a bright side.

Maine has the happiest lightning victim alive. He is Edwin E. Robinson of Falmouth, struck by lightning June 5, 1980. That bolt did miracles for him. It restored the sight and hearing he'd lost nine years earlier and made hair grow again on his bald head.

But the record holder for being struck and living to tell the tale is Roy C. Sullivan, a former forest ranger in Virginia's Shenandoah National Park. He's been struck—and set afire—by lightning seven times.

Lightning, I found out, only strikes the earth 20 percent of the time. When a bolt comes within 90 feet of the ground, the terrified earth itself lets loose with a tremendous "return stroke" of radiant light that shoots up to join the lightning bolt. This wards off the blow.

The good news is this. The chances of being killed by lightning this year are one in a million. It's 16 times more likely you'll die falling down stairs.

JACKSON LAB—SCIENCE ON MT. DESERT

MOUNT DESERT ISLAND — Ever think of Maine as one of the world's foremost centers for research? Even those who laud and magnify Maine seldom picture Maine as a pioneer and leader of the world in science. Yet Maine is, thanks in part to the Jackson Laboratory on Mount Desert.

Jackson Lab is bigger than 95 percent of all the independent research laboratories in the United States. More than 475 people work here.

In its specialized field—genetic research with experimental animals—the Jackson Lab at Bar Harbor is unequaled in the number of its professional research staff and unmatched in the size of its animal colony—three million mice. Jackson Lab is the world's largest center for mammalian genetics research. The lab buildings on scenic Mt. Desert are worth more than $20 million.

One more figure of a different calibre. About mice. Specially bred mice are the stock-in-trade at Jackson Lab. Over three million mice are born here in a single year.

Mice are big business. Jackson Lab sells over two million mice a year to research labs in 49 states and 22 foreign countries. And earns well over $5 million from such mice sales. The reason for all the mice is the study of genetics. Genetics is the key to new knowledge at Jackson Lab. In lay terms, 'genetics' is the study of genes. And genes are the factors of heredity which are passed along from generation to generation.

The Maine connection to genetics came to Mount Desert through Clarence Cook Little, president of the University of Maine in the 1920s.

Heredity or genetics is the scientific field first investigated in 1866 by an Austrian monk, Gregor Mendel. Mendel experimented in his monastery garden with peas, breeding into generations of peas a specific 'family likeness'. Mendel's theories were rediscovered about 1900, a few years before young Clarence Cook Little entered Harvard in 1906. Little, fascinated by genetics as an undergraduate, began using mice to study the transmission of hereditary characteristics.

Little started his important study of cancer in mice. And at the same time he climbed the academic ladder, becoming assistant dean at Harvard (1916-17); then research associate at Carnegie Institute; and then came his Maine connection.

From 1922-25, Little served as president of the University of Maine. His liberal ideas about funding higher education caused him to lock horns with Governor Percival Baxter. But during his years as president of the University of Maine, Little also directed a small research lab at Bar Harbor. The lab was lent to him by George B. Dorr, the man responsible for putting together the land gifts which became Acadia National Park. During his summer work at this lab, Little grew to know two summer residents of Mt. Desert especially well—Edsel Ford and Roscoe B. Jackson of Detroit. These men talked Little into leaving the presidency of the University of Maine to become president of the University of Michigan.

Based on his friendship with Roscoe B. Jackson, Little won financial support to start the Jackson Lab at Bar Harbor. He began that lab in 1929 with $50,000 and a dozen people working in one building. Little directed the lab until his retirement in 1956. He also served as president of the American Cancer Society from 1929 until 1945. He died in 1971.

Cancer research is and has always been a major effort at Jackson Lab. The basic research is devoted to the study of how a normal cell turns into an abnormal wild cell, which grows and multiplies crazily—hallmark of cancer. Jackson Lab researchers have explored how and why viruses inside a cell can lie latent, doing no harm for years, then suddenly explode into active infection, hurting the cells, making those cells multiply and passing on the infection to other cells in the body.

Jackson scientists studied how two infected cells divided and made four infected cells, and how the four made eight, and how the eight divided again and became 16 infected cells—until the infection spread cancer throughout the body.

Jackson scientists studied mice, generations of mice, to test the theory that 'mammary cancer agents' can be passed through the milk of a mother mouse to her offspring, developing the first clear evidence of the virus theory of pass-along cancer. This inherited, latent potential is 'switched on' by genetic or environmental factors; and the Jackson work is focussing on how the latent potential can be kept quiet, asleep, harmless, by other genetic and environmental factors.

Jackson mice serve as the models for many human illnesses and constitutional disorders. In scientific terms mice have many similarities to humans.

But the life span of the mouse is short, three years or less. They live quickly. They are weaned six weeks after birth; they begin breeding 12 weeks after birth; so it is scientifically possible to test quickly in generation after generation the effect of genes upon illness. In other words, to test what can be passed along, and then study how that pass-along effect can be controlled.

Here is the genealogy of a Jackson-strain mouse. Take two mice that are brother and sister and mate them. Then select a brother and sister from their offspring and mate them. Do this for 20 generations and at the end the offspring will be as genetically identical as two individuals can be. That is the key to "Jax mice." After the scientists have bred one genetically 'fixed' strain of mice, they can start another fixed strain, with inbred differences this time. Then they compare the genetic differences to see the effects of inherited genes. And what are the benefits of all this?

Jackson scientists have, for example, paved the way for successful organ transplants in modern surgery. Their studies discovered the genes that determine the acceptance or the rejection of tissue grafts.

Jackson studies paved the way toward immunology—through 'preimmunization' of the host with a serum or tissue taken from a donor who is resistant to the infection.

Almost half of all the work done at Jackson Lab is related to cancer. Immunology is one prime field; virology of cancer cells is another; a third is the biochemistry of cancer cells and the function of cholesterol in the membranes that surround each cell.

Mice are an unexpectedly endearing aspect of science at Jackson Lab. The mice here can be as charming and amusing to watch as the mice which are family pets. But the scale here is enormous.

For its vast programs in genetics, cancer and inherited diseases of all kinds, the Jackson lab has a resident colony of almost a million mice.

These produce three million babies a year.

Taking care of these mice is a mammoth job, which requires a crew of 131 professional mice caretakers.

Mice are big eaters. At Jackson Lab, mice eat over 800 tons of specially prepared mouse food a year; and a local industry supplies over 500 tons of pine shavings to use as cage bedding. The mice drink 22 million gallons of water. And it takes 39 full time staff to clean the cages, and fill the water bottles. Jennie Sawyer, senior mousekeeper, alone tends to one room with 10,000 mice of eight different inbred strains. "Working with the mice every day, you get to know their different characteristics. And you really develop quite a feeling for them" says Mrs. Sawyer.

When Steer Clear looks like a poor Cinderella among her sister yachts around Bar Harbor, or when the skipper and crew feel turned off by the hordes of humans in Bar Harbor, we go ashore and visit the mice.

A GHOST FROM GERMANY IN BAR HARBOR

BAR HARBOR — When the giant liner QEII dropped her anchors in Bar Harbor in July 1981, the ghost of an earlier sea-going palace, an enemy of England, stirred.

It was the ghost of the German luxury liner, Kronprinzess Cecilie, which fled to sanctuary in Bar Harbor in 1914, at the start of World War I.

Aboard her were 1,216 passengers, including two men from Portland, Maine, and over $10 million in gold and silver bullion.

After sailing from New York, the Crownprincess Cecilie was 900 miles out in the Atlantic on July 31, 1914, when a coded message for her captain was flashed into her radio room. The mysterious message, signed Siegfried, stated that the royal family was ill. Those were the code words which meant that Germany was at war with England and France, and that the German luxury liner should seek sanctuary in the nearest neutral port. The captain chose Bar Harbor, Maine.

Two brokers from Portland, Henry Beaumont Pennell Jr. and Walter S. Hammons were aboard. Pennell was first to notice the ship had reversed course. "I was at a dance in the ballroom, and went out on deck for air. The moon, which had been over our stern, was now suddenly over our bow. Moments later, the ship's captain announced Germany was at war. He ordered the ship darkened, all lights extinguished and said we were headed back to the States."

For almost four days and nights the blacked-out luxury ship fled for safety, speeding through fog and night with no horns blowing, no lights showing. Some irate and rich passengers offered to pay five million dollars to buy the ship and put her under the protection of the American flag. The captain ignored such offers. He knew that down in the ship's hold were $10 million in gold and silver, withdrawn from U.S. banks just before sailing from New York. He knew German army reserve officers, called back to duty, were aboard in mufti. He knew he was being pursued by French and British ships, determined to capture his vessel and its wealth in gold and silver bars. So he headed to the neutral port and quiet sanctuary of Bar Harbor. But he had no local knowledge of the waters.

Aboard however was C. Ledyard Blair, of the Eastern Yacht Club, Marblehead, who had often sailed the Maine coast. Blair, a mere yachtsman, piloted the giant liner into Bar Harbor, dropping anchor at 5 a.m., August 4, 1914, to the amazement of Bar Harbor residents. Henry Pennell, the Portland broker, finagled a ride ashore, phoned the Portland Express Advertiser and gave the first eye-witness story.

First, the gold and silver were ferried ashore, and loaded on special trains of steel cars. Long strips of paper were laid in the aisles. Over $10 million in gold and silver were piled onto the paper. Four men armed with guns rode in each car until the bullion was off-loaded in New York and taken back to the bank vaults whence it had come a week earlier. Then almost $1,000 in gold dust was swept up from the paper. (Today the same cargo would be worth $150 million.)

The Bar Harbor post office sent out for emergency helpers to handle the 3,000 sacks of mail taken off the ship.

After the bullion had been taken off, first and second class passengers were ferried ashore to catch trains to New York and Boston or to take the coastal steamers. But 700 poorer passengers in steerage class were kept aboard, while officialdom wondered what to do with the massive German luxury liner.

Local seamen suggested she could run to Boston and still keep inside the three mile limit of U.S. territorial waters and therefore be safe from attack. Local skippers recommended that the German luxury liner steer a course past the Cranberry Isles, back of Isle au Haut, past Matinicus, Monhegan, Portland and thence to Boston. The captain of the luxury liner cursed the proposal. He said his liner was no rowboat, and set off

Wave-rounded rock beach. On a run to spend a sheltered night in Winter Harbor, we anchored for an island walk and picnic here. But the holding ground was poor, so we skipped lunch ashore.

to Washington to see a young official in the Navy Department, named Franklin Delano Roosevelt. Roosevelt arranged for the Crownprincess Cecilie to be towed to Boston, escorted by two U.S. destroyers, to prevent attack by French or British warships hovering in wait just outside the three mile limit.

The German luxury ship spent the next two and a half years at anchor in Boston harbor. When the U.S. entered World War I, in April 1917, the navy converted her into a troopship, and renamed her the U.S.S. Mt. Vernon.

A Maine man, Capt. Douglas Dismukes, was the first captain of the Mt. Vernon. Capt. Dismukes, later became the first superintendent of the Maine Maritime Academy, in 1941. On a return trip to the U.S. from carrying troops to France, the former German luxury liner was torpedoed by a German submarine, on Sept. 5, 1918, and 36 men were killed. She limped into Boston, was repaired and went back to duty.

The QE 2's visit to Bar Harbor in July, 1981 was less adventurous. But her visit stirred the ghosts of the other great luxury liner which had dropped anchor in Bar Harbor unexpectedly on the outbreak of World War I.

FIGHT AT PETIT MANAN: GULLS VS. TERNS

PETIT MANAN — This is the story of how and why wildlife scientists deliberately killed 550 gulls on a nine-acre Maine island.

They did it by poisoning bread which they put into the gulls' nests on Petit Manan Island.

The reason they committed mass murder was to bring back the terns to their traditional nesting sites on Petit Manan, from which invading gulls had driven them.

The extermination of 550 gulls and the subsequent return of about 1,200 terns have both been successful, say the scientists. The scientists directly involved were Thomas Geotell and Douglas Mullen, managers of the National Wildlife Refuge at Petit Manan in Washington county.

Action began in May, 1984, but only after public meetings with concerned citizens and after the proposal to poison gulls had been approved by environmental officials. Thousands of tax dollars and hundreds of hours of work by scientists were invested before a single gull was killed.

Some think that all the brain power, paperwork and money expended might better have been used toward solving human problems than solving a fight over nesting sites between gulls and terns on a remote island far Downeast. But Petit Manan Island was acquired in 1974 by the U.S. Fish and Wildlife Service because of its value as a nesting site for terns, a beautiful seabird whose numbers in Maine have declined by 40 percent in recent years.

In the 1970s, the tern colony on Petit Manan was the largest in Maine, numbering thousands. Tern colonies had been on Petit Manan for 100 years. During most of that time, virtually no herring gulls or black-back gulls nested there. But by 1977, the aggressive gulls began shoving out the smaller terns. The gulls took over. By 1980, terns had completely abandoned the island, driven away by big black-back gulls.

Gulls had earlier driven terns from many favorite nesting sites on other Maine islands. Maine's gull population had climbed to about 150,000, while the tern population had been cut almost in half within 10 years.

Under the terms of the Fish and Wildlife Act of 1956, the agency is authorized to ''take such steps as may be required for the development, advancement, management and conservation and protection of fish and wildlife.''

So in May 1984, Fish and Wildlife scientists baited every gull nest on

Petit Manan with cubes of bread poisoned with minute amounts of a chemical compound called DRC 1339. Gulls, scavengers that they are, gobbled up the poisoned bait before other non-target birds could get it. Within 48 hours, 550 gulls died. The unconsumed bait was collected and buried.

The poison DCR 1339 acts as a kidney depressant. A gull's kidneys fail to function; toxic waste in the gull's bloodstream causes uremic poisoning. Within 12 hours the gulls who have eaten the poisoned bait become lethargic and fly home to rest in their nests. Within 24 to 48 hours, they become comatose and die.

The terns, terrified from their habitat by aggressive gulls, apparently heard the news that Petit Manan was safe again. For, by the next summer, 1,200 terns were back on the island; and Petit Manan became once again a flourishing tern colony.

If nothing more is done, say wildlife scientists, Maine tern populations will probably continue to decrease as they have done over the past 40 years. The few remaining unprotected tern colonies may be taken over by gulls. Then the tern populations would be concentrated on Maine's four protected sites—Machias Seal Island, Matinicus Rock, Eastern Egg Rock and Petit Manan.

WORKING THE MUD FOR MONEY: CLAMS

FRENCHMAN BAY — Make mine mussels. Easy to get. Easy to cook. Succulent to eat. But today we went clamming. Result was too few clams and too many sore backs. Clams was once slang for dollars. People once said: "This tie set me back 10 clams." Maybe the expression ought to be revived, because the clams spell dollars more than ever before.

Strong-backed, hard-working diggers on a good clam flat can dig two bushels on one low tide and earn $120 a day. However, diggers like these are the high-liners; lots of diggers, especially part-timers, earn only beer and gas money.

I know a pair of diggers—diggers usually work in pairs for safety— who work the flats downeast. In a beat-up metal skiff, powered by an outboard which looks filthy but works well, these burly, bearded men don't look like big money-makers. They come back to the dock caked

388

in stinking mud, intimidating in their huge, high rubber boots, swinging fearsome clam forks. They unload string bag after string bag filled with succulent Maine clams. They get paid in cash on the spot, as much as $250 between them for four hours of hard digging on a good day.

After watching them come in and unload at the wharf one wet gray day, I went back aboard Steer Clear and got out my copy of "The Ocean Almanac," to learn about clams.

The world's oceans contain so many millions of clams that the number is uncountable; they come in 15,000 species in 70 families. Some are as small as the tiny nut clam, three-tenths of an inch, and others grow as big as the giant clam of the East Indies, which is five terrifying feet long. Clams grow so densely in places that one patch of Dogger Bank fishing grounds is reported to have more than 4.5 million of tiny clams in a 700-square-mile area.

The "steamers" we get in Maine are more complicated creatures than you'd believe from looking at them. They have gills for breathing, a heart, liver, kidney, stomach, mouth and intestine. Their blood is colorless, and we drink it, in clam broth.

This eagle was found by U.S. Fish and Wildlife agent Bill Snow, killed by gunshot along the Penobscot River. A leg band identified it as an eagle transplanted to a nest at Machias. Maine's eagle population hovers at about 165. Close to 40 bald eagles are born in Maine each year, about 10 in the downeast coast.

A clam breathes, eats and then purges itself through a pair of tubes, which it pushes out through the crack between its two half-shells. Water is sucked in through one tube, bringing in food and oxygen, and the clam's waste matter is flushed out through the other tube.

Female clams discharge eggs by the millions into the ocean, where they are fertilized externally. The tiny embryos, if they survive, begin to grow into clams in two weeks. One female hard-shell clam was recorded as producing 24 million eggs in a single spawning. Only a fraction are fertilized and fewer live long enough to grow into full-sized clams, which takes two to four years in hard-shells.

In Maine, clams are harvested the hard way, by hand, by diggers using long-pronged, short-handled clam forks. One drawback to this method is that about 50 percent of the small juvenile clams, hidden close together in the mud, are hit and hurt by the digging fork. Once their shells are broken, they are quickly eaten by fish, ducks, gulls or crabs; a loss which cuts in half the size of future clam harvests.

Pollution has reduced the clam diggers' territory. In New York about 35 percent of the 450,000 acres of hard-shell clam flats are too polluted to be harvested. Pollution plus the "red tide" disease closes many of Maine clam flats.

The hard-shell clams used to be, and sometimes still are, considered an aphrodisiac. Indeed, their scientific name is Venus mercenaria. Clam meat contains as much iron as beef liver; yet one serving of clam meat contains only 70 calories, because its fat content is so low.

American Indians used the quahog clam shell for wampum or money. When Dutch settlers governed New Amsterdam, later New York, they recognized clam shell wampum as a legal currency. Then America's first counterfeiters set up a wampum factory on Long Island, and flooded the market with counterfeit wampum.

Legend has it that the first clam chowder was concocted in Maine by sailors from northern France when they were shipwrecked on the Maine coast centuries ago. The story goes that the Breton sailors salvaged the ship's crackers, salt pork and potatoes; then dug a mess of clams on the beach and threw the whole concoction into a big cooking pot called a "chaudiere." Our word chowder derives, they say, from the French word chaudiere.

In Maine it sounds sacrilegious to scoff at clams. But, make mine mussels—and spare my back and spare my decks from clam flat mud.

Getting set to part company. Steer Clear (with flag on stern) has just bought lobsters from a friend in Frenchmans Bay, and they will be eaten within the hour.

BLUE HILL AND JONATHAN FISHER

BLUE HILL — This friendly harbor is where Steer Clear often comes for two days of rest after a long cruise Downeast. The walk from the one-room yacht club into town is a mile-long stroll on a road jewelled with lovely old houses.

Another good reason I enjoy Blue Hill is Jonathan Fisher.

Jonathan Fisher was the epitome of the competent Yankee, the tinkerer who does everything and does it well. He was appointed parish parson in Blue Hill from 1794 and died in 1847. But that is a conventional backdrop to the very unconventional doings of this amazing Blue Hill parson.

Besides saving souls, the Reverend Jonathan Fisher built his own home, farmed his own fields, built his own surveying instruments, mapped the whole area, invented the circulating miter saw, invented a shingling machine, painted scores of landscapes and portraits, wrote 3000 sermons, invented his own shorthand, carved his own typeface and alphabet, printed his own books. He hand-bound his hand-printed books in cat-hide, stripped from his own dead cats. He was tone deaf; but he made and played his own flutes.

Thanks to Roland M. Howard and the Historical Society of Blue Hill, the amazing output of the most versatile man in Maine history has been preserved in the Jonathan Fisher Home and Museum.

In one exhibit, next to Fisher's enchanting primitive painting of Blue Hill, is a clock he made while a Harvard student in 1790. He made the inner works of the clock from scratch. He used a broken wine glass as the alarm, set to waken him at 4 a.m. He painted the intricate face of the clock; and then inscribed it with phrases in Hebrew, French, Latin and Greek. He taught himself most of these languages, after graduating from Harvard. As a missionary to the Indian tribes, he learned their Indian languages too; and rode 300 miles some months on horseback as a missionary, travelling as far as New Brunswick. He mapped the Indian territories using his home-made surveyor's instruments. Those maps were used as evidence in Maine's famed and precedent-setting Indian land-claim case 150 years later.

Because he wrote so many notes and journals for himself, Fisher invented his own shorthand. He built his own filing boxes where he stored more than 3,000 of his sermons, his books and his "how-to-do-it" instructions. His "how-to-do-it" files tell how to make cement, how to color ivory scarlet, how to dry furs, how to preserve eggs for two years, and how to mend broken china by boiling flint glass in river water for six minutes, beating it to a fine powder, and grinding it well with the white of an egg on a painter's slab.

The Reverend Jonathan Fisher was a man to boggle the mind. Fisher cut the lumber he used to build his handsome home. He painted the pictures for its walls. He designed his local school buildings, complete to innovative sloping floors so students in the rear could better see the teacher. He even designed extra strong hinges for the school desks he made. He tapped maple trees, made syrup, kept production records, planted and preserved his own strawberries, dug clams, a bushel or two on a tide, caught and salted down his own mackerel, wrote treatises in Greek, Hebrew, Indian dialects, French and German. He wrote music for his church. In a single shot he once brought down 23 pigeons; and the thrifty Yankee skinned his own dead cats to make his gloves as well as bind his books.

To see his prodigious range, and the excellence of his total life, is to see and marvel at the endless talents of those matchless men who first settled Maine and the nation. They did everything. They did it all, from preaching sermons to skinning cats, from writing Greek hexameters to brewing strong spruce beer to publishing a treatise on Infant Baptism. Such a man was Jonathan Fisher, appointed parish priest of Blue Hill almost 200 years ago.

PLACENTIA ISLAND

PLACENTIA ISLAND — The most treasured gifts sometimes come not with flourishes and trumpets, but so quietly that the gift is almost a secret. This is the case with an island called by the strange name of Placentia.

Placentia Island is 500 acres of wooded Eden at the mouth of Blue Hill Bay, a few miles offshore from Bass Harbor on Mount Desert. Almost uninhabited for the past 40 years, except for one elderly couple, Placentia is close to the heart and deep in the history of Maine, and has been for hundreds of years. The happy news is that Placentia is now protected and safeguarded forever, thanks to a remarkable man and woman.

On a fair day, when wind and tide were favorable, this man and wife used to row their wooden dory five miles from Placentia to the mainland and back. They did it when they were both in their seventies. They made this trip together only five of six times a year, to buy supplies. For the other 360 days and nights of the year, they lived remotely, happily and very simply on Placentia. This very private couple bought the uninhabited island in 1948, and their plain lifestyle had minimum impact upon it. They lived in a small, secluded camp at one end, and burned only downed, dead wood for warmth and for cooking.

I met them only once, years ago, when they were gathering driftwood on the beach. We had come ashore from Steer Clear for a swim and a walk after a long day's cruise.

In the spring of 1981 the Maine Chapter of the Nature Conservancy came to a most happy agreement with the wonderful couple about protecting the future of Placentia.

After 10 years of discussions, Nature Conservancy bought the island for the cost of a modest annuity for the 72-year-old inhabitant-owners, which allowed them to live undisturbed on their island till their days were done. The purchase was no easy matter; and it should never be an easy matter to buy another's island paradise. The Conservancy had to undertake an intensive fund-raising drive. Through contributions of hundreds of individuals and foundations, the goal of $190,000 was reached. The figure includes the annuity, acquisition costs and funds to pay property taxes and stewardship costs on the 500-acre island in the years ahead.

Placentia Island is the best documented nesting place for the American bald eagle on the Maine coast. Records show eagles nested here continuously from the 1920's until 1979. That year, a storm blew down the tree where they nested. But eagles usually have alternate nesting places in the same locale. They came back to Placentia. This area between Blue Hill Bay and Frenchman's Bay is home to at least 18 pairs of eagles, one third of the entire eagle population of Maine.

Stirred by my meeting with the owners, who lived on Placentia together for over 30 years, who rowed their dory to the mainland five times a year, I've delved into records to find the island's history.

I wanted first to find out about the name Placentia. It was long assumed to be a French name, derived from the word "plaisance," meaning pleasure; and the early French explorer, Samuel de Champlain, was credited with christening the island.

But another story is that a Portugese navigator brought the name Placentia to North America. He was in these parts in the early 1500s, a century before the French, and Placentia was the name of a town in his native Portugal. He named a large bay, a harbor and a town in Newfoundland Placentia; then a century later the French brought the name with them from Canada to the coast of Maine.

In the Revolutionary days of 1776, a call was issued to the inhabitants to establish a Committee of Correspondence. The Atlantic Neptune survey of those days shows Grand Placentia. In 1786 Col. James Swan, that high-flyer from Boston, bought 20 islands in the bay, Placentia among them. Later, Swan's fortunes crashed. From a debtor's prison in Paris, France, Swan mortgaged Placentia to Michael O'Mallery, along with 13 other islands. Long and bitter litigation followed, with Daniel Webster involved as one of the lawyers. By 1820, a federal census showed 37 people living on Placentia. In 1828 Robert Mitchell, a strong, energetic farmer with a wide reputation for clearing land fast and building endless stone walls, bought half the island for $210, and in 1839 Francis Gilley bought the other half for $237. An island cemetery contains Mitchell's grave.

Not long after, the town of Tremont established its Poor Farm, reputed to be a hard and harsh place, on Placentia. In 1909, the island was cut over extensively for pulp wood, and all inhabitants left. During the 1930's the island belonged to Charles Welch of Boston, and the Church of Christian Scientists briefly held title to it.

In 1948 the couple who rowed to the mainland in their dory bought the island and quietly loved and cared for its 500 acres for 33 years. Thanks to their caring, it is forever in the custody of The Nature Conservancy; and eagles again raise their young on Placentia Island.

ON ANCHOR AT IRONBOUND: DEPENDING ON THE INVISIBLE

IRONBOUND ISLAND — Ironbound is the right name. The hard high rock cliffs around this small island east of Mount Desert looked forbidding and hostile. The rain poured. The wind gusted. The hour was late. The engines were coughing ominously. My decision was to anchor for the night at Ironbound. It was the night I learned to love my anchor.

Anchor—the word sounds dull; and to look at an anchor is boring.

But on a storming night, anchored alone in an offshore island, an anchor gets more prayers, more anxiety and eventually more gratitude than men and women give to almost any other inanimate object.

When you are thrust awake and scared at midnight by the fury of a gale battering your little boat and angry seas trying to tear you adrift, your cruising life is tethered to a lump of steel you cannot see, buried in mud you can not visualize.

At Ironbound, I got hit by a scary, storming night, alone with only a Danforth anchor to hold me, an anchor so light that a small woman can lift it off the deck. My Danforth anchor weighs only 30 pounds. My boat weighs many tons. The sea pounding us weighs more than a man can calculate. And how much ruthless force is in that 40 mile an hour wind, which is trying to dash me and my boat against the nearby ledges? Too worried to sleep, too anxious even to lie still, I climbed out of my bunk and went topside, out into the storm and inched my way forward to the bow.

Mount Desert Island, Acadia National Park. This beautiful sea coast park of more than 40,000 acres is visited by 1.5 million people. It is the only national park in the U.S. donated by landgrants from private individuals, including John D. Rockefeller. Steer Clear's favorite, quiet anchorage here is in Somes Sound.

A check on the lines seemed to show the anchor under the angry sea was holding well. Rain-soaked and worried, I crept back off the foredeck and huddled in the cabin below. For comfort, I took a little pamphlet about anchors and anchoring from the ship's library and read.

Danforth anchors were designed by a Maine man, Robert Danforth Ogg, born in Gardiner in 1918, long-time resident of North Windham, officer of the Danforth-White Company, long a Portland firm.

The booklet told me that a four-pound Danforth has as much holding power as a 500-pound concrete block. I sat in that storm-lashed cabin figuring my 30 pound Danforth was as strong as a mammoth 3750 pound rock. Comforting. But was my arithmetic right?

Steer Clear came through the night, not budging from the bulldog grip of that 30 pound anchor into primeval mud. In gratitude, the next morning I telephoned Ogg, the man who designed my savior. I reached him coming in from a swim on the beaches of California.

"Take comfort" he said "Danforths are holding boats the world around. The tiniest is a six ounce toy, used to anchor duck decoys. The biggest weigh 40,000 pounds. They use 12 of these big ones to hold oil drill rigs through gales from the North Sea to the Java straits. And Danforth anchors got their first tests, their baptisms by storm and sea, off mid-coast Maine."

Bob Ogg and his uncle brought their anchor business to Maine from California in 1958. "We did some of our most rugged testing off the White Islands, outside of Boothbay Harbor. We anchored 30 and 40 foot boats out there through the fiercest storms, with instruments aboard measuring all forces of wind and wave. This anchor is able to take the damndest punishment nature can hit you with."

Ogg emphasizes that scope, the length of line and chain from boat to anchor, should be as much as seven times the ocean depth. Anchor on a stormy night in 15 feet and you need 105 feet of scope out. Anchor in 50 feet and a wise sailor puts out 350 feet to help take the strain, if there is swinging room and enough anchor line aboard.

Oddly, Ogg compares an anchor to a kite. "One sinks and holds you in place, while the other soars and you hold on to it. But each must be perfectly proportioned, balanced and shaped to penetrate the medium in which it operates. Kites and anchors are kissing cousins."

It is reassuring to know that Danforth anchors, Maine-bred, are holding men and their boats in safety the world around tonight. But now I promise that I'll appreciate and love and take good care of my anchor, its shackles, its chafing gear before I put it through another night like the night-of-the anchor off Ironbound Island.

EPILOGUE

Clear up an old mess, and start a new mess. A boatman's work and a writer's work is never done—thank God!

Yesterday I cleaned up the writer's mess, made through the Maine winter, while this book was in work. I've cleaned up and hidden from sight the old charts, logbooks, papers, early drafts, notes, reminders and all the paraphernalia which proliferates around a book in its birthing room.

The room looks naked but neat. Empty the way a son or daughter's room is empty after they have moved out on their own. The mess you hated is gone. And suddenly, you miss the mess.

Putting away good stories, material I liked but which never made it into this book, is one of the guiltiest parts of cleaning up after the birth of a book about the Maine Coast. So many good places, good people, so many treasured times—all left out because there was no more room. Like packing a suitcase, and having to leave behind on the bed some favorite shirts or tie or shoes. You don't reject them at all. But they wouldn't fit inside the case.

I've left out three times more stories about the Maine Coast and Steer Clear's happy encounters with people and places than are between these covers. Perhaps some of your favorite places have been left out. Many of mine have been.

Today I'm starting a new mess, a boatman's mess. I'm off to the boatyard, to the real thing. It is still only March in Maine. But the sun is out, the ice is gone, the mud is underfoot. And the winter cover is off Steer Clear. I'm headed for the boatyard, carting sanders, paints, tools, new zincs, lots of elbow grease and a nice old song singing in my heart. The time to mess about in boats is here again. Soon Steer Clear and I will be off again together, gunkholing our Maine coast.

A few old loves just get better and better, the longer they are together. A man, his boat and the coast of Maine are three gifts of God which seem to get better, the more they rub off on each other.

So I'm off to enjoy the mixture as before.

One final wish to you: May the Coast of Maine bring you exhilaration and joy.

Buttermilk Cove
November 1, 1987—March 20, 1988

Rowing Piper to an island shore during the last of her 12 summers of cruising the Maine coast aboard Steer Clear. She can never be replaced, but her memory forever permeates Steer Clear and the island shores where Piper explored and swam.